# Therapeutic Justice

"In this book, Karen Snedker has set the stage for the next generation of mental health court reform. This innovative book mixes sociological insights with concrete dialogues taken from interviews with court participants, judges, prosecutors, probation officers and more. The author points to the many ways mental health court has been positively transformational; but in her guide to the future she also helpfully notes some not so obvious ways where we may go awry. Practical considerations combine with the importance of going beyond psychology and inviting sociology to play a larger role in the future development of therapeutic jurisprudence."

—David B. Wexler, *Honorary President, International Society for Therapeutic Jurisprudence, Distinguished Professor Emeritus of Law, University of Arizona, USA, and Professor of Law, University of Puerto Rico, USA*

"In Therapeutic Justice, Karen Snedker offers a nuanced analysis of both the promise and pitfalls of mental health courts—and therapeutic justice more generally. This case study draws on both quantitative and qualitative data, including the experiences of mental health court clients, to explore not only how well mental health courts work, but also what more can be done to enhance their therapeutic potential, what success in this context means, and how it should be evaluated. Students, academics and practitioners alike will find much to appreciate in this thoughtful and thought-provoking book."

—Katherine Beckett, *Professor of Sociology and Professor of Law, Societies and Justice Program, University of Washington, USA*

"This book is a breath of fresh air in its in-depth analysis of what mental health courts are really about—what works, what doesn't, and how these courts can be improved. Through in-depth interviews with litigants, court personnel and others, and through sociological analysis, she focuses on some of the issues that are often obscured in the academic conversation (training—or lack of it—of court personnel, including judges; unconscious bias in the selection process; the difficulty in erasing stigma; the relationship between court success and the presence of Crisis Intervention Teams; the extent to which the 'net' is widened, reduced, or made deeper; the role of pressure from DA offices; how being a mental health court judge can be a 'career killer' for a judge), and that are so important if we are to understand how mental health courts work in practice, and how we can improve upon them further. Not recommended reading, but compulsory reading for all in this court process and all who take these issues seriously."

—Michael L. Perlin, *Founding Director, International Mental Disability Law Reform Project and Professor Emeritus of Law, New York Law School, USA*

"Using mixed methods including extensive observations of mental health courts (MHCs), interviews with MHC team members including judges and clients, and administrative data, Dr. Snedker offers a comprehensive approach to the efficacy and future of MHCs as a part of the "contemporary criminal justice system." Case studies of clients illustrate how being mentally ill and involved with the criminal justice system are mutually reinforcing, and the "powerful impact of the legal system" on the lives of individuals entangled in that system. Rightly so, Dr. Snedker reminds the reader that MHCs are not "preventative" or a "panacea," but "reactive entities." As such they need to evolve towards a model of care and away from a model of control…She offers her finding that to continue to be impactful MHCs must "innovate," and "align mission, resources, and practice."… Dr. Snedker concludes that while MHCs may be one response to addressing a set of social problems, they may also contribute clients being stigmatized and tethered to the criminal justice system. Through her thorough data collection and thoughtful analysis, Dr. Snedker provides hope that MHCs will ultimately evolve as social welfare initiatives serving rather controlling the clients they convene. This is a powerful and significant reframing of MHCs and, in turn, larger issues of criminal justice reform. This book should inform the debate among practitioners and scholars alike. I congratulate Dr. Snedker on her wonderful contribution moving the conversation about mental health and other problem-solving courts forward."
—Stephanie Hartwell, *Professor of Sociology, University of Massachusetts Boston, USA*

"Dr. Snedker's work provides a thorough and well-rounded examination of the mental health court experience. Her research addresses the underlying process and theory of mental health courts but also provides an empirical analysis of outcomes as well as client case studies. This provides a voice to the clients but also a deeper understanding of this unique court process. In using this approach Dr. Snedker is able to speak to mental health courts influence on criminal justice and public safety outcomes but also to their ability to transform clients' lives. Conversely, her work also highlights a number of areas where mental health courts can improve and to address these Dr. Snedker suggests a number of progressive reforms that would push the mental health court experience further into a therapeutic justice framework. This book will be important to mental health practitioners who work at the intersection of the criminal justice system, as well as academics who conduct research in this area. Perhaps most importantly this book offers a comprehensive understanding of the potential for those mental health courts currently working in this setting as well as those who aim to make a difference at the intersection of mental health and the criminal justice system."
—Bradley Ray, *Assistant Professor, Indiana University, Purdue University Indianapolis, USA*

Karen A. Snedker

# Therapeutic Justice

## Crime, Treatment Courts and Mental Illness

Karen A. Snedker
Seattle Pacific University
Seattle, WA, USA

ISBN 978-3-030-07676-4     ISBN 978-3-319-78902-6  (eBook)
https://doi.org/10.1007/978-3-319-78902-6

© The Editor(s) (if applicable) and The Author(s) 2018
Softcover re-print of the Hardcover 1st edition 2018
This work is subject to copyright. All rights are solely and exclusively licensed by the Publisher, whether the whole or part of the material is concerned, specifically the rights of translation, reprinting, reuse of illustrations, recitation, broadcasting, reproduction on microfilms or in any other physical way, and transmission or information storage and retrieval, electronic adaptation, computer software, or by similar or dissimilar methodology now known or hereafter developed.
The use of general descriptive names, registered names, trademarks, service marks, etc. in this publication does not imply, even in the absence of a specific statement, that such names are exempt from the relevant protective laws and regulations and therefore free for general use.
The publisher, the authors, and the editors are safe to assume that the advice and information in this book are believed to be true and accurate at the date of publication. Neither the publisher nor the authors or the editors give a warranty, express or implied, with respect to the material contained herein or for any errors or omissions that may have been made. The publisher remains neutral with regard to jurisdictional claims in published maps and institutional affiliations.

Printed on acid-free paper

This Palgrave Macmillan imprint is published by the registered company Springer International Publishing AG part of Springer Nature
The registered company address is: Gewerbestrasse 11, 6330 Cham, Switzerland

*For Steve*

# Preface

I come to study MHCs for both personal and academic reasons. My life has twice been touched by mental illness and random acts of violence. On December 31, 2007 my friend Shannon Harps was stabbed to death within feet of her Capitol Hill apartment in the early evening by James Anthony Williams. Williams had a long history of criminal behavior and mental illness. Then, six and half years later on June 5, 2014, Aaron Ybarra entered Otto Miller Hall on Seattle Pacific University's campus shooting several students and killing Paul Lee. I have worked as a Professor at SPU since 2006 and, although I did not personally know Paul, I was shocked by the shooting event and its aftermath. Mr. Ybarra also had a history of mental illness.

In the case of Shannon's killer, a panel was created to investigate why Williams was a free man when the slaying occurred. His long history of mental illness and criminal activity was known to the appropriate agencies—including 248 infractions committed in prison while serving an 11-year sentence for randomly shooting a man in 1995 and a host of violations he committed after his 2006 release. He had been assessed for involuntary commitment but according to psychiatrists did not meet the standard. "It is our worst fear—a random predatory violent killing," stated the county prosecutor during a news conference about the case (Seattle Times, January 30, 2008). Williams had spent time in *City* Mental Health Court (MHC) not as a client but on the MHDT (mental health diagnosis and possible treatment) pathway.

In the case of the SPU shooting, Ybarra's first contact with police occurred in 2010 when he called 911, telling dispatchers "he was suicidal and had a rage inside him" and according to the police report "he wanted to hurt himself and others" (Seattle Times, June 6, 2014). Ybarra had been referred to Snohomish County Mental Health for possible involuntary treatment, but was at this time—as in subsequent times—determined "not detainable." According to police reports, he had alcohol problems which resulted in an arrest on a drunken driving incident in 2012. He reportedly eschewed his medications and "he reported hearing the voice of one of the Columbine killers in his head, 'telling him to hurt people'" (Seattle Times, June 6, 2014). Despite all of this, he was able to legally purchase a gun which he used to kill one student, injure two, and terrorize countless more. It is not clear what would have prevented the shooting at SPU, but it raises questions about the exceedingly high standards for involuntarily commitments and the lax legislation about attaining guns legally, despite clear mental instability and trouble with the law.

In my role as a bereaved friend, concerned citizen, and as a social scientist these incidents raise questions about mental illness, treatment, and criminality in our society. Furthermore, it raises specific questions about the role of MHCs in contemporary criminal justice system. Who belongs in MHCs? Do they work even when we experience tragedies like the death of Shannon? Can MHCs reduce the likelihood of these worst-case scenarios? Why was Mr. Williams, with his long history of violent criminal behavior, released from prison? Would he have benefited from the full MHC program (as opposed to MHDT)? Would a MHC have helped Mr. Ybarra—who did not have a violent history toward others—stay on his medication, receive substance abuse treatment, receive social support, and avoid violence? It is these important issues that frame the book. While there are no easy answers to these troubling questions, this book provides some insights about how and when MHCs work.

This book represents a coming together of various scholarly interests and academic disciplines. It reflects the intersection of my three main research interests including crime, urban sociology, and public health (especially mental health). I approach this project as a sociologist with a longstanding interest in law and crime in an urban context inspired by books that try to show the relevance of law in the everyday lives of people (e.g., Ewick and Silbey's *The Common Place of Law*). However, I am also informed by my training in health sciences after being a NIH postdoctoral fellow and now as a Clinical Assistant Professor at the University of Washington's School of Nursing in the Psychosocial and Community Health Department. Employing a socio-scientific framework, I detail the organization, culture and efficacy of two MHCs. I explore the role of MHCs in our society from academic and policy perspectives. I am attempting to straddle two audiences—academics and practitioners—in linking research to policy. Academic scholars' critiques of the court system help to guide the exploration and analysis of MHCs while I am also cognizant of the need to reshape and improve MHCs for those working within the system. At the same time, as a person who has been deeply touched by mental illness and violence, I approach this investigation with compassion and hope that MHCs can provide a path to more humane treatment for those suffering from serious mental illness.

Seattle, USA                                                                 Karen A. Snedker

# Acknowledgements

My discovery of mental health courts (MHCs) was fortuitous. In January 2010, I arranged to have a group of students attend a Municipal court proceeding as a supplemental activity to a Sociology of Law class I was teaching. My friend Adam Eisenberg was a sitting commissioner of the court at the time and suggested that my class observe MHC as he was presiding that day. He thought I might find it fascinating. He was certainly correct. That was my first day in MHC and I knew that I needed to study these courts. Memories of Shannon's case came flooding back. I could not stop writing notes while in court and that day represented the beginning of the research that culminated into this book. I am indebted to Adam for bringing me into the world of MHCs. I never intended for that day to alter my research trajectory as it did, but I am forever grateful.

There are many people in the court system that provided me with support during the data collection phase. I appreciate the generosity of all of the MHC team, especially Steve Connolly. He was an amazing resource and I am personally indebted to him. I appreciate all of the time and support he offered me at every stage of this project, especially the practical support in connecting me with clients as well as offering feedback on sections of the final manuscript. I am extremely grateful to the MHC clients I spoke with in court and interviewed during the course of the book. Not only were my respondents generous with their time but also amenable to the interview questions and sincere in their responses. I hope that I have accurately captured their sentiments and intent. While I owe many people for assisting me this book, any mistakes are entirely mine.

I owe great thanks to my many colleagues at Seattle Pacific University including my department chair Kevin Neuhouser. He provided continual support of my research agenda around this book. My Lectio group was also supportive as we met bimonthly to talk about life—work and family balance. I suspect my continual reference to "the book" grew tiresome but they listened and urged me on nonetheless. I am grateful for SPU's Center for Faculty Scholarship as some of the qualitative data collection for this book was supported by SPU Faculty Research Grants. I am personally grateful to the former and current Directors of the center, Margaret Diddams and Margaret Brown, for their support of my research agenda. Dominic Williamson, at SPU's Center for Educational Technology & Media, assisted me with tables and figures. I also thank Erin Powers for her support, as a friend, and transcribing some of the early interviews. And for Katie Schultz for expeditiously and thoroughly transcribing the majority of the interviews for the project. This work in its earlier form benefited from presentations at various forums and conferences including class presentations (Seattle University Law School, University of Washington School of Nursing) and academic talks (University of Washington West Coast Poverty Center; University of Washington's Deviance Seminar, Umeå University, and the American Sociological Association). In these forums, I received constructive criticism and encouragement. Also I owe thanks to Lindsey Beach and Katie Corcoran who were co-authors on a related paper (sections which appear in Chapter 5). I am especially grateful to Lindsey for reading a draft of the book and offering insights and critiques that sharpened the final version of the book and for carefully indexing the book. Also Heidi Rettinghouse read chapter drafts and offered both encouragement and feedback on the external validity of the work for which I am indebted. I also received helpful comments from Pete DeSanto on the final manuscript. I am grateful to anonymous reviewers for comments on the early stages of this project as well as support my editors, Josie Taylor, Becky Wyde, and Stephanie Carey.

During the process of data collection, analysis and writing successes and travails were shared by many. I thank my former grad school friends, Danielle Bessett and Lynn Krage who were continually encouraging. Also to my University of Washington colleagues and friends. I am thankful for support from the University of Washington, especially the department of sociology and Jerry Herting.

I am also grateful to a wonderful group of friends (UW graduate students) who had to listen to me talk about this book for years on end at our weekly dinner at my home. Thank you, Tim Thomas, Michelle O'Brien, and Mike Esposito for enduring the tedious details about the book and for sharing in this journey with me. Thank you for reminding me to have perspective. Tim, thank you for sharing many hours at Solstice and other cafés as we worked on our research. Your friendship and support was significant. I am also indebted to other friends for their support and for being patient with me when I was unresponsive to Facebook posts, phone calls, emails, and others forms of communication, especially my long-time "book club" pals, Jennifer Knight, Kris Kirwan, Robin Crabtree, Callie Greenfield, Gail Hoffman, and Heidi Walter. I missed many a book club (and often did not read the book when I was there) due to a preoccupation with the book. I am also thankful to other good friends who always believed that I would write this book especially Doug Angel, who is an author and judicial team member himself, and endured my disconnection during this crucial process. Members of my church community, Phinney Ridge Lutheran Church, were also supportive of this work especially my former pastor and his wife, Paul and Donna Hoffman. At one of our dinner parties Donna reminded me that I needed to tell the stories of the men and women whose lives I was invited into—it became both my duty and privilege (culminating in Chapter 6).

I am especially grateful to my SPU research group: Jennifer McKinney and Sara Koening. The three of us assembled as a group to aid one another along through the difficult process of finding time to do research and write at a teaching-intensive university. I consider the support from this group a tremendous resource. Not only did we meet almost every week to work on research throughout this entire project—as we have done for more than 8 years—but they provided critical feedback on *every* chapter of the book. During this time we were all working on books and I feel extremely lucky that we shared such a momentous time together. Moreover, their friendship, support, and insights were integral to the completion of this work. I am privileged to have these intelligent women as my colleagues and friends.

I also need to thank my family for their tremendous emotional and material support. I am grateful beyond words to my mother-in law, Barbara Pfaff. She gave me unbelievable emotional support, witnessing firsthand (as she sometimes lives with us) the trials of writing this book and provided much needed nourishment in the way of family meals, childcare, and most of all love. A great loss to our family occurred during the process of collecting fieldwork for this book, my father-in-law, Edward Pfaff succumbed to cancer. I know he would be proud of this accomplishment. My parents, Judy and Clive Snedker, provided continual unwavering love and encouragement. At every moment, they believed in my ability to succeed and supported my ambitions. My mum often asked about the book's progress, but also knew when not to ask or press me about it. Their never-ending faith in me brought me confidence and strength. My sisters, Sarah Fox and Clare Raggio, also offered encouragement. A family friend and lawyer, Bob Melhalf, always encouraged my pursuit of higher education, and we always got together when I went home to visit family to talk about law and the book. I am touched by his confidence in me.

I am ever grateful for my two sons, Arno and Jonas, whose love and spiritedness provided amusing distraction, keeping me grounded in what matters most. In writing this book, I hope that how we care for people who are mentally ill in our communities will improve for the sake of a better world for them and future generations. My entire family encouraged me on a daily basis to persist in spite of the many obstacles for which I am forever thankful.

Finally, I owe an endless amount of thanks to my husband, Steve Pfaff, with whom I have shared all of my successes and all of my disappointments. This has not been an easy task to bear, but one that he has done willingly and generously. This book would never have been possible without his love and support. Not only did he tirelessly read and edit this document, providing positive and constructive feedback, which challenged me to provide more clarity to my writing and analysis, he was a constant source of support. He always believed in me and the book, even when I did not believe it was possible myself. For all of this and more I dedicate this book to him. I hope that I will be able to give him in return the love, support, and inspiration that he has and continues to give to me.

# Contents

1 Mental Health Courts as the "New Generation" of Problem-Solving Courts     1

2 Beyond Adversarialism?: Collaboration and Therapeutic Goals     29

3 Clients and Therapeutic Agents: Court Selection and Team Dynamics     83

4 Therapeutic Justice in Action: Court Process, Reviews and Sanctions     131

5 Reducing Recidivism and Pathways to Success     183

6 Stories from Clients: How Mental Health Courts Can Change Lives     229

7 Conclusion: From Therapeutic Justice to Social Work Criminal Justice     263

| | |
|---|---|
| **Appendices** | 293 |
| **References** | 307 |
| **Index** | 321 |

# List of Figures

Fig. 3.1  Screening, selection and case processing in MHCs  92
Fig. 5.1  Predicted number of arrests two years after
exiting *City* MHC  186

# List of Tables

Table 4.1  Court compliance and sanctions in MHC  158
Table 7.1  MHC reforms: From therapeutic justice
to social work criminal justice  266

# 1

# Mental Health Courts as the "New Generation" of Problem-Solving Courts

Monique, a woman in her early fifties, entered the criminal justice system in 2012 on multiple charges of assault (two separate cases) and a harassment charge. She was heading straight to jail. A plea on her cases ranged from 10 to 90 days[1] in jail. If Monique had gone through the traditional court system, given her underlying mental illness, alcoholism and housing instability, time spent in jail would probably do little to curb future contacts with the law, contributing to the "revolving door" of criminal justice. But Monique was offered a different path—mental health court (hereafter MHC)—which she accepted. In choosing to participate in MHC, a relatively recent court innovation, Monique avoided time in jail, was linked to critical social and treatment services and cleared her criminal record. At her graduation from MHC, she was hopeful about her future trajectory.

One afternoon in 2014, Monique was sitting in the gallery of a criminal courtroom waiting for her case to be called for the last time. As the presiding judge called Monique's case and Monique found her seat next to her defense attorney, it was clear to her—and to many of us—that this was not a regular court review. After two years on probation, Monique was about to graduate from MHC.

She was smiling but obviously a bit uneasy as the gravity of what was to come sunk in. The presiding judge asked to first hear the probation report. Monique's probation officer addressed the court with what turned out to be a long monologue recounting her path, recognizing her struggle and praising her ultimate success. The city prosecutor also expressed pleasure with Monique's accomplishments and then requested that the court dismiss all charges. The defense attorney joined in the acclamation, highlighting Monique's commitment to court requirements in spite of a long and arduous path. The judge proclaimed, "I want to congratulate you. I know it has been hard. You persevered through the difficulties and you continued on. The Court is happy!" Then the judge stood up, stepped down from the bench, and shook Monique's hand, congratulating her and giving her a certificate of completion. Beaming, Monique held up the certificate and exclaimed, "It makes it official!" She is now legitimately done with MHC and the charges that brought her into court were dismissed.

Everyone in the courtroom laughed and clapped. Once everyone was back in their seats, the judge invited Monique to say something to the court. Slightly nervous, she addressed the judge, "I am really grateful to the court and probation. I talked to a lot of people, they told me to do the time and not to spend two years on probation. But the time I spent in jail motivated me not to go back [to jail]." She detailed the support from her treatment provider and probation officers. She concluded by thanking the court and all the lawyers who contributed to her accomplishment, exclaiming "I did not do this by myself!" Monique exited the courtroom happy to be free from criminal justice interference in her life.

What happened in court that day may represent the dawn of a new era in the history of criminal justice. The success of Monique's journey through MHC, despite parental death and abandonment, teen pregnancy, mental illness, and chemical dependency issues, owes to her strong motivation. But features of the court structure and culture were also pivotal to her success. A supportive team, balancing accountability through frequent monitoring and creative sanctions, worked together to alter Monique's trajectory and help make her graduation possible. From Monique's perspective, the court was helpful despite her early hesitation to opt-into the court. In the end she was proud to have successfully managed to fulfill the court obligations and felt optimistic about her life.

Monique's case (detailed more extensively in Chapter 6) highlights that *how* law operates in people's lives can have powerful effects. This book examines the complex relationship between mental illness, criminal behavior and the legal system within MHCs. The book's approach draws on the longstanding area of social inquiry that explores the relationship between law and society. Whereas a strictly legal approach focuses on the crime, legal facts and redress, a sociological approach focuses on the social construction of mental illness, the people who are mentally ill in the criminal justice system and public policy responses. Studies adopting a socio-legal orientation go a step further, treating the law as a human product which is shaped by social institutions and culture, examining how the larger political and social context influence the legal sphere and those positioned within it. In the case of the criminal justice system, socio-legal scholars address questions related to the impact of reforms and innovations within the law on practitioners (e.g., legal actors), recipients (e.g., defendants, victims) and society at large and explore how those same individuals, groups and organizations shape laws and produce legal change. It is the *process* that is being sought after in the spirit of Roscoe Pound's renowned proclamation of "law in action"[2] that brings the social effects of law into center view.

The use of socio-legal framing underscore this book. I see the law and legal system as a political, economic and cultural phenomenon and like others rely primarily on qualitative research methods to see how law works on the ground (Ewick and Silbey 1998; Lens 2016; Nolan 2001). This study explores law as an institution and as a behavioral system (Sutton 2001) with a focus on a specific penal innovation: problem-solving courts, which include MHCs. Used as an umbrella term, problem-solving courts refer to a different understanding of a case as a "problem to be solved, not just a matter to be adjudicated" (Berman and Feinblatt 2005, 5). The design of these courts specifically address certain types of crimes (e.g., drug charges) and categories of offenders (e.g., people with mental illness and/or substance abuse issues) and embrace a treatment orientation. Examining how these problem-solving courts—with a specific focus on mental health courts—are structured, culturally defined and practiced reveals broader trends within society. This book uncovers insights about the relationship between law and society, between different categories of people in the legal system and the everyday workings of the law. Before detailing the emergence of problem-solving courts and MHCs specifically, I first provide a brief historical discussion of punishment practices in the United States, highlighting an important shift in penal policy through these court innovations.

## Shifting Punitive Penal Practices

Historically, laws and criminal justice practices have oscillated between rehabilitation and punishment, only infrequently settling on a balanced ideal between the two imperatives. In the nineteenth century, reformers responded to the number, or perceived number, of people with mental illness in jails and prisons by campaigning for specialized facilities leading to a decline in jails and prisons (Torrey et al. 2010). In the beginning of the twentieth century, reforms moved toward treatment and rehabilitation in the legal arena. This is best illustrated by the birth of the juvenile justice system, created by Progressives in 1899 to specifically address the needs of a special class of offenders. The progressive argument was that young people's age and level of development demand differential treatment in the name of justice. This progressive reform reflected an understanding of criminal behavior in juveniles as at least partially related to broader external social forces, especially family functioning and structure. This orientation necessitated differential treatment of the young, notably specialized procedures and punishment (Erickson and Erickson 2008). While drawing parallels to the juvenile court system, Berman and Feinblatt (2005) also highlight the distinctiveness of problem-solving courts which addresses some of the pitfalls associated with court treatment of juveniles. Notably they reference the role of the defense attorney, greater accountability, measuring effectiveness and realistic expectations. These changes in structure and function draw insights from earlier progressive agendas.

For most of the latter part of the twentieth century and the early part of the twenty-first century however, American criminal justice has tended to err on the side of punitiveness informed by a "culture of crime control" (Garland 2002). From this standpoint, crime is viewed as a serious social problem that needs to be tightly controlled and punished. This "grand social experiment" of increasing punitiveness is what Clear and Frost (2014) call "the punishment imperative." This "new penology" (Feeley and Simon 1992) of crime control is centered on the management of the crime problem, shifting the focus away from rehabilitation and toward more efficient means of control and penal severity. This trend is evidenced in policies such as "three strikes laws," "mandatory minimum" and "truth in sentencing" guidelines, and trying juveniles as adults in criminal proceedings. At the local level, the popularity of the "broken windows" theory (Wilson and Kelling 1982) among politicians and police enshrined a putative link between low level criminality and more serious criminal behavior. On the streets, this led to policy changes whereby police targeted minor level offenses in response to growing concerns about crime, social decay and physical disorder. The law—as it often is—was thus called upon to address a series of social problems not all of which were directly related to crime. The results were a far cry from the rehabilitative ideals of the past.

The devastating "drug wars" and a general fear of crime were clear factors in the new penal regime focusing on expanding the so-called "prison-industrial complex" (see Selman and Leighton 2010). It was not merely rising crime rates that fueled increasing rates of punishment but the framing of crime as out of control and politically charged definition of crime as a major social problem (Beckett 1999; Clear and Frost 2014; Garland 2002). The forcefulness of this shift in response to crime was driven by media accounts and the politicization of crime that influenced changing public discourses on crime. Beckett (1999) argues that crime and drugs became framed as social control issues which was reflected in "get tough" approaches and "law and order" campaigns that dominated political races at every level of government in the latter part of the twentieth century. Politicized "anti-crime" campaigns and subsequent policies shifted the focus away from rehabilitation and reintegration to deterrence, retribution and public safety as the focus of criminal justice. This was particularly influential in the political campaigns of the "war on crime" (1960s and 1970s) and "war on drugs" (1980s and 1990s) eras. The combined effect of these social control strategies led to mass incarceration with dire effects, felt disproportionately by poor and minority groups (Alexander 2012).

Clear and Frost (2014) contend that the current discourse is shifting *away* from "tough on crime" to "smart on crime" rhetoric and policies. While fiscal concerns related to the economic recession and strained public budgets were a motivating factor in these shifts, they argue that changing media coverage and new social scientific research on the cost and consequences of mass incarceration are crucial factors explaining the current shift in penal policy. The U.S. may be on the verge of a new era of criminal justice focusing on more pragmatic and rehabilitative practices. In Clear and Frost's (2014) account of the "waning of the punitive ethic" they introduce a new "justice reinvestment" framework. The problem-solving court movement can be understood within that context, especially in light of the central role judges play as they adjudicate between social and legal factors in the court process.

Problem-solving courts are part of an effort to swing the pendulum back from increasing punitiveness and "punitive jurisprudence" (Miller and Johnson 2009) to the rehabilitative ideal of an earlier era but as a "distinctively new innovation" (Nolan 2001, 186). Some of the same forces that led to the development of the juvenile court system a century ago are behind the formulation of problem-solving courts today, particularly evident in the case of MHCs. Of course, a full embrace of the rehabilitative ideal would go far beyond the boundaries of the criminal justice system by moving into prevention and early intervention *before* people are entangled in the criminal justice system. Although criminal justice policies are largely reactive—responding to defendants once they are brought before the court—the broader trend of which the courts are a part—is an attempt to balance punishment and treatment, so as to correct the overemphasis on the former in previous decades.

Despite the gains made by the treatment orientation, the punitive imperative runs deep in our political culture and still resonates in society and the criminal justice system, with negative effects reverberating throughout society (Alexander 2012; Clear and Frost 2014). However within the scope of the criminal justice landscape, the growing presence of problem-solving courts represent an important legal development, one that recognizes the broader social context which influences the relationship between mental illness and criminal justice in the case of MHCs. The more explicit integration of social aspects of defendants within the law hold great possibility for individuals within the criminal justice system, their families, the communities in which they live and the broader society. It is this potential—with full recognition of constraints and shortcomings—for individuals with mental illness within the criminal justice system that inspires this book.

## Problem-Solving Courts

Proponents of alternative judicial models argue that the one-size-fits-all adversarial criminal justice system is neither proper, nor effective for all types of crimes and all categories of offenders. In the last twenty years, problem-solving courts have arisen to address various types of offenses and categories of offenders. These courts are sometimes referred to as problem-oriented courts, because they are not "solving" the underlying social problems but are "oriented" toward their amelioration (Berman and Feinblatt 2001; Freiberg 2001). Problem-solving courts are a type of specialty jurisdiction courts (Petrila 2003) known simply as treatment-oriented courts. Even if they do not necessary solve social problems, these courts are set-up to address the underlying social factors related to criminal behavior. They reflect the broader "infusion of the therapeutic ethos into America's criminal justice system" (Nolan 1998, 77).

In response to growing concerns about the efficacy of the traditional criminal justice model in addressing crime, especially in the case of drug-related offenses, problem-solving courts emerged in the late 1980s and early 1990s. Drug courts were the first problem-solving court model and appeared in 1989 in an attempt to combat, or at least reduce, the connection between drug abuse and criminal behavior (Nolan 2001). As a judicially-supervised treatment program for defendants with drug abuse issues, drug courts focus on ways to address the underlying problems among non-violent substance abusers who are in the criminal justice system. The assumption of the drug court movement is that drugs are a driving force behind criminal behavior and that addressing addiction reduces recidivism and enhances community safety.

Whereas the first problem-solving courts were drug courts, reformers have developed a "new generation" of problem-solving courts. In the subsequent decades, pioneering courts have proliferated—referred to by some as a "quiet revolution" (Berman and Feinblatt 2005)—to address a range of special populations (e.g., veterans) and offense types (e.g., domestic violence) including community courts, domestic violence courts, and Veteran's courts. In general, problem-solving courts rely on a more holistic approach, linking the individual to the larger social context and the broader genesis of criminal behavior. In practice, this means understanding that the individual's crime and conditions (e.g., mental illness, substance abuse, etc.) are related to social-structural conditions (e.g., poverty, homelessness, lack of healthcare, unemployment, etc.) and working toward better treatment, housing and employment outcomes as the key to criminal desistence. One of the most promising of this "new generation" of problem-solving courts are MHCs oriented toward addressing the connection between mental illness and criminal justice involvement.

## Mental Illness and Criminality

Despite recent assertions that there are "signs" that things are changing in the criminal justice system, reflected in the decline in the U.S. correctional system population, this is unambiguously not the case with the number of mentally ill offenders represented in the jail and prison population. An unmistakable trend in contemporary criminal justice is the rising number of individuals with mental health diagnoses under the supervision of the criminal justice system. This is a crisis with local, regional and national implications. The data tell a bleak story. The U.S. Department of Justice reports that 56% of inmates in state and 45%

of inmates in federal prisons have mental health problems, of which 24% and 14% respectively had a recent clinical diagnosis or treatment by a mental health professional (James and Glaze 2006). The most recent report on mental health problems in jails and prisons states that 26% of jail inmates and 14% of prisoners met the threshold for serious psychological distress (SPD) in the past thirty days, with percentages higher for female and white inmates.[3] There were no significant differences in meeting the threshold for SPD between prisoners incarcerated for violent versus property crimes. Moreover 44% (jail inmates) and 37% (prisoners) had a history of mental health problems(Bronson and Berzofsky 2017). An additional problem is that among the incarcerated mentally ill population, approximately three-quarters of those incarcerated in state or local prisons are *also* substance abusers or are substance-dependent (James and Glaze 2006; Vogel et al. 2007). The problem of mental illness in the criminal justice system—coupled with chemical dependency issues for many—has become unavoidable. Growing media attention on crimes committed by individuals who are mentally-ill add to public demands for action.

The mental health crisis in the criminal justice system is driven, at least in part, by the failure of other social institutions, especially the mental health system. The warehousing of individuals with mental illness in jails and prisons is thus not just the result of aggressive policing, but previous governmental and judicial decisions that largely dismantled the network of mental institutions across the country. It is tied to well-known broader cultural and structural issues such as deinstitutionalization (policy that led to closing down federal and state psychiatric mental hospitals) and insufficient support for mental health treatment and facilities. Although the many criticisms of the previous mental institutional model were valid and have been noted elsewhere (see for example, Whitaker 2010; Torrey 1997, 2014), the result of deinstitutionalization without putting into place a viable community mental health system had detrimental effects. People with mental illness are now afforded greater civil liberties, making it much harder in many jurisdictions (including the study site for this book) to involuntarily (civilly) commit a person. The irony is that many are now confined in jails and prison serving time on criminal charges or awaiting competency evaluations. This means that institutionally we have moved from a system based on a right to treatment for patients with mental illness to being based on commitment on the basis of dangerousness.[4]

The goal of caring for people with severe mental illness in the least restrictive setting is laudable and efforts toward community-based alternatives are re-emerging (Heilbrun et al. 2015). The community care model is premised on treating individuals with severe mental illness in the community, but the reality falls short of that promise. However the early efforts of the National Mental Health Care Act of 1946, National Institute on Mental Health, and Community Mental Health Care Act of 1963—while not successful in the goals of deinstitutionalization and funding and organizing a community care model—did change the public dialogue about mental illness, treatment and criminal justice. In the wake of these efforts, court-based initiatives did set the groundwork for present-day MHCs (Goldkamp and Irons-Guynn 2000).

While there are many complexities surrounding the process of deinstitutionalization and its consequences, in terms of the relationship to the criminal justice system one thing is clear: the number of individuals with serious mental illness who are now under the criminal justice apparatus as opposed to the mental health system has ballooned. Many characterize this move as criminalization of mental illness. The public is beginning to realize these trends, as witnessed by headlines from *The Atlantic* to *The New York Times* brandishing titles such as "America's Largest Mental Health Hospital is a Jail" (Ford 2015) and "The Mentally Ill, Behind Bars" (April 6, 2014).

The now outsized role of the legal arena—courts, jails and prisons—in the lives of people with mental illness is a stark reality. Many scholars argue that the criminal justice system is the *de facto* mental health apparatus—the new mental institutions (Schneider et al. 2007). Some explicitly link the two populations, showing that there is a negative correlation between the prison and mental health populations (Erickson and Erickson 2008). In a national survey by the Treatment Advocacy Center, the overrepresentation of people with mental illness in jails and prisons as opposed to hospitals is about 3 to 1 (Torrey et al. 2010). In fact, there has been a transference from one institution—the asylums—to another—the prisons. Scholars refer to this transference from one institution to another as transinstitutionalization (Slovenko 2002) or transcarceration (Torrey 1997). Transinstitutionalization is an umbrella term for the shift in the institutions that oversee the severally mentally ill population, and includes prisons, boarding-houses and nursing-homes. Transcarceration refers more specifically to transferring people with mental illness from asylums to jails or prisons. This process makes criminal justice agents, as opposed to trained medical personal, responsible for overseeing individuals with mental illness. The criminal justice system is the new apparatus to "monitor and control the mentally ill" where "punishment [is] the primary response and the paucity of mental health treatment" characterizes the systemic approach (Erickson and Erickson 2008, 39, 40).

This institutional transformation is related to the underlying orientation of penal settings. The social construction of mental illness as a criminal justice problem, premised on the failure of individual responsibility, led to increased incapacitation. This diverges significantly from the earlier medical orientation toward mental illness, based on the need for medical attention that promoted institutionalization for the purpose of treatment. A *model of care* for people with mental illness was displaced by a *model of social control* of people with mental illness. Although this shift from care to control was underway before the transference from asylums to prisons, it was partially responsible for the public outcry and the shutting down of the asylums in the first place. Given that both mental institutions and prisons/jail are "total institutions" (Goffman 1961) used to house "social deviants," they are premised on incapacitation and not a transformative change within the continuum of confinement and social control (Harcourt 2006). The "disciplinary technologies" (Foucault 1995 [1978]) used to control individuals with mental illness in asylums is comparable in many ways to the criminal confinement in jails and prisons.

It comes as no surprise that the prison system is ill-equipped to handle the massive influx of prisoners with mental illness, especially the large number with severe mental illness. The everyday conditions of incarcerated individuals with mental illness are grave. Treatment of their mental health needs is generally inadequate. Moreover the staff and leadership within the prison system is ill-suited to handle the needs of the mentally ill given the lack of training about mental illness and engaging with this population. While in jail or prison, behavior by individuals with mental illness are subsequent to more punishment and greater victimization; the prevailing conditions have serious negative outcomes including excessive use of force by correctional officers, segregation and isolation and self-harm and suicide (see Erickson and Erickson 2008). Prisoners who are mentally ill present management problems for staff and find themselves in solitary confinement at greater rates than other prisoners and for minor violations that are largely, if not entirely, related to underlying mental illness with sometimes fatal consequences (Pfeiffer 2007). Moreover, inmates with serious mental illness on average stay in jail longer, have higher recidivism rates, and incur greater costs (Torrey et al. 2010). All of this despite that most of people with mental illness who are arrested did not commit major crimes but committed misdemeanors or minor felonies related to symptoms of mental illness.[5]

In short the environment of America's jails and prisons are grim for people suffering from mental illness. Things are starting to change. Modifications in staffing priorities are illustrative of both a new management strategy and a shift toward more humanitarian and rehabilitative approaches. For example, Cook County Jail in Chicago recently hired a clinical psychologist as its director, a change in priorities in line with estimates that one-third of the jail population are mentally ill.[6] MHCs represent an important counter-trend—a hybrid approach— and the revitalization of a therapeutic orientation focused on treatment and care. Yet MHCs still operate within the social control apparatus of the law.

## The Advent of Mental Health Courts

The increase in the number of mentally ill individuals involved in the criminal justice system coincided with a demand for alternative approaches toward offenders with mental illness. Since the late 1990s, the number of MHCs in the United States has grown tremendously, with over 300 courts in operation today (Fisler 2015).[7]

Since their emergence in 1997 in Broward County, FL, MHCs have become a movement. According to the most recent estimates by the National GAINS center, there are 348 mental health courts across the country. Others put the numbers slightly higher at over 400 courts in the U.S. with 346 adult mental health courts and 51 juvenile mental health courts (Goodale et al. 2013). Many of these courts are now in their second or third decade of operation. MHCs are often distinguished by their tenure and categorized accordingly as first or second generation courts with first generation courts as early adopters.

Mental health problems and co-occurring conditions (or dual diagnosis as it is also referred) such as chemical dependency frequently render traditional criminal justice methods inappropriate or, at least, ineffective, contributing in large measure to the "revolving door" problems in the criminal justice system (Bernstein and Seltzer 2003). Furthermore, critics contend that punitive criminal justice policies are especially cruel, discriminatory and ineffective toward those with impaired competence and heightened vulnerability. Rising caseloads and frustration among judges, lawyers and court administrators led to development of problem-solving courts. Public opinion, too, indicates a lack of faith in traditional criminal justice approaches in the managing people who are mentally ill (Berman and Feinblatt 2001). Clients in MHCs are generally facing manifold disadvantages reflecting the intersection of homelessness, mental illness, substance abuse, unemployment and imprisonment (Kushel et al. 2005). These factors combine to make individuals in MHCs complex in their treatment needs and especially vulnerable to punitive treatment.

In response, reformers have introduced innovations and new strategies which reorient the criminal justice system, especially the courts, in how they work with individuals with mental illness with a focus on diversion and rehabilitation. A range of alternative approaches and diversionary strategies have been proposed and employed. In their Sequential Intercept Model (SIM), Munetz and Griffin (2006) provide a conceptual framework for diversionary strategies to address the challenges of mental illness in our communities and the interconnection with the criminal justice system. The rationale for this approach are threefold: treatment appropriateness, cost savings and humanitarian grounds (Heilbrun et al. 2015). Focusing on community-based alternatives for offenders, their model identifies five "intercepts."[8] Ideally intervention occurs at the earliest point. MHCs represent one diversion option within the third intercept (jails/courts). The SIM details two opportunities to intervene and divert individuals from the criminal justice system *before* MHC even become an option and two stages *after* a possible MHC intervention. In some ways this point of intervention is the last chance to divert an individual from incarceration and a criminal record.

Many jurisdictions around the U.S. have created specialized MHCs to address the problem in addition to other points of intervention. The dueling imperatives of the social construction of mental illness as a criminal justice problem, on the one hand, and the treatment paradigm on the other, is a tension that underpins the MHC model. The nature of problem-solving courts and specifically MHCs as "blended institutions" (Miller and Johnson 2009; Nolan 2001) is related to these broader structural and cultural shifts. The advent of MHCs illustrates the way that broader social forces shape the demands and role of the criminal justice system.

MHCs, as a part of the larger re-orientation towards non-adversarial criminal justice practices—an approach described as a "radically new" (Perlin 2013)—are designed to addresses the needs of defendants with mental illness. MHCs have been largely modeled on drug courts (Griffin and DeMatteo 2009) which were at the forefront of the problem-solving court movement (Nolan 2001). Like all problem-solving courts, MHCs are holistic and committed to rehabilitative and therapeutic ends with court-ordered and court-supervised treatment (Almquist and Dodd 2009; Schneider et al. 2007), but they are specifically targeted towards those defendants with serious mental illness. They treat defendants with mental illness as a special population by linking them to community-based treatment and services to reduce recidivism and entanglement in the criminal justice system (Goodale et al. 2013). MHCs are intended to balance a rehabilitative ideal with a public safety model but often confronts the tension between serving society by ameliorating crime and protecting and treating vulnerable defendants.

Despite the very swift emergence and diffusion of MHCs, research on court process and the effectiveness of these courts has lagged behind. Most studies of MHCs focus on program evaluation and outcomes. There is reason to be hopeful about the future of MHCs based on re-offending and treatment outcomes. Participation in MHCs may lead to better outcomes for defendants and society. What remains underexplored are the *mechanisms* by which MHCs work and for which defendants they prove most effective. Through a detailed examination of court process and interviews with legal actors and MHC clients, I illustrate how MHCs operate and identify practices that work (and do not work). Moreover, I show that the focus on treatment and therapeutic ends based on teamwork leads to a shift in punitive components of court that can be clearly seen in the social practices and rituals of the court, making the experience unique and potentially transformative. Employing a case-based study design with quantitative and qualitative elements, this book explicitly addresses some of the methodological limitations and limited research of previous studies (Griffin and DeMatteo 2009; Lurigio and Snowden 2009) especially the lack of qualitative data.

The previous era of mass incarceration, coupled with deinstitutionalization, created a national crisis. Inadequate investment in the mental health care infrastructure fostered a system whereby jails and prisons became the nation's default mental health facilities in which police officers are on the frontlines performing tasks more appropriate for social workers. Furthermore, incarceration with minimal opportunities for treatment functioned as standard criminal justice practice. This book focuses on one response to the crisis. Studying MHCs contributes to our understanding of the intersection of criminal justice and mental health and insights gained from this study will assist in evaluating and reforming MHC practices. This study is the most ambitious to date in addressing the nexus between mental illness, criminality, and recovery through the lens of alternative courts and the practice of therapeutic justice.

## Case Study Research Design

This book is based upon the logic of case-study research (Gerring 2007; Ragin 1992). Case-based methods give greater insight into the broader treatment court phenomenon. In case study research a single case or small number of cases yield detailed descriptions of key social phenomenon. Case studies of MHCs allow me to explore hypotheses from the existing theoretical literature and further examine the *processes* that may account for existing research findings.

I conducted two highly contextualized studies of MHCs using purposive sampling. The selection of cases reflects a hybrid approach by relying on both the "diverse case" and the "most similar case" design selection strategies (Gerring 2007). The two case study sites are different from other MHCs because they were early adopters of problem-solving strategies. Both courts are first generation courts and reflect the earliest institutional form of MHCs, which differ from courts that developed later. They are also both competency and therapeutic courts which is atypical of MHCs in the country (Finkle et al. 2009). While these matched cases are similar on key dimensions—urban context, court tenure, staffing—they vary on one important factor, namely the types of offenses handled (misdemeanor vs. felony cases). Both courts began as misdemeanor courts but one expanded to take on felony cases. This difference allows me to focus on a major distinction that characterizes first and second generation courts. Insights from these two courts are valuable for understanding the future challenges faced by MHCs and problem-solving courts more broadly. These courts are at the forefront of this trend towards alternative models of criminal justice and hence uniquely situated to serve as case studies for the growth, change and development of MHCs.

The data in this book come from two case studies in a West coast city–*City* MHC and *County* MHC. I avoid naming the courts to ensure confidentiality of my interview respondents. I observed court proceedings and collected detailed observations of court hearings in both *City* and *County* MHCs. I also conducted 48 in-depth interviews including 41 interviews with MHC team members from both courts between 2013 and 2016. All statements are confidential and team members are referred by their professional role (e.g., defense attorney) and not linked to the court in which they work. For those professionals with whom there were less than three in that position he/she is referred to simply as MHC team member. I gathered additional data, quantitative and qualitative, focusing on *City* MHC including interviewing 7 clients from *City* MHC. I use "defendant" throughout the book to refer to the pre-opt-in (or opt-outs) and "client" for those who opt-into MHC. I think the change in language denotes a change in status, though not all team members liked the term. I use pseudonyms for all client references, from both interviews and court observations. The client interviews provided valuable perspectives because their side of the court experience is often unexamined. To ensure confidentiality, I use pseudonyms for all client references from both interviews and court observations. Case studies demonstrate how the process, clients, and proceedings in many ways deviate from "business as usual" in American criminal justice. Courtroom vignettes and interviews reveal the ways the goals of the court shape the actors and the social roles they play. The quantitative portion analyzes a cohort of exiters from *City* MHC in 2008, explaining patterns of criminal recidivism. Together these data paint a fuller picture of MHC from multiple perspectives. The MHC case studies showcase the mission of the court as applied in practice and sheds light on why MHCs are expanding across the country. (See Appendix A for more details on methods and study design including data collection, descriptive characteristics of interview respondents, and quantitative analysis models.)

*City* MHC adjudicates cases within city boundaries while *County* MHC has a larger jurisdiction beyond the city to the broader county lines, encapsulating several other smaller cities, and neighboring areas. Like other first generation MHCs, these two courts began as a response to public concerns over rare, but highly publicized cases of violence perpetrated by people with mental illness. The local jurisdiction evaluated how better to address issues of mental illness and the criminal justice system and recommended establishing a MHC. The court's mission centers on better serving the community by addressing public safety, reducing criminalization of persons with mental illness, and promoting systems integration. Planning for the MHCs involved key stakeholders from across the county. They adopted a collaborative approach to create an effective pilot program which expanded into permanent courts.

Both courts are located in an urban downtown corridor. Like many West coast cities, the metro area has a visible concentration of people who are homeless and struggling with mental illness. The urban context links contemporary issues about quality of life campaigns (e.g., social disorder and "broken windows") to incarceration and mental health services and treatment. While *City* MHC takes cases largely from the downtown core, *County* MHC has a larger catchment area, taking cases from the rest of the county. *County* MHC also has satellite courts as it expands beyond the city boundaries to include the entire county. *County* also takes *City* cases and there are several clients with cases before both courts. A court may also consolidate several cases. For example because a client in *County* MHC might also have a charge pending in *City* MHC, *County* MHC might decide to track all of the cases together under one jurisdiction to simplify review hearings, prevent extending probationary period, and incentivize compliance.

*City* and *County* MHC are similar in many ways. They are comparable in terms of mental health eligibility criteria and amenability assessment. Both courts mandate that the accused have a demonstrable mental health diagnosis (usually Axis I based on DSM-IV criteria[9]) which is consistent with other MHCs (Almquist and Dodd 2009; Goldkamp and Irons-Guynn 2000). In both courts, defendants volunteer for MHC by opting-into the court process. The clients must be amenable and willing to participate in treatment; most clients usually have a history (often extensive) of mental health treatment. As is typical of problem-solving courts, both courts have specialized dockets and a dedicated MHC team (McNiel and Binder 2007; Schneider et al. 2007; Steadman et al. 2001). Team members hold a pre-court meeting to discuss the court calendar in detail. Both courts also have a similar probationary period of approximately 2 years; the potential to graduate early based on compliance is present in both. Moreover, both courts have two functions—a competency and therapeutic court—centralized in one court. There is some cross-over in staffing, as some of the team members have worked in the other court at a prior point in their careers.

The basic organization of *City* MHC has remained largely the same since it began, although some of the daily practices and procedures have shifted over time. By contrast, *County* MHC has changed substantially, and the differences between the courts make for instructive comparison. The key difference between the courts is in the type of cases handled: misdemeanor versus felony cases. As is typical of many first-generation courts, *City* MHC only processes misdemeanor cases (McNiel and Binder 2007; Redlich et al. 2005). *County* MHC does take felony cases, as is more typical of second-generation courts. Felony charges are referred to as "felony drop-downs"; once a defendant officially enters into MHC the court reduces the charge(s) to a misdemeanor. The result is a unique type of "hybrid model," as a MHC judge put it. Cases do not stay at the felony level but they are also not truly treated as misdemeanor offenses either. A defense attorney explained the shift in *County* MHC to include felony cases as follows:

> I think when the mental health courts first got set up, it was primarily for low-level offenders – trespass and indecent exposure and that kind of thing. What it has become, particularly in [*County*] MHC, is a lot of higher-level crimes, a lot more felonies. A lot more co-occurring disorders and a population that is more difficult to serve because they have more complex issues – sex offences, arsons, things that make housing difficult… now our population has shifted to the more serious offenders.

In fact *County* MHC has transformed from a misdemeanor only court to one in which felony cases consume about half of its caseload. This has caused considerable tension as more serious offenders enter MHC. Team members, most notably probation officers, worry that the court is moving away from its stated mission of addressing mental illness to a more complex set of factors. According to the critics, the expanded pool of potential MHC clients are at higher risk of reoffending and require more intense supervision, putting a strain on resources and discretionary authority necessary for adequate supervision (these concerns are discussed in greater detail in Chapter 2).

# Book Outline

This book provides a better understanding of the *social processes* by which MHCs operate. Chapter 2 examines the theory of therapeutic jurisprudence and highlights the centrality of this orientation for MHCs. I outline the major paradigm shifts characteristic of MHCs—treatment orientation and collaboration and describe my formulation of "therapeutic justice." I detail the mission of MHCs and the changes in court structure and culture, noting how a treatment orientation works in practice of a less adversarial model of criminal justice. The chapter examines net-widening arguments—expanding the number of individuals under the control of the criminal justice system and the intensity and severity of criminal justice intervention—around wider, stronger and denser nets. The chapter ends by revisiting the court's mission.

Chapter 3 illustrates the key principles of MHCs in the two case study sites detailing the selection process, treatment plans, conditions of probation, and the services offered to those opting-into the court. The chapter reveals how clients decide to opt-in or opt-out of the MHC and the ways in which some involuntarily get catch in the web of MHC. It details the MHC team members and specifically considers the role of the judge and other members of the team as therapeutic agents in dispensing therapeutic justice.

In Chapter 4, I explore MHCs in action and how the court process influence client experiences. The chapter focuses on court reviews and the sanctioning process. How the court responds to compliance and non-compliance is consequential for clients, having both therapeutic and anti-therapeutic effects. I highlight the role of procedural justice and harm reduction frameworks in the working of the court. Throughout the chapter, I detail how MHCs treatment orientation is on display formally before the judge and informally with team members in ways that enhance and impede therapeutic justice.

Chapter 5 focuses on assessing the efficacy of MHCs using quantitative and qualitative data. Focusing first on criminal recidivism, the chapter describes reductions in criminal behavior post court-exit using administrative court data. Incentives at opt-in, mental health treatment usage, and completing MHC are associated with reductions in the likelihood of new crimes after exiting from *City* MHC. Drawing from interviews with MHC team members, the role of incentives, mental health treatment and graduation are explored further. Data illustrate the relationship between benefits offered to clients at entry and rewards throughout the court process. Findings highlight compliance levels with MHC conditions and the role of rituals in positive outcomes for clients. The chapter ends with a discussion on how to assess success, calling for a more expansive understanding.

Chapter 6 details seven MHC case histories. By giving voice to clients, I uncover the experiences of those within the court and detail their pathways of sucess (and thier setbacks). The stories illustrate the court's influence on recidivism and *how* MHCs impact the lives of individuals. The interviews of MHC clients exemplify the ways in which experience in MHC influence their quality of life including the management of mental illness and substance use, housing stability, employment status and family relations. I examine how MHC participation encourages other pro-social and healthy behaviors that can lead to changed lives. The narratives reveal the potential of MHCs by highlighting some success stories based on court observations and interviews. Toward the end of the chapter I provided a nuanced explanation of why MHCs do not work for all clients.

In the conclusion, I turn to the implications of therapeutic justice for MHCs and broader social policy. This chapter summarizes the unique features of MHCs and their important role in contemporary models of criminal justice. It details key strengths and identifies current limitations within the MHC model. Pointing to the future, the book concludes by charting out some improvements in the functioning and effectiveness of MHCs in line with a kind of *social work criminal justice*. I return to the key paradigms shifts that characterize MHC and offer some reforms based on "best practices" for the next generation of MHCs and problem-solving courts more broadly. MHCs, as an innovative therapeutic model of jurisprudence, represent an important step toward reforming contemporary criminal justice practices.

## Notes

1. In mainstream court, the amount of jail time would depend on whether Monique was willing engage in treatment for her mental illness. Monique also had the option of having her case go to trial.
2. This idea is part of his broader perspective of sociological jurisprudence.
3. The standardized general population for SPD threshold is 5%.
4. In California for example, involuntary commitment standard mandates that a person has to meet the following criteria: (1) be dangerous to self/others; or (2) unable to provide for basic personal needs for food, clothing and shelter. The Oregon standard is almost identical with slightly different wording: (1) be a danger to self/others; or (2) be unable to provide for basic personal needs and is not receiving care necessary for health/safety. The second criterion is elaborated to include 4 components (a) have chronic mental illness; (b) have had two hospitalizations in previous three years; (c) have symptoms/behaviors substantially similar to those that led to the previous hospitalizations; and (d) will continue to physically or mentally deteriorate to either (1) or (2) if untreated. In Washington state, there are three standards but they fall along the same two dimensions as in the California and Oregon statutes: (1) be a danger to self/others/property; or (2) be in danger of serious physical harm from failure to provide for essential human needs of health or safety; or (3) have severe deterioration in routine functioning evidenced by loss of cognitive or volitional control and not be receiving essential care (Treatment Advocacy Center, http://www.treatmentadvocacycenter.org/home-page, retrieved August 12, 2016).
5. https://www.nami.org/Learn-More/Mental-Health-Public-Policy/Jailing-People-with-Mental-Illness, retrieved January 28, 2018.
6. The new director instituted a mental health transition center so that once individuals with mental illness are in jail they are linked to mental health treatment and job skills training. At the time of the news story this only included 40 graduates but the results were encouraging in that 1/3 were pursuing education and 2/3 were employed (See NPR May 19, 2015, "Clinical Psychologist to Head Chicago's Cook County Jail").
7. According to the Justice Center, The Council of State Governments along the West coast there are 53 MHCs in total (34 in CA, 8 in OR and 11 in WA). Retrieved on September 1, 2016 from http://www.samhsa.gov/gains-center/mental-health-treatment-court-locator/adults.

8. The five intercepts include: (1) law enforcement/emergency services; (2) booking/initial court hearing; (3) jails/courts; (4) reentry; and (5) community corrections/community support.
9. In 2013, the American Psychiatric Association issued the DSM-V. The revised edition discarded the multiaxial system of diagnosis (formerly Axis I, Axis II, and Axis III) and instead lists all disorders in Section II, thus blurring the lines between Axis I and Axis II which represents key distinction in MHCs. In interviews I asked court liaisons about the latest DSM and whether or not eligibility criteria had shifted or if there were any plans to reevaluate eligibility based on the revisions. A court liaison stated "No. [name of state mental hospital] is still using the old DSM. I don't even have training in the new DSM. I don't know what the reasoning behind it is."

# References

Alexander, Michelle. 2012. *The New Jim Crow: Mass Incarceration in the Age of Colorblindness*. New York: The New Press.
Almquist, Lauren, and Elizabeth Dodd. 2009. *Mental Health Courts: A Guide to Reserach-Informed Policy and Practice*. New York: Council of State Governments Justice Center.
Beckett, Katherine. 1999. *Making Crime Pay: Law and Order in Contemporary American Politics*. Oxford: Oxford University Press.
Berman, Greg, and John Feinblatt. 2001. "Problem-Solving Courts: A Brief Primer." *Law & Policy* 23: 125–40.
———. 2005. *Good Courts: The Case for Problem-Solving Justice*. New York: The New Press.
Bernstein, Robert, and Tammy Seltzer. 2003. "Criminalization of People with Mental Illnesses: The Role of Mental Health Courts in System Reform." *The University of the District of Columbia Law Review* 7: 143–62. https://doi.org/10.3366/ajicl.2011.0005.
Bronson, Jennifer, and Marcus Berzofsky. 2017. *Indicators of Mental Health Problems Reported by Prisoners and Jail Inmates, 2011–2012*, 1–17. Washington, DC: U.S. Department of Justice. https://www.bjs.gov/index.cfm?ty=pbdetail&iid=5946.

Clear, Todd R., and Natasha A. Frost. 2014. *The Punishment Imperative: The Rise and Failure of Mass Incarceration in America*. New York: New York University Press.

Erickson, Patricia, and Steven Erickson. 2008. *Crime, Punishment, and Mental Illness: Law and the Behavioral Sciences in Conflict*. New Brunswick: Rutgers University Press.

Ewick, Particia, and Susan S. Silbey. 1998. *The Common Place of Law: Stories from Everyday Life*. Chicago: University of Chicago Press.

Feeley, Malcolm M., and Jonathan Simon. 1992. "The New Penology: Notes on the Emerging Strategy of Corrections and Its Implications." *Criminology* 30: 449. http://scholarship.law.berkeley.edu/facpubs.

Finkle, Michael J., Russell Kurth, Christopher Cadle, and Jessica Mullan. 2009. "Competency Courts: A Creative Solution for Restoring Competency to the Competency Process." *Behavioral Sciences & the Law* 27: 767–86. https://doi.org/10.1002/bsl.

Fisler, Carol. 2015. "When Research Chllenges Policy and Practice: Toward a New Understanding of Mental Health Courts." *The Judges' Journal* 54 (2): 8–13. http://www.courtinnovation.org/sites/default/files/documents/JJ_SP15_54_2_Fisler.pdf.

Ford, Matt. 2015. "America's Largest Mental Hospital Is a Jail." *The Atlantic*, August 10, 2015. https://www.theatlantic.com/politics/archive/2015/06/americas-largest-mental-hospital-is-a-jail/395012/.

Foucault, Michel. 1995. *Discipline and Punish: The Birth of the Prison*. 2nd ed. New York: Vintage. https://doi.org/10.2307/2065008.

Freiberg, Arie. 2001. "Problem-Oriented Courts: Innovative Solutions to Intractable Problems." *Journal of Judicial Administration* 11 (January 2001): 8–27.

Garland, David. 2002. *The Culture of Control: Crime and Social Order in Contemporary Society*. Chicago: University of Chicago Press.

Gerring, John. 2007. *Case Study Research: Principles and Practices*. Cambridge: Cambridge University Press.

Goffman, Erving. 1961. *Asylums: Essays on the Social Situation of Mental Patients and Other Inmates*. New York: Anchor Books.

Goldkamp, J. S, and C. Irons-Guynn. 2000. "Emerging Judicial Strategies for the Mentally Ill in the Criminal Caseload: Mental Health Courts in Fort Lauderdale, Seattle, San Bernardino, and Anchorage," 1–83. http://www.ncjrs.gov/pdffiles1/bja/182504.pdf.

Goodale, Gregg, Lisa Callahan, and Henry J. Steadman. 2013. "Law Psychiatry: What Can We Say About Mental Health Courts Today?" *Psychiatric Services* 64 (4): 298–300. https://doi.org/10.1176/appi.ps.201300049.

Griffin, Patricia A., and David DeMatteo. 2009. "Mental Health Courts: Cautious Optimism." In *Problem-Solving Courts: Justice for the Twenty-First Century*, edited by P. Higgins and M. B. Mackinem, 91–113. Santa Barbara: Praeger.

Harcourt, Bernard E. 2006. "From the Asylum to the Prison: Rethinking the Incarceration Revolution." *Texas Law Review* 84: 1751–86.

Heilbrun, Kirk, David DeMatteo, Heidi Strohmaier, and Meghann Galloway. 2015. "The Movement Toward Community-Based Alternatives to Criminal Justice Involvement and Incarceration for People with Severe Mental Illness." In *The Sequential Intercept Model and Criminal Justice: Promoting Community Alternatives for Individuals with Serious Mental Illness*, edited by Patricia A. Griffin, Krik Heilbrun, Edward P. Mulvey, David DeMatteo, and Carol A. Schubert, 1–20. Oxford: Oxford University Press.

James, Doris J., and Lauren E. Glaze. 2006. *Mental Health Problems of Prison and Jail Inmates*, 1–12. Washington, DC: U.S. Department of Justice. http://bjs.gov/content/pub/pdf/mhppji.pdf.

Kushel, Margot B., Judith A. Hahn, Jennifer L., Evans, David R. Bangsberg, and Andrew R. Moss. 2005. "Revolving Doors: Imprisonment Among the Homeless and Marginally Housed Population." *American Journal of Public Health* 95 (10): 1747–52. https://doi.org/10.2105/AJPH.2005.065094.

Lens, Vicki. 2016. *Poor Justice: How the Poor Fare in the Courts*. https://books.google.com/books/about/Poor_Justice.html?id=kCugCgAAQBAJ.

Lurigio, Arthur J., and Jessica Snowden. 2009. "Putting Therapeutic Jurisprudence into Practice: The Growth, Operations, and Effectiveness of Mental Health Court." *Justice System Journal* 30 (2): 196–218. https://doi.org/10.1080/0098261X.2009.10767926.

McNiel, Dale E., and Renée L. Binder. 2007. "Effectiveness of a Mental Health Court in Reducing Criminal Recidivism and Violence." *American Journal of Psychiatry* 164 (9): 1395–403. https://doi.org/10.1176/appi.ajp.2007.06101664.

Miller, JoAnn, and Donald C. Johnson. 2009. *Problem Solving Courts: A Measure of Justice*. Lanham: Rowman & Littlefield.

Munetz, Mark R., and Patricia A. Griffin. 2006. "Use of the Sequential Intercept Model as an Approach to Decriminalization of People with

Serious Mental Illness." *Psychiatric Services* 57 (4): 544–49. https://doi.org/10.1176/ps.2006.57.4.544.

Nolan, James L., Jr. 1998. *The Therapeutic State: Justifying Government at Century's End.* New York: New York University Press.

———. 2001. *Reinventing Justice: The American Drug Court Movement.* Princeton: Princeton University Press.

Perlin, Michael. 2013. "'The Judge, He Cast His Robe Aside': Mental Health Courts, Dignity and Due Process." *Mental Health Law & Policy Journal* 3 (1): 1–29.

Petrila, J. 2003. "An Introduction to Special Jurisdiction Courts." *International Journal of Law and Psychiatry* 26 (1): 3–12.

Pfeiffer, Mary Beth. 2007. *Crazy in America: The Hidden Tragedy of Our Criminalized Mentally Ill.* New York: Carroll & Graf.

Ragin, Charles C. 1992. "Introduction: What Is a Case?" In *What Is a Case? Exploring the Foundations of Social Inquiry*, edited by Charles C. Ragin and Howard S. Becker, 11th ed. 1–52. New York: Cambridge University Press.

Redlich, Allison D., Henry J. Steadman, John Monahan, John Petrila, and Patricia A. Griffin. 2005. "The Second Generation of Mental Health Courts." *Psychology, Public Policy, and Law* 11 (4): 527–38. https://doi.org/10.1037/1076-8971.11.4.527.

Schneider, Richard D., Hy Bloom, and Mark Heerema. 2007. *Mental Health Courts: Decriminalizing the Mental Ill.* Toronto: Irwin Law.

Selman, Donna, and Paul Leighton. 2010. *Punishment for Sale: Private Prisons, Big Business, and the Incarceration Binge.* Lanham: Rowman & Littlefield.

Slovenko, Ralph. 2002. "The Transinstitutionalization of the Mentally Ill." *Ohio Northern University Law Review* 29: 641–60. https://doi.org/10.3366/ajicl.2011.0005.

Steadman, Henry J., Susan Davidson, and Collie Brown. 2001. "Mental Health Courts: Their Promise and Unanswered Questions." *Psychiatric Services* 52 (4): 457–58. https://doi.org/10.1176/appi.ps.52.4.457.

Sutton, John R. 2001. *Law/Society: Origins, Interactions, and Change.* Thousand Oaks: Pine Forge Press.

Torrey, Fuller E. 1997. *Out of the Shadows: Confronting America's Mental Illness Crisis.* New York: Wiley.

———. 2014. *American Psychosis: How the Federal Government Destroyed the Mental Illness Treatment System.* Oxford: Oxford University Press.

Torrey, Fuller E., Aaron D. Kennard, Don Eslinger, Richard Lamb, and James Pavle. 2010. "More Mentally Ill Persons Are in Jails and Prisons Than Hospitals: A Survey of the States." May: 1–22. http://www.treatmentadvocacycenter.org/storage/documents/final_jails_v_hospitals_study.pdf.

Vogel, Wendy M., Chan D. Noether, and Henry J. Steadman. 2007. "Preparing Communities for Re-Entry of Offenders with Mental Illness Wendy." *Journal of Offender Rehabilitation* 45 (1–2): 167–88. https://doi.org/10.1300/J076v45n01.

Whitaker, Robert. 2010. *Mad in America: Bad Science, Bad Medicine, and the Enduring Mistreatment of the Mentally Ill*. Philadelphia: Basic Books.

Wilson, James Q., and George L. Kelling. 1982. "Broken Windows: The Police and Neighborhood Safety." *The Atlantic* (March): 29–38.

# 2

# Beyond Adversarialism?: Collaboration and Therapeutic Goals

Pushing through the heavy double doors to enter a MHC, it is difficult to impress upon an outsider the different legal world that awaits inside. MHCs are located inside criminal court buildings, and in many ways look like traditional courtrooms with the familiar layout, furnishings, and people.[1] The hierarchy is clear with the judge's bench set back and elevated from the rest of the courtroom. The two opposing counsel tables are positioned on either side of the courtroom in front of the judge, symbolizing the adversarial nature of traditional court. The jury box is located on either side of the courtroom. In some courtrooms a low half-wall or gate separates the gallery, where defendants, clients and visitors sit awaiting court hearings. The gallery is located at the back of the courtroom, physically reinforcing the power differential and spatial distance between defendants and representatives of the legal system. While on the surface the design of MHCs reflects a typical courtroom and the actors seem to represent conventional legal agents, an atypical context—oriented toward complex social issues—lies therein.

It takes time and extensive observation to understand the organization and workings of these courts. Partly this is due to the almost constant milling around; the coming and going of actors in and out of the courtroom (both while the court is on and off the record) and the noise associated with the opening and closing of doors (both to the outside hallway and internally from the jail causeway where in-custody defendants are escorted).

## Therapeutic Justice

In this book, I offer a new perspective on problem-solving courts based on key paradigm shifts that characterize this court innovation. The potential for law to have therapeutic implications is paramount. The focus on therapeutic goals moves law toward substantive justice. The integration of extra-legal factors in the resolution of legal matters, coupled with an emphasis on individual's well-being, shifts some of the emphasis away from procedures and rules. This change in orientation towards outcomes is reminiscent of Max Weber's classic distinction between formal law and substantive justice. MHCs attempt to balance formal law and substantive justice, favoring just outcomes over the formality of law. A focus on outcomes and not just procedures and rules orients the court toward ethical and sometimes political goals. The challenge of this orientation is the lack of predictability that is often associated with courts favoring this form. Another concern is an interventionist role of law that can lead to disparate treatment by individual cases, raising legal concerns around due process and equal treatment before the law.

I use the term therapeutic justice in this book's title to underscore the importance of the philosophy of therapeutic jurisprudence (I detail the theme of therapeutic jurisprudence later in the chapter) as well as to highlight the focus on outcomes—substantive justice—and not merely formal case processing. This should not be confused with promoting a certain ideological version of justice but rather a focus on the welfare of both defendant and society (which need not be at odds). Enhancing treatment and welfare is central to the philosophy, organization and cultural practices of MHCs. In large part, it is the members of the court team that bring therapeutic justice into action.

Decades ago, David Wexler (1973, 337) raised concerns about "procedural safeguards in a system of therapeutic justice." While he never explicitly defined the term therapeutic justice, he warned against "paternalistic power" in an overreaching, boundless therapeutic state. In part, it is the elasticity of mental illness itself that creates the potential for a social control-oriented therapeutic state anchored in judicial process. The issues raised by Wexler remain important. His precautionary insights underpin the limits of attaining therapeutic justice within the criminal justice framework. My usage of the term therapeutic justice reflects these concerns. It is through the extension and merging of a criminal justice model with a medical and social work model, while preserving legal safeguards, that MHCs have the best hope of achieving therapeutic justice. This kind of individualized, "wraparound" approach incorporates social service elements and verges on what I call *social work criminal justice*, a point I return to in the conclusion.

I find that Wexler's fears of an "unbridled therapeutic state" are not on display in the everyday working of MHCs in my case studies. MHCs do not abandon concerns about formal law and legal rules. In fact, quite the opposite; the legal process and protections are integrated into how MHCs work. Some MHCs tailor court practices further toward the goal of therapeutic justice than do others. There may be a danger in going too far, in which the law is overshadowed. Several team members I interviewed articulated this concern, warning about a slippery-slope in applying treatment court principles toward "law as therapy." The tension between therapy and punishment (Paik 2011) is important for understanding the potential and limits of therapeutic justice. The therapeutic mission of the court raises concerns about expanding or deepening the reach of the criminal justice system into the lives of some of the most vulnerable in our society.

## Mission

The underlying mission of MHCs is anything but standard criminal justice. The main goals of MHCs are similar to all problem-solving courts: to reduce recidivism (reducing jail and contacts with the criminal justice system) and enhance public safety. What differentiates the mission of MHCs from other problem-solving courts and traditional criminal courts is the additional focus on addressing mental illness, connecting people with mental illness to mental health services and treatment, and improving the well-being of clients. MHCs attempt to achieve their goals in different ways from other problem-solving courts and traditional courts. Realizing these goals, however, is a serious challenge. The goals that inform *City* and *County* courts are similar to those stated by other MHCs in the country and internationally (Almquist and Dodd 2009; Schneider et al. 2007) but the focus on social support, services and quality of life of mental health clients in these courts stands out, advancing a public health objective within the criminal justice system.

Many saw the mission of MHC in broader ethical terms tied to society, seen in the following statement by a judge:

> We want this person to be better, not only just sort of altruistically – I am a person and I want to see people do better in their lives, but also from a systemic point of view, if they are doing better, they are not committing new crimes. They are not creating victims, causing resource drains, etc.

Judges, like other MHC team members, wanted to see clients "out of the system." Upon seeking the appointment to MHC a judge summarized that MHC was an "innovation… a place where it was possible to promote wellness and recovery."

Every MHC team member expressed "buy-in" to the mission of the treatment court while recognizing that each team member has a different role to play in the legal process. For some the MHC approach is truly an alternative to the traditional court model, approaching the problem from a "different angle," as a defense attorney put it. MHC team members referred to the court's mission in similar ways. A prosecutor highlighted two key components: "promote public safety and reduce recidivism." When probed to identify their "ultimate goal" of MHC, team members gave varied answers. A probation officer explained that getting clients "reintegrated back into society is my ultimate goal" while a prosecutor argued that addressing "the mental health need that will address the criminal behavior" was paramount. A team member stated, "It is for community safety, for victims' safety, for the benefits of the defendant also and their family." For some it was more political against the broader system of mass incarceration, for example a court liaison pronounced the mission is "to lower recidivism rates, to promote mental health wellbeing, to work against this punitive system."

Even when a defense social worker talked about reducing recidivism as the "ultimate goal," he acknowledged that "to foster a healthier community" is also part of MHCs. Even prosecutors highlighted the goal of "having graduates be in a position to be a productive member of society." Some went even further, as did a certain probation officer who claimed that "defendants are also part of the community" and that providing access to mental health treatment aids in reducing "the criminalization of mentally ill people, and reducing jail time." For many the mission of MHC is a clear attempt to "decriminalize mental illness and to help people who are mentally ill get stable in the community" characterized a defense social worker and to protect people with mental illness from being prosecuted from the perspective of a defense attorney. A judge reflected that "individuals shouldn't be punished because they have a serious mental health problem."

Believing in the mission of the court does not mean that MHC team members were naive and unaware of its limits. A court liaison confessed:

> I know that there are flaws in [the MHC], but I do think that it is a good idea. I think it is an imperfect solution but I think that it can be tweaked… I do think it is a lot better than letting people sit in jail and they get no treatment and minimal treatment and then you release them. That is a horrible solution and it will never, ever, ever work.

I found that a prevention orientation prevails among MHC team members working in the court.

MHCs embrace a holistic criminal justice approach that responds to the conditions associated with mental illness and other circumstances that contribute to the presence of people with mental illness in the court system. The key to improving the likelihood of a successful intervention and shaping an alternative life trajectory—away from future court entanglements—is social support, access to housing and other social services. In theory, the different parties—judges, prosecutors, defense attorneys, probation officers, social works and court liaisons—work together to address the individual needs of each client, all the while being cognizant of community safety. Team members intervene in the lives of clients around mental illness, substance abuse, and housing needs; they work collaboratively to develop a workable treatment plan to increase stability, thus reducing contact with the criminal justice system, which, in turn, brings about greater public safety. The consensus I found was that in order to alter behavior, clients needed some combination of stability, support, and treatment.

## Mental Illness and Criminal Behavior

Many MHCs are premised on the idea that mental illness is related to criminal behavior (Schneider et al. 2007). Some MHCs see mental illness as *the* cause or at least a contributing cause of criminal behavior, as in the case of *City* MHC whose website designates mental illness as the "key issue." Other MHCs see an indirect or even ephemeral connection between mental illness and crime such as *County* MHC whose website focuses on a "nexus" between symptoms and circumstances leading to criminal behavior. It focuses on treatment for clients for the "mental health issues causing them to commit crimes or be part of the criminal justice system." However, team members from both courts referred repeatedly to a direct link between un-treated or under-treated mental illness and criminal behavior, but often linked mental health to other issues outside the criminal domain. A court liaison referred to focusing on those defendants who are "genuinely mentally ill." A defense attorney described the process of MHC to a potential client, clarifying that the goal is to "Get you the right treatment, get you the housing." For many MHC team members linking clients to broader services is key. In order to reach those goals another defense attorney declared, "We need to make our clients more stable and medication compliant so they can remain in society and be successful."

*City* MHC traces a more direct link between mental illness and crime. Its understanding reflects the criminalization hypothesis which argues that criminal behavior is often the consequence of untreated mental illness and that the solution is to provide psychiatric services to mentally ill individuals (Abramson 1972; Peterson et al. 2010). However, support for this perspective is waning as social research suggests quite the opposite; only a small subgroup of offenders (~10%) exhibit a direct link between mental illness and criminal acts. For the majority the link is indirect or mediated by other circumstances (Johnston 2012; Morse 1999; Skeem et al. 2011) and often linked to the paucity of mental health services and not illness per se (Fisher et al. 2006). The pathways to criminality for those with serious mental illness are heterogeneous (Peterson et al. 2010) and there is noteworthy research debunking the claim that people who are mentally ill are more violent than others (Metzl and MacLeish 2015). The same criminological theories used to understand the general population can explain offenders with mental illness (Silver 2006). Nevertheless, rare but horrendous violent episodes and the associated media coverage link dangerousness and mental illness in the minds of many Americans (Angermeyer and Matschinger 2003). Reflecting the emerging consensus, *County* MHC assumes an indirect relationship between mental illness and a person's presence in the criminal justice system. This position reflects a broad understanding of the cumulative disadvantages by which mental illness can lead to negative life events and increased contacts with the criminal justice system. For critics such as Johnston (2012), the segregation and coercive treatment of a stigmatized population without adequate evidentiary support of it key assumptions (nexus between criminal behavior and mental illness) suggests that MHCs lack legitimacy (as does their denial of individuals rationality, will and autonomy).

Despite that the fact that scientific evidence does not support certain assumptions of MHC programming, I found overwhelming support among MHC practitioners for a direct connection between mental illness and criminal justice involvement. In a competency evaluation, where the case was dismissed and referred to one of the state's mental hospitals for possible civil commitment, the judge stated "I'm worried about you. You might not be able to take your meds. You might hurt someone." In talking about the mission of MHCs, one probation officer described the court's mission as being "to take people in the legal system with criminal charges whose behavior has been, if not primarily, significantly influenced by their mental health issues and their deficits in their treatment." The court then intervenes with assessment, connecting clients to treatment organizations and monitoring in the hope of inhibiting future legal troubles. However, all the team members I spoke with stated something like "of course it doesn't always work out quite that simply."

While existing studies suggest a weak link between mental illness and criminal behavior most MHC team members see a clear association between the two as foundational to the courts. Many said something similar to this probation officer's account of the court's mission:

> I think the sort of mission of the court as it's described in general is sort of accurate, you know… So, you know, the idea being that if you change something in their mental health treatment, either how much, whether they're taking meds or participating in treatment, and encourage them and sort of hold them accountable to do it, it will decrease their legal problems because the legal problems are tied to the mental illness.

Undoubtedly, for most MHC team members, the court's goals were bigger than the individual defendant. For example, most saw the mission of the court as being directly related to changing the public view of mental illness and distancing it from its publicized criminal association. Recounting how she understood the connection between mental illness and criminal behavior, a judge declared "You are not seeing a criminal who is mentally ill. You are seeing a mentally ill person who is engaging in criminogenic behavior. That is a huge difference, and it is not just word play."

In practice MHC team members are acutely aware of the complex and sometimes tenuous relationship between mental illness and criminal behavior. MHCs can offer "immediate relief," they cannot solve the broader criminalization of mental illness (Bernstein and Seltzer 2003, 148).[2] The court and team members help to alleviate circumstances, such as lack of housing and lack of social support that create the stress and instability that heightens probability of criminal behavior. For many team members housing was central as the other issues represent even greater challenges without stable housing. Part of the approach in MHC, as opposed to mainstream court, is "to take into account the wider stresses and triggers" reflected a judge. MHC team members make efforts that are individualized for the client, combining treatment, rehabilitation, housing and social support (Schneider et al. 2007). A prosecutor suggested that part of the challenge is due to the inability "to define the relationship between the history or the current status of the mental health problems" which multiple team members related to the complexity around alcohol, drug problems and homelessness. Both social scientific evidence and client evidence (from interviews) suggest that untreated mental illness is not the prime driver of criminal behavior. Regardless, the mission of MHCs is linked to criminality leading to a philosophical change in court orientation and functioning.

## Paradigm Shift

The goal of MHCs is to reduce the "revolving door" of criminal justice for people with mental illness. One of the ways MHCs try to fulfill their mission is through a philosophical shift toward a less punitive, less adversarial style of criminal justice. MHCs diverge from the traditional court model in key ways characterized by two major paradigms shifts. First, MHCs are treatment courts and thus committed to rehabilitative and therapeutic ends. Second, they are premised on a non-adversarial team model approach.

### Therapeutic Jurisprudence

Problem-solving courts are often associated with therapeutic jurisprudence (Schneider et al. 2007; Daicoff 2000; Hora et al. 1999; Perlin 2013) and MHCs are underpinned by these principles but the practice of therapeutic jurisprudence are not confined to specialty or treatment courts and best understood on a continuum (Rottman and Casey 1999). Partly this orientation stems from the early modelling of MHCs after drug courts. "Therapeutic jurisprudence" entered into the lexicon of the criminal justice system in the late 1980s in the field of mental health law. The writings of David Wexler and Bruce Winick are seminal. They defined therapeutic jurisprudence as "the study of the extent to which substantive rules, legal procedures, and the roles of lawyers and judges produce therapeutic or antitherapeutic consequences" (Wexler and Winick 1991, 981, emphasis added). The insight is that how law is enacted through courts have both intended and unintended consequences for people who come "before the law" (Ewick and Silbey 1998). The therapeutic jurisprudence perspective regards the law as a social force that can have both positive and negative therapeutic outcomes. An explicit aim of therapeutic jurisprudence is to bring into focus the emotional and physical well-being of individuals. The law can either help heal both individual defendants and members of society or it can lead to greater stress and injury.

Seeing law as a social force, Christopher Slobogin's (1996, 767) redefinition of therapeutic jurisprudence is particularly relevant given the central role social scientific research plays in the evaluating it in practice. He refers to one definition of therapeutic jurisprudence as "the use of social science to study the extent to which a legal rule or practice promotes the psychological and physical wellbeing of the people it" (1996, 767, emphasis added).

Therapeutic jurisprudence as an interdisciplinary project calls for linking social scientific inquiry and law. The principles of therapeutic jurisprudence guide courts in fundamentally different ways than the traditional non-therapeutic court model. Emphasizing therapeutic matters does not necessitate an undermining of legal issues including constitutional rights (e.g., due process) for the sake of therapeutic goals. In the case of MHCs, *both* legal and therapeutic concerns are addressed. Winick noted that therapeutic jurisprudence does not suggest that therapeutic interests take precedence over other rights but he argues that whenever they are in tension, the theory of therapeutic jurisprudence does not provide ready tools to adjudicate the conflict. There are some notable critics of this shift towards therapeutic jurisprudence and therapeutic rehabilitation[3] (see Johnston 2012; Seltzer 2005 for excellent discussions).

Therapeutic jurisprudence was originally formulated around mental health law and thus its application to MHCs is participially compelling. However, it has expanded to multiple domains within and outside of the law. It has spurred a new wave of alternative approaches to law and legal practice. Daicoff (2000, 466) describes therapeutic jurisprudence as one of almost a dozen "vectors"[4] in the comprehensive law movement eschewing the traditional "adversarial, litigative model." In her discussion of these alternatives she argues that this emergence revolves around a goal of establishing a "more comprehensive, humane, and psychologically optimal way of handling legal matters." This new orientation acknowledges the "importance of concerns beyond simply the strict legal rights, duties and obligations of the parties" (2000, 466, 470).

The philosophical orientation toward therapeutic jurisprudence leads to shifts in the social practices of the law as an alternative cultural framework (Nolan 2001; Schneider et al. 2007). Wexler links therapeutic jurisprudence to collaboration; he promotes it as an alternative counter to the "culture of critique" in which the "two sides" of adversarial framing encourage "debate rather than dialogue" (2000, 450). Going forward, the law must address how the practice of adversarialism influences those who practice the law as well as those caught up in it.

## Collaboration and Reduced Adversarialism

MHCs are less adversarial than traditional courts. A collaborative approach characterizes problem-solving courts including MHCs. The team model and the treatment orientation shift the court's focus toward therapeutic ends including mental health and chemical dependency treatment, housing, social services, and social support. A judge recounted that "The adversarial system is I am going to win and you are going to lose" which, while a stereotype, is a stark contrast to a collaborative model operating in MHC. For a prosecutor, "it is very rare that you can be in a legal position where you are in a collaborative and therapeutic approach" which is what led him to seek out a rotation in MHC.

This "teamwork" approach includes new social positions and new social roles as different parties work together across the traditional demarcations of prosecution and defense. The working MHC team includes the standard legal actors—judges, prosecuting attorneys, defense attorneys, and probation officers—but they also include new members such as defense social workers, court liaisons (also referred to as court monitors[5] or court screeners) and victim's advocate (only in *County* MHC). Court liaisons[6] serve in a "neutral" position acting as a link between defendant and court personnel as well as "gatekeepers" of the court screening process. Whether or not a deferent fits the criteria is a clinical decisions decided by the court liaison. The importance of this new position and having an "independent third party" makes MHCs unique. Defense social workers assist defense attorneys and work with clients to connect them to social services, benefits, and housing. The victim's advocate serves as the contact person between the victims and the prosecutors and the court. In addition, other service providers and treatment professionals are involved in the team and offer insight. Ideally, the professional legal staff has training or expertise in the focused area (e.g., mental health, chemical dependency) which was not formalized in the two MHC in this study.

There are both subtle and dramatic changes in social roles in the court. The same positions exist but operate in a new capacity with "role refinement" (Schneider et al. 2007). While each position still has a specific agenda with associated training and expertise, there are underlying goals of the court that unify team members, facilitating greater compromise. For the prosecution, the goal is to work with defendants, offer recommendations and support for MHC clients for the sake of reducing criminal recidivism, addressing public safety concerns and ensuring the well-being of the defendant. Prosecutors in MHC are less concerned with their conviction record and caseload management that perhaps in other courts. Filing charges, what type of charge, and reduction of charges are still prosecutorial decisions. Although zealous representation is maintained, for the defense counsels the goal is not necessary to get the "best deal" for a defendant but to consider the long-term criminal justice entanglements. Probation officers, often referred to as Mental Health Specialists, supervise clients while in the community. They are tangentially involved in the process during the early stages, unlike in mainstream courts where probation officer are unable to offer any input prior to disposition. Probation officers do not respond to violations with automatic revocations, in which clients are thrown out of MHC or into jail as an automatic sanction. For judges there is less discernment over complex legal issues and more time spent communicating (including active listening) with team members and clients. While judges still act as the neutral arbiter of cases, they collaborate with and listen to the team throughout the entire process. Judges in *City* and *County* MHC are on two year rotations with substitutes and pro-tems as needed (especially used in *City* MHC).

The differences in how the law is practiced in MHCs, how judges address defendants, and general case processing are striking. Tensions do arise when team members operate from their traditional professional frame of reference without fully considering other team member's perspectives and the broader mission of the court. Under the current structure, especially in *County* MHC, a prosecutor detailed that "we lead the meeting, we call the cases, we direct the conversation, and we look to everyone for the oral updates." She was not sure if this was perceived well from the team but it reflected how she was trained, representing a carry-over of traditional adversarial criminal justice. Conversely, in *City* MHC the defense team often led the pre-court meeting and there was more joint decision-making on calling cases before the judge. There are "entrenched interests" that "interfere with our collaborative approached" noted a judge. Different parties can prioritize different goals and hence exhibit some degree of adversarialism, but it is still a far cry from traditional judicial adversarialism. But for some, like a prosecutor, "The role is not left at the door, but because the team involves the same player most of the time, there is a lot of trust amongst the team and respect for each other." As one court liaison summarized it, "You will never get defense and prosecution to fully agree on anything. They never should, that's their job, to disagree. But I have seen them work very well together." Even if all parties at not in agreement it is important that "everybody's positions are at least heard before we go to court" according to a prosecutor; this process helps to build trust.

A defense attorney admits there is less adversarialism, "So there aren't as many opportunities, I think, for the adversarial process to come out. I guess it comes out when we are negotiating, but I feel like I am always trying to negotiate for the best recommendations, no matter what" while another defense attorney stated that the adversarialism comes in "on the front end" before client opt-ins. A court liaison described the dissent that sometimes occurs positively: "Overall everyone is understanding on some level that we are here to do something positive... Even if people don't agree, it doesn't turn into... a personal attack." Alternatively, a different court liaison suggested more consensus would be beneficial, "I think you would have to really integrate things between the liaison and probation and the prosecution. You would have to present that unified front and we don't." In fact a judge remarked that most of the time "the judge is going to follow the rec [recommendation from the MHC team]" but in situations of disagreement we "let the judge decide" stated a prosecutor. Often times there is agreement, a prosecutor appreciated that under such a collaborative model "You are given the discretion to be reasonable."

I do not mean to exaggerate the contrast between the adversarialism of the mainstream court system and the collaborative nature of problem-solving courts. The characterization of the criminal justice system as primarily adversarial is not an accurate depiction but some level of adversarialism is built into the criminal justice system. This is an ideal-type (and Hollywood version) of criminal justice that focusses on combative trials between opposing counsel. Likewise, collaboration is not confined to problem-solving courts. Research on plea bargaining and court process (Yngvesson 1994) demonstrate how legal actors work together to construct a compromise. Not only is this type of collaboration typical of mainstream criminal justice but necessary for the system to function. There is a lot more collaboration in practice in the mainstream court system than its adversarial structure would suggest.

MHC team members insisted that a dualistic understanding of the traditional court system as adversarial and the treatment courts as non-adversarial is misleading. In fact, a probation officer reflected on working in a different county in a non-treatment court commenting that "it was just as collaborative as it is here." He went on to describe how the collaboration worked:

I would go into the judge's chambers and say, Judge, here is what we have going on with this. I would go to the prosecutor, I would go to the public defender, and we would kind of just hash out what we were looking at in terms of what was going to be coming up on the docket that day with their mental health people on the caseload.

Although this was not a MHC, members of the court recognized the needs of defendants with mental illness and attempted to address them. This example illustrates that collaboration is not exclusive to MHCs or problem-solving courts. However, although all courts have elements of collaboration and adversarialism, MHCs clearly favor collaboration and it is that shift in the balance towards a team model that sets MHCs apart from traditional criminal courts.

MHCs are more intentional about fostering collaboration, making their approach distinct. Judicial dialogue illustrates the significance of the shifting balance toward collaboration in the orientation and practices of the court. Judges often refer to the "collaborative nature of the court" explicitly in exchanges with defendants. For example, during an initial welcoming of a client to the MHCs, one judge declared that "This is a different type of court, a collaborative court" while another proclaimed that "This is a treatment court with a team that is going to work with you." If the collaborative and therapeutic orientation was the standard norm of criminal justice it would not need to be stated so fervently and at the center of the initiation ritual into the court.

In treatment courts the organizational and cultural shift actively promotes a collaborative framework by placing them in a broader therapeutic orientation. Team members participate in joint decision-making related to treatment and punishment attempting to bring about positive therapeutic outcomes (Goldkamp and Irons-Guynn 2000; Watson et al. 2001). A treatment-oriented team of professionals attempts to resolve the root causes of involvement with criminal justice system by connecting clients to social services and treatment. As expressed by a defense attorney:

> I think it creates a team of people who understand that traditional approaches aren't going to work, and so you can keep banging your head

against the wall doing the same thing or you can think outside the box. That's what a mental health court does really well. It certainly creates additional accountability and monitoring that traditional courts don't really have access to anymore.

The collaborative and therapeutic orientations within the team shift the focus toward treatment ends by developing an individualized, personal treatment plan for each client and working together toward successful adherence to court conditions. MHCs focus on intervention, supervision and judicial monitoring through a supportive but accountable structure. There is variation in what extent therapeutic jurisprudence organizes any particular MHC and the level of consensus or adversarialness that pervades it. But to be a MHC there needs to be a therapeutically-oriented multidisciplinary team responding to a client's mental health issues and associated life stressors. Even those MHCs on the modest end of the therapeutic commitment are still qualitatively different from mainstream courts. In practice there is a range in the level of court adoption of therapeutic jurisprudence and collaboration and how well different courts actualize these principles in court proceedings and team dynamics.

## Court Organization and Cultural Practices

These two paradigm shifts impact the structure and culture of the courts in significant ways (Berman and Feinblatt 2005; Miller and Johnson 2009; Rottman and Casey 1999). While there is variation in MHCs (Fisler 2015) they all have central features that separate them from the traditional case adjudication process. The altered philosophical orientation toward therapeutic outcomes and the team model has everyday implications for the workings of the court. Combined, they reflect an awareness of the complexity in treating mental illness and its co-morbidity with alcohol and drug abuse. The focus on treatment and therapeutic ends based on teamwork leads to a shift in the punitive orientation of courts. A treatment orientation leads to different organization and ordering of the court (e.g., express reviews) and focus/

content (e.g., housing, treatment, relationship with case manager) as well as different priorities and value orientations. Structurally, there are new social positions and new social roles and a transformation of roles (Nolan 2001; Schneider et al. 2007). The team work model is premised on working together across prosecution and defense. There is also a non-traditional view of standard roles within the court system, as well as the inclusion of new team members reflecting cultural shifts in the norms of the court.

The structure of MHCs is different than traditional courts and the broader philosophical orientation of therapeutic jurisprudence results in organizational shifts in MHCs. First generation courts faced early challenges in setting up the court process and the team as "there wasn't any clear template except sort of theoretically on how this would work." In the early days, without a dedicated staff or courtroom, a team member referred to the court as a "triage unit." Both courts have substantially evolved structurally and culturally since their inception.

The courts operate on separate dockets and have a designated staff including judges. The inclusion of a pre-court meeting (one hour before the court calendar begins) is a significant change in the organization of the court and a clear illustration of collaboration toward joint goals. Culturally, this collaboration-based model leads to a different set of social roles and norms.

Scholars raise legal and ethical concerns with MHC in general (Casey 2004) and specifically around the team approach and the pre-court meeting. Some argue that these meetings lack legal legitimacy (e.g., neutrality, due process, and open justice). This concern is about procedural safeguards. A judge articulated some of the legal issues around collaborative decision-making:

> Sometimes in a pre-court meeting you might say, 'Oh, how about this sanction,' because that is what you think might be right, but then the other person might say, 'Well, actually, that's not going to be good for him or her because they have this going on, so how about X sanction.' Then you can kind of give and take a little bit and say, OK, 'let's on consensus get to this.' The issue is are you giving away client privileges or information without the client being there. It is a legitimate issue.

All members of the team, except for the judge, are present at the daily pre-court meeting. While there is variation in judicial presence, both courts in this study did not allow the judge to be present in the pre-court meeting. Interestingly, historically *City* MHC allowed the judge to be present. There was some indication that this norm might be changing in line with a state Supreme Court case permitting judicial presence. As expressed by a judge,

> Personally, I think that it would be helpful to have a judge be present there, to be able to discuss the issues and to be a little bit more informal and open about things that we can do, especially in terms of problem solving, coming up with creative solutions. On the bench I can only do so much.

Another judge was in favor of the judge being present, "we are not really talking about outcomes… just receiving information… everything is fine." He went on to argue that it was indeed beneficial for the clients to have the judge receive more information in a collaborative court. Similarly another judge added, "it would make the calendar go a whole lot faster." Judges expressed worry about participating in *ex-partae* communication. A clear exception came from a judge who took this issue seriously and emphasized the importance of the judge not being in the pre-court meeting to alleviate many of the legal concerns. Despite some renewed interest in sitting in, almost all judges suggested that if the team is working well, the judge's presence may not be required.

Most team members were not in favor of having the judge present. A court liaison summarized the reasoning:

> I think if the judge was in the meetings, that the meetings would go on forever, and it would just turn into a debate. I don't think that is necessarily productive. I think that if the judge needs to be informed of something important, that's what the role of the liaisons or the other team members need to be sharing on the record… I can't imagine how difficult that would be for a judge, to know that much personal stuff and trying to make a judgment that is fair.

At this pre-court meeting, the MHC team members meet informally (while some eat lunch) to go through the day's calendar and discuss each defendant's case (e.g., status, progress, compliance, etc.). During the pre-court meetings—the *backstage* where there is no audience and the presentation of self (in face-to-face interactions actors perform to manage the impressions that others have of them) is more authentic— team members share recommendations and conversation and negotiations occur (Goffman 1959). This informal meeting prior to court is where much of the "work" happens and where "candid conversations" occur or in the words of a prosecutor where we can "hash things out." During the meetings, a defense attorney described a productive meeting as "when we are really talking about how we are going to help a person together, and bouncing around ideas." While this does not always happen, when it does it illustrates the potential of collaborating towards therapeutic ends. Once the meeting is over the actors immediately go to the *frontstage*—a guarded presentation of self before an audience in line with normative expectation based on social position (Goffman 1959)—where formalized exchanges take place in from of the judge in the courtroom drama (Nolan 2001; Miller and Johnson 2009).

The pre-court meeting often makes for a much smoother and more efficient hearing before the judge. Sometimes it is clear that a joint recommendation was reached in the pre-court meeting discussion and in these cases the prosecutor and defense presentations to the judge might be similar. When everyone is in agreement, collaboration is most evident. But at other times there are differences in opinions and some adversarialism appears as different parties represent competing interests and different perspectives. There are also backstage moments in the pre-court meetings where adversarialism is evident. Yet a probation officer described how collaboration persists amidst dissent:

> We will meet in the pre-court meeting today, we will go over everything. It certainly makes it a lot more cohesive on the decision-making processes. There are not a whole lot of surprises – not to say that there are not disagreements, but everybody at least knows where they are coming from. There are no surprises! You know that I am be asking for 30 days. You know that I'm going to be doing this. I know that you are advocating

that they don't go to jail. So let's just agree to disagree on this. Then, at the same time, there are situations where we all say, this person doesn't need to go to jail and here is what we need to do on working getting this person back on track, great. Let's go in there and pitch that to the judge.

This quote illustrates how there is still adversarialism—often on display during the pre-court meeting—but expressed within a collaborative framework.

Disagreements are usually friendly and professional and most often occur behind closed doors. Most members of the team recognize that they have different roles to play and must do their jobs zealously and advocate for their positions. For example, defense attorneys might not want to consolidate cases on behalf of their defendant if the new charge is easy to challenge legally. At other times, there is fundamental agreement by all parties during the pre-court meeting but adversarialness was presented by the opposing legal counsels before the judge. For example, defendants often demand that their attorney present a certain position to the judge. Defense attorneys, reflecting their obligation to represent their client's interest and wishes, sometimes make requests to the judge knowing that it is not feasible, probable, or even in the interests of the defendant or community safety but are important to make for the sake of their clients. Release motions are prime examples of this tendency to represent defendant's wishes even if there is little likelihood of the motion being granted.

## Competency

The structure and culture of the *City* and *County* are shaped by having a competency court—a subspecialty court—<u>within</u> the therapeutic court. The therapeutic component is the traditional function of a treatment court. The competency function of the court shapes the overall therapeutic orientation of the court. In MHCs questions of legal competency and a defendant's ability to proceed with the court case are varied. The term "competent," as used here, is in reference to the legal category of a defendant being competent to understand the charges brought against him/her and one's ability to assist in the defense. A court liaison clarified competency as "they [defendants] understand what is going on and they can make some kind of decision about whether they want to work with the court or not." Rather than having a separate court assess whether or not a defendant is competent, MHCs are serving this dual function assessing competency in the same courtroom with the same team as the therapeutic court with "centralized expertise" according to a judge. Practitioners and researchers claim that having these two elements in the same court with the same professional staff is better for both the defendants and the public (Finkle et al. 2009). Other MHC team members reflected on the benefits of the dual court model. For example, a court liaison stated that "It is a benefit to have it all in one court, in a therapeutic sense, the people who have the experience, the skill, knowledge... versus keeping it [competency evaluations] in the mainstream court." A prosecutor suggested another benefit that if they are found competent "we can capture then right then" and offer assistance. These sentiments are reflected in client experiences. In Vicki's case, a MHC client in *City* MHC (see Chapter 6 for her full story), competency was raised. She reflected on the dual roles of the court: "When you are in mental health court, there are actually two different sides in the court. One of them is just [to] judge whether someone is competent. That is a whole different – that is what I dealt with at first." Having them integrated, in the same place, made the process "smoother" given the complexities surrounding competency and mental illness and alleviates some concerns about issues of competency in MHCs (Perlin 2013).

There was substantial variation in the degree of competency cases. In *County* MHC competency hearings are less frequent (the court ordered 66 non-recalled (competency evaluations) in 2015) while competency hearings are more common in *City* MHC (with a monthly average of approximately 30 in 2010); in fact, some *County* MHC team members described *City* MHC pejoratively as a "competency court" rather than a MHC. The legal concept of competency is ambiguous and a binary classification may be "artificial" (Winick 1996, 37). The fluidity of competency assessments poses challenges for MHC defendants and team members; a court liaison described competency as something that "shifts rapidly." This is true more generally of mental health as articulated by a judge's metaphor, "It is like playing chess on a beach of sand where the board is always changing. Because… mental illness can shift moment to moment." This perspective on competency permeates the MHCs in this study and explains why there might be several competency evaluations of the same client or defendant within the same year (especially in *City* MHC) as many viewed competency as changing from day to day.

MHC cases are sometimes entangled with the civil court system such as when defendants are held in confidential civil proceeding. While civil commitment hearings can occur at any time in the court process, it often happens in the early stages of a case. This can cause long delays in the competency evaluation process.[7] In some cases, the civil system holds an individual before the court has a chance to have a competency hearing. When competency is raised in MHCs it activates a series of steps in the legal process. To begin the process a competency evaluation is ordered. The next issue is whether or not the defendant[8] is in-custody or out-of-custody and if an in-custody defendant can await the competency evaluation out of custody or must have it arranged in the jail. There are many considerations, but at the forefront for judges is the seriousness of the alleged offense. Judges habitually cite public safety concerns in release motions. However, having a competency evaluation in-custody must be scheduled in less than two weeks (often right up to the fourteenth day). Out-of-custody, it can be extended to several months, or even longer, with six months typical. For out-of-custody cases, there are a series of review hearings scheduled while awaiting the actual competency evaluation to receive status updates and further connect defendants with services. Once the court receives a defendant's psychiatric evaluation, there is a court hearing to discuss the expert's findings.

Next, competency hearings include a review of the psychiatric evaluation by judge, prosecutor and defense attorney. During a competency hearing both attorneys may take exception to the forensic report presented to the court. A judge engages in a colloquy (legal name for the exchange) with the defendant during a competency evaluation, hearings often aided by defense counsel. The goal of the colloquy is two-fold. First, does the defendant understand the nature of the charges against him/her? Questions are asked such as, "do you know who is seated to your right (in the position of the defense attorney)? What does she do? What is the role of the prosecutor? Judge? What is a jury trial?"

These questions aim to get a simple description from the defendant about court actors and procedures. Judges or defense attorneys asking the questions are careful to steer the defendant away from any specific details related to the charge(s) or the alleged criminal incident; however, in practice defendants often blurt out relevant and often damaging information about the alleged crime which is quelled quickly by defense attorneys.

Second, the colloquy aims to reveal if the defendant can assist in his/her own defense. This line of questioning focuses on a defendant's present state of mind and often tries to conjure up recent statements made to counsel prior to the start of court that day. The first set of questions can seem superficial and less therapeutically oriented while the second set of questions are directly of a therapeutic nature. Moreover, these different types of questions reflect competency as "contextualized inquiry" (Winick 1996, 37) where individuals may be competent for one purpose and not for another.

During competency hearings judges mostly focus on the first group of questions whereas defense attorneys, with more experience working with specific defendants, address the second line of questioning. Often a defendant has a clear understanding of the court actors and judicial process but cannot assist council due mental illness symptoms. This distinction becomes clear with deeper person-specific questions. All parties must be satisfied with both prongs of the criteria or the judge orders a contested hearing. Based on the forensic evaluation, supplemented by court observations, members of the team easily reach consensus in most competency cases. However, if there is a disagreement then a contested hearing is scheduled.

Consistent with state law once the court issues a competency finding, team members (defense, prosecutor and judge) agree upon a redacted version of the forensic evaluation that protects the privacy of the defendant in terms of hospitalization, medications and diagnosis. Defense counsel brings forth the redacted version of the psychiatric evaluation and the court enters it into the public record with little or no debate. Judges then declare that "the privacy issues of defendants needs to maintain medication and diagnostic personal information outweighs the public interests."

If there is a finding of "not competent" or "not able to proceed," the court dismisses the case and either refers or detains the defendant, known as "dismiss and refer" or "dismiss and detain." If "referred" this means the defendant must wait to have a mental health evaluation by a Mental Health Professional (MHP) within (72) hours. If "detained" the defendant is sent to the state mental hospital for evaluation and possible civil commitment. If the individual is "not competent, but not committable" the phrase used by a prosecutor, then they are untethered to either the mental hospital or the criminal justice system which is a cause for grave concern. If the court issues a finding of "competent," the defendant can proceed to the opt-in or opt-out phase of the court process depending upon eligibility, amenability, and defendant's interest in participating in MHC. The competency process is intermingled in the everyday practices of MHC as there is not time set aside in the court calendar for competency cases. Having an integrated competency function—mixed calendars—within MHC highlights its therapeutic function, but also can have some antitherapeutic effects as the shift from a status review to a competency evaluation can be jarring and disruptive for clients as well as reduce the time devoted specifically to MHC clients.

## Goals and Values of Therapeutic Justice

Collaboration and principles of therapeutic jurisprudence have led to cultural changes. The court is oriented towards different goals and different values (treatment, elements of a harm-reduction perspective, etc.). As such, rehabilitative or restitutive ends shape exchanges and responses (especially to violations or issue of non-compliance) as opposed to purely punitive ones. There is also a shift in power dynamics, as witnessed through the pre-court meeting as well as the deference sometimes afforded to team members' expertise from the judge. Although there is still a hierarchical power structure with the judge at the top, it is a flatter pyramid structure, with less formality and more informal meetings (e.g., pre-court meeting). An example of the informality is that attorneys usually sit while addressing the judge, reflecting a less formal exchange than a traditional courtroom where attorneys stand when speaking to the judge. Newcomers to the court, especially attorneys with less experience in MHC and private attorneys, often stand. This is counternormative to a frequent observer and introduces formality and hierarchy, especially in the case of the private defense attorneys. Sitting next to the defendant at the same level symbolizes a more collaborative relationship. A latent result of this practice is the exchanges often run smoother with repeat players (Galanter 1974)—that is regular MHC legal agents (judges included)—in the proceedings.

One of the ways that MHCs work toward therapeutic ends, as opposed to punitive ones, is in the language used by MHC professionals. As a critical element of culture, language conveys messages to people about status, which is an important element in the problem-solving court movement (Miller and Johnson 2009). Both MHC courts refer to a defendant as a "client" or "participant," seeing language as an important start toward more therapeutic ends. A prosecutor talked about "personalizing it [court]" and making "a conscious effort not to refer to them as defendant." MHC team members refer to clients personally using their last name, as opposed to status terms such as defendant. Judges use words such as "we" and "us" to convey the "team" approach to be more "inclusive" remarked a judge. This shift is consistent to notions of "personalized justice" and the individualized nature of the court (Nolan 1998).

When addressing clients, some judges refer to "responses to noncompliance" instead of "sanctions" for violating court conditions. The former was supposed to symbolize a less punitive tone creating conditions for success as opposed to punishment.

A defense attorney referenced the important of language changes in relation to stigma:

> I think that… we do try to de-stigmatize a lot. We have actually had meetings where we have discussed that, even with the judge present, where he said, OK, I really would like to talk about how this looks to everybody else in the audience, and the other clients that might be doing the court watch. Instead of saying violations, why don't we say, 'There are the issues we are here to discuss today, because that sounds a little bit better. These are the consequences of your actions, not the sanction.'

Not all team members appreciated this shift in language. A probation officer remarked that

> The defendants understand that these are violations, they understand that these are sanctions, they weren't born yesterday. Almost all of them to a fault have been on probation before. They understand how the system works. They don't need to be coddled by saying 'the court response'.

Modifying the court language also occurs in competency evaluations where team members refer to the hearing as "ability to proceed" as opposed to competent. Rather than referring to defendants as "incompetent," a term with stigma attached, court actors typically refer to the process of a competency evaluation or hearing by the verdict or finding as "not able to proceed" or "unable to assist counsel."[9] In the words of a judge, "we don't inflame or exacerbate the mental illness that is going on." In some cases judges refer to legal language and refer directly to the legal statute to avoid any unnecessary embarrassment, stigma or shame for the defendants. This view was expressed by many team members, such as a court liaison:

> I think people would get labeled and we wouldn't have expectations that people can recover. I tell a lot of people that recovery is the model now… I said, it is no different than a medical disorder, and it is medical, but we both talked about the stigma. This person feels that there shouldn't be this stigma.

The negative effects of "incompetency" labeling by a judge or legal agent, even if unintended, can be detrimental to individuals (Winick 1996). Beyond deprivation of liberty, such labeling influences the social and personal identity—how others view clients and how they view themselves. Avoiding mental health diagnosis and terms about mental competency in public proceedings may reduce stigma and have positive therapeutic effects. At the same time naming something with mental illness terms can have therapeutic benefits as defendants gain insight into their mental health conditions and when such acceptance opens up therapeutic opportunities such as MHC. Therapeutic and antitherapeutic possibilities are real and must be balanced as the loss of agency and dignity around a negative mental health classifications can be consequential. Erring on the side of stigma reduction and protecting client's social identity is consistent with therapeutic justice but it has its limits. A central therapeutic goal is to decriminalize and reduce stigma around mental illness.

## Stigma Remains in MHC

While MHCs can work to diminish social stigma, they can unwittingly reinforce it. MHCs are treatment courts with a therapeutic focus. Avoiding stigmatizing labels is one of the fundamental goals (Fritzler 2003). Nevertheless, there is a certain residue of stigma inherent to the criminal justice system MHCs cannot eliminate. Clients are very aware that they are not free to do as they desire but are encumbered in the criminal justice system and are required to follow the courts' orders. One probation officer commented that stigma "creeps back in" to the working of the court, largely through the structure of the court itself.

Some research on the experience of being in MHCs suggest that it only adds to the stigma of mentally ill individuals. According to one study the very existence of MHCs is part of the problem: "Mental health courts create stigma by segregating people by illness and then defining their uniqueness and irresponsibility in terms of the illness" (Wolff 2002, 434). Moreover MHC practices reinforce mental illness as a "master status" (Fisher et al. 2006).

Of course, the name itself might be part of the problem. Another probation officer with a long tenure linked the stigma of the court to its name: "We had talked originally when the court started about not even calling it Mental Health Court, because we thought just by that name on the calendar, somebody would see that and know they were mentally ill." Likewise, a different probation officer acknowledged that because of the name and being in the criminal justice system, "no matter what, there is going to be that stigma." The name of the court may impede clients from wanting to enter, as a prosecutor suggested, saying "I have heard through their attorneys that somebody might be mentally ill and they don't want to be connected with other mentally ill people or mental health court." A defense attorney revealed that some clients did not want to be associated with "the crazy court." Clients felt the sense of stigma in being in MHC was different than traditional court; while both have stigma attached, MHC has two stigmas: mental illness and criminal. Jennifer confessed the stigma she feels in society underpins MHC, even if in name only:

> I don't know how people would go about doing this, but I feel like my mental illness and addiction defines me. I feel like that is who I am. It is part of who I am... I think the mental health part kind of reinforces it, that feeling of that's who you are. You are in this group of people.... I am not normal anymore, and the mental health court, I think, reinforces that, because of the name of it... I don't think it is purposefully, really, but just how it is.

This perspective, that the name itself is stigmatizing, was echoed by most probation officers and a few other team members. One judge joked that at least they did not label it mental illness court or something far worse. He also articulated that perhaps we should use a general umbrella term like "therapeutic courts" with different tracks. He intimated that some problem-solving courts might benefit from a label, such as Veterans court, because the label "veteran" is a source of "pride" and can induce group solidarity, but no such benefit confers to MHC. The label around mental health is itself stigmatizing. Many have long been critical of mental illness labels, as related to social disadvantages, including stigma, enhancing a self-fulfilling prophecy effect (Scheff 1974; Winick 1996).

Similarly, a defense attorney suggested that the informality and team model was misleading in that there is still some stigma because "we are still within the confines of being a court... It is a different culture, but it is still a court. It is kind of feet in two worlds." She went on to articulate the complexity around the level of stigma in MHCs:

> In a weird way it [MHC] de-stigmatizes mental illness. But at the same time, it is hard to say, because you have pulled out the mentally ill and

said, 'No, you go over here,' which seems to stigmatize more. But within the context of the mental health court, you are more understanding that mental health issues can drive these kinds of behaviors, so it is kind of a double-edged sword like that.

A probation officer emphasized this duality, most notable in *County* MHC where the incentives are much greater. Another probation officer stated that it can be de-stigmatizing but is depends on the offense and client. She characterized the process as "kind of topsy-turvy because of the felony drop-downs. Because you have people who are desperately wanting to get mental health diagnosis. Which is usually the opposite [of most other cases]. Because a lot of the people who opt-out deny that they are mentally ill." She reflected upon the direction of incentives based on the type of offense (felony vs. misdemeanor), noting that the former offenders were given an incentive to have a mental diagnosis while the latter eschew the stigmatizing label "mentally ill." The stigma reducing potential is related to net widening arguments.

## Criticism of MHCs: Net Widening

Court innovations in the criminal justice system may lead to "net widening" and expanding the number of individuals under the control of the criminal justice system and the intensity and severity of criminal justice intervention (Castellano and Anderson 2013). Net-widening refers to expanding the actual number of people who get caught up in the "net" of the criminal justice system. Net-widening is a serious concern especially in the case of individuals with serious mental illness. Austin and Krisberg (1981, 165) define three forms of "net-widening": wider nets, stronger nets, and new nets. The issue is not only expanding the number of people in the criminal justice system, but increasing the duration or severity of criminal justice interventions in people's lives, greater intensity of treatment, and the introduction of new organizations to the criminal justice system. Each of these aspects of net-widening is relevant to the case of MHCs.

## Wider Nets

It is clear that the net has gotten wider; those at the margins of society who were previously incapacitated in asylums and mental hospitals are now increasingly represented in the criminal justice system (Erickson and Erickson 2008; Harcourt 2006). However, this trend predated the advent of MHCs and other problem-solving courts. Due to the ordering of these institutional interventions MHCs are not responsible for negative outcomes caused by deinstitutionalization. In the case of MHCs, a wider net would translate into more individuals being brought into the criminal justice system for the purposes of being in MHC or because new laws or police tactics funnel individuals into MHC who would otherwise not have received police intervention with the expectation of accessing services (Bernstein and Seltzer 2003). New laws or enforcement which criminalize homelessness (Beckett and Herbert 2009) and crimes against poverty are factors and have implications for MHCs, since many individuals who are homeless are also impacted by mental illness. There is evidence of a wider net, including some who end up in MHCs that might not have otherwise been apprehended. Nevertheless, net widening does not appear to have been the result of purposive policy because new laws have not been created to capture more people for the sake of problem-solving courts.

Likewise, there is no indication that agents of the criminal justice system—police or prosecution—are criminalizing new behaviors or prosecuting certain offenses more than before due to the emergence and expansion of MHCs. In fact, quite the opposite seems true. A police officer active in the Crisis Intervention Team (CIT)—a division of the police department trained to respond to possible crimes involving individuals with mental illness—reported that his team works actively to "divert" people with mental illness from jail and the court system.[10] The police officer recounted that they are "bypassing the whole [criminal justice] system"—in favor of treatment, housing, case managers or family intervention. He explained how this works in practice:

> They have the crisis diversion facility, where it is set up where you have somebody who has an arrestable offense... It is a qualifying misdemeanor

offense, and in lieu of taking them to jail, they voluntarily agree to go directly to the solution center to get resources immediately. As long as they [the individual with mental illness] meet the terms of that, the charges go away.

From this officer's perspective, the idea that an officer on his team would make an arrest so that an individual could enter into MHC was preposterous. In fact, he found the MHC selection criteria so restrictive that it makes it hard to refer cases that resulted in an arrest to *City* MHC. He informed me that "77 percent of the [crisis] interactions were not qualifying admission. They are automatic declines for that program… they don't even qualify to get in the door there. So that [MHC] is not really a viable option." Of course given that there are only approximately five police officers in the CIT, regular police officers are making the majority of arrests for those who come into MHC. These officers, especially those without advanced CIT training, are likely more inclined to make an arrest to terminate an encounter but they seem unlikely to do so with the intention of channeling cases to MHC.

Some argue that the existence of MHCs might encourage people to commit crimes to enter the criminal justice system for the sake of accessing services (Wolff 2002). This form of the net widening argument asserts that people with mental illness, some of whom are homeless, might engage in criminal behavior to get access to free housing, food and services. Interview data did not support this claim. MHC clients told me countless times that jail was a major deterrent to criminal behavior, so much so that many opted into to MHC to avoid jail time. Monique, a MHC client, exclaimed that, "Jail was terrible. I do not ever want to go back there again" (Monique's story is detailed in Chapter 6). Given the conditions of American jails, the stigma around the label "criminal" and the level of planning required to commit a qualifying offense, make this an unreasonable explanation, save for marginal cases. Although the time under court supervision is much longer for MHC clients, for many the time is jail is reduced.

As alternative courts, MHCs have access to specific resources— housing and spaces in treatment programs—to incentivize participation. To the extent that these services and resources are not available to non-clients, there could be a perverse incentive to expand time under the supervision of the criminal justice system for people with mental illness as well as misallocation of scare resources (Boldt 2009). Some might argue that people try to get into MHCs in order to access services that are in short supply (Johnston 2012). In both *City* and *County* MHC some service spots are prioritized or set-aside for MHC clients or those who opt-in. It is also the case that MHC clients, especially those with co-occurring disorders and complex needs, may gain access or priority to housing or treatment beds or program otherwise unavailable. These are incentives to opt-into MHC, although with declining resources, incentives (such as housing and treatment options) are being substantially reduced, especially in the case of *City* MHC. Still team members noted that while resources have been reduced, there are still earmarked funds for the court.

Given limited financial investment, there is no evidence from these two MHCs are functioning as a pipeline to social services. The number of clients who opt-in is not high enough nor the services generous or expansive enough to support this explanation. Housing may be a "carrot" used to encourage people to enter MHC, however, if a client is not amenable to treatment (for mental illness and possibly also substance abuse) it may not be offered. The MHC team is aware that certain clients are not ready for treatment and thus not ready for court. This perspective was often articulated in court hearings before the judge. For example, a representative from a supportive housing agency commented to the judge about a client that "He seems interested in housing but not interested in his mental health." The additional resources available in MHC did draw some clients into the court in the first place but they were already caught in the "net" of the criminal justice system. I find limited evidence for the widening of the net in the case of MHCs, but the other practices raise serious concerns.

## Stronger Nets

The stronger net critique refers to the greater intensity of treatment or the increasing duration or severity of criminal justice interventions in people's lives. Much of the broad concerns about net-widening in MHCs center on the deepening and strengthening of the net. Concerns about clients being punished or confined out of proportion to the crime committed dates back to (Bentham 1969) and his attack on general deterrence theory. Wexler's (1973, 299) critique of the therapeutic state raises concerns about conditions or interventions that are "out-of-proportion to the crime or deviant act omitted." As well as "undermine goals of deterrence" (Johnston 2012, 536). This happens in four ways in MHCs.

First, defendants awaiting competency evaluations may experience stronger nets. Sometimes the urgency of an evaluation can encourage judges to keep a defendant in jail. Take for example the case of a young man who was in-custody awaiting a competency evaluation. He stated "My rights have been violated. I've been here [in jail] for 3 weeks. I'm not safe here. I'm not an alien. I am a human being." Expressions of injustice are not unusual from in-custody defendants. But his objection taps into the serious ethical concerns around extensive detainment of people with mental illness. The waiting time for an evaluation is much shorter in jail (legally mandated to be completed within two weeks) but can take months out of custody, typically upwards of six months. Concerns about the mental decline (referred to as decomposition) of individuals with mental illness, lack of access to medication and appropriate treatment in jail are also serious concerns. Defendants can also be ordered to a process of restoration which includes being medicated involuntarily to see if the defendant can be "restored" for a competency hearing.

Second, while considering opting-into MHC some individual are awaiting treatment leading to more time in jail. A defense attorney described a situation in which a defendant is currently in jail and is considering MHC while waiting for a treatment bed. She argued that the defendant could get credit for time served and get out today:

> or we need two or three weeks to get treatment and housing set up, invest this 2 or 3 weeks and sit in jail waiting. That is a huge problem for us. That's kind of a tension, because we don't want to just let people out without a treatment plan, but the longer they wait, the more likely they say, 'Forget this, I can do my time and be done.'

A similar exchange illustrated the deepening of the net. A client was waiting in jail voluntarily for a treatment bed, as a precondition for entering MHC. In a status hearing to review progress toward release directly into a treatment facility, the court learned that the defendant needed to stay in jail longer than anticipated to await a coveted space.

> *Defense*: Client is waiting patiently for in-patient bed date. She is still willing to continue with this [mental health court].
> *Defendant*: I'm changing. Sober! Not the same person I was when… I am tired of being an addict. It's hurtful, it's dangerous, it's dirty. I want to change. I want to be somebody… I want to be a better person. I know I have been an addict for 15 years (1/2 my life). I have been using drugs, alcohol and crime for a long time I want to change. I need help .
> *Judge*: You are doing a lot towards that.

The client expressed willingness to wait in jail given her public [in court] awakening to addiction. It was this reasoning that lead some team members to justify stronger nets.

Third, clients who are charged with misdemeanors agree to strict conditions of compliance in exchange for a reduced sentence or a dismissed sentence at the end of a probationary period (approximately two years). Some of the charges that bring clients in MHC are behaviors which could arguably be de-criminalized. Researchers have found that for MHC non-completers who return to traditional court, the majority of their cases were dismissed (Ray et al. 2015a). This raises concerns about the charges: if they were subsequently dismissed were they appropriate for MHC in the first place?

Opting-into MHC leads to more time in the criminal justice system, but not usually jail, on the current charge. Defense attorneys shared this concern when advising defendants. The conditions of release and the length of the probationary period, compared with the opt-out recommendation, often deterred defendants from opting-into MHC. A defense attorney stated that MHC clients:

are held to an even higher standard than somebody [who] may be in a mainstream court. You can have the same charge and someone in mainstream court does two days in jail and they are done. They never come back to the court. Then someone in mental health court, could have the same thing and they have this probation. They have already done jail time, the same amount of jail time and now they have this probation where they can continue to get jail if they are not getting the help that they need. Sometimes I feel like that is a conflict with what we are trying to do.

Fourth, the expansion of social control through court monitoring in problem-solving courts adds to its net widening effects (Boldt 2009; Miller and Johnson 2009). While under probation there are more opportunities to be out of compliance and sanctioned based on the increased length and intensity of supervision. It is in cases of non-compliance that concerns arise that MHC clients may be treated more harshly than traditional defendants. This concern includes spending more time under the supervision of the criminal justice system and, in some cases, more time in jail (for non-compliance) if they opt-into MHC than if they had opted out. This was a concern that many team members articulated across professional roles.

The biggest concern expressed by team members was about stronger nets leading to increasing levels of punishment and treatment intensity. Many probation officers (and some defense attorneys), especially those who embrace a harm-reduction approach, were concerned about clients being punished for "failing MHC." Concerns about stronger nets was best articulated by a probation officer who stated that "we don't want to set people up to fail." He went on to describe that in the early days of the court the first judge and prosecutor held the view that:

> If somebody comes into mental health court and they have a sixty day jail recommendation from the prosecutor and they served, you know served thirty days of it and then they did the mental health court thing, so they're not serving that second thirty, so to speak. And then they do mental health court: six months later they bomb out and they get revoked. The agreement was that they wouldn't do more jail than if they had just done the jail from the get-go.

A defense attorney described another case where trying and failing the treatment plan in MHC led to more time in jail:

> A client had done 90 actual days waiting to go to inpatient, went to inpatient, opted in, and then was not successful. Then got more jail time revoked. The original jail rec had been 90 days with no treatment. If he had pled to the originally jail rec, he would have been free.

For many working in this court, concerns about stronger nets were overblown. From their perspective, the stronger net associated with MHCs is justified given the voluntary component of the court. Even a court liaison who was very critical of injustice and bias in the criminal justice system was unpersuaded. In response to my question about stronger nets, she stated forthrightly, "No, it doesn't concern me and the reason it doesn't is because we are a voluntary court… if they don't want to be on probation for two years, they don't have to be. They don't have to be with us." So ultimately many team members understood the ability to make the choice as client empowerment. A probation officer explained further,

> So, while it's true that there's more supervision and more contacts than there would be normally, that's fully explained out front, so it's part of the opt-in. They don't have to opt-in. So you could say their deal is better, you know, rather than having to serve jail they don't have to do any time in jail, but they have to do two years of mental health court conditions.

Following from this perspective, many MHC team members understood the stronger net criticism represented a short-view. A judge described how the current public defenders agency works with defendants to reevaluate and consider "foregoing the short-term rewards for gaining long-term benefits" in the case of entering MHC and spending more time on probation than if they served time in jail. Similarly "there might be [in the] some short-term more involvement with the criminal justice system, but my belief is that in the long-term there will be less involvement and that it would be better for the community" declared a judge. Noting that "they probably would be in jail again on another charge" a judge justified the intensive, net-widening, MHC model. Acknowledging a stronger net argument and the potential for increasing amounts of punishment "I don't think it is a problem" declared a judge taking a long-term view around client well-being. In general most team members reverted back to MHC is in the "client's best interest" argument. The time in MHC would link the client with needed social services and a support structure aimed at altering the individual's life trajectory.

Concerns about stronger nets were more evident in the interviews with teams from *City* MHC and less so in *County* MHC. This owes to the type of defendants recruited and the incentive structures of the courts. In the case of *County* MHC, rather than the net getting stronger it might even be getting weaker as the jurisdiction and the time under the supervision of the criminal justice system for felony cases, once reduced to misdemeanor charges, is reduced quite substantially. Even if a client is revoked from *County* MHC, the possible jail time is limited to the misdemeanor offense (a limit of less than two years). Even so, team members recognized that MHCs can inadvertently be more punitive. Accordingly a judge articulated an informal metric that is useful in making sure not to be excessively punitive. For example, this judge mentioned taking the mid-point of the possible sentence (for the felony drop-down) and then subtracting time served from that point which I witnessed in practice during court observations. While a judge declared that "I don't think I've ever given anymore more jail time then they would have gotten before [if they opted-out]" there are no clear standards in place to guarantee this outcome.

While the majority of clients I interviewed expressed gratitude for the better treatment they received from MHC, they also highlighted its "burdensome conditions." Monique detailed her experience in MHC as "better for me because they were more lenient" as opposed to traditional court. This was not the case for all of the clients I interviewed. Jennifer opted into the court because she was offered a dismissal of the charges upon successfully completing the court, but toward the end of her time in MHC when we spoke she expressed regret or at least suggested that this might not have been the best decision: "I don't even know if I would have gotten jail time. I spent more time in jail because of relapsing than I would have if I had just done my time. I don't even know." Experiences like these go to the heart of some of the criticisms about strengthening the net of the criminal justice system.

Interesting, one way that judges try to protect against possible tendencies to stronger nets in MHCs is around fines. In MHC judges are cognizant of the injustice of monetary fines. A judge articulated this prevailing norm to waive fees "if there are fees that I can alleviate or get rid of, I will" which is counter to national trends in the criminal justice system (Harris 2016). MHC, per se, do not necessitate stronger nets, but they do occur and team members ought to be more mindful of the potential dangers and establish more formal safeguards.

## New Nets

The third form of net-widening centers on "new" nets. This refers to the transfer of authority from one agency to another or the involvement of new agencies in the criminal justice system. In the case of MHCs, this includes the role of new agencies and social service providers in the everyday practice of the court such as case managers, housing specialists, treatment providers and other social service agents. The addition of case managers' perspectives can give rise to new dynamics between case managers, defense and prosecuting attorneys, and judges (Castellano 2011). Treatment compliance, treatment intensity and the role of case managers and treatment providers are integrated into the workings of the court in ways that can be bad for clients.

The new nets in MHC are largely related to treatment, both mental health treatment and in many cases substance abuse treatment. *County* MHC specifically states that the court is set up to foster cooperation between "two systems that have traditionally not worked closely together – the mental health treatment system and the criminal justice system." Medication is often a requirement of MHC participation detailed in treatment plans (under the supervision of psychiatrists or treatment providers). Concerns about coercive treatment, being forced to take medication, are expressions of the new net argument (Bernstein and Seltzer 2003; Casey 2004; Nolan 2003). Although the court does not make medication decisions, judges do remind clients that they "need to comply with their treatment" or "follow their doctor's orders," or simply "you need to take your medication." Within the MHC structure, clients' right to refuse treatment is hampered, reducing potential therapeutic effects of treatment (Winick 1994).

Requiring some clients to take pharmaceutical drugs is controversial and raises ethical issues (Hughes and Peak 2013). For some MHC team members this is a compelling concern. While judges are aware of this issue, many referred back to the voluntary nature of the court and that the burden rests heavily on defense council to properly inform and educate their clients on the possibility of required medication as a condition for court compliance prior to opting-in. Clarifying what it is the court actually does, a judge spoke of the limited power of the court in client medication decisions, "What we force them [clients] to do is go to a doctor and stay on the doctor's recommendation. We do not have the ability at this point in time to be so specific [about medication prescriptions]." A notable exception came from one judge who admitted that "I struggled with it [coercive treatment] all the time, but I don't have a better answer."

Discussions around taking prescribed medications are frequent in MHC, but tensions are rarer. A court liaison recounted one such case with a bipolar client with chemical dependency currently participating in an outpatient mental health treatment program. Concerned that the client was not complying with medication requirement, she asked the judge to order daily medication monitoring. The client protested before the judge according to the court liaison,

> 'I disagree,' he told the judge. I really like this case because he still said, 'OK, I'm still willing to do this but I disagree, but okay.' He got on daily med monitoring, and he ended up getting the reward for most changed person by the mental health agency. It was just amazing. He had housing, he was stable, he started looking into school… It [MHC] gave him insight, because you have a whole team that is normalizing you.[11] You can go into a court system and a judge can tell you, 'You are doing a good job.' These people come from families that have never, ever, ever heard that. It gives people the opportunity to work through stigma, to be

empowered, to have their basic needs met, which you don't have that, you can't do anything else.

This case suggests that MHC team members justify new nets around management of mental illness for the sake of client well-being. Multiple team members detailed cases of setting up a plan for clients' medications to be monitored and have even made arrangement with pharmacies and fire houses. These are clear examples of new nets in the lives of MHC clients that lack formal oversight and client protections.

Mandatory medical treatment or coercive treatment raises questions about newer nets which also relates to stronger nets. Tensions around treatment and medication compliance also explain much of the time that defendants stay in jail when they might have been released otherwise. I found evidence from both MHCs of these "new nets" and some evidence of their being used as indirect social control mechanisms (stronger net). Being out of compliance with treatment for mental health and chemical dependency is a frequent pathway leading to court sanctions. In the cases of court sanctioning this leads to greater punitiveness. In others, the inclusion of new perspectives might mitigate a violation and explain problematic behaviors in ways that moderate the court's response. It depends on how the new actors' perspectives are integrated into judicial decision-making. The role of discretion is clear in MHCs and fully cognizant by team members, a judge exclaimed there is "a lot of discretion" in MHC which he understood as "benefit to our participants and our team." This is highlighted in Paik's (2011) discussion of evaluation compliance in drug courts. She finds that in many review hearings case managers were present and sometimes called upon by the judge to offer testimony that did not necessarily benefit clients. However, in the majority of the cases I observed the inclusion of additional actors, such as case managers, bettered the clients' circumstances as they were called upon to mitigate concerns and showcase the client's support structure, even in the case of non-compliance.

For MHC clients the involvement of non-legal agents did raise additional concerns. Some saw their involvement as creating more opportunities to "mess-up" and get into trouble with the court. In the case of Norm, a client in *City* MHC (see Chapter 6 for Norm's full story), an altercation with a treatment provider led to a criminal charge. It is unclear if Paul was not in MHC or if the treatment provider was not familiar with MHC that the incident would have been dealt with differently. Other clients found that the inclusion of additional service agents expanded the web of social support and provided more voices of encouragement. Shima said that "they helped me out." It was clear that "they" referred to case managers, housing specialists, therapists in addition to the MHC team. For her, being in MHC "reminded me that they believe in me enough, and I need to start believing in myself… You hear other people telling you that you have so much to live for, but in my mind, it is hard for me to really realize that." However, most of the clients I interviewed were indifferent and did not see any effect of these "new nets" in their court experience. For some clients, prior entanglements with the criminal justice system might have altered their perceptive, in a way normalizing outside interventions in their lives and in the court experience.

## "Nets" Revisited

Although net-widening is a serious concern among socio-legal scholars and criminal justice advocates, in general, most team members were not overly concerned. This was in some ways inconsistent with the clear de-criminalization message summarized by a judge that "you should not be punishing people because of their mental health" a view widely embraced by the entire team. For many the lack of concern revolved around the voluntarily nature of the court as well as the fact that "they are going to be touched by the criminal justice system no matter what," as a court liaison put it. Another team member understood it in comparative terms, "we are keeping them in jail a bit longer until their housing is ready or whatever, and I can see from the defendant's side that might seem unfair, but also the benefit is so great."

Even so there was a genuine concern about fairness, articulated by a prosecutor: "we are in the business of justice, we have to makes sure that we are not unnecessarily punishing the defendant." One judge stood out as an exception noting his preference is to avoid holding defendants in jail while waiting for housing or an in-patient bed, "I have been encouraging us [MHC team] to think of different ways to do that, and providing structure so we have safety in the community, but being out in the community." Notable exceptions also came from a few probation officers with a strong treatment orientation and clear harm-reduction leanings. Probation officers voiced concerns about increasing levels of punishment for minor offenses or violations especially in relation to respective charges outside of the MHC system (if the individual had opted out of MHC and had the case processed in mainstream court). Surprisingly, few team member expressed concern for treatment intensity or additional oversight by treatment agencies.

Net concerns were generally discounted by judges with one stark exception; she explicitly raised questions about protecting against these nets: "How do you keep them from getting trapped in the system?" A few judges entertained conversations about the issues but most found this line of thought unconvincing. It was not that they callously dismissed these concerns but rather that they saw things from a different vantage point. First, they argued that if an individual opted out, served a sentence and then committed a new crime, they would probably be back in jail anyway so it was not a fair comparison to focus on the one offense that brought them into MHC. As one judge explained, "Is it reasonable to consider the accrued number of offenses and cumulative time in jail rather than just the first offense?" If correct, the stronger or denser net argument starts to break down. This point was articulated by most judges calling for a broader picture and longer time horizon. Judges linked participation with access to benefits and services which alters a defendant's calculus in deciding whether or not to opt-into MHC. From this perspective, it is not just time spent under the supervision of the criminal justice system or number of days in jail that need to be considered, but rather the cumulative time in jail over possible multiple offenses if the individual were not in MHC.

In comparing the two courts, concerns over "net-widening" are more compelling for misdemeanour offenses (*City* MHC) and less so for felony cases (*County* MHC), as charges are already reduced substantially at opt-in in the latter. Concerns about stronger and new nets are most convincing in the case of violations or revocations whereby clients are sanctioned with additional oversight (e.g., meetings and reviews), new commitments (e.g., community service) and/or confinement (e.g., jail). While it is true that many MHC clients are extensively intermingled with the criminal justice system that would likely be the case with or without MHCs. Yet concerns about wider, stronger and new nets remain.

The net arguments raise valid concerns about the breadth and depth of criminal justice intervention but also misses part of the therapeutic outcomes embedded in MHCs. Achieving reductions in crime, enhanced community safety, higher rates of treatment participation and greater stability for clients, takes time. Part of strengthening the net is in response to how the court—as a social institution—can best assist clients in meeting their treatment needs in order to stabilize their lives and reduce future criminal justice intervention. MHCs work to provide defendants with opportunities to live in the community while on probation, as is consistent with alternative diversions strategies (e.g., Sequential Intercept Model, Heilbrun et al. 2015). The trade-off is greater supervision and, in this way, an extension of the criminal justice net. Some criticism regarding net widening might be due to gaps in stated mission and court practices and the drifting away from initial goals of MHC.

## Mission Alignment

New organizations often experience "mission drift" as time passes and the organization expands (Meyer and Rowan 1977). This is also true for MHCs. In both MHCs, team members voiced concerns about changes the court was undergoing by referencing "mission drift" as well as "mission creep." "Drifting" in the overall mission in terms of the process, including types of charges and defendants offered MHC.

Drift suggests a change that is not purposeful or planned and without team input. MHC team members in both courts talked about a kind of mission drift, however these concerns were more pronounced in *County* MHC. In the case of *County* MHC, the change was intentional on the part of the prosecutor's office, but reflected a shift away from the collaborative nature of the court. Expanding to felony cases, like many second-generation courts have done, makes sense in light of recent evidence of reduced recidivism among completers (Ray et al. 2015b), reduced risk of violence from clients (McNiel et al. 2015), and the greatest reductions in criminal justice costs for felony problem-solving courts (Steadman et al. 2014).

This shift in the level of seriousness in the type of offenses accepted creates additional challenges around supervision as expressed by some MHC team members. This moves the court away from "original mission" of the court a view voiced most loudly by staff in probation (not surprisingly given their supervisory role of clients and concerns about liability). Probation officers declared that the "mission had changed"—in the beginning "the court was really going for the neediest population, and then the in and out of jail a lot… the frequent fliers." Another probation officer reiterated this position that

> we're seeing a different, a very different population as opposed to the kind of, people shouting on the bus kind of people, the psychotic wandering around on the street, kind of people. We're seeing a lot more people with serious criminal histories, serious underlying personality disorders, and a lot of drug issues.

Drift in the court's mission is related to issues around eligibility assessments. A probation officer articulated that "Our criteria has gone right out the window!" He explained why this change was happening—the court "make all these exceptions, we, our numbers are low, and we need to justify our existence." It went beyond the probation department, judges also expressed concerns about widening the doors of MHC given public safety concerns. A defense attorney discussed the population prioritization characterizing the court and voiced that concerns are justified as "our initial core audience… now they are getting missed." This was echoed by a defense social worker who adamantly stated that the "Court is not doing its mission." He went on extensively about the case that inspired the creation of the court and asked rhetorically "Are we doing anything for him… so that this does not happen again?" which he answered "No! The seriously mentally ill and isolated are being missed." Prioritizing "safety concerns" as the main focus for decisions is behind the shift, argued a defense attorney.

I did not hear concerns about mission drift in *City* MHC. In fact many stated that the court has stayed quite consistent, such as a probation officer's reference that the "basic goals are somewhat intact" to its stated goals over the last several decades.

Concerns were less frequent and less tied to the mission in the case of *City* MHC. The changes were understood as modest and more natural. For a court liaison the court has "evolved organically" and the informal shift in criteria raises questions of equality:

> I see the benefit of it, but I also struggle with that organic growth, I feel, [it] enmeshes people's roles in a way that is very confusing... organic growth makes the eligibility very, very flexible... To me that doesn't seem fair [Why some cases are excluded?]

On the few occasions when there was reference to mission drift in *City* MHC, it was around competency. MHC team members from *County* suggested that *City* drifted to being a "competency court" as opposed to a MHC. While it is true that *City* holds many more competency hearings than *County* MHC, it is still an active MHC centered on its original mission around serving defendants with minor charges related to mental illness.

Many team members argued that the courts should be true to the stated mission while others were more open to expanding the eligibility criteria. Team members were clear that MHCs need to be aligned with the needs of the clientele. For instance, a court liaison asserted that "if we ever wanted to expand the definition of the court, we would have to expand what the court does, and we would have to change it. I don't think this court is made for Axis II. Do I think a court could be made for Axis II, probably, but I don't think it is this one." In the case of changing eligibility criteria, other structural and cultural practices and resources need to follow.

Drifting away from the mission has implications for the everyday practices of the court and for net-widening arguments. Even if the mission is clear, the court can also experience drift related to the court practices and organization, known as "model drift." "Model drift" refers to the organizational model and changes in practices around collaborative decision-making, caseloads and revocations (Skeem et al. 2006). Model drift is related to personnel issues and team functionality. This occurs if the organizational framework increases caseloads of key personal, notably probation officers. While about 40 cases was the target caseload for *City* MHC that has not been realized. In fact it is about 65–75 with a combination of MHC's and MHDT's with a smaller proportion MHC clients. In *County* MHCs the caseloads are lower, ranging between high-thirties and fifty, and closer to the suggested rate. In terms of the "sort of model drift," a probation officer clarified that it is less about caseloads and more about staffing and the team model:

> There really did used to be more of a team focus in decision-making, including hiring... I know like when [name of probation officer] came on board, all of us got to be on an interview panel, once personnel saw that he met the minimum requirements and stuff, and that completely gone away.

A large part of model drift is related to the power between the two sides of a traditional adversarial system. In some ways the collaborative model is supposed to turn the adversarial structure on its head but the shift toward taking more serious felony offenses has reverted *County* court to a more adversarial structure. Not all team member were pleased with the new focus and structure. One probation officer stated it plainly:

> Right now it seems like all the power has kind of shifted to the prosecutor's office, and it's unfortunate too, because I think particularly defense right now, we have a really strong team and a really good social worker and all the attorneys are good, and they're completely left out of this felony drop-down process. And so... that's really a huge imbalance.

This shift has led to changes in certain positions, of which probation is the most vocal and perhaps the most affected. Several probation officers described how they used to have more freedom in how they handled their clients without requiring "the judge's permission" but increased strictness in the structure and accountability resulted from a lawsuit, according to a probation officer. One characterization of the shift was toward more paternalism and less autonomy, "we [probation] end up spending a lot of time… playing 'Mother, May I?' And then writing little violation reports, missed one appointment." The model drift negatively influenced the team model and was differentially understood by team members.[12]

The idea of mission drift and to a smaller extend model drift have implications for arguments about net-widening, especially in terms of more punishment and stronger nets. While there may not be strong mission drift sentiments in both courts, there were concerns about slight shifts away from a therapeutic orientation. In reference to the stronger net of more punishment, especially for those who opt-into MHC, try and fail, a probation officer noted, "this wasn't true in the beginning, but it kind of drifted this way." To understand how therapeutic justice works (and does not work) and how it relates to the process of "net-widening" we must now turn to the court process directly.

## Notes

1. The MHCs in this study use the same courtrooms as traditional criminal courts. There has not been, but could be, a concerted effort to create/design separate treatment courtrooms.
2. Bernstein and Seltzer caution against an over-reliance on MHCs.
3. The version of therapeutic rehabilitation that MHCs embrace, according to Johnston, is the "one that narrowly focused on the causal relationship between certain mental illness and crime" (551).
4. Also see Daicoff (2000, 466–467).
5. A court liaison disliked the term court monitor as it connotes less status, she felt that the disrespect she experienced from the team and the judge made her feel more like a "secretary" or a "hall monitor" which "increased confusion with the defendant." She compared the position to a licensed mental health professional with clinical expertise

and should undergo a title change such as Forensic Mental Health Practitioner.
6. In both courts, the court liaisons are affiliated with a non-profit community mental health agency. In *City* MHC it is the largest provider of "mental health, substance abuse and behavioral health services" in the county. In *County* MHC the court liaisons were contracted with a different agency which was the source of much discontent. Upon follow-up court observations and interviews *County* MHC switched to the same outsider provider as *City* MHC, eliminating many of the previous concerns.
7. In one case after a civil competency hearing for over one year the case in MHC was dismissed in the interest of justice.
8. I use the term defendant and not client as the individual is not yet eligible for MHC. If the individual is found able to proceed then MHC becomes an option.
9. On several occasion a new prosecutor kept referring to a defendant as "incompetent" which was atypical for MHC. I spoke with a team member after court and she told me that the team has talked to him and encouraged him to alter his language. Several weeks later I observed another competency evaluation and he switched his language to "unable to proceed." He was now socialized into the cultural practices of MHC. Alternatively a judge clarified that he uses "competent" at it is seen as positive.
10. All police office in this city where the court cases studies are located must undergo a mandatory 36 hour CIT and de-escalation training. To become CIT certified, an officer must complete an additional 40 hour training course, and ongoing training is required to maintain certification. Subjects covered in the training include an overview of mental disorders, recognizing types of mental illnesses, and communicating with mentally ill individuals.
11. The language of normalization is interesting and ties to the idea of restoring clients to functional members in society (a theme that comes out in court rituals such as graduations).
12. In fact *County* MHC had a kind of "intervention" in the year after I conducted the majority of my research interviews in order to foster a more communicative and collaborative team.

# References

Abramson, Marc F. 1972. "The Criminalization of Mentally Disordered Behavior Possible Side-Effect of a New Mental Health Law." *Hospital and Community Psychiatry* 23: 101–5.

Almquist, Lauren, and Elizabeth Dodd. 2009. *Mental Health Courts: A Guide to Reserach-Informed Policy and Practice.* New York: Council of State Governments Justice Center.

Angermeyer, M. C., and H. Matschinger. 2003. "The Stigma of Mental Illness: Effects of Labelling on Public Attitudes towards People with Mental Disorder." *Acta Psychiatrica Scandinavica* 108 (4): 304–9. https://doi.org/10.1034/j.1600-0447.2003.00150.x.

Austin, James, and Barry Krisberg. 1981. "Wider, Stronger, and Different Nets: The Dialectics of Criminal Justice Reform." *Journal of Research in Crime and Delinquency* 18 (1): 165–96.

Beckett, Katherine, and Steve Herbert. 2009. *Banished: The New Social Control in Urban America.* Oxford: Oxford University Press.

Bentham, Jeremy. 1969. "An Introduction to the Principles of Morals and Legislation." In *A Bentham Reader*, edited by Mary Peter Mack, 86–87. New York: Pegasus.

Berman, Greg, and John Feinblatt. 2005. *Good Courts: The Case for Problem-Solving Justice.* New York: The New Press.

Bernstein, Robert, and Tammy Seltzer. 2003. "Criminalization of People with Mental Illnesses: The Role of Mental Health Courts in System Reform." *The University of the District of Columbia Law Review* 7: 143–62. https://doi.org/10.3366/ajicl.2011.0005.

Boldt, Richard C. 2009. "A Circumspect Look at Problem-Solving Courts." In *Problem-Solving Courts: Justice for the Twenty-First Century*, edited by Paul Higgins and Mitchell B. Mackinem, 13–32. Santa Barbara: Praeger.

Casey, Timothy. 2004. "When Good Intentions Are Not Enough: Problem-Solving Courts and the Impending Crisis of Legitimacy." *SMU Law Review* 57: 1459–520. https://doi.org/10.3366/ajicl.2011.0005.

Castellano, Ursula. 2011. *Outsourcing Justice: The Role of Nonprofit Caseworkers in Pretrial Release Programs.* Boulder: Lynne Rienner Publishers.

Castellano, Ursula, and Leon Anderson. 2013. "Mental Health Courts in America: Promise and Challenges." *American Behavioral Scientist* 57 (2): 163–73. https://doi.org/10.1177/0002764212465616.

Daicoff, Susan. 2000. "The Role of Therapeutic Jurisprudence within the Comprehensive Law Movement." In *Practicing Therapeutic Jurisprudence: Law as a Helping Profession*, 465–92. Durham: Carolina Academic Press.

Erickson, Patricia, and Steven Erickson. 2008. *Crime, Punishment, and Mental Illness: Law and the Behavioral Sciences in Conflict*. New Brunswick: Rutgers University Press.

Ewick, Particia, and Susan S. Silbey. 1998. *The Commone Place of Law: Stories from Everyday Life*. Chicago: University of Chicago Press.

Finkle, Michael J., Russell Kurth, Christopher Cadle, and Jessica Mullan. 2009. "Competency Courts: A Creative Solution for Restoring Competency to the Competency Process." *Behavioral Sciences & the Law* 27: 767–86. https://doi.org/10.1002/bsl.

Fisher, William H., Eric Silver, and Nancy Wolff. 2006. "Beyond Criminalization: Toward a Criminologically Informed Framework for Mental Health Policy and Services Research." *Administration and Policy in Mental Health and Mental Health Services Research* 33 (5): 544–57. https://doi.org/10.1007/s10488-006-0072-0.

Fisler, Carol. 2015. "When Research Chllenges Policy and Practice: Toward a New Understanding of Mental Health Courts." *The Judges' Journal* 54 (2): 8–13. http://www.courtinnovation.org/sites/default/files/documents/JJ_SP15_54_2_Fisler.pdf.

Fritzler, Randal B. 2003. "10 Key Components of a Criminal Metnal Health Court." In *Judging in a Therapeutic Key: Therapeutic Jurisprudence and the Coirts*, 118–23. Durham: Carolina Academic Press.

Galanter, Marc. 1974. "Why the 'Haves' Come Out Ahead: Speculations on the Limits of Legl Change." *Law & Society Review* 9 (1): 95–160.

Goffman, Erving. 1959. *The Presentation of Self in Everyday Life*. New York: Anchor Books.

Goldkamp, J. S., and C. Irons-Guynn. 2000. *Emerging Judicial Strategies for the Mentally Ill in the Criminal Caseload: Mental Health Courts in Fort Lauderdale, Seattle, San Bernardino, and Anchorage*, 1–83. http://www.ncjrs.gov/pdffiles1/bja/182504.pdf.

Harcourt, Bernard E. 2006. "From the Asylum to the Prison: Rethinking the Incarceration Revolution." *Texas Law Review* 84: 1751–86.

Harris, Alexis. 2016. *A Pound of Flesh: Monetary Sanctions as Punishment for the Poor*. New York: Russell Sage Foundation.

Heilbrun, Kirk, David DeMatteo, Heidi Strohmaier, and Meghann Galloway. 2015. "The Movement Toward Community-Based Alternatives to Criminal

Justice Involvement and Incarceration for People with Severe Mental Illness." In *The Sequential Intercept Model and Criminal Justice: Promoting Community Alternatives for Individuals with Serious Mental Illness*, edited by Patricia A. Griffin, Krik Heilbrun, Edward P. Mulvey, David DeMatteo, and Carol A. Schubert, 1–20. Oxford: Oxford University Press.

Hora, Peggy Fulton, William G. Schma, and John T. A. Rosenthal. 1999. "Therapeutic Jurisprudence and the Drug Treatment Court Movement: Revolutionizing the Criminal Justice System's Response to Drug Abuse and Crime in America." *Notre Dame Law Review* 74: 439–538.

Hughes, Shannon, and Terry Peak. 2013. "A Critical Perspective on the Role of Psychotropic Medications in Mental Health Courts." *American Behavioral Scientist* 57 (2): 244–65. https://doi.org/10.1177/0002764212458273.

Johnston, E. Lea. 2012. "Theorizing Mental Health Courts." *Washington University Law Review* 89 (3): 519–79.

McNiel, Dale E., Naomi Sadeh, Kevin L. Delucchi, and Renée L. Binder. 2015. "Prospective Study of Violence Risk Reduction by a Mental Health Court." *Psychiatric Services* 66 (6): 598–603. https://doi.org/10.1176/appi.ps.201400203.

Metzl, Jonathan M., and Kenneth T. MacLeish. 2015. "Mental Illness, Mass Shootings, and the Politics of American Firearms." *American Journal of Public Health* 105 (2): 240–49. https://doi.org/10.2105/AJPH.2014.302242.

Meyer, John W., and Brian Rowan. 1977. "Institutionalized Organizations : Formal Structure as Myth." *American Journal of Sociology* 83 (2): 340–63. https://doi.org/10.1086/226550.

Miller, JoAnn, and Donald C. Johnson. 2009. *Problem Solving Courts: A Measure of Justice*. Lanham: Rowman & Littlefield Publishers.

Morse, Stephen J. 1999. "Craziness and Criminal Responsibility." *Behavioral Sciences & the Law* 17 (2): 147–64. https://onlinelibrary.wiley.com/doi/abs/10.1002/(SICI)1099-0798(199904/06)17:2%3C147::AIDBSL336%3E3.0.CO;2-X.

Nolan, James L. Jr. 1998. *The Therapeutic State: Justifying Government at Century's End*. New York: New York University Press.

———. 2001. *Reinventing Justice: The American Drug Court Movement*. Princeton: Princeton University Press.

———. 2003. "Redefining Criminal Courts: Problem-Solving and the Meaning of Justice." *American Criminal Law Review* 40: 1541–65. https://doi.org/10.3366/ajicl.2011.0005.

Paik, Leslie. 2011. *Discretionary Justice: Looking inside a Juvenile Drug Court*. New Brunswick: Rutgers University Press.

Perlin, Michael. 2013. "'The Judge, He Cast His Robe Aside': Mental Health Courts, Dignity and Due Process." *Mental Health Law & Policy Journal* 3 (1): 1–29.
Peterson, J., J. L. Skeem, E. Hart, S. Vidal, and F. Keith. 2010. "Analyzing Offense Patterns as a Function of Mental Illness to Test the Criminalization Hypothesis." *Psychiatric Services* 61 (12): 1217–22. https://doi.org/10.1176/appi.ps.61.12.1217.
Ray, Bradley, Brittany J. Hood, and Kelli E. Canada. 2015. "What Happens to Mental Health Court Noncompleters?" *Behavioral Sciences & the Law* 33 (6): 801–14. https://doi.org/10.1002/bsl.2163.
Ray, Bradley, Sheryl Pimlott Kubiak, Erin B. Comartin, and Elizabeth Tillander. 2015. "Mental Health Court Outcomes by Offense Type at Admission." *Administration and Policy in Mental Health and Mental Health Services Research* 42 (3): 323–31. https://doi.org/10.1007/s10488-014-0572-2.
Rottman, David, and Pamela Casey. 1999. "Therapeutic Jurisprudence and the Emergence of Problem-Solving Courts." *National Institute of Justice Journal* 240 (July): 12–19.
Scheff, T. J. 1974. "The Labelling Theory of Mental Illness." *American Sociological Review* 39 (3): 444–52.
Schneider, Richard D., Hy Bloom, and Mark Heerema. 2007. *Mental Helath Courts: Decriminalizing the Mentall Ill*. Toronto: Irwin Law.
Seltzer, Tammy. 2005. "Mental Health Courts a Misguided Attempt to Address the Criminal Justice System's Unfair Treatment of People with Mental Illnesses." *Psychology, Public Policy, and Law* 11 (4): 570–86. https://doi.org/10.1037/1076-8971.11.4.570.
Silver, Eric. 2006. "Understanding the Relationship between Mental Disorder and Violence: The Need for a Criminological Perspective." *Law and Human Behavior* 30 (6): 685–706. https://doi.org/10.1007/s10979-006-9018-z.
Skeem, Jennifer L., Paula Emke-Francis, and Jennifer Eno Louden. 2006. "Probation, Mental Health, and Mandated Treatment: A National Survey." *Criminal Justice and Behavior* 33 (2): 158–84. https://doi.org/10.1177/0093854805284420.
Skeem, Jennifer L., Sarah Manchak, and Jillian K. Peterson. 2011. "Correctional Policy for Offenders with Mental Illness: Creating a New Paradigm for Recidivism Reduction." *Law and Human Behavior* 35 (2): 110–26. https://doi.org/10.1007/s10979-010-9223-7.
Slobogin, Christopher. 1996. "Therapeutic Jurisprudence: Five Dilemmas to Ponder." In *Law in a Therapeutic Key: Developments in Therapeutic Jurisprudence*, 763–93. Durham: Carolina Academic Press.

Steadman, Henry J., Lisa Callahan, Pamela Clark Robbins, Roumen Vesselinov, Thomas G. McGuire, and Joseph P. Morrissey. 2014. "Criminal Justice and Behavioral Health Care Costs of Mental Health Court Participants: A Six-Year Study." *Psychiatric Services* 65 (9): 1100–104. https://doi.org/10.1176/appi.ps.201300375.

Watson, Amy, Patricia Hanrahan, Daniel Luchins, and Arthur Lurigio. 2001. "Mental Health Courts and the Complex Issue of Mentally Ill Offenders." *Psychiatric Services* 52 (4): 477–81. https://doi.org/10.1176/appi.ps.52.4.477.

Wexler, David B. 1973. "Therapeutic Justice." *Minnesota Law Review* 57: 289–338. https://doi.org/10.3366/ajicl.2011.0005.

———. 2000. "Therapeutic Jurisprudence and the Culture of Critique." In *Practicing Therapeutic Jurisprudence: Law as a Helping Profession*, 449–64. Durham: Carolina Academic Press.

Wexler, David B., and Bruce J. Winick. 1991. "Therapeutic Jurisprudence as a New Approach to Mental Helath Law Policy Analysis and Research." *University of Miami Law Review* 45 (5): 979–1004.

Winick, B J. 1994. "The Right to Refuse Mental Health Treatment: A Therapeutic Jurisprudence Analysis." *International Journal of Law and Psychiatry* 17 (1): 99–117. https://doi.org/10.1016/0160-2527(94)90039-6.

———. 1996. "The Side Effects of Incompetency Labeling and the Implications for Mental Health Law." In *Law in a Therapeutic Key: Developments in Therapeutic Jurisprudence*, 17–58. Durham: Carolina Academic Press.

Wolff, Nancy. 2002. "Courts as Therapeutic Agents: Thinking Past the Novelty of Mental Health Courts." *Journal of the American Academy of Psychiatry and the Law* 30 (3): 431–37. http://jaapl.org/content/30/3/431.full.pdf.

Yngvesson, Barbara. 1994. "Making Law at the Doorway: The Clerk, the Court, and the Construction of Community in a New England Town." In *Law and Community in Three American Towns*, edited by Carol J. Greenhouse, Barbara Yngvesson, and David M. Engel, 54–90. Ithaca: Cornell University Press.

# 3

# Clients and Therapeutic Agents: Court Selection and Team Dynamics

Before therapeutic justice has a chance to be realized, defendants (or family members) have to find a MHC or be found by a MHC team member, legal agent or social service provider. Once referred, a defendant is diverted to MHC and undergoes the eligibility and opt-in process. If a defendant accepts the court's conditions, he/she becomes a client in MHC. Before I discuss client experiences in MHC I first turn to the selection process and the therapeutic team that engages directly with clients on their journey in MHCs. Case processing and reviews are the focus of the next chapter.

## Entry into MHC

Monique's experience in *City* MHC (her case was introduced in Chapter 1 and further detailed in Chapter 6) illustrates the selection and opt-in process. Even though Monique lacked a lengthy criminal record and had limited prior contact with the criminal justice system (harassment and property destruction charges[1] and several infractions), she was going to jail on assault and harassment charges. Even in mainstream court, the amount of jail time would depend on whether Monique was willing to engage in treatment for her mental illness. The prosecutors' office was willing to offer a sentencing recommendation with minimal jail time (10 days) but with treatment expectations and 2 years of probation—this is known as a MHC "opt-out" recommendation (mental health diagnosis and possible treatment (MHDT) track). Defendants with mental illness who choose a MHC opt-out offer often face similar requirements as MHC clients but without the support from the MHC program. If Monique was unwilling to agree to treatment, the sentencing recommendation would be approximately 90 days in jail, referred to as a "straight jail" sentencing recommendation without treatment conditions attached. Even if she had agreed to the plea with no treatment requirements, at a later date the judge in mainstream court can mandate assessment and possible mental health treatment (MHDT).

The prosecutor offered Monique MHC with no jail time on the condition that her charges would be dropped if she successfully completed the court obligations. She fulfilled the first requirement for entry—eligible diagnosis—as she has a severe mental illness. In fact, Monique had a long history of mental illness and treatment participation; her mental illness led to institutionalization in a mental health hospital more than two decades before she entered *City* MHC. She also expressed willingness to re-engage in mental health treatment, fulfilling the second requirement—amenability—for a MHC offer. This made her a "good fit" for MHC.

MHC clients like Monique are given an option to enter MHC in hopes of altering their criminal trajectory by receiving social support, mental health treatment (which sometimes includes chemical dependency treatment), and, in some cases, housing. However, accepting a MHC offer comes with strict conditions and frequent supervision by probation and the court. Monique was apprehensive but willing to commit to MHC. Ultimately, despite periods of non-compliance, she successfully graduated from MHC. Not all cases that come through MHC are as successful as Monique's but all go through a similar selection process.

## Stages of Selection

There are three stages of the selection process in MHCs (Wolff et al. 2011). The first stage is the initial screening in which team members determine the eligibility of charges and evidence of mental illness. In the second stage—assessment of eligibility—there is a more in-depth review of other key factors. The final stage of eligibility screening requires both client and judicial approval of the opt-in recommendation. In this study, the MHCs have a similar multi-level sorting process and the selection process is driven by two key components—eligibility and amenability; these represent the first two phases of selection which, although distinct, are often assessed simultaneously.

The first part of the initial screening—a pre-phase of initial screening—is the referral process. Clients must be referred to MHC. Referrals can come from a variety of different sources, such as attorney, judges, police officers, family members, court liaisons, or flagged case files.[2] Referrals to *City* MHCs most commonly come from public defense attorneys, according to interviews with multiple team members, which is consistent with prior research (Steadman et al. 2005). In *County* MHC felony referrals largely come from the local prosecutors' office as well as prosecutor's offices from other neighboring cities (especially *City* MHC). There is a certain amount of "outreach" by the MHC team members from both courts. A defense attorney detailed how this referral and outreach process often works at the public defender's office:

> [I start my day] going to the jail and screening everyone that has been picked up in the last 24 to 72 hours to see if there are competency issues or mental health issues, discussing with them the possibility of going to mental health court for a courtesy hearing, if that is something that they might be interested in, and just trying to pick out people who might be a good fit for the court from that perspective.

A court liaison reflected similarly:

> So part of my duties, my everyday morning duties is I go to the [name] jail in arraignment calendars, and I am outreaching clients there. So I am

literally pulling people into our court, not just getting referrals from other legal entities.

Once referred to MHC, the next stage of the selection process begins. In the second part of the initial screening stage, defendants must be deemed eligible to receive an offer to participate in MHC. While there is a team aspect to the selection process in general, the primary decision-making agent is the court liaison. A court liaison described what she is looking for in the initial assessment, which lasts approximately one hour: "Part of that is my own assessment of their symptomology, making sure that I don't have any competency concerns."[3]

To be considered for MHC, a defendant must have an eligible psychiatric diagnosis, usually former Axis-I[4] mental health illnesses, described as "severe and persistent," such as schizophrenia, schizoaffective disorder or bipolar disorder.[5] A defense attorney described that the "diagnostic eligibility is pretty stringent"—having to be on the specific list of Axis-I diagnosis—with limited discretion to expand. Even though MHC eligibility includes all serious mental illness there are other mental health conditions that are excluded. After the initial assessment a court liaison must obtain a defendant's consent for a release of information from medical and social service providers. Dual diagnosis complicates the opt-in process in determining fit. From one judge's account, given the mental health focus, the standard practice is that if a defendants "primary diagnosis is mental health, they get to opt-in, whereas if their primary diagnosis is substance abuse, they don't get to opt-in" but he feels free to deviate from that rubric. Similar perspectives were expressed by various team members. There are discussion about shifting toward a co-occurring disorder court (a reform I raise in the conclusion).

Once a defendant has been found eligible, he/she needs to be amenable to mental health treatment—that is expressing a willingness to engage in the management of his/her mental illness. Court liaisons assess a defendant's amenability based on their prior engagement with mental health treatment and treatment readiness is used as a marker. During the screening phase, after defendants give consent, court liaisons talked about "record gathering" which takes about two weeks, according to one court liaison. The court liaison "screens" potential clients, which includes interviewing the defendant and collecting data from past mental health service providers. The court collects baseline substance use tests (e.g., Urine Analysis (UA) and Blood Alcohol Content (BAC)) to "ensure transparence and amenability," in the words of a court liaison. At the same time court liaisons are constrained by "resource issues" and working to connect defendants with services and "getting people funding" through the state and federal government assistance program.

Court liaisons talked about the role of motivational interviewing and "being able to talk to people and see if they have something that they want to have different about their situation." A court liaison identified those who are "intrinsically motivated" as the ideal candidates for MHC. It is with the amenability assessment (during the second stage) that more discretion occurs as subjectivity is more pronounced. A court liaison called this stage "fuzzy" and another court liaison described the selection process as, "It basically means your judgment as to how willing this person is to engage in treatment."

During the defendant interview and subsequent meetings a court liaison stated that "I try to talk to them and try to figure out what is really going on. They can have the diagnosis, but if they are not eager or willing to take the steps get the treatment, I can't make people do that. It is not fair to them, and it is not a good use of resources." For many this may mean not being ready to opt-in on the current case because "Some people are so impaired or so contrary—their illness, their personality." In addition to motivation level, concerns about "false diagnosis" to get defendants into court inspired another court liaison to state that it was incumbent upon the team to "screen that out."

The court liaison is trying to assess a defendant's level of motivation for MHC, which is clouded by other defendant concerns. Defendants "number one motivation" is to get out of jail or stay out of jail and a court liaison told me she must "cut through that." This was a widespread issue for court liaisons—assessing the veracity of defendant's willingness to engage in treatment with their desire to be released. Jail complicates the assessment of defendant amenability and a court liaison cannot "be foolish and believe everything that people tell me." It has become more difficult to ascertain treatment amenability with felony-dropdown cases in *County* MHC. Given the seriousness of felony charges a court liaison detailed the challenge, right now we are taking charges that are significantly violent, and so you have to really take into account criminal history. You really have to look at that, the current pending charges, the way that somebody talks about their diagnosis or their symptoms, their insight, kind of assess for their motivation for change.

A court liaison described the selection process as having "many moving pieces to it," which can be complicated by co-occurring disorders and/or homelessness.

During the amenability assessment, court liaisons gather a defendant's history with treatment providers, prior level of engagement and past compliance but "on some level the nexus between the mental illness and the crime" influences assessments, according to a court liaison. A court liaison recalled a prosecutor specifically asking her to explain "What is the nexus of the mental illness to the crime?" which is consistent with how prosecutors talked about eligibility in interviews. This determination goes beyond a mere diagnosis, a court liaison stated plainly, "it isn't just a matter of people having a specific diagnosis. The prisons are full of people with diagnoses, but to look at the interplay with the person's diagnoses, the incentive that the criminal matter gives them." There is a disconnect between the extensive focus on a mental health and criminal behavior connection (and its centrality to MHC) given how this is challenged by social scientific data.

In addition to the eligibility assessment, a court liaison "monitors clients in a short-term conditions of release basis." A court liaison described the job as "a go-between" who is "assessing, coordinating, developing treatment plans, reporting to the judge." Many team members understood the role to be "neutral" which can be a "weird fine line" in which court liaisons must focus on the "factual information with regard to client compliance and treatment."

Many team members, especially court liaisons, defense attorneys, and defense social workers, did not see their position as compelling them to persuade defendants to enter MHC, even if there is "pressure to bring people in" from other areas of the court. A court liaison declared:

> I'm not going to sell this program to anyone. That is just the therapist in me. You don't beg someone to go into therapy. They are not going to get

anything from it. I try to bring people into this court that I really think will succeed.

There was also a sense that this type of court can really benefit certain clients as described by a court liaison, "I tell everybody who comes in that this is a very friendly court. It is a squishy court. You are not going to find another court that is as friendly."

Once a defendant is deemed eligible the court liaison sets up a treatment plan and distributes it to the team. In *County* MHC a court liaison stated that I "work with probation and the state," which often takes place during the pre-court meetings. The obvious absence of defense in the court liaison's description of the screening and selection process is notable. While some of the discussion take place during the pre-court meeting and defense may be present for those conversations, it is another example of the prosecution-heavy or defense-weak imbalance of *County* MHC (a point I reference in the conclusion). In some cases (e.g., domestic violence) the perspective of the victim's advocate is consequential, a prosecutor noted that "I can't imagine a case coming in that the victim wasn't on board."

The final phase of the selection process is the approval stage. After being offered the option of participating in MHC, defendants must voluntarily agree to enter MHC and the judge must accept the opt-in decision. During the time before opt-in or opt-out (i.e., the pre-adjudication phase), while exploring MHC, defendants are placed on MHC conditions of release or a "tryout" as characterized by a prosecutor.

While out of custody, a defendant must comply with the conditions of release for a few weeks, or even months, to ensure that a client is willing and able to fulfill court expectations. There is some variation in the length of time for the opt-in process and it can last up to several months. In *City* MHC the court liaisons described the range of time as typically from two to four months, with some defendants taking up to ten months to complete the opt-in process. Court liaisons expressed a desire to keep it on the lower end of the range being "mindful" of concerns from the attorneys regarding the trial process and a defendant's right to a speedy trial. The time allotted to the opt-in process varied by court liaisons, reflecting their different philosophies and styles. One court liaison talked about preventing it from becoming a "drawn out process," especially in an effort to pursue "perfect compliance" from clients. Despite the more serious charges adjudicated in *County* MHC, the opt-in process is faster: as one court liaison put it, "the court doesn't want somebody to be in our process of screening for a long time." One *County* court liaison aims for a thirty day window.

During this time potential MHC clients come to court for check-ins and are in frequent contact with defense social workers and court liaisons while the client stabilizes, largely related to mental health stabilization. The broader team can also assess how amenable the defendant is and the treatment plan may undergo revisions. In some cases, such as if a new charge was committed while on pre-opt-in conditions of release, the defendant may be re-assessed and deemed not amenable by the court, causing their MHC offer to be rescinded. Out-of-custody defendants considering MHC also attend official hearings, known as a courtesy hearing or a "look-see." This hearing is meant to emphasize the defendant's choice in the opt-in process and expose possible clients to the court's structural and cultural practices. This is a kind of anticipatory socialization process similar to other MHCs (McNiel and Binder 2007).

To enter MHC, clients must agree to a set of conditions and the judge must accept the opt-in recommendation. The MHC team, mostly at the direction of the court liaison and the prosecutor, prepares a set of conditions for participation. These are similar to the conditions of release prior to official opt-in. In additional to mental health treatment, clients must agree not to commit new criminal law violations, abstain from drugs and alcohol, participate in chemical dependency assessment and treatment if so required, and comply with other court conditions based on the charge type or plea agreement (e.g., no contact orders) as outlined in the sentencing conditions. Those who enter the MHC program receive individually tailored treatment plans—a mental health treatment plan with specific group meetings and appointments with treatment providers which is consistent with a therapeutic jurisprudence orientation (Wexler 1996). MHC clients must submit to periodic reviews, which occur more frequently in the beginning (e.g., weekly or bi-monthly) and become less frequent (e.g., 6 weeks or more) as familiarity with the court increases and compliance is maintained. The expected MHC probationary period, wherein defendants are expected to comply by these conditions of release, is two years (with some variation at sentencing for less but not more,[6] as well as room for early graduation). The probationary clock starts once a client opts-in and in some cases (e.g., competency raised) the clock pauses.[7]

A probation officer, with an awareness of net-widening critiques, described the conditions of release this way:

> I think the conditions aren't set to hurt them. It is just to get them that level of structure that they need. None of the conditions in our COS [conditions of sentence] or CORs [conditions of release] are outrageous. The only thing we would write in is anything significant. But for the most part, they are to attend mental health treatment and take medication. Obviously, if you are taking medication you can't use drugs or alcohol. That is self-explanatory. If you start making threats to harm others, we have to look at that. Commit no new criminal law violation – that is on any probation. [And] You can't possess weapons.

Once a defendant agrees to the court conditions a client proceeds to the opt-in hearing. Although there is not a singular initiation ritual, there are some commonalities in the invitation to MHC. In an opt-in hearing a judge made it clear how important it was to abstain from alcohol, "alcohol and medication [together] make everything worse." During the opt-in hearing a MHC judge rules that a defendant "voluntarily, knowingly and intelligently" entered into MHC and in some cases pleads guilty to a charge(s) and in other case are given the option of a dismissal of charges. Then the client formally enters MHC. Following is a typical welcome statement: "Welcome to MHC! This is a different type of court, a collaborative court." Or consider another invitation upon a client's entry into MHC: "Welcome to MHC! This is a treatment court. We understand it will be hard. We will ask a lot of you but the team is here to provide support along the way." The ritual of initiation can be helpful for clients, focusing on group involvement and social support in the court process instead of inflicting more stigma or shame. A judge articulated why MHC is so different from her perspective, "When I opt people in, I always told them this is an incredibly different court than any other court, because we get to see you not just on your bad days, which is really when judges get to see people, but also on your good days." A team member described the process as a "really welcoming reception."

During the opt-in hearing a judge often tries to make clear the trade-offs of MHC and court expectations. In addition to the normal welcome, there is sometimes a warning. One judge declared "This is going to be hard work. 'Are you ready to sign up?' The benefit for you is that you will have access to lots of support and services. The flipside of the coin is that we expect a lot of you." In an opt-in hearing before the judge, a client said, "Your honor, I will do the best I can." Setting a tone of accountability, the judge replied candidly "This is not a do the best you can court." As a probation officer summarized it, the team is "constantly having to challenge and support" clients.

The selection process is extremely important as it determines the pathway into and through MHC that a defendant may take. For a court liaison the screening process represents a preview of the whole court experience, "a microcosm of what is going to happen or how you are most likely to be throughout mental health court for two years." While there is some potential for opting-into MHC at a later stage in the traditional court process, it primarily occurs during the early stages of case processing. (See Fig. 3.1 for the multiple pathways in and out of MHC.)

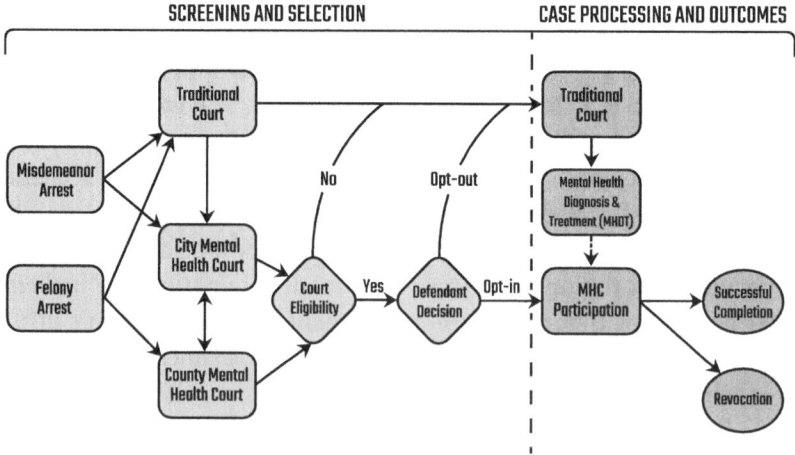

Fig. 3.1 Screening, selection and case processing in MHCs

## Selection Process: Bias and Underrepresentation

Selection and sorting occurs at both the institutional- and individual-level. First, MHC staff must determine whether or not to offer a court invitation to a defendant. Second, defendants self-select by volunteering to participate in MHC. There are two stages of selection into the court introducing possible selection bias. The first stage of sorting is the referral process whereby certain groups become over- or under-represented in the court (Steadman et al. 2005). Once defendants are referred to MHC they have been found eligible and amenable, which further sorts and selects clients. Although there are multiple referral pathways to MHC that safeguard against any category of defendants being completely overlooked, there are still clear cases of underrepresentation.

Researchers report that socio-demographic characteristics (e.g., sex, race and age) influence patterns of selection (Luskin 2001; Steadman et al. 2005). Women, older defendants and whites receive referrals at higher rates. A probation officer claimed, "young white women are more likely to be offered charge dismissals and that, in general, the court is 'tougher' on men." *City* MHC has a higher proportion of white men than other demographic groups and women are offered more dismissal of charges than men. Nationally, female inmates had higher rates of mental illness problems than men and white inmates reported higher rates of illness (James and Glaze 2006).

Both MHCs are underrepresented in the number of clients from racial and ethnic minority groups. Given the overrepresentation of minorities in the broader criminal justice system this raises an equity gap. Disparities around mental illness may be associated with lack of access, inhibitory help-seeking behaviors and stigma that result in not having a diagnosis. The lack of responsiveness to issues of racial and ethnic justice was sometimes a hindrance to increasing client minority representation.

Minorities are untapped groups and underserved populations who might benefit from treatment courts. A court liaison spoke of immigrant populations which could benefit from MHC but are deterred by deportation issues and stigma; the effect of stigma in dissuading individuals from opting-in was a point also emphasized by a judge. The court liaison further spoke about the lack of cultural sensitivity by the court that limits racial and ethnic diversity, asserting that a lack of institutional trust and lack of awareness of potential biases by team members influenced who was offered and who opted-into MHC. For example, she argued for a need to invest more in building relationships and nourishing trust with minority defendants. She provided an example of a case involving an immigrant client. The MHC team wanted to move the client to a different city that was closer to their residence (still with the *County* MHC) and the court liaison protested, stating that the client knew her and understood this court's process. She told the team,

> They [the client and family] are overwhelmed with the system. It is intimidating… Don't start a new system for them. They know how to drive here, they know how to walk up to this floor.

But the team pressed and when she offered the option to the client and his father they asked if the court liaison would be there. I told him "No" and the father responded, "I think we should stay here because we already know how to get here, we already know the people."

An overall lack of racial/ethnic awareness pervaded much of the court. A disconnect was also seen in a case with an African-American male client. The same court liaison suggested that while this client can come across as "angry" and "resistant" it was dependent upon one's approach with him, "Then you just approach him in a different way, whereas if you treat him as if he is resistant, he will end up being resistant." She suggested that this was a subtle way that race comes into play in the court process. The lack of attention to race and cultural differences was stunning to several court liaisons, "I don't know how many times different people in the court will say, 'Well, I've never thought about race. I've never looked at it that way'." This limitation was evident in my interviews with white team members, most of whom suggested that bias was not a problem or that they had not considered it. I found a clear pattern in who perceived a racial/ethnic disparity in court participation and experiences and who did not. Minorities and women were more likely to mention this as a concern. Several white male team members, including judges, did not find any issues with this. A team member stated matter-of-factly that "I haven't thought of it." For all of the minority team members this was a source of frustration and/or bewilderment.

Several judges were aware of the court being "racially unbalanced" in the words of a judge, but few wrestled with the racial and ethnic make-up of the court with one notable exception. On the one hand this judge saw "racial disparity issues on the forefront of everything we do now" but also claimed that "I will never look at the race of the defendant in making a ruling." Despite this declaration he was cognizant of this issue, revealing how it shaped his behavior "I try to be mindful of what the perception is going to be by the defendant, of other participants in the court. I try to think of do I have any implicit bias. I try to recognize any biases or issues that I might have on a case."

Beyond the selection bias and racial and ethnic underrepresentation, a few MHC team members, especially defense social workers and liaisons, suggested that the broader criminal justice system introduces the initial bias. A court liaison characterized it as a "biased institution, it is oppressive." Nevertheless, she acknowledged that "mental health court is an effort to combat" the "many problems" with the court and jail/prison system. For many team members it was the broader criminal justice system that constrained the potential for positive therapeutic outcomes. However, the court can be more or less therapeutic depending on the team members and the court process itself. Once moving beyond the selection process at the institutional level, individual factors enter in.

At the individual-level defendants must decide whether or not to volunteer for MHC. Prior research reports that defendants' acceptance or rejection of MHC offers is not a significant source of selection bias, except for mental health status (Steadman et al. 2005) which does significantly influence the opt-in rates. This was a point confirmed in my interviews, whereby higher functioning defendants are seen as more likely to be in MHC (and be successful). *City* MHC has a lower opt-in rate than reported by other MHCs, suggesting there might be some unmeasured selection bias operating. For example, based on seven MHCs, researchers found that about one third of referred defendants were not found eligible for MHC due to their mental health status and almost all of the defendants found eligible accepted the offer of MHC as an alternative to mainstream court (Steadman et al. 2005). In *City* MHC 64% of defendants who were offered an opportunity to participate in the court opted-in (based on 2008 data).

The combination of legal and treatment-related factors influence the selection and referral process, including the presence of warrants, diagnosis of depression and reported use of illegal drugs around the time of admission(Luskin and Ray 2015). In addition to socio-demographic characteristics, prior criminal history, felony conviction, and crimes against persons also decrease the chance of diversion (Luskin 2001), which in turn decreases the likelihood of being offered MHC. This point was expressed by a defense attorney, "We self-select, I think, for the people… who can get benefits." She described this as a problem because this process brings in those "with really significant criminal histories or really significant charges in the end" which may not always be the best fit for MHC. A defense social worker declared that minorities "are not making it to MHC due to criminal history and access issues which influences amenability" and when they do, "Young black man not getting the benefit of the doubt… getting revoked more than necessary." The combination of overreliance on criminal history led to clients being "branded" and early revocation which for a defense attorney was a "really disturbing inequality." A court liaison suggested a generational effect in terms of education and training. The education in the past was all about "being colorblind" but that can "promote institutional racism to be colorblind, that that is negating somebody's experience and how can you help them if you negate their experience. Right now, definitely there is a colorblind culture to our court, and that needs to go away."

In sum, Wolff (2002) argues that that MHCs engage in "preferred selection" or "cream skimming" practices, selecting for the least risky defendants. In many ways MHCs select the "best" defendants to participate. For example a defense attorney offered this account in response to a question about "skimming":

> As for [MHCs] taking more low-risk offenders, that may be partly true but I think that may be because we cannot engage with some of our most mentally ill clients in the program because they tend to be the ones whose cases are dismissed due to not being competent.[8]

This "cherry picking" neglects the most vulnerable defendants. "We like the people who are nice," suggested a defense attorney, selecting for clients that are easier to work with. Under a "preferred selection model," MHC staff are taking good risks by only offering participation to defendants experiencing less intense mental health symptoms and those who have less prior criminal activity. Bias raises fundamental questions of equity for those individuals who are sorted out of this therapeutic environment.

Politics of the court, tensions between different team members, and funding issues can also influence the selection process. Concerns about selection bias were not universally shared by all court members and some wrestled with this issue more than others. A court liaison struggled with bias in the selection process and realized that it falls squarely on her: "I recognize that who gets in obviously depends on me, right, and I have biases." A judge suggested that if any bias did exist, it is in the referral process of which court monitors/liaisons are the "gatekeepers," conveniently laying the problem prior to entering the court and outside of judicial authority. Reforms to enhance awareness of possible bias in the selection process and general underrepresentation of certain groups are important (and addressed in the Conclusion). Referral and selection processes may ultimately influence success in the court which highlights this critical stage in the broader MHC process (an issue examined in Chapter 5).

## Client Participation in MHC

The decision-making process for defendants is driven by several factors. The court provides incentives to enter MHC, including access to housing, treatment and social support from MHC team members. It also includes small items such as food gift cards and bus passes. The specifics of the opt-in offer influence client decisions to participate in MHC. But with a defendant's acceptance of a reduced sentence (or dismissal of charges) and access to valued resources, comes a host of expectations and a built-in accountability structure to monitor their compliance.

MHCs provide assistance with access to housing which, while not sufficient to meet demand, represents a resource that draws some defendants into the court. At the opt-in stage, housing and treatment beds can be compelling incentives for defendants. Other social services and support are integral to clients' long-term experiences in the court. For many MHC clients I interviewed, the court helped with housing. In a forthright tone, Norm, a MHC client, explained the connection between housing and being in MHC: "The court set me up in housing. I got housing through the court. That is the main reason I went into mental health court. They gave me a year's worth of housing, for 1/3 of my income. I was homeless at the time." In Norm's case he opted in for a more intensive criminal justice intervention in order to receive housing which reflects the limited social safety net more broadly and the widening of the net.

Others, like Shima, only received temporary housing but the stability and support she received from court appointed housing was decisive in the early days of the court. The temporary housing was clearly beneficial in a broader sense of her recovery: "They [MHC] have gotten me housing. They have helped me find a place… It was clean and sober housing, just for girls… It worked out." Others, like Jennifer, recognized that the court helps some people with housing needs but the "court didn't help me." In talking about her current housing situation she told me, while "It is not what I would choose in the long run, but I was homeless for awhile, and then in a skuzzy motel for awhile, and then lived at the YWCA for awhile, and now I am in my own apartment." It is not clear why she did not receive more housing assistance given her sub-standard and unstable housing. In some ways Jennifer's general frustration with the court process was related to the lack of housing assistance offered to her at opt-in which was probably related to availability and limited resources.

The most influential incentive to enter MHC for clients I interviewed was a reduced sentence or dismissed criminal charge. The incentive structure in the two courts is very different, because of the types of offenses considered, which has implications for overall levels of defendant participation. In *City* MHC those who opt-in are offered three possible conditions of sentence: (1) dismissal of charge(s) if the defendant successfully completes the MHC requirements (sometimes referred to as a dispositional continuance, stipulated order of release, or continuance for dismissal); (2) a deferred sentence, whereby a guilty plea is required with the opportunity for dismissal if all conditions are satisfied; and (3) a suspended sentence, which requires a guilty plea and the charges will remain on the defendant's record even if all MHC conditions are satisfied. Several constitutional rights are waived during the opt-in phase (e.g., speedy trial waiver, right to a trial by jury) as well as in some cases clients must agree to the facts in the police report (stipulation of facts). A defense attorney tried to make this clear to defendants as they consider MHC, "And if you are not doing it [abide by MHC conditions], we have no legal recourse. There is no trial. A probation violation has a much lower standard. They don't have to prove it beyond a reasonable doubt."

The majority of MHC clients fall under the third condition of sentencing category and must plead to a guilty charge in order to opt-into the court. However, clients I interviewed in *City* MHC—among the more successful clients—were more likely to be offered a dismissal of charges. Many clients expressed a desire to keep their "records clean" or "avoiding having a record" as the central reason for opting-into MHC. There is clearly a stronger incentive to opt-into MHC for clients with no criminal record (or a limited one). Beyond serving time in jail, there are a host of additional reasons to avoid or reduce one's criminal record as it can have adverse effects on housing, employment, family, social stigma and self-identity.

In *County* MHC the same sentencing options (i.e., dismissal, deferred, or suspended) for misdemeanor cases exist as in *City* MHC. The majority of cases are "felony drop downs" so clients must plead guilty to a misdemeanor charge(s)—it about "50 percent of cases" according to multiple team members.[9] This represents a strong incentive on the front-end for most clients to reduce their felony charge(s). Even if the charges are revoked the client will likely spend less time in jail, not in prison, as was the case if convicted prior to MHC.[10] A probation officer described the incentives in *County* MHC:

> So the benefit of coming into our court [MHC] is you lose the felony, you don't have the felony conviction, you don't get points, you don't risk going to prison, and the most [prison time] you can get is one year, maybe two if they do two misdemeanors consecutive.

Reduced sentencing was the cause of frustration for probation officers given concerns over levels of dangerousness and questions of amenability and fit.

The pressure from the *County* prosecutor's office to bring in more felony cases was apparent and the source of most of the discontent among MHC *County* team members. It produces a challenge in assessing amenability to the court and seems to be counter to a net-widening argument—that is that those facing more serious jail time are offered the greatest reductions, reducing the time under the supervision of the criminal justice system. In talking about the incentives to opt-into MHC a probation officer stated that incentives are clear but that this can also be problematic. It can be difficult to assess how serious a defendant is in wanting to engage in managing mental illness and working with the court: "there are people who say, 'oh, I want this better deal,' because they get a better deal." This led a court liaison to be more stringent in her opt-in recommendations and in cases where the motivation seemed to be "I don't want felonies, I don't want to serve jail time" she admitted, "I just screen out."

The incentives for clients work in the other direction in *City* MHC making it less attractive to opt-into MHC; in fact sometimes the concern around opting-in is the small amount of jail time at stake in some misdemeanor offenses. In *City* MHC this raises concerns about net-widening. In articulating the role of incentives, a defense attorney indicated:

> It all goes back to the carrot or the stick. People have to come to mental health court because they are facing a lot of jail time or because we have a lot to offer them. Suddenly, especially with these felonies the jail time is not particularly threatening, and we have got not a lot to offer them [due to budget cuts] – it makes us less effective.

Available court resources and court imposed punishment enters into defendants calculations of opting-into MHC. For example, the more resources the court can offer clients on the one hand, and the more jail time (to be reduced) on the table, on the other hand, can increase the likelihood of agreeing to MHC.

Similarly, a court liaison suggested that incentives are all on the front end, a point vocalized by others, which is a problem:

> We have had cases where people are very sick and they do very sick things when they are sick, and those are the ones that we want very much to help. I feel like it would probably be a better idea to drop their crimes down at the end. I don't know if that is legal, but I feel that would be their carrot on the stick a little more.

The metaphor of a "carrot on a stick" is an apt metaphor for MHCs as it is not a carrot *or* a stick, but both fused into one tool. The desire to limit sanctions led others to suggest "the stick is but a painted carrot" (Miller and Johnson 2009, 104).

In both courts the declining material resources and social assistance from which the court can draw from pose a serious challenge, as it alters client decision-making. MHCs are caught up in the broader fiscal crisis characterizing mainstream criminal justice. A defense attorney stated:

> It is a hard sell. Come to this court and have all these additional responsibilities and all these additional ways that you may end up going back to jail that you otherwise wouldn't have. That is hugely problematic, which means that the sell is much easier for someone who is facing a lot of jail time, who we are saying you can get out a lot sooner. Or someone who is going to have all the same probation conditions anyway, so why not come work with us.

The list of court conditions for opting-into MHC can be arduous and in some cases too burdensome, deterring participation. Even judges recognized the "onerous requirements." The set of expectations that defendants who opt-into MHC have to agree to may be more demanding that mainstream court. A probation officer described the conundrum this way, "there are definitely more conditions and more supervision in mental health court than there are in regular probation."

Sobriety conditions are a deterrent for defendants in the decision-making process. This also influenced how attorneys advised their clients. A defense attorney remarked that "I think there are also people that don't want to abstain from alcohol, abstain from drugs, and in any other probation system they are not going to be randomly UA's [urine analysis] and in ours they are." A probation officer explained that in the decision-making process at the opt-in/opt-out stage some defendants say "I don't think I want to do that. I don't know if I'd make it, it just seems like too much."

Defendants must volunteer for MHC. For MHC team members the voluntary requirement indicates that an individual is willing to work with court personnel to manage his/her mental illness and, in some cases, chemical dependency issues. A probation officer characterized the voluntary component as a signal in the following way: "having the people that are actually recognizing that, 'I do have these problems, I do need help, I want help.'" In practice, the notion of voluntariness is complex.

In research on mental health treatment the notion of voluntariness is often challenged. Consent is a potential safeguard to an overreaching "therapeutic state" (Wexler 1973), but participation in MHCs may not always be fully voluntary (Redlich 2005) reflecting legal coercion (Boldt 2009). I find that constrained choice predominates. A defense social worker further clarified that for some clients it is not "informed consent." Among team members, it is understood in terms of "engagement as opposed to coercion" suggested a defense attorney. For clients, the voluntary component of MHC was understood as a choice but one made under duress with the threat of more jail looming over them and with various competing emotions (Bernstein and Seltzer 2003). Clients in MHC might also receive pressure to opt-in from others including family members and the criminal justice system, creating a kind of "therapeutic alliance" (Skeem et al. 2007) which reduces the defendant's full capacity of voluntary consent and thus deepens the net of the criminal justice system in their lives.

Nevertheless, when a defendant opts-into (or opts-out of) MHC the act is an assertion of their agency, albeit limited. Defendants do not have to agree to participate in MHC, a point emphasized by the majority of team members. In fact many defendants do not choose to enter MHC due to the length of the probationary period and behavioral expectations mandated by the court. In the decision-making process, clients who agree to enter the court often do so in a way that reflects a long-term time horizon, taking a broad view of how MHC might improve their life in the future. A judge noted "I guess foregoing the short-term rewards for gaining long-term benefits." However just because defendants do not opt-into the court does not mean they are exempt from some of the conditions normally associated with MHC.

## "MHC Lite": Both In and Out of MHC

If a defendant decides not to opt-into MHC or is found ineligible for MHC, the case is referred back to traditional court. However, some defendants become involuntarily intermingled with MHC, while not technically MHC clients. Those defendants within this group are required to complete MHDT[11] as a condition of their sentence given by any judge. A defense attorney characterized the MHDT as "mental health drive through" as this group do not receive the same level of care. Ineligible defendants—based on their lack of amenability—might also be harder for the court to work with while having the greatest need for the court's intervention. Apart from the MHDT group, most often when a defendant decides not to opt-in or is found ineligible for MHC the defendant is put on a different pathway in mainstream court.

There are different pathways to becoming an MHDT defendant: (1) defendants who were never considered for MHC; (2) defendants who are found eligible for MHC but chose not to opt-in (also called opt-outs); and (3) defendants who are found ineligible (either due to diagnostic criteria or a lack of amenability) by the court. A court liaison described the group:

> They didn't opt-in or some of them will go to a different court and the judge will decide or the prosecutor will decide or the police will recommend that they have a court condition like that… They have to get a mental health evaluation that will say what's going on with them, and treatment recommendations.

MHDT individuals are exclusively in *City* MHC. MHDT defendants are required to receive mental health treatment based on assessment as a condition of their sentence. They have fewer court-ordered requirements and receive reduced access to court resources and support compared to MHC clients. In many cases, MHDT defendants are assigned MHC probation officers with supervision and hearings in the MHC. Many team members informally referred to this group as "category 3" or "cat 3" for short,[12] implying their non-traditional entanglement in MHC is a third form of (partial) participation; the first category refers to defendants who opt-into MHC, the second are competency cases where "ability to proceed" is raised and the third category are the MHDT defendants who partially participate in MHC but do not receive the full array of services.

A probation officer compared MHDT defendants to general probationers in mainstream court: "They had mental health problems. They had a diagnosis. They have treatment regimens. They had medication regimens, but I didn't have any real teeth to enforce that." With more resources available in MHC (as opposed to mainstream), probation officers can do more to assist their client's mental health needs. A MHC probation officer articulated the difference between the MHDT group and MHC clients: "the support for the program is much higher" as well as the "MHC program is much more forgiving for relapses and missteps. We say let's go back and try again." The MHDT group posed some particular challenges for the court, as described by a probation officer: "So obviously working with the Category 3s is a lot more difficult, because they don't have a lot of the resources that are available to them. But they have all the same problems."

In theory, MHDT defendants have fewer court hearings and less contact with probation, but there is the potential to increase the frequency of court contact based on defendant's needs and level of non-compliance based on probationary discretion. In practice, MHDT defendants are often assigned to a MHC probation officer but their reviews are not necessarily heard by MHC judges. While most probation officers treat these client groups as distinct, other officers "do not feel bound by their sentence structure nor their MHC program enrollment." In practice the "high functioning [MHDT] cases" can be handled in the same way as MHC clients who opt-in, and are required to complete weekly UAs and more frequent reviews. A probation officer stated frankly that "I still do the same type of things for the people that are Category 3's [as I would for full MHC clients]." For some MHC probation officers, just because some MHDT defendants were not offered MHC or chose not to opt-in "doesn't mean they won't benefit from MHC style supervision." This example illustrates how the court presents constrained choices rather than fully voluntary decision-making if it is not made clear to defendants that they may have many of the same requirements imposed on them if they choose to opt-out of the MHC program. I did not find evidence that defendants are made fully aware of the MHDT pathway. If similar conditions and oversight characterize MHC clients and MHDT defendants, even in some cases, it reduces how meaningful the opt-in "choice" really is.

In some cases, MHDT defendants are held to similar standards of treatment compliance as MHC clients without the additional incentives or resources. For example, although a defendant might not have to abstain from chemical substances in the conditions of sentence in mainstream court, a probation officer handling the case may impose this as a new condition in response to defendant's behavior (e.g., new criminal law violation). To address non-compliance a probation officer might add a new level of supervision more similar to MHC clients. For this reason, the MHDT group can be understood as "MHC lite" (a point explored further in Chapter 5) with broad implications for net-widening arguments, as some MHDT defendants are in some ways involuntarily caught up in the "web" of MHC. This may work to a defendant's benefit in the long run, but it also imposes a stronger net, such as more contact with probation and more review hearings. For probation officers, the frustration around MHDT defendants was that they do not have the resources to provide the needed assistance. Some probation officers expressed desire to move some defendants to MHC from the MHDT pathway.

MHDT defendants can opt-into MHC post-sentence, and while this is not typical, it does happen. A probation officer detailed one such case in which Sally, a client, who did not opt-into MHC until several months into the process on the MHDT track. He described Sally as a young woman with major depressive disorder with psychotic features. She was estranged from her husband and without family support (her divorced parents were living out of state) and "kind of up here by herself" according to the probation officer. The incident that led to her incarceration is fairly typical of many individuals in MHC: She was intoxicated at a bar, after being denied access to the bathroom, and an altercation occurred. Sally was charged with harassment and assault. According to her probation officer, Sally was not on her medication, was homeless and hopeless. Upon meeting with this defendant, the probation officer tried to "delve into it" and begins to establish trust:

> I don't normally do this with Category 3's [MHDTs], but I told her to come back the next week. I wanted to see her. I wanted to make sure she was okay. So she went to the shelter. She came back the following week, so I started developing a relationship with her. Why is this happening? Why don't you have housing? Why are you drinking? Why aren't you on your meds? Why aren't you seeing your case manager that has been set up for you?

After building a relationship over several months he asked Sally why she didn't opt-in. Her answer, as recounted by her probation officer, revealed a lot about the incentive structure of MHCs for individuals facing minor charges with limited jail time. This probation officer recalled that Sally did not know why she did not opt-into MHC—a similar view expressed by many clients I interviewed. At that point, he told her about the benefits available to MHC clients, emphasizing housing, food gift cards, and bus passes. Although Sally was given all of this information at an earlier stage in the process the probation officer reflected that she might not have opted-in because she was "not ready" and did not "see the benefits." The timing of the opt-in offer and decision comes at a stressful and often unstable time. After an arrest, getting out of jail is a paramount concern for defendants, obscuring long-term planning. A probation officer argued:

> What wound up happening [to Sally] was the court was giving her credit for time served at sentencing, so she didn't have any jail time hanging over her, so whatever they were saying wasn't really important. She just wanted to get out of jail. So somehow there was a little bit of a disconnect at sentencing that she heard getting out of jail, versus 2 years of probation, which she wound up getting anyway, but the services that

were available to her at the time, when she was not making good decisions on her own because she wasn't taking meds, she just wanted to get out.

With the assistance of probation, and working with the court liaison, Sally opted-into MHC and received housing and the other benefits. Without this intervention, Sally would have missed the opportunity to receive the full benefits of the MHC, raising concerns about which defendants receive an offer for MHC and who is overlooked. Her case also illustrates the net widening process and the role of team members in client trajectories.

## Therapeutic Agents and the MHC Team[13]

A team member's position influences the performance of the team and also shapes their contact with the defendant. Notwithstanding variation in individual personalities, the social positions individually and collectively (as a part of a team) take on a unique role within the MHC team. From the therapeutic jurisprudence perspective courts and staff are seen as "therapeutic agents" (Wolff 2002); team members work collaboratively with a "mindset" toward therapeutic justice (Schneider et al. 2007). Each member of the MHC team holds a different position with associated role expectations. This leads to varying abilities to influence therapeutic and substantive goals. In some cases, individuals are balancing traditional court functions with new norms and expectations based on the therapeutic orientation of treatment courts. In other cases, individuals do not have a counterpart in mainstream court and are navigating entirely new social roles.

The danger with the therapeutic orientation is if it shifts toward therapy. A defense attorney succinctly stated "we are a therapeutic court and not therapy." A defense social worker expressed similar concerns when judges acted more like "counselors and asked too many questions that are not directly about the court process or compliance." The tension between therapy and punishment and blending legal and treatment logic is present in the everyday working of MHCs. Finding the appropriate balance is a critical component of therapeutic justice.

## Judges

Most of the research on court actors and therapeutic jurisprudence focuses on judges as the central figure and characterize them as "therapeutic agents" (Wexler and Winick 1996) emphasizing the power of the judge in problem-solving courts. The quality of interactions between judges and clients, judicial tone and overall engagement is cited as important to positive MHC outcomes (Fisler 2015; Wales et al. 2010). Under a therapeutic model, judges are characterized by legal agents as both a "cheerleader and stern parent" (Chase and Hora 2000), illustrating the dual role of support and accountability with therapeutic effects as well as the potential for paternalism (Petrila 1996), even if not the intent (Casey and Rottman 2000). A judge referenced that "the judge's role is really to be a cheerleader [for clients], really give positive feedback and give consequences when appropriate, and really just engage." Some judges reflected on their role as "more protective." In all of these accounts the judicial role is understood as distinct in MHCs, so much so that some have described that judges in MHCs "cast their robe" aside (Perlin 2013: 5).

Judicial effectiveness in treatment courts is different and reflects several themes including their level of "buy-in," demeanor and temperament, and leadership. In addition to these key factors, judicial consistency also matters. While there is an appointed MHC judge for a two year period in both courts, there have been times in *City* MHC where multiple judges rotate through MHC, impeding the development of a relationship with clients and team members needed to be an effective therapeutic agent.

### "Buy-In"

"Buy-in" is a term used to describe a judge's understanding and appreciation of the court's treatment orientation and therapeutic practices. A judge who buys-in treats presiding over a MHC as a distinct and important role. Mission buy-in from all team members is a necessary foundation for the working of the court but pivotal from the bench. A probation officer put it bluntly, "I don't think you can be in mental health court without having some sort of empathy with the situation and trying to help solve these people's long-term problems." Team members more often referred to judges as having empathy or compassion. A judge clearly shared this orientation:

> It is very important to have empathy for people – to really try to understand what they are going through, and under that you, you are not going through it as a judge and no one else is, but that person is going through that. That is what I really try to understand with people and treat them – really try to be empathetic to their plight.

All judges I interviewed believed in the mission of the court and attempted, some more successfully than others, to produce therapeutic justice. "On all sides, it is we just want to help them get better, it will help everybody" was how a judge understood the court's broad mission. Another judge articulated that judging in MHC requires a different non-legal approach, "you are not trying to decide legally is this right or wrong. You might be trying to decide what's the best way to get to a certain outcome."

For many team members, buy-in was really about judges having the right "intent." For a court liaison this reflected a "rehabilitation perspective, that treatment-oriented perspective, and being educated [about mental illness]." Clarifying this further, a probation officer stated, "I think there needs to be a certain understanding of the mental health process and how things go." A defense attorney contrasted judges in therapeutic courts to judges in mainstream courts, declaring, "In mainstream [court] the judge might not understand—understand where the client is coming from, understand the mental health issues, understand what really needs to help that person get better or to stop them from violating their probation." Team members linked understanding to knowledge and training but also to judicial practices. A probation officer noted that some judges do not "really understand mental illness… chemical dependence and criminal personality."

It is critical for a MHC judge to be guided by the court's mission and understand the challenges with working with people with mental illness. A court liaison spoke of "insightfulness" and suggested judges need to have an "understanding [of] themselves in relation to this court… and not always necessarily get bogged down in the legality of it or the paperwork or the administration piece of it. It is humanistic." To achieve therapeutic justice judges need to shift their orientation away from purely legal matters to therapeutic ones.

Another court liaison described a judge who he believed did this well:

> He tries to make good decisions, and he tries, most of all, to be compassionate, which you don't find in many judges. He is a very good judge for this court. I know that some people wish that he would be harder. Like I said, even some days I do. But if he were a hang 'em high judge, he wouldn't be for this court, because we work with people who have a chronic history of making bad decisions, and we can't expect them not to.

In practice buying-in to MHC for judges means "engaging" and a judge emphasized that "It is really important to slow it down and talk to them [client]." Talking about the "human engagement side" of MHC a judge highlighted the opportunity MHC gave to "learn how to not pathologize" which starts with not seeing people who "walk in the door… as a problem."

Most team members expect judges to preside in a clear and organized way, balancing support and understanding with accountability and firmness when necessary. But in theory most team members endorsed the notion that mistakes or non-compliance were part and parcel of MHC client behavior. Judges who understood that would be more therapeutic according to a court liaison:

> Everyone makes mistakes, and when they fall [make mistakes] throughout the program, when they relapse, you are not treated like, 'You are horrible, you failed, you are done.' It is just, OK, this is what you did, what happened. Where are your other needs? When someone gets approached with that attitude, then they are more likely to succeed and you see that. So having a judge with that frame of mind, I've seen that be really helpful [for client success].

Judicial buy-in to the court's therapeutic mission is a necessary but not sufficient condition for success. A defense social worker suggested that all prior judges "bought into MHC" but they all proceed differently—some more effectively than others. It matters <u>how</u> a judge translates judicial buy-in to the running of the court. A probation officer gave an emotional assessment about a judge, "His heart seems to be in it and I believe that he wants to be a good MHC judge" but he isn't "very effective" given his lack of knowledge and training around mental illness. Beyond believing in the mission of the court, judges need to be trained to preside in MHCs (which is not formalized) as well as have the right demeanor and temperament given the therapeutic and antitherapeutic effects of judicial action.

## Demeanor and Temperament

The judge sets the tone of the court. Their words, affect and style shape interactions with clients and the team. One judge stated that being a judge in MHC "means setting a tone in the courtroom that you expect the other attorneys and providers to sort of model." Judicial demeanor and temperament is even more important in treatment courts where judges spend more time in conversation with clients and have more exchanges with potentially therapeutic outcomes. For many team members this proved pivotal and a probation officer stated, "There is a certain judge demeanor that needs to come across" which includes patience, listening and empathy in the words of judges. Being "even keeled" was how a prosecutor described the most effective judge he worked with in MHC. For judges this meant having time to "build up a rapport" with clients.

Differences in style may reflect personality styles and idiosyncrasies but research finds patterns and variation in judicial style and temperament ranging from pleasant, to neutral to unpleasant (Mack and Anleu 2010).[14] In both MHCs judicial style ranged from neutral to pleasant with only a few observations of or interview references to disrespectful or unpleasant judicial tone or style.[15] A defense attorney explicitly stated of a successful judge that "she is doing it in that tone that is not condescending, not judgmental. I feel like people are open to have a conversation with her." A team member described a judge the following way: "He has been very fair with the clients and I like the tone of his courtroom. He is also very consistent, which I greatly appreciate." An effective judicial style is pleasant, but direct and clear, described by a probation officer as "holding them accountable and supporting them all at the same time." Team members described judges who are "clearly directed and willing to take action" were the most beneficial for the court.

Unpredictability characterizes MHC proceedings and for a judge being able to stay calm and respectful amidst outbursts or heated emotional exchanges reflects the appropriate judicial style. Recounting a practical way this occurs in court he explained, "One minute there could they could be like calm and lucid and the next minute they could tell you to fuck off, or vice versa. I don't put much stock in it when they tell me to fuck off." He contrasted this with a problematic response to such an exchange where a judge was offended and held the defendant/client[16] in contempt. It is important for judges to be aware of affect and remember in the words of a judge that "it isn't about me" implying it is about the clients.

A court liaison contrasted an effective MHC judge to an ineffective MHC judge:

> Well, we had one judge who was very smart, very detail oriented, like that, but it was painful to work in the court because of the way the judge addressed the defendants… because of the lack of respect, humiliating people who were mentally ill, and there is nothing you could say about it, certainly not. And, yeah, it was very, very painful to see. We endured and the person left and the next judge we got was like night and day, very good, very thoughtful, very appreciative [of the team].

Team members saw judges who were organized in running the court and straightforward with clients as more effective. Alternatively, judges who were seen as less effective by team members were those who were verbose and tended to meander or, at worst, lecture the court. A team member reflected that a judge "talks out loud in a way to try and figure out what he's trying to say… He forgets he's on the bench and he's not a teacher. He teaches. And a lot of his style would be better for teaching." Displaying the appropriate demeanor and temperament were clearly connected to judicial effectiveness, along with a judge's ability to be an integral part of the team.

## Team Players

All team members saw the judge's position as important, even if the judge was not always effective. A defense attorney saw the judge's role as critical "even though he doesn't have any say in our decision-making process [which takes place during the pre-court meeting]," reflecting the limits of judicial leadership. Most MHC team members expressed esteem for judicial authority but some discontent in how that role was performed. Although there are some similarities in how MHC team members and clients viewed judicial effectiveness, there was often a disconnect between a judge's self- assessment and the team's evaluation.

MHC team members described effective judges as team players but not necessary leaders of the team, but certainly "a facilitator" as described by a prosecutor. This point was frequently reiterated including by another prosecutor who stated that tone captures judicial leadership: "I do see the judge as the leader of the team, in the sense the judge, he or she, sets the tone." Judges described themselves as "problem-solvers" and "leaders of the team." I found that the most effective judges in therapeutic court knew when to assert their authority and when to defer to team expertise in a collaborative manner. The consensus amongst team members was that with a well-functioning team judges can be less "hands on." While several judges also expressed the view that they could be less directly involved, it was not always consistently practiced. A judge noted that:

> I see the judge in the best-case scenario as being a leader of the team, which is different than being the boss of the team, which means setting sort of behavioral expectations and modeling behaviors among – I am going to treat you this way and you need to treat each other this way. I think it means setting agendas and sort of facilitating discussion around strategic planning and helping to troubleshoot issues as they arise.

Another judge described the role as "a neutral decision maker." A probation officer suggested that "Still kind of being in the role of the judge... They [effective MHC judges] didn't see themselves as separate from the team. Some of the other judges, to be honest, had a hard time adjusting [to MHC]."

For many team members the challenge of indirect leadership was related to judges' inability to recognize the gaps in their mental health expertise. Many MHC team members would like to see a greater awareness from judges of what they know and what they don't know and a willingness to rely on expertise from the team in the latter. One team member expressed the concern concretely, "You have judges... who think they know something about mental health and substance abuse, and criminal personalities, and they don't. They think if they read the DSM-IV they understand mental illness." But as a court liaison said, the judge needs to "listen to our recommendations" and "trust decisions or information that the 'professionals' are providing," a point emphasized by many. There are judges who were mindful of their limited mental health expertise and fully recognized that "we as judges are not psychiatrists." This led him to "rely on others [expertise]" such as when requesting a clinical recommendation.

Many team members identified a judge's ability to solicit and integrate feedback as central to an effective and functioning team. Speaking about a judge, a team member stated that "he doesn't ask for feedback... he's afraid of conflict." Alternatively, while describing effective judges, a probation officer identified a willingness to listen to the team:

> You could go back and talk to them beforehand and say, we want to kind of like stir this person up a little bit about how important this is, but we don't really want to throw them in jail, so.... It was even almost like, the subtle way of how you talked about it was giving the judge a hint on what to do.

A court liaison highlighted the importance of being "appreciative of the team," having an "open door" policy welcoming feedback and open communication about the functioning of the court. She linked this positive approach with client benefits: "I think it is the respect, because if that judge is respecting the team, then you know the judge is respecting the clients."

Relying on the team's recommendation and expertise was an adjustment for some judges. A judge suggested that his time in MHC changed his judicial approach and his thinking evolved into greater reliance on others' insights. Reflecting on the collaborative model in MHC, he stated that it was the "team approach" that informed "a lot of what I did." He further clarified:

> I actually gave a lot of weight to my probation officers, because they were very good and did a lot of work. They are the ones that are face-to-face with the person… we actually had some really good public defenders at the time, too. I gave a lot of weight to what they had to say. A lot of times everybody was on the same page.

**Judicial Consistency**

Part of judicial leadership and court functionality is judicial consistency. A court liaison stated it succinctly, "I do think it super-important to have a consistent judge." This was particularly true in *City* MHC, where for two years (the standard judicial appointment) the MHC judge had many administrative responsibilities (outside of MHC) which took precedence over presiding over MHC. Team members and clients alike raised this as a problem. A court liaison expressed the view that the judge "spread herself too thin." A probation officer recounted a case when a defendant came into court and was out of compliance with the conditions of his release, but the judge told the client he was going to get another chance. The client was looking forward to the next review. If the same judge was not at the subsequent reviews, this type of support and encouragement is lost:

> They come in a month later and they don't see that judge and then the judge will make a completely different decision. You are giving a little bit of inconsistency to the people who already have life inconsistencies. They need to know what to expect.

Consistency in having the same judge hear reviews for the same client over the course of their case varies depending on the commitment from the presiding MHC judge. Most took that role seriously and were in court dependably even informing clients of scheduled absences.

Anxiety about judicial variability was also felt by clients who were unsure of what to expect from the bench both when they were in and out of compliance.[17] In talking about some of the challenges as a client in MHC, Monique stated that "I think having a more consistent judge [would have helped] because she was gone a lot." However she explained that "She was happy when she saw different judges because the normal judge was tougher on her and asked her hard questions." Later in the interview she admitted that although the judge was tough she was "more involved in our cases then other judge." Likewise, Jennifer asserted that "It is nice to have that continuity and to have them [the judge] know your case... I think it makes the whole experience more... coherent." Isaiah, a MHC client, expressed that while different judges can offer "different views," it would be "beneficial" to have the same judge, especially when clients are in compliance. He wanted to receive positive affirmations from the same judge.

Judges play a central role in adjudicating between social and legal factors in the court process. With a well-functioning team, the judges' role is not at center stage. While judges play an important role in the team model, emphasizing the judge overshadows other significant roles that are integral to how MHC can deliver therapeutic justice. Other members of the MHC team act as therapeutic agents framed by a treatment philosophy.

## Lawyers

The literature on therapeutic jurisprudence focuses on judges and lawyers, especially defense attorneys in the case of criminal law and the quality of counsel is seen as necessary for court sucess (Perlin 2013). In MHCs defense attorneys sometimes act as "therapeutic agents," engaging in preventative lawyering. In line with therapeutic jurisprudence, preventative lawyering refers to a proactive style with an awareness of potential legal conflicts and law-related psychological harm (Stolle et al. 2000; Winick et al. 1999). This approach considers the client's well-being, trying to anticipate how legal procedures and court processes can produce antitherapeutic outcomes and result in what experts call "psycholegal soft spots" (Birgden and Ward 2003). Psycholegal soft spots (Wexler 2000) refer to the psychological and legal implications of attorney communication with their clients about legal matters. Practicing law as a therapeutic agent is related to lawyering with an ethic of care (Menkel-Meadow 1992) and lawyering as a helping profession (Stolle et al. 2000). In her comparison of adversarial and collaborative lawyering, Daicoff (2000) identifies active listening, focusing on clients, respect, personal responsibility, compassion among other positive characteristics of collaboration.

Defense attorneys spoke about being "zealous" in protecting their client's rights and best interests and their unwillingness to pressure defendants to enter MHC. However, they also suggested that, in many cases, they tried to offer clients a long-term perspective, highlighting possible benefits of court structure (meetings with probation and support from team), treatment regimen (including groups, therapy, and/or medication) and possibly housing. At times, defense attorneys reported a tension between the team model and the short-term interests of their clients, which was particularly acute in situations where defendants had less serious charges and limited jail time. This tension was also felt by other team members. For example, a court liaison suggested that defense attorneys focused on getting the best deal for their clients and making legal challenges might not be a good fit for MHC: "Maybe if you feel really strongly about getting people out of jail, maybe that is not the right court for you." Trying to "balance and navigate… privileged information is tricky" according to a defense attorney and sometimes not divulging information leads to tension among team members. Central to defense's perspective is focusing on "doing right by my client" and keeping the team "client focused" which includes both legal and therapeutic factors. Defense attorneys clearly understood their duty through a therapeutic lens: to act "reasonably calm" and work collaboratively to "figure out a way to actually work with them."

A judge saw attorneys as therapeutic agents especially in terms of conversations during the opt-in/opt-out phase as clients are sometimes "driven by the defense attorney" and the level of encouragement or discouragement for the court. He highlighted the attorneys are also "counselors" and attorney temperament in dealing with clients with mental health issues is important, of which all lawyers do not have. While prosecutors were working in a therapeutic court they did not see themselves, nor did others see them, as therapeutic agents per se, reflecting their more distant role that prosecutors have with clients. However, prosecutors still practiced with a therapeutically-oriented philosophy.

## Probation Officers

Previous research on treatment courts characterizes judges and lawyers as important therapeutic agents, leaving probation largely unexamined in the everyday workings of MHCs. Yet once a defendant enters MHC, clients interact the most probation officers, who hold the greatest potential to bring about therapeutic outcomes. Much of the work by probation officers with clients is done behind the scenes, in collaboration with other team members and social services agencies. In court before the judge, the main task for a probation officer is to present reports on client's progress and level of compliance with court conditions for court reviews and offer recommendations, especially in the case of non-compliance.

Data from both MHCs suggest that probation officers matter more in the practice of therapeutic justice than previously recognized. The supervision of clients with mental illness is different from traditional probation across key dimensions, including exclusive and reduced mental health caseloads and problem-solving strategies as a preferred method for addressing treatment non-compliance (Skeem et al. 2006). Probation officers are even referred to as Mental Health Specialists in *County* MHC, emphasizing their therapeutic role.

Probation's dual-role of "care and control" or "care and supervision" leads to key distinctions between "the therapeutic relationship and the dual-role relationship" (Skeem et al. 2007, 406). Probation officers in their supervisory roles talk and comfort clients as well as dole out punishments. Although MHC probation officers are not therapeutic providers, based on my observations probation officers are therapeutic agents within the framework of care and control. Probation officers described themselves as "effectively massaging the relationship between the bench and the defendant." Of all the team members probation officers have the most contact with MHC clients. They are pivotal in the functioning of MHC and vital to client experiences with the court. Interviews with clients highlight probation officers dual-roles. Robert, a MHC client, described his probation officer as "more like my case manager than my probation officer." This was also expressed in other client interviews. When Shima got out jail [for the last time] for violating a no-contact order, her probation officer made arrangements for supportive housing while she was still in jail. Shima recounted that she was "grateful" and described the supportive scene when she was released from jail to go for her housing interview:

> I am doing my makeup and trying to look better. My clothes were kind of wrinkled… As I was doing this and waiting for him to pick me up. So I got out and he said, 'I know you need a cigarette. We have an hour before your interview.' He got me from jail, walked down to Rite-Aid [to get a cigarette]… walked there from the courthouse, sat outside, and smoked.

The supportive exchange and knowledge of stress-reducing activities (smoking) to calm her down before the interview was vital for Shima. In fact, she was so connected to her probation officer that his departure from the court had the potential for anti-therapeutic effects. She felt "abandoned." However, upon meeting her new probation officer, Shima told me that the relationship worked from the beginning because it started out with trust. Shima was able to transfer the trust from her former probation relationship to a new probation officer. She told her new probation officer, "I know [name of former probation officer] put me with you because he knew that would be a good fit." She also told me that her new probation officer was "awesome" and "his vibe" and style was tough but caring: "It was hard, but when he was hard, he wasn't being mean or trying to make it feel like your worthless, you have so much ahead of you, stop." Shima's case underscores how "caring becomes blended with fairness" (Skeem et al. 2007, 406). Given this therapeutic relationship, it is not surprising that in client interviews probation officers were most often cited as the key team member in their court experience, integral to their perceptions of fairness with the court process and in their accounts of success in MHC.

Probation officers vary in prior experience and style but described their role similarly in both MHCs even with different clientele. A probation officer stated that despite different backgrounds of probation officers "From our court, we all, I feel, are very open-minded in this process." However, not all probation officers were viewed in a therapeutic light. There were tensions expressed by MHC team members based on different philosophies and styles of probation work. A court liaison made a clear distinction between probation officers who "assist versus penalize." A few clients also expressed some discontent about how their probation officer proceeded with their cases and a tendency, by a select few, to be overly punitive to non-compliance. Underlying this tension is the varying levels of support for a harm reduction perspective (versus zero-tolerance) a point explored further in Chapter 4.

## Other Therapeutic Team Members

Other team members do not consider themselves therapeutic agents or even see the purpose of the team in those terms. Team members with training as defense social workers were less inclined to see their roles as therapeutic in the context of the criminal justice system. A court liaison expressed a consistent tension in working in MHCs given a social work background,

> [The] challenge that I have as a social worker is it is a court, it is a court of law. It is not a harm reduction court. There is abstaining, there are penalties, there are sanctions. In a social service world, we are flexible, we adopt treatment plans to accommodate that, and not necessarily penalize. It is complicated, right, in terms of the client's accountability and engagement and all that stuff, but a court of law, ultimately the court will take action if someone is not in compliance. So that's the challenge.

Another court liaison refused to call it a "therapeutic team," instead she referred to a "knowledgeable team, a team that knows how to have the patience and understanding in working with clients whose situation might be very difficult." Interestingly, court liaisons who are on the frontlines screening potential clients into or out of MHC see themselves in a less therapeutic sense. One explained:

> I think it is really important as a liaison, that you don't get overly involved in a therapeutic sense with somebody, because some people end up wanting to maintain the relationship when they entered the court. There is no female mental health court probation officers [in *City* MHC], so for some people, females, that is an issue… that we are not here to be a therapist… Things that we say are not confidential. Our privilege lies with the court.

Nevertheless, the position of court liaison clearly has therapeutic and anti-therapeutic effects. The neutrality of the role of court liaison enhances its therapeutic effects as they are not part of the adversarial criminal justice model. When talking with potential clients, a court liaison recounted a typical exchange, "I tell them, 'I am a clinician for the court. I am neutral. I don't work for the defense, I don't work for the prosecution.' Then they calm down… which decreased their anxiety, which increased amenability." With a higher level of trust, the court liaison and the defendant (soon to be client) can start working on a possibly therapeutic course of action (including housing, treatment providers, federal subsidies, and other forms of support).

In court hearings, attorneys and judges call upon the court liaison for expertise, perspective and additional information. They often act as an intermediary between the court and the defendant. They provide "ancillary support." As a court liaison explained once a client officially opts-in, "I really like to just see how they are doing and give them some encouragement. I do think that sometimes it is just nice [for client] that you haven't forgotten about them." Even though court liaisons do not see their role as therapeutic, in the practice of working in MHC, they are therapeutic agents. How and in what ways they engage with clients has positive and negative effects to their well-being.

## Assessing the Therapeutic Team

Stability and trust are key factors related to the functioning and effectiveness of the team model. It is clear from all team members that while the positions in MHCs are the same in many ways to positions in traditional courts the norms and role expectations are different. Any team member's ability to be a successful therapeutic agent is dependent, at least to some degree, on the broader team. This is most acute in the case of probation. Most of the probation officers stated in some way that they felt they were important in the team, though not always appreciated. They considered themselves "more invested" and having "an emotional attachment" to the clients, which gave them special "insight." A probation officer reflected upon a functioning team in which probation's participation was seen as an important part of the overall functioning of the team:

> It was just nice to know that I had all these different entities that were helping me make decisions and back me up… there was accountability with a lot of these decisions that were being made on all parts – prosecutor, public defender, and then the judge would take your input and you actually felt like you were part of it.

A major limitation of MHC is the extent to which therapeutic styles vary by court actors, especially judges, as described by a court liaison: "But in actuality sometimes I think it depends on who you get. It depends on the judge. It depends on who our prosecutor is. It depends on the defense attorney. It depends on how they are feeling that day." Efforts to continually foster a therapeutic orientation into the culture of the court reduces this judicial variability. Many team members from both courts described *County* MHC as marked by "tension" which impedes the ability to deliver therapeutic justice and contrasted *City* MHC as a "well-functioning team" with long-standing team members.

A consistent and effective team with good judicial leadership is necessary, but there are challenges in recruiting and retaining team members. For judges, the feeling that bench appointments in MHCs, and problem-solving courts more generally, have a lower legal status may be related to perceptions from clients. Vicki stated happily that "I didn't have to go in front of an actual court and be judged" and Monique relished that MHC clients "do not have to face a real judge or a real courtroom." A defense attorney characterized MHCs as "a career killer" for a judge—a point she also made about other treatment court attorneys. A judge shared that while the experience in MHC was enriching, it was not legally or intellectually challenging and that it was a great "break" from traditional court practices. Her ambition toward a higher court judgeship deterred her from pursuing a return to problem-solving courts, noting that it would be "an unusual career trajectory to go to a lower level court." Despite the lower status, there are benefits of practicing therapeutically for judges in terms of increased job satisfaction (Chase and Hora 2000).

Most of the judges that I spoke with sought out their MHC judicial appointment or were approached by the current presiding judge. But they were reticent to take another MHC rotation due to "burnout" and "exhaustion" unless someone perceived as unfit was pursuing it. It was characterized as "the most difficult calendar we have" by a judge. This perspective was articulated nicely by another judge describing her typical speech at graduations:

> I ended up telling graduates…. that they gave me a lot more than I gave them. I hope that I gave them sort of a safe place to come in and get help and talk about how they were doing. They gave me an entire world view shift, an entirely different way of looking at why people are in crisis and how we can help them feel strong about getting out of crisis, which is a pretty profound.

Many judges expressed that they had changed as a judge because of time spent in MHC and that the approach extends to mainstream court. A judge declared "I love therapeutic justice, because you don't have to be a mental health court judge… to do it."

Working in MHC was a positive experience for many probation officers. Being able to provide clients with "resources in order for them to attain those goals is a lot more rewarding [that in mainstream court]." Even though court liaisons do not claim to be therapeutic agents, they did express professional satisfaction. For example, a court liaison described how everyone can benefit from MHC,

I think it is a really good opportunity for our clients. I think it is a good opportunity for attorneys to learn more compassion, and knowledge that there are ways that people can help themselves I feel really honored to be able to be in court and explain certain things [about clients] to the judges. As a professional, I think it is great.

All team members expressed positive sentiments about working in MHC. Therapeutic justice depends on a functioning team that trusts each other, is flexible, and respects each other's expertise. It requires investments of time, energy and resources and an "ethic of care." Finding team balance—between support, encouragement and accountability—represents a real challenge for therapeutic agents in MHCs but is imperative for therapeutic justice. A court liaison articulated this tension saying, "I don't know how you strike that balance between I care about you and, by the way, if you mess up I'm going to throw you back in jail."

Team members have great influence during the court process but also influence the selection process—who gets into MHC and who does not—which limits the reach of therapeutic justice. Only those clients who are in MHC are exposed to the therapeutic team model. If a defendant is not selected or chooses not to opt-into MHC, the team has limited opportunities to have a therapeutic effect through the court process—with the notable (and problematic) exception of MHDT defendants. Some defendants miss out completely on the opportunity to receive therapeutic justice given their lack of insight into their mental illness or lack of readiness during the decision-making process and/or gaps in the referral process. Added pathways into MHC at later stages could alleviate this limitation. Once fully immersed in MHC, how team members respond to compliance and non-compliance illustrates therapeutic justice in action, a point to which I now turn.

## Notes

1. Both charges were dropped due to a lack of a complaint filed.
2. The flag is an administrative tool directing future cases from a defendant to MHC, creating bureaucratic efficiency with the intent of positive therapeutic outcomes. All parties usually must agree for the flag

to be removed (or remain) and then the presiding judges authorizes an official removal. In court observations I never witnessed a difference in opinion between attorneys or judges on questions of flag removal.
3. If there are competency concerns the assessment is suspended and the competency process begins.
4. However many team members referred to other kinds of cases coming into MHC, such as a court liaison described "I'm sorry, but the cases we get, they are not all eligible by the standard definition of the diagnosis. A lot of them are Axis II. We have to make it clear why they are not eligible based on that, and we get a lot of blow-back for that… I do think we work with Axis II, I do think we work with some antisocial and I do wish that sometimes there was more punishment for that."
5. *City* MHCs also takes individuals with developmental disabilities, brain injuries and dementia. This is unusual and represents a small portion of cases.
6. There are exceptions to the two year jurisdiction in cases of domestic violence and DUIs which are up to five years.
7. If an individual is waiting on a competency evaluation, it stops the clock on probation and jurisdiction until the evaluation is resolved. This also happens if an individual has received a warrant, the clock resumes once the warrant is resolved. So, sometimes there can be clients in MHC for three to four years, such as in the case of Jennifer, because of all the stopping and restarting.
8. This comment reflects the fact that in MHCs defendants with the most severe mental illnesses are not found legally competent and thus unable to proceed in MHC. Thus, there is a selection bias based on a defendant's competency and ability to proceed as there is no possible opt-in offer for these defendants.
9. It was approaching 65% felony cases according to a prosecutor on a follow-up interview.
10. This assumes that the case was not plead down to a similar misdemeanor charge during the plea bargaining process in mainstream court or the defendant was found not guilty at trial.
11. It might be more appropriate to talk about evaluation as the court does not mandate diagnosis. The inclusion of possible treatment also seems important to include. A preferable acronym could be Mental Health Evaluation & Possible Treatment (MHEPT).

12. However, not all embraced "category 3" term. A court liaison adamantly stated "I don't care for that term." In fact *City* MHC has repeatedly tried to phase out the term "cat 3" and refer them as non-MHC clients who have MHDT obligations.
13. In this section I refer some interview respondents as MHC team members due to the sensitive nature of critiquing judges to protect confidentiality.
14. Mack and Anleu (2010) detail five types of judicial demeanor: (1) welcoming or good-natured; (2) patient or courteous; (3) routine, business-like, or impersonal; (4) impatient, rushed, inconsiderate, or bored; and (5) harsh, condescending, or rude.
15. Court observations suggest only rare occasions where a judgmental and disrespectful tone was used. A social service provider reflected on some of the exceptions in MHC, "I've seen judges who are incredible, who are really demeaning, talking down, really simple... They are aren't dumb. You see the client just looking at them, like, 'what is your problem?'" (see a notable example on page 209).
16. It was not clear at what stage this episode took place. It could have been a MHC client (opted in) or a defendant whose ability to processed was raised or a defendant considering MHC.
17. A notable exception was Robert. He told me "It doesn't matter" because the focus is really on probation which was very consistent.

# References

Bernstein, Robert, and Tammy Seltzer. 2003. "Criminalization of People with Mental Illnesses: The Role of Mental Health Courts in System Reform." *The University of the District of Columbia Law Review* 7: 143–62. https://doi.org/10.3366/ajicl.2011.0005.

Birgden, Astrid, and Tony Ward. 2003. "Pragmatic Psychology Through a Therapeutic Jurisprudence Lens: Psycholegal Soft Spots in the Criminal Justice System." *Psychology, Public Policy, and Law* 9 (3–4): 334–60. https://doi.org/10.1037/1076-8971.9.3-4.334.

Boldt, Richard C. 2009. "A Circumspect Look at Problem-Solving Courts." In *Problem-Solving Courts: Justice for the Twenty-First Century*, edited by Paul Higgins and Mitchell B. Mackinem, 13–32. Santa Barbara: Praeger.

Casey, Pamela, and David B. Rottman. 2000. "Therapeutic Jurisprudence in the Courts." *Behavioral Sciences & the Law* 18: 445–57.

Chase, Deborah J., and Peggy Fulton Hora. 2000. "The Implications of Therapeutic Jurisprudence for Judical Satisfaction." *Court Review* 37: 12–21.

Daicoff, Susan. 2000. "The Role of Therapeutic Jurisprudence Within the Comprehensive Law Movement." In *Practicing Therapeutic Jurisprudence: Law as a Helping Profession*, 465–92. Durham: Carolina Academic Press.

Fisler, Carol. 2015. "When Research Challenges Policy and Practice: Toward a New Understanding of Mental Health Courts." *The Judges' Journal* 54 (2): 8–13. http://www.courtinnovation.org/sites/default/files/documents/JJ_SP15_54_2_Fisler.pdf.

James, Doris J., and Lauren E. Glaze. 2006. *Mental Health Problems of Prison and Jail Inmates*, 1–12. Washington, DC: U.S. Department of Justice. http://bjs.gov/content/pub/pdf/mhppji.pdf.

Luskin, Mary Lee. 2001. "Who Is Diverted? Case Selection for Court-Monitored Mental Health Treatment." *Law & Policy* 23 (2): 217–36.

Luskin, Mary Lee, and Bradley Ray. 2015. "Selection into Mental Health Court: Distinguishing Among Eligible Defendants." *Criminal Justice and Behavior* 42 (11): 1145–58. https://doi.org/10.1177/0093854815601158.

Mack, Kathy, and Sharyn Roach Anleu. 2010. "Performing Impartiality: Judicial Demeanor and Legitimacy Law & Social Inquiry Performing Impartiality: Judicial Demeanor and Legitimacy." *Law & Social Inquiry* 35 (1): 137–73. https://doi.org/10.1111/j.1747-4469.2009.01180.x.

McNiel, Dale E., and Renée L. Binder. 2007. "Effectiveness of a Mental Health Court in Reducing Criminal Recidivism and Violence." *American Journal of Psychiatry* 164 (9): 1395–1403. https://doi.org/10.1176/appi.ajp.2007.06101664.

Menkel-Meadow, Carrie. 1992. "Is Altruism Possible in Lawyering." *Georgia State University Law Review* 8 (2): 385–419. https://doi.org/10.3366/Ajicl.2011.0005.

Miller, JoAnn, and Donald C. Johnson. 2009. *Problem Solving Courts: A Measure of Justice*. Lanham: Rowman & Littlefield.

Perlin, Michael. 2013. "'The Judge, He Cast His Robe Aside': Mental Health Courts, Dignity and Due Process." *Mental Health Law & Policy Journal* 3 (1): 1–29.

Petrila, John. 1996. "Paternalism and the Unrealized Promise of Essays in Therapeutic Jurisprudence." In *Law in a Therapeutic Key: Developments in Therapeutic Jurisprudence*, 685–705. Durham: Carolina Academic Press.

Redlich, Allison D. 2005. "Voluntary, but Knowing and Intelligent? Comprehension in Mental Health Courts." *Psychology, Public Policy, and Law* 11 (4): 605–19. https://doi.org/10.1037/1076-8971.11.4.605.

Schneider, Richard D., Hy Bloom, and Mark Heerema. 2007. *Mental Health Courts: Decriminalizing the Mentally Ill*. Toronto: Irwin Law.
Skeem, Jennifer L., Paula Emke-Francis, and Jennifer Eno Louden. 2006. "Probation, Mental Health, and Mandated Treatment: A National Survey." *Criminal Justice and Behavior* 33 (2): 158–84. https://doi.org/10.1177/0093854805284420.
Skeem, Jennifer L., Jennifer Eno Louden, Devon Polaschek, and Jacqueline Camp. 2007. "Assessing Relationship Quality in Mandated Community Treatment: Blending Care with Control." *Psychological Assessment* 19 (4): 397–410. https://doi.org/10.1037/1040-3590.19.4.397.
Steadman, Henry J., Allison D. Redlich, Patricia Griffin, John Petrila, and John Monahan. 2005. "From Referral to Disposition: Case Processing in Seven Mental Health Courts." *Behavioral Sciences & the Law* 23 (2): 215–26. https://doi.org/10.1002/bsl.641.
Stolle, Dennis P., David B. Wexler, Bruce J. Winick, and Edward A. Dauer. 2000. "Integrating Preventative Law and Therapeutic Jurisprudence: A Law and Psychology Based Approach to Lawyering." In *Practicing Therapeutic Jurisprudence: Law as a Helping Profession*, edited by Dennis P. Stolle, David B. Wexler, and Bruce J. Winick, 5–44. Durham: Carolina Academic Press.
Wales, Heathcote W., Virginia Aldigé Hiday, and Bradley Ray. 2010. "Procedural Justice and the Mental Health Court Judge's Role in Reducing Recidivism." *International Journal of Law and Psychiatry* 33 (4): 265–71. Elsevier Ltd. https://doi.org/10.1016/j.ijlp.2010.06.009.
Wexler, David B. 1973. "Therapeutic Justice." *Minnesota Law Review* 57: 289–338. https://doi.org/10.3366/ajicl.2011.0005.
———. 1996. "Therapeutic Jurisprudence and the Criminal Courts." In *Law in a Therapeutic Key: Developments in Therapeutic Jurisprudence*, 157–70. Durham: Carolina Academic Press.
———. 2000. "Practicing Therapeutic Jurisprudence: Psycholegal Soft Spots and Strategies." In *Practicing Therapeutic Jurisprudence: Law as a Helping Profession*, edited by Dennis P. Stolle, David B. Wexler, and Bruce J. Winick, 45–68. Durham: Carolina Academic Press.
Winick, Bruce J. 1996. "The Jurisprudence of Therapeutic Jurisprudence." In *Law in a Therapeutic Key: Developments in Therapeutic Jurisprudence*, edited by David B. Wexler and Bruce J. Winick, 645–68. Durham: Carolina Academic Press.

Winick, Bruce J., David B. Wexler, and Edward A. Dauer. 1999. "Preface: A New Model for the Practice of Law." *Psychology, Public Policy, and Law* 5 (4): 795–99. https://doi.org/10.1037//1076-8971.5.4.795.

Wolff, Nancy. 2002. "Courts as Therapeutic Agents: Thinking Past the Novelty of Mental Health Courts." *Journal of the American Academy of Psychiatry and the Law* 30 (3): 431–37. http://jaapl.org/content/30/3/431.full.pdf.

Wolff, Nancy, Nicole Fabrikant, and Steven Belenko. 2011. "Mental Health Courts and Their Selection Processes: Modeling Variation for Consistency." *Law and Human Behavior* 35 (5): 402–12.

# 4

# Therapeutic Justice in Action: Court Process, Reviews and Sanctions

MHCs counter traditional punitive and stigmatizing criminal justice practices. Upon an invitation to therapeutic court a judge understood that the model is "rehabilitation and recovery" in contrast to a punishment orientation. The two different sides of MHC—"legal side and human engagement side"—was how one judge understood treatment courts in practice. Therapeutic practices in MHC are premised on the idea that traditional deterrence principles and punishment practices, pervasive in the mainstream criminal justice system, do not work for most people who come through the doors of MHC.[1] A defense attorney detailed a disconnect between standard criminal justice practices and problem-solving courts, highlighting the unique needs of MHC clients:

> In traditional courts, the idea is punishment, taking somebody out of the community for the sake of protecting the community, and hoping that they learn their lesson and they think, 'Well, I don't want to offend because I don't want to go back there [jail].' Our population doesn't always have that kind of insight, so taking them out of the community doesn't necessarily alter their behavior, but what does alter their behavior is stability, treatment, medications.

An integral part of a treatment court model is a process grounded in principles of fairness—both real and perceived. For a judge, therapeutic justice in action meant he asked three guiding questions: "What just happened? Why did it happen? What's the best response?"

Among the most important goals of MHCs are reintegrating clients and restoring the self which can be achieved through *rituals* within the court.[2] Observations of court proceedings reveal that more is going on than simple opt-ins and compliance reviews. Therapeutic moments occur in the everyday practices of the court and can be "discovered simply by being attentive to the emotional dynamics of the courtroom" (Rottman and Casey 1999, 14–15). Emotions are an integral part of problem-solving jurisprudence (Miller and Johnson 2009). Positive rituals—sometimes filled with emotions—within the MHC process can serve as a counter to the traditional criminal justice practices and markedly reduce stigma (Goffman 1986).[3]

## Procedural Justice in the Court Process

It matters how people are treated by legal agents and how clients perceive their court experiences. Fairness is an elementary societal value (Lens 2016). Court outcomes may be less important, in terms of satisfaction with a legal issue, than the psychological factors related to the court process. Positive emotional reactions in court hearings for MHC clients are tied to reduced coercion and procedural justice (Poythress et al. 2002). Being treated fairly and with respect, as opposed to experiencing procedures perceived as arbitrary or unfair, inform people's perceptions of the court experience. Everyday hearings and reviews shape clients' perceptions of fairness which subsequently influence behavior both in and out of court. Court experiences shape future trajectories and entanglements with the legal system. Tyler (1996) has long argued that perceptions of fairness have implications beyond the specific court case, influencing individual's self-conceptions and everyday behaviors and attitudes toward the law. This dynamic may be even more important in treatment courts.

MHC organization can alter the delivery of therapeutic justice. MHCs and other treatment courts operate within a procedural justice framework, centrally defined by perceptions of fairness with dignity at its core (Perlin 2013).[4] Treatment courts and procedural justice were seen as going "hand-in-hand" according to a judge. Procedural justice includes several elements—having a voice, being treated with dignity, perceiving concern, and perceiving fairness in the process (Canada and Watson 2013; Kaiser and Holtfreter 2016; Wales et al. 2010). In fact, researchers suggest that procedural justice may be a mechanism to explain success and positive experiences in MHCs (Canada and Watson 2013; Kopelovich et al. 2013; Poythress et al. 2002; Ray and Dollar 2014). Judges are the main contributors to a client's perception of procedural justice. MHC clients' experience lower levels of coercion and are overall more positive about the program compared to participants in an assisted outpatient treatment (AOT) program, which seems to be the result of greater perceived procedural justice from the judge (Munetz et al. 2014). Effective MHC judges are fully aware of this and adjudicate cases accordingly. In line with a procedural justice orientation, a judge explained that in MHCs we are "making sure we abide by those principles [procedural justice], which I have really taken to heart… In general those kinds of principles really apply in therapeutic court."

Most of the clients I interviewed felt that they were treated much better in MHC and that it was less punitive than the ordinary judicial process. Almost every client I interviewed mentioned at least one aspect of procedural justice. For Vicki—a notable exception—questions of legitimacy plagued her view of the case from the beginning (detailed in Chapter 6), which impeded her buy-in to MHC as well as her openness to seeing any part of the court process as fair. Nothing the MHC team could do would lead her to see the court experience as just. She recounted: "Coming to court, it is just procedural. It is not that I am being judged. There is no back and forth. You go up there and they say, great, good, go. The amount of time that I am in front of the judge is a minute or two." Vicki's reference to the reviews as "just procedural"—a set of formal steps—is out of line with the practices of procedural justice, which include depth and mutual investment of which Vicki was uninterested.

According to the clients I interviewed, the judge greatly influenced procedural justice. Clients described how the temperament and tone of the judge, especially "treating me with respect," shaped experiences in court. In contrasting a less effective judge—whose demeanor and approach was "really harsh and not real personal"—to an effective judge, Jennifer stated that the latter "was just matter of fact, and then when you are doing good, he just made me feel good." Isaiah stated unequivocally that "The judges have been great."

"Giving voice" is important for procedural justice and evident in judicial dialogue with clients. Judges invite clients to more fully participate in court hearings and ask pointed questions to solicit client involvement in verbal exchanges. Describing the difference between MHC and mainstream courts a judge focused on "interactions with the individuals" and "speaking directly to the individual." Judges often asked clients "What is it that is important to you [about being in MHC]" in judicial-client conversations. For some clients, the opportunity to speak directly to a judge was in stark contrast to previous court experiences. In mainstream courts, lack of voice and limited involvement psychologically removed individuals from the process, making it less therapeutic. Monique recalled:

> I have been in court systems before when I got my DUIs [Driving under the Influence]. Your public defender, I always had a public defender and never had a paid lawyer defending me, they basically can represent you and you don't have to say much of anything. You just go there, sit in front of the judge for a minute, and they do what they are going to do.

Exchanges characterized by respect, politeness and dignity enhance client willingness to actively participate in the court process during both standard reviews and in the case of displeasure (Dollar and Ray 2015). Judicial discretion and direct interactions provide greater opportunities for respectful dialogue (Ray et al. 2011) and just outcomes (Lens 2016). Robert, a client, articulated this response to a question about how to improve the court process:

No, there is no way they could do that [improve the process], keep it the way they are doing it now. If there is an easier way, they would have done it. But all the way around, I got treated real good. All the way around, I don't have no complaints. They never disrespected me or anything like that, anything of that sort. They never did that. They respected me.

Robert's emphasis on respect was critical in his story as it was for other clients. While Norm expressed frustrations with the court, he was always positive about the team's fairness: "I like everybody. I like [probation officer]. He is a nice guy. I like the attorneys. The prosecutor seems reasonable. They always seem reasonable." A judge advocated for respectful treatment of clients and highlighted its practical implications, "If people treat them [the clients] differently, then they feel worse about themselves. But if you can treat them with some dignity, be empathetic to them and everything else, too, you can at least help them out and get back on that road."

Showing concern is another element of procedural justice. Shima perceived MHC judges as different, declaring "I believe — I'm not saying the judges in regular courthouses don't care, but they don't put the effort to trying to put more help into finding help for me. I felt that they always worked for me." She described that even when she went to jail she felt respected and felt that the judge cared about her, believing in her ability to succeed: "But I had support, and the judge was wonderful to me. I went to jail several times when I was with [probation officer], and it seemed they always got me out. Judge [name] put faith in me." Procedural justice is not enough to guarantee therapeutic justice, but it provides a foundation. Probation officers' relationships with clients gives legitimacy to the whole court process consistent with research that identifies the role of other team members (other than the judge) in a client's perceptions of procedural justice (Canada and Watson 2013). Both procedural justice and therapeutic justice demand a client-centered approach in managing the court calendar.

## Shifts in Organization and Court Practices

Practicing therapeutic justice in court entails integrating aspects of procedural justice which, in turn, leads to shifts in organization. A therapeutically-oriented court approaches the use of time differently, demanding greater flexibility in the running of the court. MHCs adjust the amount of time given to clients during court exchanges, as well as broaden the focus of the substantive interactions. Creating a balance between efficiency and effectiveness lays squarely on the judge. Even in MHCs, despite the focus on spending time with clients and getting underneath client issues, judges can err in both directions, impeding therapeutic justice. For example, according to a probation officer, there are MHC judges that spend "too much time" talking on the record with clients which heightened anxiety. The challenge of judicial-client exchanges was described by a prosecutor as a "very delicate balance of how much to interact" to make clients comfortable and reduce anxiety as well as "remain judicial." By dragging the court review on for several extra minutes, a judge reduces the expected therapeutic effect with some clients.

There are also judges who are so concerned with being efficient and watching the clock that the whole flow of the court is off. For instance, a judge always wanted to get on the record at exactly 1:30 p.m., when the court is scheduled to commence.[5] In theory this is commendable, but in practice it was problematic; trouble ensued when cases were not ready. Per court practice, defense and probation teams were meeting with clients prior to their cases being heard. It was informally understood that the first several minutes of court, especially in *City* MHC, were devoted to preparation and brief meetings with clients. This judge seemed unware of the norm, despite many years on the bench and well into her tenure as a MHC judge. She started court promptly and abruptly asked which cases were ready to be heard. Impatiently, the judge proceeded to sit on the bench, pressing the prosecution to call a case or work through administrative matters (best suited for later, during a lull in the court calendar). Rather than signifying effective time management, it led to some unease in the courtroom—for both team members and clients—as the court was on the record but no cases were being officially heard.

Effective judges are cognizant of client apprehension and sometimes must sacrifice a degree of efficiency for the sake of therapeutic justice. This is particularly pertinent during court reviews. Judges need to effectively adjudicate between cases and discern which clients need more time investment on the record and which cases need to be processed quickly. The ability to manage the court calendar relies on non-legal skills, which not all judges possess, such as the ability to read behavioral cues from clients. As other MHC team members know the clients the best, an effective judge relies on the team for insight into client personalities and behavior. Probation, prosecutors or defense can inform or "prep" the judge prior to court or signal informally during court to limit questioning of a particular client, especially in the case of full compliance.

A probation officer noted that many judges need assistance in dealing with mental illness. She recounted, "judges, a lot of times, don't really know how to handle mentally ill people – to not let them escalate and to keep everything really short, and so we would have notes about that, 'needs to be really short, clear.'" A judge offered an example of how subtly a team member might indicate important information about a client:

> We [MHC team] got so good at signals. Sometimes, for example, one of my [team members] would sometimes write in italics in his reports – the information that he thought I needed to know, but shouldn't be discussing in court. It went to everyone. There was nothing *ex parte* about it.

This judge would offer appreciation to this team member and recalled thanking him for "helping me know how to approach this person." The end result was a more therapeutic exchange. Court reviews represent opportunities to showcase the principles of procedural justice and enhance the dispensing of therapeutic justice when the team works collaboratively, especially with an awareness of court-induced client anxiety.

## Client Anxiety

Coming to court, especially for reviews, produced anxiety for clients. Anxiety limits both procedural justice and therapeutic justice in MHCs. Clients talked about the difficulty of sitting in court, sometimes for hours, waiting for their cases to be called. MHC team members recognized that being "tangled up with the court" was stressful and that going to court "makes them [clients] really nervous." Judges must manage the calendar to "have it be a non-stressful environment. It's stressful for people to sit for four hours" remarked a team member. Often clients wait long periods of time for their cases to be heard due to the priority of in-custody cases.[6] A court liaison compared going to court and being in front of a judge to going to the dentist:

> I can imagine some people that are mentally ill, or they have had poor experiences with the criminal justice system through their own doing or just being knocked around, that that is not something that they voluntarily go do. It is like, I don't want to go to the dentist. I go because I have to. Would I opt-into go to the dentist? No.

Client anxiety was often exacerbated when speaking before the judge about their behavioral compliance. Monique, a client who successfully graduated from the court, spoke about it this way:

> I was always nervous on court days, because I don't like to go in with the judge, and especially if there was something that I had done wrong. So my experience is I was fearful, anxiety, my anxiety level was up through the roof. But I went in there every time, I never missed a court date, and faced whatever they were going to give me. Believe me, it was a lot nicer to be able to go in there when you had nothing wrong, your month review. It was like, 'Oh, thank God, I don't have that anxiety level now.'

This perspective was expressed by other clients. For instance, Robert told me that he was nervous while waiting in court for his case to be called, "I get anxious. I keep thinking that something will pop up to make me go to jail…" This was not completely assuaged by being in compliance. Robert went on to say, "I knew I was clean, though, so that couldn't have been it. I knew that part." For others, compliance abated any anxiety, as in the case of Isaiah, who declared, "I have no fear… I am not anxious… I'm doing what I am supposed to do."

Usually, if a client is in compliance with court conditions, the case is called first and clients can leave court, as a reward. Unfortunately this is not always the case, especially if there is an influx of in-custody cases or if the client's lawyer is not in court when the prosecutor is ready to call the case. This was often so for Jennifer, who had a non-MHC defense attorney which was atypical, adding to her anxiety and stress as seen in the following exchange:

> *Interviewer:* What are the hearings like? When you go in for your reviews, what is that process like for you?
>
> *Jennifer:* It depends on if I had a good month or not, basically. For sure, one of the times they did all the cases. I was the very last person to go, so I didn't go until 4:00. I was freaking out. I went in the bathroom and was punching the wall. I didn't really have anywhere to be. I don't know, it is weird.
>
> *Interviewer:* Just sitting there is hard.
>
> *Jennifer:* Yeah, and that time I didn't know how the review was going to go. I had messed up kind of.
>
> *Interviewer:* There was a lot of anxiety?
>
> *Jennifer:* Yeah, and I have problems with irritability in general, and then not knowing… But usually I just meet with my lawyer and meet with [probation] and they tell me the exact same thing. Then it is usually not a big deal. There was one time I didn't know, because I had taken some tincture, like Echinacea, but it had alcohol in it, so I tested positive for the EtG [Ethyl Glucuronide or ethanol]. I didn't know if they were going to believe me. I was really nervous about jail.

For Jennifer, the anxiety was curbed by a good meeting with her lawyer and probation officer prior to the court hearing; if there was a violation she would have a better sense of how it would be presented. Of course, judicial responses vary, which leads to additional client uncertainty. Some attorneys orient their pre-court meeting with clients in full awareness of this anxiety and help to prepare them for the upcoming hearing before the judge. A defense attorney explained:

That's my concern, is just the anxiety of the client and the judge asking questions. I've had clients say, 'Is he going to ask me any questions today?' There have been times where certain clients, I know that they get very anxious in front of the judge, and I'll say, 'Remember the judge likes to ask you what's happened since the last time you were in court, so let's have an answer prepared.'

The stress, anxiety and sometimes embarrassment around court appearances can limit its therapeutic effects. In the case of Monique, anxiety limited her willingness to express voice, "I always said something but I didn't want to," reducing the benefits associated with procedural justice. The judicial review process can lessen client anxiety, more so when clients are in compliance.

## Reviews: Accountability, Compliance and Sanctions

The MHC program aims to provide support and monitoring to clients. People with mental illness within the criminal justice system may not have the necessary "insight" into mental illness, as a team member suggested, and thus other tactics need to be used to assist them in their management of their mental illness and other life demands. Hence, supervision, social support, and accountability are built into the structure and culture of MHCs. These elements are integral to the review process. Judges and team members often talk about the "structure" the court provides. But there is a tension between social support and accountability.

There are two important levels of review for MHC clients, reflecting the *backstage* and *frontstage* of the court process (terms defined in Chapter 2, p. 47): probation meetings and court reviews. Reviews, by probation and the judge, are structured to be more frequent in the beginning of a client's court process and reduced in frequency as time in the court increases. The duration and frequency of probation meetings often begin with meeting several times a week, decreasing to weekly, and possibly ending with monthly meetings based on a client's compliance with court conditions. If out of compliance, clients may meet with probation weekly or every other week until issues are resolved. But as noted by a probation officer, "This is a fluid process, so duration in the court program does not always result in less frequent reviews. If they are struggling, they may come in every week or every week for a while until we can address the issues with their compliance."

Clients are more frequently monitored by probation officers than any other team member. Regular probation contact serves multiple purposes. First, they represent a clear reminder to clients of the court's expectations. Second, reviews provide opportunities for clients to build a relationship with their probation officers, having frequent opportunities for positive affirmation. Third, they act as an intervention point in case a client struggles with compliance to their conditions of release or sentence. If reviews are too far apart and a client has a crisis or gets off-track from their treatment regimen, it becomes more difficult to reorient a client to court expectations, increasing the likelihood of negative sanctions and court failure. In talking about the purpose of reviews, a probation officer stated his position:

> I know that certainly my goal being in this mental health court is to have regular reviews, to see them on a weekly basis, be constantly in contact with their case managers and their housing managers. But at some point I want to taper them off of me. I don't want them to be dependent on my continually making sure that things are done for them. Go from monthly to six weeks, to two months [for court reviews], seeing me from weekly to maybe bi-weekly, to monthly. Then when they are done, it is not such a drastic change in accountability and lifestyle.

In practice, the team approach and therapeutically-oriented probation officers have implications for interactions with clients. For example, a probation officer stated, "When they come in, they miss their appointment, I don't go, 'Oh, you missed your appointment, I am setting for a [court] review.' I say, 'Why did you miss your appointment?' and then we can strategize from there."

The purpose behind frequent probation reviews carries over to official reviews—"status updates"—before the judge. The point of court reviews is to check-in and provide support as clients follow the regimented set of court conditions, including mental health treatment, maintaining sobriety and complying with all parts of the program as outlined in the sentencing conditions. A probation officer described the therapeutic effect of frequent judicial reviews,

> There is a real big value, I think, to the clients that are coming in on a monthly basis and getting kudos from the judge. It feels a whole lot different than every time to come to court for a review and they are telling you, 'Why aren't you doing this, you need to do this, I'm going to put you in jail.' They come to court on a monthly basis and they say, 'Congratulations, keep up the good work. I'm looking forward to seeing you next month.' They walk out of there, head held high and feel like they are a little more invested in it. They don't want to let the courts down, versus leaving the court saying, 'Screw this, I'm not coming back.'

Requiring frequent court reviews, especially early in the program, does two things. First, it reminds clients of court expectations, much like frequent probation meetings. A court liaison emphasized a similar point, "I think having regular reviews is good. It reminds the person that they are going to be held accountable." Second, it provides the client opportunities to "to appear before the judge in <u>compliance</u>, rather than out of compliance" (emphasis in original), according to a probation officer. He went further arguing that it is not only beneficial for the client to feel good when doing well in court, but also "it's good for the judge to see him [the client] doing well." The effect on a judge of seeing clients in compliance may lead to more judicial investment in a client or a greater willingness to be understanding in instances of non-compliance. The notion that coming in frequently to be praised has therapeutic effects applies both to being in and out of compliance. When in compliance, clients receive positive affirmation and are encouraged to continue to adhere to court conditions. When out of compliance, clients might be better able to sustain momentary setbacks if they have a positive relationship with the team and have received prior praise from the judge. A judge may also praise a client for honesty in the case of non-compliance, which can turn a potentially antitherapeutic exchange into a more therapeutic one.

These two types of reviews—probation and court reviews—are related, and ideally reinforce each other. Just prior to the official court review, clients briefly meet separately with their probation officer and defense counsel. Working to counter the known stressors associated with court reviews, meetings with probation officers prior to court can reduce anxiety. A probation officer recounted:

> There are not going to be any surprises [for the client]. You are not going to come to court thinking that everything is going to be fine, and then I'm going to go in front of the judge and go, 'I think they need to go to jail.' That just breaks down the whole relationship that I've built up.

Most of the time the probation meeting prior to a court review lessens anxiety and promotes a trusting relationship between a probation officer and a client, but it can be derailed by judicial actions. A probation officer described the therapeutic relationship and its challenges due to judicial intervention:

> We always say in mental health court, be honest with us, be honest with us, tell us, so it is not fair for me to say, you be honest but then I'm not going to tell you what I'm recommending, even if it is a difficult recommendation. The worst is when you recommend jail, and the judge doesn't go for it, and then you have to work with somebody, 'You just said you wanted me to go to jail.'

When a judge does not follow probation's recommendation, it strains the client-probation relationship and the team-judge relationship.

Both types of reviews are integral to the efficacy of MHCs and, based on interviews, it is clear that both are fundamental to success. Monique spoke at great length about the social support she received from the "good team," especially from probation and the court liaison. Coming to court was a clear incentive for good behavior for many clients. Monique reflected that "the court system in place also has this big role of what I was doing… I knew every month that I was going to have to go in front of that judge. I wanted a good report and not a bad one." How compliance and non-compliance are characterized in court reviews, and what sanctions are imposed, is critical to client trajectories and the MHC process.

## The Sanctioning Process

During court reviews, probation officers offer status updates on the client's progress. Although it does matter how probation presents cases, the judge is the ultimate arbiter offering positive sanctions or imposing negative sanctions. Reviews represent opportunities to re-evaluate some conditions of a client's sentence, including the frequency of monitoring and supervision by internal and external agents (e.g., probation and treatment facilities). Mental health stability and sobriety are serious challenges for clients in MHC. There is a sense that the court needs to take client progress one day—or one review—at a time.

There are competing philosophies to address non-compliant behavior in treatment courts and competing styles of responding to non-compliance influence therapeutic justice. Team members vary in their sanctioning philosophies, which has implications for the court process. There are two models on display in MHCs: graduated sanctions and harm reduction. The graduated sanctions model—or escalating sanctions—reflects a range of sanctioning options designed to respond to violations in a step-wise punitive fashion. In MHCs this is largely modeled after drug courts. According to a defense attorney, graduated sanctions reflected "the kind of increasing nature of punishments" and is more in line with the accountability side of the court. Proponents of the harm reduction model advocate for reducing the harm inflicted on the individual as well as society at large. Underpinning the harm reduction model is a recognition that while completely abstaining from a particular behavior (e.g., alcohol use) is beneficial, it is not always realistic or even possible for a client and punishment can be antitherapeutic. To the extent that the latter orientation exists in MHC, it reflects the supportive and understanding side of the court.

The model of "zero tolerance" that pervades other parts of the criminal justice system is antithetical to the premise of treatment courts. MHCs impose jail time as a response to a serious violation (e.g., new criminal charge), in stark opposition to a zero-tolerance perspective where any non-compliance could be punished by jail or revocation from MHC. Observational data suggest that the working culture in MHCs rests on a hybrid model—not fully harm reduction but not exactly a graduated sanctions model either. All team members, with two exceptions, supported some elements of a harm reduction philosophy, and all eschewed a zero-tolerance framework. Overall a collaborative approach stimulated a "problem-solving" orientation to client issues according to a judge that result in "creative solutions… and not just following cookie-cutter approaches."

## Integrating Elements of a Graduated Sanctions Model

One probation officer argued for graduated sanctions as the preferred model and was adamant against any use of a harm reduction model—which was counter-normative to the rest of the MHC team. In fact, the probation officer recalled a recent meeting with the judge, who referred to the court as "a harm reduction court" and he replied, adamantly, "No, we are not. We are not a harm reduction court. Our goal is abstinence. Our goal is not to reduce your use and go on from there. Our goal is abstinence. It has to be." He went on to detail why a harm reduction model will never work in MHC, "because it is a biological imperative that if you have crossed that line and you start using… The people over here [MHC], if they are using a little bit, they are using a lot and they are out of control and they are reoffending." Similarly a prosecutor, who clearly embraced the mission of the court, was in clear opposition: "I think harm reduction has a place. It is just not within the court." The complex needs of MHC clients increased resistance to adopting a harm reduction approach as well as the integrity of the court and public safety concerns.

For those who were skeptical of a harm reduction model, a graduated sanctions model represented a more workable philosophy for the context of the criminal justice system. A probation officer gave a detailed description of what this means in practice:

> Graduated sanctions, which simply means… [that] the first violation is usually a non-sanction, which is 'stay sanction'. 'OK, you did your violation, it is your first violation, let's just get you back on track. What can we do to help move past that'…If it is a criminal law violation,, there is really no way I can avoid a sanction…So after the first violation, if there is another violation, it is usually maybe community service, maybe increase – depending on what they are not doing, if they are not reporting, we try day reporting. If they are reporting and there are still UAs [Urine Analysis], maybe we do day reporting with breath or UAs, just so they have that 30 days of being checked. They know if they start violating, that they could go to jail, which is a good component. It just goes from there. If there is a third violation, depending on what it is, we might actually start looking at maybe work crew. If they have some disability, we might look at community service. If they can't do community service or work crew, then we might have to look at some jail time, depending on what they are doing. Unfortunately sometimes you have to go right to jail, depending on the violation.

A team member, with experience both as a defense social worker and a probation officer in MHC, stated that the court used graduated sanctions. She made a clear distinction between social services and the courts: "I'm not a big proponent of harm reduction within the criminal justice system. If they are just at a mental health agency, they are not out committing crimes – a lot of our crimes are against people." In the case of positive drug test, as a probation officer she stated rhetorically, "Do I throw them in jail when they have one positive UA? No, I try to do the least restrictive. I also try to look at what is going on with the person." In this case she sees harm reduction strategies as a possible risk to public safety.

A prosecutor stated, "We use graduated sanctions to a certain extent. I've seen cases where we have had work crew and then we have imposed the paper [reflective essay]. If it was a true graduated sanction, it wouldn't occur that way. You [MHC team] tailor it to what the actual violation was in front of us." This prosecutor didn't see the court as using a graduated sanctions approach because the severity of the sanctioning did not follow a certain order. Judges also shared this understanding that the court integrated some elements of graduated sanctions but not entirely:

> What we would do is kind of that graduated sanctions depending on the violation, whether or not it was having somebody do increased appointments with their treatment provider, whether it is mental health, PTSD, chemical dependency, whatever it was.

Interestingly, a judge suggested that a modified graduated sanction philosophy currently underpins the court, but he was exploring moving to a more harm reduction approach. Another judge argued that graduated sanctioning was explicitly dependent upon the violation.

Even those who understood MHCs as using a graduated sanctions approach saw it as distinct in its application from other courts. For instance, a judge who advocated for more harm reduction acknowledged:

> When we do graduated sanctions, ours are more fluid. We will navigate that a little bit. So I think they [courts that use graduated sanctions in a traditional way] say, well, there really isn't much discussion. There is a violation and this is the sanction. In our court, we don't follow that path completely. We will say graduated sanctions, but our sanction might be something different than the next person, because in that individual circumstance, this sanction is more effective than with that person.

There is an inherent tension between these two philosophies in the daily operation of MHCs. One probation officer discussed the idea of graduated sanctions at length and stated that it is more appropriate for drug court as it is "much more structured, and it's much more predictable, and it's much more linear. And I think that's appropriate for the population that it's trying to work with." While there is some variation, most MHC team members expressed some version of harm reduction approach or somewhere between that and a graduated sanctions model.

## Harm Reduction Insights in MHCs

A harm reduction philosophy can be in direct contrast to graduated sanctions. There was tremendous support—both vocally and in practice—for harm reduction from the bench. Some judges stated rather unmistakably that they thought the MHC used a harm reduction approach. A judge expressed that, "It is almost all harm reduction." He referred to his approach to sanctioning as "compliance-based" and trying to get a client "to do something" as opposed to "punishment as a deterrent." Another judge talked about the use of graduated sanctions in mainstream court and compared it to a harm reduction approach in treatment courts, "I'm talking about the mainstream court… Yes, the harm reduction issue, I totally understand that in specialty courts, right. I guess I was looking at the contrast." A judge described a harm reduction orientation in the following way:

> To me what harm reduction means is how do you mitigate the harm that a person is inflicting upon themselves or potentially on others who are around them. So, for example, have they gone from… shooting up heroin three times a day to smoking weed sometimes. That is probably harm reduction in a typical analysis. They have gone from getting into fights at bars to occasionally shoplifting because they need food.

Another judge suggested that practicing with a harm reduction philosophy reflected a "sense of fairness and justice."

Support for this approach carried over to other positions in the team but with some cultural adjustments. For some team members the move toward harm reduction represented a dramatic shift in how they understood their role. A prosecutor detailed this challenge:

> It is a difficult way to shift your thinking, because it is very clear as a prosecutor. There are people who have broken the law and you are going to hold them accountable, and you will ask for appropriate justice… I still want accountability in mental health court, but… mental health court is a little bit of a shift in thinking… These courts [problem-solving courts] are designed differently, and there is a lot of harm reduction involved in it that you don't necessarily see in other courts.

For others, the approach was more consistent with their professional role but reflected an institutional shift in the court. A probation officer summarized what he thinks harm reduction looks like in MHC:

> My philosophy for working with clients in mental health court—and actually even outside of mental health court—is not so much last time we did two days [of jail time], so this time we have to do four days, which is what graduated sanctions is. My philosophy is, this person is at Point A and we need to get them at Point B, and so what is the sanction, what is the court intervention that is most appropriate and most likely to have success in getting them from Point A to Point B.

In our conversations about how to improve MHCs, a defense attorney explicitly referred to a harm reduction emphasis as a necessary MHC reform:

> Maybe more acceptance of the harm reduction model for certain people. This could be difficult of how you carry it out. Some people can be expected to abstain and some not. But I think allowing for more harm reduction would capture some of those people who are on the margins.

A defense social worker and advocate for harm reduction adamantly called for more education and training for the team around research and "best practices." She argued that "the studies have shown that it takes eight to nine tries for somebody to get through a successful completion with a CD [chemical dependency] treatment." Given the dual-diagnosis of mental illness and chemical dependency for many MHC clients, the court may need to better incorporate the research on relapses into the sanctioning practices.

For many team members a harm reduction approach matched with therapeutic encouragement of small improvements, in hopes of more substantial life changes in the future. A probation officer affirmed, "We all realize, I think, that the most important thing for the people is that they are making an effort. They are making strides, and I feel it is unfair for somebody who is making strides or making an effort to punish them." He clearly advocated, as most did, that elements of a harm reduction within a team approach is the appropriate model for treatment courts. For another probation officer it was clearly a part of his socialization into the court. He was told by a veteran probation officer that, "The mental health court is a harm reduction model." After an explanation of the tenets of a harm reduction approach, the new probation officer laughed and said that he was unaware that his approach to supervision had a specific name replying, "Oh, I've been doing that for ten years. And didn't know what it was that I was doing."

A harm reduction philosophy allows for building rapport with clients, strengthening the therapeutic relationship, which was central to how most probation officers understood their role in MHC, especially in how probation officers confronted clients' non-compliance and framed judicial recommendations. With a harm reduction philosophy, when a client has a problem (e.g., relapse), the client comes into probation to explain and actively "problem solve" together. The resolution might involve more contacts with probation, meetings with treatment providers, medication compliance, or other support. From the perspective of a probation officer, the point was that, "They tell me, we work it out, and they realize that it is not always going to end this way [going to jail], and it helps because they are the ones that participated in the change in behavior."

For many team members, a harm reduction approach was explicitly about considering the context and thinking about appropriate responses, given the violation and the client's needs. For a probation officer, practicing harm reduction did not mean ignoring problematic behaviors:

> I would not look the other way, but I would say, 'I know you are drinking, but you are not committing any new crimes. You are not selling drugs, or you are not beating your wife, and you are not doing those types of things, so I am going to work with you on this aspect'... I am certainly not going to take you out of society, put you in prison or put you in jail because you drank or you had a relapse... Consequently, those people started to develop a rapport with me, that, 'I can be honest with this guy and he is not going to throw me in jail.'

A probation officer responded that graduated sanctions was not the guiding principle in MHC and that <u>context</u> is the crucial determinant:

> Last time when they engaged in this behavior, let's say a relapse, we put them in jail for three days. Now, six months have gone by and they've made some improvements, some things have changed... maybe they had housing, lost housing, back in housing... But they're in a different situation now... but rather than saying, 'OK, they lapsed again, and last time we gave them three days so the thing to do right now is to give them six days,' I say, 'OK, they lapsed again, what are the circumstances,' because you don't just look at the violation, you have to consider the context. And so, OK last time, they stopped going to groups, they were hanging out with the wrong crowd, they decided that they were going to go partying and they went on a week-long—I'm going to use an extreme example—they went on a week-long alcohol and crack binge. This time, last month we found out that the client's sister had a miscarriage, that their case manager had turned over two weeks ago and was no longer there, last week was the anniversary of their father's death, and this time it went on a two-day bender and went to detox, or went to the sobering center, and went to their group on Monday, reported their lapse, started going to AA meetings...

This probation officer stated that these are completely different situations and even though on paper they are both violations—failure to abstain—probation must react differently to have therapeutic effects. In the second scenario, sanctioning is not necessary because "they've got a better foundation, and they're also a little bit closer to getting back to the point that they need to be at, than they were in the prior relapse. Their attitude is different, their supports and their resources are different." The probation officer suggested that during court he reported that the client "screwed up" but came in immediately, was apologetic, detailed what happened and went to AA meetings. In such a case, there is no need for a court imposed sanction because the client is back in compliance and actively engaging with probation and treatment.

Another probation officer described a case where a client, with a minor violation (not coming in for a probation appointment), contacted probation to explain:

She showed up for court today, so I recommend that she be found in violation of 'not reporting,' but I want to acknowledge all of the good things that she has done. So they know that they are going to be called to the table even on the most minor one and it is not always going to result in a negative issue. So I feel like the court needs to be kept apprised of the situation. So her contacting me was a positive that came as a result of her not showing up.

This probation officer's assessment highlighted the need to balance accountability with building a relationship with a client within a harm reduction framework, as well as an awareness of the importance of praise.

Court observations were full of examples of a harm-reduction framing in cases of non-compliance. Take for example the following exchange that took place at a review hearing. A probation officer, who embraced a harm-reduction orientation, discussed a client's level of compliance over the last three review hearings:

*Probation*: Two reviews ago she was at 41 percent medication compliance which improved to 50 percent at her last review. Today she is at 74 percent compliance (23 out of the last 31 days). While we are still not where I'd like to see it, this suggests that [name of client] is making a concerted effort to comply. I'm very pleased with that. Next month she informed me that she will be in 100 percent compliance which is a noble goal. I appreciate her willingness to work on this. I ask the court to find [name of client] in moderate compliance.

*Judge*: I have to say that the last time you were here you significantly improved. What is going to make the difference for more improvement?

*Client*: I'm taking my meds with dinner. It's the best time. It's been working quite well. I missed because I was not at my place for dinner. I'll be at 100 percent next time.

*Judge*: We are almost three-quarters of the way there. What's going to change?

*Client*: I'll be there for dinner call. That's when I need to take them. I need to be there for dinner.

*Judge*: That's a nifty goal. Do you think you can get there?
*Client*: Yes.
*Judge*: I'll remind you at you next review.
*Client*: No, you'll hear about my 100 percent!
*Judge*: I'm looking forward to it. I'll find you in compliance today.

The judge's tone was calm and friendly, the judge gave the client time to talk and have her voice heard, evoking critical elements of procedural justice. The judge was reaffirming and encouraging, but pushing for more accountability. His ruling did not modify her compliance as suggested by probation, but merely stated she was in compliance illustrating the subjective nature of compliance and how harm reduction principles influence the working of MHCs.

This was not the case for all clients, such as Norm, who recounted a recent court review that did not go well and was not consistent with harm reduction leanings:

> I had a dirty UA once. I had a charge once. That was about two months into it. Then I had a 90 percent medication compliance once. [Name of probation officer] thought that was fine, but the judge thought different. Then I've had this problem before, once before. It is someone taking drugs every day and then they stop for eight months and they take them once and then stop again. That is pretty darned good.

From Norm's perspective the judge couldn't see the progress he was making and referred to the judge as a "stickler" who misinterpreted his laughter [to himself]. For Norm, the lack of contextual understanding undermined the therapeutic effects—although he was not in perfect compliance he was making progress and expected some recognition. This example—which contradicted many of the observations I witnessed in MHCs—illustrates that just because many judges promote harm reduction in theory, putting it into practice is more complicated.

## Individualized Harm Reduction

For many team members their philosophical approach to sanctioning was not an either/or, but a hybrid model embracing elements of both graduated sanctions and harm reduction models. Some team members were suspicious of a whole-hearted embrace of harm reduction because they are operating within the rules and responsibilities of the criminal justice system, not in the community as a social service agency where a public health perspective would be appropriate. A judge held this perspective:

> The problem is, first of all, we are a court, so I am sworn to uphold the law. So there are some real ethical limitations for me winking at someone and saying, 'That's okay,' and legally their behavior is not. So that is a real challenge when you are the voice of the justice system or a probation officer, for example, cannot probably in good conscious say illegal behavior is okay, in a way that a caseworker might very well be able to say that and say it appropriately. The other thing is that we can't sort of... in good conscious we can say it is okay to go hurt people a little bit, or it is okay to only be a little bit dangerous to the community. So that is a really complicated conversation in the context of the justice system.

However, for judges there was a clear difference between embracing the philosophy of harm reduction and the court's practice of using harm-reduction approaches. The same judge described how a harm-reduction approach still permeates the understanding of the court even if not officially declared:

> Did we all sort of wink at each other and understand that that is what we were doing? Absolutely, and there were time when we were cheerleading for people, literally, when we heard day by day about clean UA's. Just get through this week, that's awesome, right, and knowing the minute that they're off probation they were probably going to use within an hour.[7]

This perspective was echoed in other interviews with team members. A prosecutor suggested that in practice MHCs incorporate harm-reduction elements. She articulated that this occurs best on a case-by-case basis informed by client familiarity and a trustworthy team, especially reliance on probation's expertise:

> They call it the harm reduction model, and there are some people who we just know, it is just not in them, for whatever reason, mental illness or whatever, that they are not going to be 100 percent in compliance through the whole program. I have to be pretty convinced of that, and I can be if I am given enough information, to go along with, well, somebody relapsed again, but let's not revoke them and send them to jail right now. Let's give them another chance. That's the thing with becoming familiar enough with people to know what to expect with them and what not to.

The centrality of the abstinence requirement illustrated a deviation from a true harm reduction framework. There is, however, an understanding that non-compliance will occur, so there is built-in flexibility in how violations are handled. Most team members suggested that it was important to keep abstinence as a goal, knowing full-well that most clients with co-occurring conditions (mental illness and chemical dependency) will violate the abstinence requirement at some point during their time in MHC. As a prosecuting attorney expressed:

> We are keeping it as a goal without getting there. For example, if you were a true harm reduction court, so when we have a dangerous individual come in on a serious violent offense and come in mental health court, we are not going to have a condition of no alcohol, no drugs or non-prescribed drugs.

A court liaison articulated the tension within MHCs and the review process, with a specific focus on substance abuse issues:

> It is a court of law. It is not a harm reduction court. There is abstaining, there are penalties, there are sanctions. It is that universal question of a mentally ill person's behavior, their compliance to treatment is poor because of their mental illness. In a social service world, we are flexible, we adopt treatment plans to accommodate that, and not necessarily penalize. It is complicated, right, in terms of the client's

accountability and engagement and all that stuff, but a court of law, ultimately the court will take action if someone is not in compliance. So that's the… challenge.

A team member expressed frustration with the debate about harm reduction and the slow move toward adopting it more forcefully, but she did see movement in that direction in the court:

> I think we are missing the mark when we are asking for abstinence, and the rest of the treatment world is on board for something that is the 'best practice' now… They [MHC team] are getting this training, but there are so many little things we could tweak to just be that much more in line with the harm reduction place.

Even within a harm reduction framework there were clear limits. A defense attorney commented that "most of the mental health court judges are really receptive to trying to give people chances, which is good. You shouldn't have 50 chances, but you should have a couple." Likewise, a probation officer summarized that, "I think because they [judges] were on board with this kind of somewhat individualized approach, more harm reduction." However given the population that opts-into MHC there is an expectation that perfect compliance, in the words of a court liaison, was "unrealistic," in line with a harm reduction philosophy.

A common therapeutic approach is trying to understand the violation and offering multiple (but not infinite) chances. The team clearly wants clients to be successful in MHC, but they also stressed accountability and the need to be in compliance with court conditions. In a specific case, court dialogue between team members reflected the tension between support and accountability and the limits to clients making mistakes and being given additional chances.

*Probation*: I would like her to succeed. There is a good treatment plan in place. On the other hand, there are non-compliance issues…. She has not always been truthful. From a probation standpoint, this is a last chance.

| | |
|---|---|
| *Prosecutor:* | We would like [name of client] to succeed… People will work with her. But she will need to work with the court. I don't know if she is willing to make that commitment. |
| *Judge:* | We will give you the opportunity to work on the plan. It is probably the last option in this court. |

Team members consistently advocated less punitive responses based on individualized assessments. This point was clearly articulated by a defense attorney:

> I've really pushed for – they used to say graduated sanctions, everything is graduated sanctions. I keep saying, no, it should be <u>individualized</u> sanctions (emphasis added). We don't… in drug court a model of your first violation is this, and your second violation is that. So I really try to push for kind of outside the box sanctions that go to the person's abilities and purely their needs, as opposed to just, well, it is their second violation, so you are going to do a day of work crew.

Highlighting the importance of a client-centered approach, a team member offered insights about the question of equity within MHCs:

> I love that our court is so individualized… That is one thing that I am really proud about with my court, is that we deal with everybody different, not because we are not trying to be equal, but we are trying to have a system that is equitable, especially when it comes to sanctions.

While there is not perfect unanimity on a preferred sanctioning philosophy among the MHC team members, the consensus clearly tends toward harm reduction and there is a preference by some judges to "lean a little but more towards harm reduction." A modest harm reduction approach occurs in practice without officially embracing this orientation. Most probation officers saw jail, and the threat of jail, as an integral part of their toolkit (this was especially true in *County* MHC where there were more serious offenses), but reserved jail sanctions for extreme cases of non-compliance. There were tensions expressed among team members about the appropriateness and efficacy of a harm reduction approach, especially in cases of recurrent

Table 4.1  Court compliance and sanctions in MHC

| Sanction type | City and County MHC |
|---|---|
| Positive | Praise |
|  | Express review/early review |
|  | Business card (only County MHC) |
|  | Reduce court contact/accountability |
|  | Day reporting (reduce or eliminate) |
|  | Probation meetings |
|  | Court reviews |
|  | Reduce/eliminate drug testing (e.g., urine analysis) |
|  | Graduation |
| Negative | Increase court contact/accountability |
|  | Day reporting (increase or reinstate) |
|  | Probation meetings |
|  | Court reviews |
|  | Increase drug testing (e.g., urine analysis) |
|  | Increase number of treatment meetings (e.g., groups) |
|  | Essay |
|  | Court watch |
|  | Community service |
|  | Work crew |
|  | Medication monitoring |
|  | Jail |
|  | Revocation |

non-compliance. For positive reviews, the issue of sanctioning philosophy is essentially immaterial as no negative sanctions are needed. Alternatively, in case of compliance, features of procedural justice are on full display. (See Table 4.1 for a list of sanctions by type.)

## Positive Sanctions

Positive sanctions are an important part of the culture of MHC, judges recognized the importance of "positive feedback [for] adults." Court reviews begin with a report from the supervising probation officer. If clients are in compliance they receive positive sanctions (rewards), such as praise and a brief review. If clients are doing well, all MHC team members offer encouragement with clear therapeutic intent. Praise, as an essential element of procedural justice, is directed to the client but on display for all in the gallery to witness. Given the authority of the court and the role of the MHC team this reward can be powerful. In discussing how it "feels good" when a judge said "I'm really proud of you," Jennifer exclaimed "Yeah, it does. If I am having a good month or whatever, and I go into court – it is not going to determine whether I stay sober – but it definitely feels good and it helps."

For many clients praise was unexpected given the context of the court system. Shima described being surprised when receiving praise from judges and prosecutors, "He, again, was an exceptional judge. Now Judge [different judge]… she was a little hard on me, but she was good. Now the prosecutor… She actually would look at me and say, 'I'm so proud of you, Shima', during court. That is when I was doing really, really good." Even when Shima went to jail on a violation she felt that the process was fair. Respect and praise, when in compliance, allowed her to frame her non-compliance wtihin a broader court experience.

Praise isn't automatic; it is tied to behavioral compliance, probation review and judicial style. For most clients, it felt good when a person in a position of authority gave them praise. But even when praise is given, it doesn't always lead to procedural justice or positive therapeutic effects. Praise was not always given. As Norm recounted "He [the judge] didn't today [offer any praise] because I missed those two meetings." Moreover, when praise is given too freely, it can lose its influence. For example, Norm stated that a different judge "always tell me that I should be very proud of myself" and that "just goes right through me." In Norm's case this might be related to his low self-worth and self-esteem. As he was not always in compliance with sobriety, the praise was unjustified and felt vapid. Norm is mentally ill, in the court system, struggling with addiction, living in substandard housing and unemployed. He is unhappy about his life and future. Norm admitted these things and the associated pain, "I feel like I shouldn't be proud of myself." So praise has to be specific to an activity or behavior and genuinely earned or it falls flat, undermining judicial authority and procedural justice. A client also needs to be in a stable mental state to be able to receive praise.

In addition to praise, clients in compliance have brief reviews in the beginning of the court calendar. Clients who are in full compliance are considered "express reviews," though this distinction is more formalized in *County* MHC. Ideally, "express" clients in full compliance are heard first on the court calendar and are reviewed quickly, as a small reward. The defense attorney, the prosecuting attorney and the judge all give accolades to the client for fulfilling the expectations of the court and hoping to induce further compliance. A prosecutor described expresses as "we give them [clients] kudos and the move to the next case." Cases with violations are heard later in the court calendar, with clients having to stay in court longer as a minor punishment.

During Norm's time in MHC he, like many clients interviewed, had positive and some "express" reviews. During one review, the probation officer began with a comment that Norm was very patient given the long wait time and offered praise and acclaim for the work he was doing to fulfill the court requirements, as well as with his life and well-being. A typical example of a court hearing for an "express" review is as follows:

*Probation*: He is doing extremely well. He is 100 percent compliant with medications. He is attending his groups, seeing his CD counselor and meetings every Wednesday with me in probation. He is currently in transition with his case manager but lives in the building with his previous one and is contact. He is dieting and exercising. He is taking care of himself in ways that he hasn't been doing before.
*Judge*: I think you are doing really well. You are going on one year of compliance. How do you feel?
*Norm*: Very good!
*Judge*: You look good!
*Defense*: He is doing great things.

This exchange was positive but could have had more of an effect if the client was seen at the beginning of the court calendar. The longer it takes to hear cases for clients in full compliance, the weaker the therapeutic effect.

Some team members called for increasing positive sanctions and referred to the formalized "express review" as a model for expansion. A social service provider explicitly stated that the MHC program needs to have "more incentives" and more rewards:

### 4 Therapeutic Justice in Action: Court Process, Reviews ... 161

The express system is a great idea, but there should be more – sometimes the expresses will sit there until 3:00. That is a special thing. It makes people excited and that is something that they were missing in their lives, the recognition that you are doing well.

In addition to praise, rewards can also be more tangible. A judge can reduce monitoring and structure as a reward for compliance, including reduced oversight (e.g., daily reporting, reduced or eliminating drug testing, lengthening the amount of time before next court appearance). A common positive sanction is striking or reducing day reporting as a first-level of reduced monitoring for complaint behavior. More frequent monitoring can also be re-introduced later as a negative sanction for non-compliance. For example, in a review a probation officer recommended to strike day reporting and all parties agreed:

*Judge*: Looks like you are doing well. Doing day reporting. UA's.
*Probation*: He was having struggles around addiction issues. We had him in custody for a while. He went to a 21-day program. Did well. He has had ups and downs – has given up at times to stay clean. He seems to have more determination this time. He's been here before. We want to see him end this program well.
*Defense*: Congratulations with completing the program [in-patient substance abuse program]. Agree to reduce day reporting to 3 times per week.
*Judge*: Great that you made it through 21 days. Great! But it is going to be harder. You have some help. But you need to stay on medications and have positive UA's.[8]

A judge who holds a therapeutic orientation is aware of the challenges of mental illness, and in many cases substance abuse, and offers support and rewards for managing co-occurring issues.

Rewards are also given in the form of small tokens and symbolic, non-cash certificates for important achievements. Sometimes in *County* MHC (not given in *City* MHC), when a client is doing well the judge gives him or her a business card during a scheduled review hearing on behalf of the team. The business cards are decorated with artwork from prior MHC clients and bear encouraging messages. The stated intent of the business card is to praise and encourage the client. During the session when the client's case is reviewed, the judge comes down off the bench and hands the client the card, representing a positive court ritual.

There is not a formal system for selection or eligibility for this reward. Informally, and often during a pre-court meeting, it is the defense attorney who suggests that a business card is warranted in the case of a particular client and upon team agreement a recommendation is given to the judge before the court hearing. There was some discussion among team members about expanding the rewards and allowing probation or other team members to offer the business cards to deserving clients, but from the perspective of a defense attorney, the judge wanted to formalize the sanction and be the one to deliver the reward.

There were concerns that giving business cards could undermine procedural justice if not delivered equitably. A defense attorney reflected on this process in *County* MHC, "I really like those things [business cards]. In our court [*City* MHC], with the different probation officers and everyone judging all behaviors differently, I feel that some probationers would get no cards, and some get all of them, and people would be watching all of that and be, 'That's not fair, that's not fair.'"

While there are a few small rewards throughout the probationary period, the ultimate reward for compliance is graduating from MHC, and in some cases early graduation. Clients that graduate from MHC receive a certificate and the judge strikes active probation and all of the associated court conditions. Praise reaches a pinnacle in the case of graduations, a ritual detailed in the next chapter.

## Negative Sanctions

Despite a therapeutic orientation, it would be a mistake to assume that MHCs do not punish clients. In fact, there are often punishments for non-compliance of the court's conditions, although the degree, type and frequency of sanctions vary both within and between problem-solving courts. The underlying goal of negative sanctions is to be therapeutic and less punitive: In MHCs punishment is not done for its own sake.

There are attempts to alter the language around negative sanctions to illustrate their therapeutic focus, as recounted by a probation officer: "For the longest time, and I even got kind of in trouble once, because I started to change the report for the court, and instead of 'violations' I put 'non-compliance', because I figured we are a therapeutic court, and instead of sanctions, it was a court response, how does the court respond." Being "mindful of the language we use," a judge liked to use "slips" to relapses to enhance engagement with treatment. The change in language is a symbolic attempt to increase the therapeutic nature of the court and the team members' relationship to clients.

A prosecutor tried to make a critical distinction between court responses to a violation compared to punishing the mental condition related to the non-compliance: "There is not stigma in being sanctioned, because we are not sanctioning you for your illness. We are sanctioning you for the actions you are taking." While this may not be the intent of sanctions, stigma and punishment still persist. The rituals that surround non-compliance issues are not automatically punitive and are not intended to increase the stigma among the clients. A judge emphasized a similar point stating "I am dealing with the conduct. It is not you [the client]… by treating the conduct, sometimes we need to treat you." He went on to clarify that problem-solving courts are "focused on the person, whereas a lot of times we are focusing on the crime… crime takes a back seat" which can increase value and self-worth reducing negative labeling and stigma.

A probation officer provided an example of the importance of framing behavior in the review ritual, highlighting how noncompliance can be socially constructed (Paik 2011):

> Say for example a client was supposed to be at 10 treatments or group meetings/therapy sessions in the past month (since his last review) and he missed 6 of them. I can come before the court and talk about the dates and times of the 6 violations and lay them out in order – one by one – or I could state that the client successfully went to 4 court required treatment sessions. While this is not ideal and he needs to be going to all of them, he is making progress. I think he is having trouble organizing all of them so we will work together to put them on his calendar so that he can make more meetings consistently by his next hearing.[9]

Clients may be out of compliance for many reasons, but they usually revolve around substance use violations, missed treatment appointments, violations of no contact orders and not complying with medication requirements. Violations often result in failed appearances at court reviews and subsequent bench warrants, as well as new criminal law violations in some cases. In response to non-compliance, during the pre-court meeting team members talk about the appropriate sanction (if any) to get the client back on course to fulfill the conditions of their sentence. While different parties do not always agree, and thus a level of adversarialness persists, members of the team engage in dialogue with one another, debating the merits of different courses of action for specific clients. Often collaboration results in a joint plan on how best to proceed with a particular case, such as how to revise the MHC plan, recommend a sanction, and giving the client another chance.

Working in MHC, many team members described a reorientation in how they thought of negative sanctions, as less of a punishment and more as a way to increase client compliance. In describing how drug courts approach violations, Chase and Hora (2000), reflect that sanctions represent the external structure of the court until the internal structure takes over; here the sanctions are the formal social control response, applied in an attempt to trigger self-control from the client in maintaining compliance with the court conditions. MHCs operate under a similar structure. Monique expressed how court supervision assisted her in staying clean and making good choices: "I think during the time I was on probation, the monitoring of my life and what I was doing was good for me, because it kept me on the straight and narrow." The external structure—i.e. the threat of sanctions imposed by the court—altered her internal decision-making process, especially with respect to alcohol usage. A therapeutic approach to negative sanctions focuses on activating the internal locus of social control through the assistance of housing, treatment and social support not punishing their way to compliance behavior.

There are a range of sanctions, some of which were described by as "creative," in response to behavioral non-compliance. Depending on the circumstances and type of violation, the court may impose a single sanction, some combination of two or more types of sanctions, or no sanction at all. All team members appreciated the use of a range of sanctions, giving them more tools to encourage client compliance. Jail was characterized as a "last resort," consistent with the research on MHCs use of jail sparingly (Griffin et al. 2002), which was more clearly articulated in the case of *City* MHC than *County* MHC. A judge offered this account: "In my recollection, it was very unusual for me to use jail in a first or second or preliminary way, unless, it was again, they sort of went from 0 to 60 overnight." A probation officer put it this way in his introduction to clients: "You need to know that every violation does not result in jail. There are different graduated sanctions, based on the severity of the violation and I will be honest with them."

Often it is during times of non-compliance that longer conversations between judges and clients occur, representing distinct opportunities for judges to engage according to the principles of procedural justice. Once again, the role of the judge is central. Ultimately the judge decides on whether to give a sanction for noncompliance. An effective judge listens to team member perspectives and the client to adjudicate a productive response that takes into account therapeutic implications. During these reviews many team members noted that it was important for judges to offer encouragement and appreciation for honesty, even amidst discussing court violations and imposing negative sanctions.

Some judges are more adamant about requiring clients to admit or deny violations on the record. This is especially on display in *County* MHC. For many clients, this practice caused additional and unnecessary anxiety. A social service agent connected with MHC stated that, "I don't think that [formal admission of violations] is helpful… I think it is really bad." He argued that it is stressful and confusing when a client has multiple possible violations to admit or deny, "They might admit one and deny another and still get a sanction for one." Even in these cases, the explanation is vital. The court prioritizes <u>why</u> a client was out of compliance and <u>how</u> the person will come back to compliance. In many instances, the probation officer has already dealt with the violation and the client is "back on track" and in many ways a sanction might be counter-productive. Probation officers often mention non-compliance to the judge in the review, but then request that the judge take no action. Consistent with a harm reduction philosophy, judges often rule to "stay the sanction" or for a "delayed sanction," barring any strong objection from prosecution. In doing so the court acknowledges the violation on the record but declines to impose a sanction, reserving the right to do so at the next review hearing if the client is out of compliance. According to a judge, typically the sanctions are not imposed.

To increase accountability, the judge can also increase monitoring and structure as a sanction for being out of compliance. One such practice is to impose day reporting (or increase the frequency) which requires clients to report daily to the court. Jennifer's case illustrates the use of day reporting as a positive and negative sanction. When she started in MCH she had to report two days per week. She violated day reporting within six months of being referred to MHC, was brought back into the court on a warrant and when she was released her day reporting obligation was increased to five days a week with random UA's and breath tests. Three weeks later, after being in full compliance, Jennifer's day reporting was reduced to three days per week. It was not until six weeks later that the day reporting was reduced back to the original two days per week. A year after she was first referred to MHC her day reporting was completely stricken. Six months later Jennifer graduated from MHC (six months earlier than the typical two-year period). In Jennifer's case there was uncharacteristically heavy use of day reporting but limited other sanctions. Extensive day reporting, with the threat of jail, largely worked in her case.

In another case, a probation officer described a client's violation of MHC conditions, including a domestic violence no contact order: "She went off the rails. Needs to stay clean and sober and not make this mistake again." Her defense attorney later stated, "She gets very emotional. She's not minimizing but feels victimized by the relationship – power and control issues… symptoms related to mental health exacerbated by contact [with her partner]." The judge, at the request of probation, added daily reporting three times per week to get her back on track with more structure. In this case, it was the prosecutor who showed less mercy and made the stakes very clear: "[name of client] needs to be on notice. She has had her one chance. Will revoke if not in compliance." The tone and firm language was uncharacteristic in MHC, even from a prosecutor.[10] On another occasion, a probation officer asked for an increase in day reporting in a proactive approach to reinforce court expectations and oversight emphasizing structural accountability in hope of reducing the likelihood of non-complaint behavior, "There's an ongoing risk of relapse but I trust that she is ready and in a good place. She knows she has the support." Increasing structure and monitoring can be therapeutic, but it also widens the net—sometimes unintentionally—by creating more obligations to fulfill and possibly more opportunities to be out of compliance.

If violations occur between court dates, probation officers often increase client contact without judicial approval; in fact judges usually respect the autonomy of probation officers and do not need to order increased probation contacts as probation has already acted pro-actively with the client. Probation officers can also advance a court date if warranted by a behavioral violation. In most cases of non-compliance, the next court review is sooner that it would have been if the client was in compliance. So more frequent probation and court reviews are clear sanctions for violating court conditions but understood within a therapeutic framework.

One of the biggest challenges to client success in the court is the management of their alcohol and/or drug addictions. The most frequent violations in the MHCs I observed were, by far, for violations of the abstinence condition. The modal response by probation and judges was to contextualize the violation and react therapeutically often offering another chance to comply. For instance, in encouraging a client to try again to achieve sobriety, a judge remarked "Getting sober and staying sober is hard work." Another judge reinforced this idea "We are a treatment court. We don't get shocked when someone has a dirty UA [Urine Analysis]. We work to get people back on track."

Several clients suggested that there is too much focus on abstinence in MHCs, which for Robert reduced his enthusiasm for the court: "Just everything revolves around using, and just that whole environment just turned me off toward the end." Norm revealed to me that he takes his drug abuse seriously and knows he "shouldn't do drugs." The overreliance on abstinence as the source of compliance led him to feel undeserving. Yet he generally complied with his mental health treatment—infrequently missing a meeting. For Norm: "They [MHC] could be more gentle if you have a relapse. I don't know how they should treat violations. If your drugs are causing problems that is a problem… The court is a punishment thing."

Most clients shared with me that they did not maintain their sobriety throughout the MHC process, leading to sanctions in many cases. Monique was ashamed of this and feared disappointing the court. She shared that "They [MHC team] want you to be honest with them and tell them when you used. I did not want to tell them ever that I used." Sometimes she did get caught and was sanctioned with jail time. Other clients seemed gratified by "fooling" probation and the court, as Vicki put it. She worked the system: "The only times I ever need to be clean, is right before I see the guy [who administered the UA], and it is already scheduled… I know that is the amount of time it needs to get out of your system." For some clients the response was mixed. For instance, Norm told me about a time he was out of compliance (with a dirty UA) and "the judge came down on him hard." At other times he evaded detection, "I've slipped a couple of times and got away with it."

Alcohol or drug relapses and cases of minimal non-compliance can result in writing an essay, usually a few hand-written pages. This type of court response allows the client to detail the circumstances that led to the violation without adding any new monitoring and avoiding a more serious sanction (such as jail). This contextualization can be useful to the team in how they actively monitor and support the client. It also offers clients an opportunity for self-reflection. The essay is usually turned into probation before the next court hearing. In the next review (after the essay was imposed as a sanction) effective judges usually reference the essay in a therapeutic way, without revealing specific or embarrassing details. In court observations, some clients expressed new insights into their behavior through the process of writing the essay and often identified a specific issue or trigger related to substance use that might aid in future mental health and chemical dependency management. In such cases, judges praised clients for awareness into their addiction, help-seeking behaviors and management of their mental illness.

The use of inappropriate sanctions can have a negative and stigmatizing effect on a client. When talking with me about the challenges of sanctioning, a probation office noted about how important it was to give the appropriate sanction. He offered the following assessment of a judge who ordered a client to write an essay about his non-compliance:

That [when a judge orders an essay] undermines what we are doing here. The idea of it was good and I understand that you are trying to keep the guy out of jail... I do like it for certain clients because I think certain clients can really benefit from it. But they have to have a certain level of cognitive ability, they have to have a certain level of reflective ability and they have to have a certain level of writing ability. Otherwise it is garbage. That is the other thing, they can reflect and be smart but if they can't write very well, then you are almost creating this different thing, this different stress, this different dynamic... where now they're feeling badly because now they are supposed to submit this writing thing to the guy with a JD [Juris Doctorate]. Then they feel badly about it and that is not at all what we want to be doing.[11]

Given to a client without the capabilities to successfully write a coherent essay, the activity reinforces stigma and adds additional sources of shame for the client.

A client who is out of compliance for a minor violation might also receive court watch—a sanction enthusiastically supported by many team members.[12] Clients with this court imposed sanction are required to attend a full day of MHC (approximately 1:30–4:30 p.m.) before their next review. In the following interview exchange, Shima explained court watch as a sanction and its impact on her court experience:

*Shima*: When I was with my friend, even before the court doors were open, both of them, both of them, I would listen, talking to them – hear them talking to another person. This is so fucked up. I can't believe I have to do watch, court watch, or do monitoring. I would be, 'You know why you hurt yourself. You messed up...'
*Interviewer*: But you would take responsibility.
*Shima*: Right, but you have to hang in there, they are offering to help us. They are not here to put us in jail. I remember [my first probation officer] – I hated being in jail...
*Interviewer*: But sometimes you had to?

*Shima*: Yeah, but I wish I opened up more to the clients [in MHC] and say, 'Hey, listen, this is going to work. Hang in there. Know that when you mess up, it is your fault. It is not the court's fault, it is your fault, it is our fault and we have to deal with the issues or the consequences.'

In the next review (after the court watch was completed) or on the day a client completed court watch, a judge will ask if they want to comment on what occurred that day. It is an opportunity to express voice and assert agency. Most clients I observed said something to the judge about being on court watch. One client expressed appreciation for the "eye-opening" experience and talked about connecting his struggles and experiences to others he saw before the court. Another client reported to the judge about doing court watch, "This had me thinking. Especially when a guy was taken to jail. I don't want that to be me!"

Court watch (as a sanction) or just waiting in court for a case to be called can also have a deterrent effect. I probed clients about whether listening to other client reviews was encouraging, discouraging or had no effect. The clients I interviewed said that sitting in court and listening to other cases (for court watch or just waiting for one's case to be called) had some influence. Monique referenced a deterrent effect, saying, "I don't know about encouraging, but I know when I saw this man who had fouled up and drank, and had to do an AA meeting every day, I thought, 'oh, my god, I don't want that happening to me.' It influenced me to watch and see what the outcome of the other clients. I did pay attention to what was going on with them." Court reviews were directed toward specific deterrence and keeping clients accountable for their behavioral choices, encouraging compliance, but limited in terms of general deterrence. According to Wexler (1972–1973: 307), "the therapeutic state is technically unconcerned with matters of general deterrence." A judge reflecting a similar point stated that "general deterrents… That thinking does not really enter into my head in the specialty courts as much, especially mental health court." It may be that "express" reviews or graduation rituals serve to recognize clients in full compliance and show those in the gallery awaiting their hearing the moral expectations of the court and how they can be satisfied, having a general deterrent effect.

For some, observing court and seeing clients succeed helped to encourage compliance and keep graduation as a reachable goal. When I asked about encouragement in the court process and watching other cases, Jennifer mentioned "graduations" saying "I think they are cool. The judge and the probation officer, they seem really proud and happy that they are getting well. I think it is sweet…That gave me something to look forward to."

In detailing the "shared energy" in MHC rituals, a probation officer characterized the court watch sanction as a way to encourage clients to make connections between themselves and others in court, reducing the reduce the social distance. A probation officer clarified the role that court watch can play in linking a client's trajectory to other people's experiences in the court and how others manage mental health and substance use treatment:

> It [court observation] does two things. One, if the client is sitting in court from 1:00-4:00 they're not doing anything bad! They are not drinking, they are not out there engaging in any crime. There is also this cool thing… You sit in court and watch these people. So there is the actual observation part where you are seeing all these different people, from walks of life and different experiences in different levels of their recovery and how they're dealing with the court. You see the people who are newbies and are still struggling with their addiction and their stability and stuff and maybe the client goes 'Oh yeah I remember when I was there and look I have come a long way.' Or they see someone who's two years into their probation and they go "wow" and they tell their story and they [the client] go 'Wow, maybe that's where I can get to!' So you see where you have been and maybe where you can get to.[13]

This statement suggests that court watch can be reinvigorating and it can help a client get back on the right course. It might also remind a client that there are others like him/her but at different points in the process of treatment. A defense attorney echoed this point by stating that during court watch:

People can see other people getting sanctions. There are two parts of it. There is the deterrent part of seeing people get sanctioned. There is kind of the supportive part of seeing them graduate and how that is... I think for most of our clients, other sanctions [jail and work crew] are not particularly effective.

Other cases of non-compliance resulted in community service or work crew. For example, community service hours or days of work crew range from a few hours to one day to about ten days depending on the violation, client circumstances, and team and judicial approach. Ideally, some portion of the total hours imposed would be completed by the next review, but there was flexibility in the number of months given to complete the community service or work crew obligation, especially in light of work/school schedules, family responsibilities, and transportation issues. This sanction invokes a moral responsibility toward work and community assistance as a response to a court violation.

For cases of serial non-compliance around taking prescribed medication (authorized by a medical professional), team members and the court intervene to impose medication monitoring. A probation officer recounted a case of a client's medication non-compliance:

> Even one day where she took her medication and I heard that little pill drop back into the cup. She would take it and then go toss it. I said show me the cup and walked in, and the judge threw her in jail. We walked right into the court and I said, 'Your Honor, she didn't take her medication.' He said, 'You are in violation and I am taking you into custody.'

While this can have long-term therapeutic effects, this is a clear example of net-widening. If a client continues to refuse medication and treatment, as the client did in this case, the result can be jail. Jail can also have anti- therapeutic effects. Judges invoke concerns about community safety in this type of action of client non-medication compliance. While in jail, individuals (both clients and defendants) can refuse medication which occurs frequently. Individuals can also decompensate in jail for a host of reasons including refusing medication, not getting the right kind of medication (e.g., there is a list of medication that are allowed) or they are in solitary confinement.[14]

## Jail as a "Last Resort"

Jail as a sanction was seen by almost all team members as an option reserved for clients with multiple violations or in extreme cases. A judge summarized the sanctioning process, saying, "We do everything up to and including jail. That would be that last resort. If we can figure out a way to avoid jail, that is the preferred method. In some cases, it became necessary." Even when jail is imposed judges spoke of "scaling back" sanctions and specifically limiting it to a few days so that the client "remembers why he is there." Another judge warned that when sentencing jail time it has to be moderate and not overly punitive; he argued that anything "beyond ten 10 days is not useful. Beyond that is useless and then you are just kicking somebody." Research suggests that three to five days is the maximum (National Association of Drug Court Professionals). The MHC teams have creative responses to violations of court conditions and mostly follow "jail as a last resort" approach as seen in the following statement by a judge during a court review:

> I am not thinking of what happens today as <u>punishment</u>. I want to get you back on track. I am worried that we are losing your focus and motivation. If I wanted to punish you I would put you in jail and I am not going to do that.

Even prosecutors saw jail in a therapeutic light, making a clear distinction between MHC and traditional courts based on community safety,

> But when you are dealing with the criminal justice system, you are not throwing them in jail or sanctioning them because they are bipolar. You are sanctioning them or doing something because of something they have done. It is not because of the diagnosis… If someone is not taking their meds, I'm not going to throw you in jail for 6 months because the only violation you have is not taking your meds. Now, if you have not taken your meds and you are threatening to kill somebody, I am going to throw you in jail for that threat, not because you are bipolar. I think it is very important to make that distinction. You are going to jail because you are now posing a threat to community safety. If you don't take your meds but you stay in your room and do whatever you want

to do, I'm not going to throw you in jail. I may ask that you do daily med monitoring or that you do something that is related to that mental illness… Jail is a place that I [use to] keep the community safe. If I don't need to keep the community safe from you… I am not going to give you jail time.

This prosecutor claimed that sanctions were based on the individual's behavior and not mental illness status. Nevertheless, in practice these two become hard to differentiate.

Many of the clients I interviewed, all of whom were relatively successful, received jail time as a sanction. Shima recalled the times she went to jail for violating the no-contact order: "I went there [jail] several, several times, and I stayed there several times for a little bit." Clients talked extensively about sanctions they received, or were worried about receiving, and the range of sanctions that were available. Variation in sanctions can occur even for the same offense. Some clients were frustrated that they received jail for being out of compliance while others received more lenient sanctions. Norm told me that court watch "sounds like that might be fun," which is probably why he did not receive that as a response for being out of compliance.

Another client also felt she once received jail too quickly. Jennifer sometimes got mad at her probation officer when she received a negative sanction but recognized that, "It is my fault, it is more about myself usually." She wished that the team was more supportive and less punitive, offering more non-jail sanctions, "I would have been happy to do a lot of community service hours. That's me, that helps somebody else, and… I don't know if everyone is like this, but the jail time for me is horrible." In interview, Jennifer admitted that "in the long run, the fear of jail would keep me sober way more than having to do community service, because I like to do that anyway."

Jail serves as a powerful deterrent for all clients and probation officers are fully aware of this. Most used the threat of jail as a tool in their care and supervision of clients. On one extreme was a probation officer who saw jail and the criminal justice system as the problem: "I'm not a proponent of jail as a solution anyway, the research on jail as a deterrent is not very good... So, alternatives make much more sense to me." At the other end was a probation officer who was unyielding in his willingness to demand jail or revocation early in the court process. Even in a therapeutic environment there is variation in jail recommendations.

The most extreme sanction is revocation or being expelled from the court. Cases can be terminated for non-compliance. In cases where the violation(s) is perceived as too great or too many a case may be revoked whereby a client exits MHC. In such cases, revocation often includes jail time (or time served) and leads to closing the case. Cases can also be closed because a client is not progressing in MHC and the court has nothing more to offer. Charges can be dropped in the interest of justice or the entire case placed on hold due to involuntary civil commitment proceeding in the case of grave mental health decomposition. Although behavioral non-compliance can lead to revocation, as with new criminal law violations, the court usually responds with varying creative sanctions. A judge described how even the process of revocation differs in MHC from mainstream court, allowing for more opportunities for clients to be successful:

> The prosecutor in mental health court will oftentimes agree to not revoke, which is a rare occasion in other courts. The parties will agree to, in essence, modify the contract to allow the defendant another opportunity, to modify the conditions. The same with the deferred sentence. They will agree to modify the conditions of a deferred sentence, so that the defendant doesn't necessarily have to build additional criminal history, because of the difficulties in complying, which is not very typical in another court. You violate, you get revoked.

In *County* MHC there are more early revocations in the case of felony-dropdowns. Rather than seeing revocations as client failures a defense attorney understood them as court failures, "if the plan didn't work then we [MHC team] have to find something else." In some revocation cases this leads to a clear example of adversarialism which can be jarring given the general collaborative nature of the court. For many of the felony drop-down cases the team was not in consensus about bringing in a case possibly setting up a client for early revocation. Take, for instance, the following example of a client who was revoked after being in MHC for one day. A court liaison at the time of opt-in expressed her opposition but the prosecutor pushed the case forward:

> I said that it was not a good fit…. He completely violated. He went out and got a new charge, and when I said, 'This charge is criminal behavior,' and I said that and it was documented. I told the state. The state asked me, 'What is your opinion,' and I said, 'My opinion is this was a criminal behavior not related to mental health. It shows low amenability, and I do not think he is proving to be a fit for this court.'[15]

In *City* MHC, clients (compared with MHDT defendants) had higher rates of case revocation (Beach 2016), reinforcing concerns about stronger nets for those who opt-into MHC. Probation officers, defense social workers and defense attorneys were especially vocal about safeguarding against punishing people for trying mental court and failing. Research on probation highlights the role of stigma and systematic bias in supervision failures (Skeem et al. 2011) which often lead to revocation. Prosecutors also expressed a grave concern about being overly punitive, even in the case of more serious charges:

> When we are looking at felony dropdowns we are looking at what is a standard range. If their standard range is 3 to 6 months, we are not going to sanction them for 12 years in custody, because that would be unfair, unless it is a very severe public safety issue… That is something that we are very mindful of, to make sure we are not penalizing or criminalizing the mentally ill.

Another judge mentioned a similar technique: "I look at the midpoint of the standard range if they had pled guilty to the felony… Sometimes I would go to the lower end of the range. Sometimes I would go to the upper end, especially if there was a new law violation." In *City* MHC often judges would take the opt-out recommendation. In another instance, when a client was revoked from MHC for failing to comply with court conditions, a probation officer reminded the judge that the role of the court is "not to punish someone for trying and failing mental health court." Maintaining a therapeutic perspective is critical even when clients are unsuccessful in MHC; it requires keeping concerns about net-widening in mind.

## Widening Discretion

Discretion is a crucial theme in the criminal justice system. Within the sanctioning process, discretion is pervasive. This is most consequential in the case of revocations. Recent research on MHC termination found that white women were less likely to be terminated and thus more likely to complete MHC (Ray and Brooks Dollar 2013). Using data from *City* MHC, Beach (2016) identifies race and sex effects on case revocation (but not the sanctioning process in general). She finds that both blacks and women experienced higher risk of case revocation than white men in the case of mental health non-compliance. This raises questions about how probation officers frame treatment violations, and how judges respond. Nevertheless, I found discretion was shaped more by probation philosophy—harm reduction verses punishment—than participants' characteristics. While there was generally a therapeutic approach to the sanctioning process in MHCs, serial non-compliance increases discretionary practices.

At some point in the MHC process, most of the clients were out of compliance. The team had discretion in how non-compliance was presented to the judge and the judge has discretion in how to respond. A probation officer reflected on the role of discretion in a way that was emblematic of how other team members responded:

> They [clients] need to have a firm boundary of what it is that they need to do, but at the same time, what is cool about mental health court is we have a lot of discretion… It is not just measure on clean or dirty [drug tests]. In general probation, a lot of it, clean or dirty. Are you compliant or are you not compliant?

Certain probation officers saw any non-compliance as sanction-worthy and were quick to revoke (and expel clients from MHC). However, the majority were unlikely to respond to incidents of non-compliance with extreme sanctions and unlikely to suggest revocation, even in the case of serial non-compliance. Non-compliance in the handling of mental health issues sets MHCs apart from traditional courts, as well as other problems-solving courts, and even clients from other defendants in MHCs.[16]

There is a lot of room for discretion in MHCs and in problem-solving courts more generally (Boldt 2009). The fact that both compliance and non-compliance can be interpreted differently raises concerns about equity in dispensing therapeutic justice. However, discretion allows for individually-tailored responses in line with the tenants of treatment courts more broadly. Most team members agreed that sanctions need to be individualized, and while aware of possible bias, it also allows for a holistic approach targeting client-specific compliance. Used judiciously, the sanctioning process can ultimately enhance therapeutic justice. While discretion can introduce bias—conscious or unconscious—and inconsistency among cases, it is probably a necessary trade-off if therapeutic justice is to work.

The court process, specifically reviews and sanctioning, can produce therapeutic outcomes, but is it not automatic. Therapeutic results are more likely when a positive ritual process characterizes the everyday working of MHCs. And rituals—when performed well—provide part of the explanation of how the MHC process reduces recidivism among clients and improves their well-being and social status.

# Notes

1. Mass incarceration and criminal recidivism rates suggest limitations to the broader efficacy of these principles. In fact, the entire criminal justice apparatus could likely benefit from integrating more of the therapeutically oriented principles outlined in this book.
2. See Snedker (2016) for a detailed account of rituals in MHC.
3. Goffman defined stigma as a "spoiled identity" which must be constantly managed. Spoiled identities are especially acute in the case of mentally ill offenders, some of whom are diverted to MHCs. MHC clients typically suffer from multiple social stigma including mental illness, criminality, substance abuse/addiction, poverty and/or homelessness.
4. While mainstream courts may also incorporate procedural justice principles, the adoption is more widespread in treatment courts.

5. After observing court for some time I was relieved to see the court finally start on time. However, I soon realized that this represented a lack of understanding of the court process—by myself and the judge.
6. There is a norm in both MHCs that if an in-custody client is the courtroom (brought down from jail) then that case takes precedent and is heard next. In *City* MHC this norm has become formalized since the most recent change in judicial leadership. There is now a sign that states: "By Order of the Bench: In Custody and interpreter cases are to be addressed first." While this makes sense for efficiency and possibly safety, it does impede the ritual and therapeutic experience. Often clients wait long periods of time—more than an hour—for their cases to be heard due to priority of in-custody cases.
7. Despite the language used, especially the use of "wink" twice, which could be misunderstood as trivializing what happens in MHC, this judge in interviews and while presiding over court was committed to the court's mission, protecting client's rights, and enhancing their success in MHC. I think the language reflected the inherent tension and challenge of treatment courts—being both oriented toward "treatment" and operating within the "court."
8. In this case the judge means negative (non-dirty) urine analysis.
9. Snedker (2016: 46).
10. This was a relatively new prosecutor for *City* MHC. Over time, I witnessed his socialization into the court where he developed a more therapeutic style.
11. Snedker (2016: 48)
12. Some were critical of court watch as a creative sanction, including a defense social worker: "they will get a few days of court watch… In some ways I think that is more of a punishment than a day at work crew or a day in jail. It is more emotionally and mentally taxing."
13. Snedker (2016: 42–43).
14. If someone becomes a real danger to themselves or others in jail there could be a *Harper* hearing (*Harper v. State 1976*) where the jail can administer forced medication for 3 days. This seems to be a rare occurrence.
15. However there were cases where serious concerns were raised at the opt-in stage and throughout the process early dissenters became strong supporters of the same client. This turnaround showcases that once

a client opts-into MHC the team advocates for client success. It also highlights the challenge of predicting client success.
16. The divergent pathways—MHC opt-in and MHDT—influence the court process and the use of discretion. Observational data suggest that those in MHC are treated differently by the same judge based on a host of factors, including being in the MHDT group.

## References

Beach, Lindsey R. 2016. "Unlocking the Black Box of Mental Health Court Case Processing : An Event History Analysis of Extralegal Characteristics & Behavior on Case Revocation." MA thesis, University of Washington.
Boldt, Richard C. 2009. "A Circumspect Look at Problem-Solving Courts." In *Problem-Solving Courts: Justice for the Twenty-First Century*, edited by Paul Higgins and Mitchell B. Mackinem, 13–32. Santa Barbara: Praeger.
Canada, Kelli E., and Amy C. Watson. 2013. "'Cause Everybody Likes to Be Treated Good': Perceptions of Procedural Justice Among Mental Health Court Participants." *American Behavioral Scientist* 57 (2): 209–30. https://doi.org/10.1177/0002764212465415.
Chase, Deborah J., and Peggy Fulton Hora. 2000. "The Implications of Therapeutic Jurisprudence for Judical Satisfaction." *Court Review* 37: 12–21.
Dollar, Cindy Brooks, and Bradley Ray. 2015. "The Practice of Reintegrative Shaming in Mental Health Court." *Criminal Justice Policy Review* 26 (1): 29–44. https://doi.org/10.1177/0887403413507275.
Goffman, Erving. 1986. *Stigma: Notes on the Management of Spoiled Identity*. New York: Simon & Schuster.
Griffin, Patricia A., Henry J. Steadman, and John Petrila. 2002. "The Use of Criminal Charges and Sanctions in Mental Health Courts." *Psychiatric Services* 53 (10): 1285–89.
Kaiser, Kimberly A., and Kristy Holtfreter. 2016. "An Integrated Theory of Specialized Court Programs: Using Procedural Justice and Therapeutic Jurisprudence to Promote Offender Compliance and Rehabilitation." *Criminal Justice and Behavior* 43 (1): 45–62. https://doi.org/10.1177/0093854815609642.
Kopelovich, Sarah, Philip Yanos, Christina Pratt, and Joshua Koerner. 2013. "Procedural Justice in Mental Health Courts: Judicial Practices, Participant

Perceptions, and Outcomes Related to Mental Health Recovery." *International Journal of Law and Psychiatry* 36 (2): 113–20. Elsevier Ltd. https://doi.org/10.1016/j.ijlp.2013.01.004.

Lens, Vicki. 2016. *Poor Justice: How the Poor Fare in the Courts.* Oxford: Oxford University Press.

Miller, JoAnn, and Donald C. Johnson. 2009. *Problem Solving Courts: A Measure of Justice.* Lanham: Rowman & Littlefield.

Munetz, Mark R., Christian Ritter, Jennifer L. S. Teller, and Natalie Bonfine. 2014. "Mental Health Court and Assisted Outpatient Treatment: Perceived Coercion, Procedural Justice, and Program Impact." *Psychiatric Services* 65 (3): 352–58. https://doi.org/10.1176/appi.ps.002642012.

Paik, Leslie. 2011. *Discretionary Justice: Looking Inside a Juvenile Drug Court.* New Brunswick: Rutgers University Press.

Perlin, Michael. 2013. "'The Judge, He Cast His Robe Aside': Mental Health Courts, Dignity and Due Process." *Mental Health Law & Policy Journal* 3 (1): 1–29.

Poythress, Norman G., John Petrila, Annette McGaha, and Roger Boothroyd. 2002. "Perceived Coercion and Procedural Justice in the Broward Mental Health Court." *International Journal of Law and Psychiatry* 25 (5): 517–33. https://doi.org/10.1016/S0160-2527(01)00110-8.

Ray, Bradley, and Cindy Brooks Dollar. 2013. "Examining Mental Health Court Completion: A Focal Concerns Perspective." *Sociological Quarterly* 54 (4): 647–69. https://doi.org/10.1111/tsq.12032.

Ray, Bradley, and Cindy Brooks Dollar. 2014. "Exploring Stigmatization and Stigma Management in Mental Health Court: Assessing Modified Labeling Theory in a New Context." *Sociological Forum* 29 (3): 720–35. https://doi.org/10.1111/socf.12111.

Ray, Bradley, Cindy Brooks Dollar, and Kelly M. Thames. 2011. "Observations of Reintegrative Shaming in a Mental Health Court." *International Journal of Law and Psychiatry* 34 (1): 49–55. Elsevier Ltd. https://doi.org/10.1016/j.ijlp.2010.11.008.

Rottman, David, and Pamela Casey. 1999. "Therapeutic Jurisprudence and the Emergence of Problem-Solving Courts." *National Institute of Justice Journal* 240 (July): 12–19.

Skeem, Jennifer L., Sarah Manchak, and Jillian K. Peterson. 2011. "Correctional Policy for Offenders with Mental Illness: Creating a New Paradigm for Recidivism Reduction." *Law and Human Behavior* 35 (2): 110–26. https://doi.org/10.1007/s10979-010-9223-7.

Snedker, Karen A. 2016. "Unburdening Stigma: Identity Repair through Rituals in Mental Health Court."*Society and Mental Health* 6 (1): 36–55. http://journals.sagepub.com/doi/abs/10.1177/2156869315598203.

Tyler, Tom R. 1996. "The Psychological Consequences of Judicial Procedures: Implications for Civil Committment Hearings." In *Law in a Therapeutic Key: Developments in Therapeutic Jurisprudence*, 3–15. Durham: Carolina Academic Press.

Wales, Heathcote W., Virginia Aldigé Hiday, and Bradley Ray. 2010. "Procedural Justice and the Mental Health Court Judge's Role in Reducing Recidivism." *International Journal of Law and Psychiatry* 33 (4): 265–71. Elsevier Ltd.

Wexler, David B. 1973. "Therapeutic Justice." *Minnesota Law Review* 57: 289–338. https://doi.org/10.3366/ajicl.2011.0005.

# 5

# Reducing Recidivism and Pathways to Success

Once a client exits the court, not returning to the court system is treated as success. Many team members, especially judges, referenced recidivism—the extent to which former clients are arrested for new crimes after being released from the criminal justice system—in discussing client success. A judge declared, "We want to see the benefits to individuals so they don't reoffend." All members of the MHC team stated that there is some degree of success and expressed hope for changed lives, illustrating the broader benefits of MHC participation, characterized simply by some as "We had a lot of success!" and "Yes. I definitely think the court works!" Assessing success was understood in relative terms. "It is fairly effective" stated a judge about MHC given the "low success rate in general in all of our courts." This same judge later stated that "we see clients' lives turn around, and we don't see that a lot in the non-specialty courts… it is more positive."

There was some variation by the two courts in how success was characterized. Most *City* MHC team members offered affirmative statements about success in comparison to *County* MHC team members whose positive declarations were laced with ambiguity.[1] It was not that team members in *City* MHC were naïve about the complexities of their clients, but rather that the team was more in sync with each other and the clients' charges were less serious. In reference to felony drop-downs, prosecutors and probation officers alike mentioned that is why the court works less well. In many cases MHCs—in this study, County MHC— are not taking "good fits" in the words of many team members and are easily revoked.

Beyond court differences, opinions varied on exactly what success looked like and how it was best assessed. For many "not getting in trouble with the law," mental health management, sobriety and stability were intermingled with criminal desistance, but for most team members reductions in criminal behavior represented a central part of success.

Summarizing a success story in general terms, a probation officer offered this account in reflecting on a past client: "He is out in society. He is working. He is not committing new crimes. He is taking his meds. He is where he needs to be." A prosecutor similarly offered an "ideal" picture of success and tied it to the heart of what MHCs are designed to do:

> I think the mission is to change someone's life, and at the end of two years they are in a completely different, stable, secure place in the community, and in their mental health and their chemical dependency treatment, and that they don't ever come back. They don't offend again.

Assessing success of MHCs is multi-faceted and can be measured at several time points. While success may be correlated with lower rates of recidivism, other forms of success are also relevant. Success in MHC is best understood by greater stability in the lives of clients—emotional, housing, and health (physical and mental)—that translate into fewer life stressors, reducing the probability of contact with the criminal justice system.

In this chapter I explore conventional conceptions of success—most notably criminal recidivism—as well as offer a broader perspective of success in MHC. During the time I observed the courts, City MHC was undergoing a scheduled external evaluation (DuBois and Martin 2013). Administrators compiled data on clients, merging criminal justice data with public health data (e.g., information from providers of mental health and chemical dependency services). I gained permission to analyze the same data which includes a population of 136 individuals (both MHC clients and MHDT defendants) who exited *City* MHC in 2008. (See Appendix A for an explanation of the methods, data and analyses.)

## Criminal Recidivism: Incentives, Mental Health Treatment and Graduation[2]

The most common metric used by academics, policy makers and practitioners to measures court success is criminal recidivism and possibly even the primary object of MHCs (Miller and Perelman 2009). Simply stated by a judge, "if clients don't return to court that is a clear measure of success." Researchers claim that MHCs "may be a moderately effective treatment for reducing recidivism" (Sarteschi et al. 2011, 18) and that MHC participation is associated with fewer arrests, increased time to first arrest, and fewer serious charges (Anestis and Carbonell 2014; Burns et al. 2013; Cosden et al. 2003; Hiday and Ray 2010; McNiel and Binder 2007; Moore and Hiday 2006; Ray 2014). A study also suggests that positive effects of MHCs are not coming at the expense of community safety goals (Christy et al. 2005). This is also true for *City* MHC.[3] *City* MHC clients have lower odds of re-arrest, a longer time to a new criminal charge, and fewer number of criminal charges two years after exiting the court (Snedker et al. 2017). (See the Appendix C for descriptive and regression tables.) Participating in MHC (for both clients and MHDT defendants) had long-lasting effects on post-court behavior several years after they were no longer monitored or sanctioned by the court. In this population, 47 percent have not been re-arrested within the two years after exiting *City* MHC and 53 percent had one or more arrests. The average client has 2.2 charges two years after exiting the court. Analysis of these data reveal key factors that alter the criminal pathways of MHC clients. Specifically, three factors—incentives offered at opt-in, connection with planned mental health treatment, and successful court

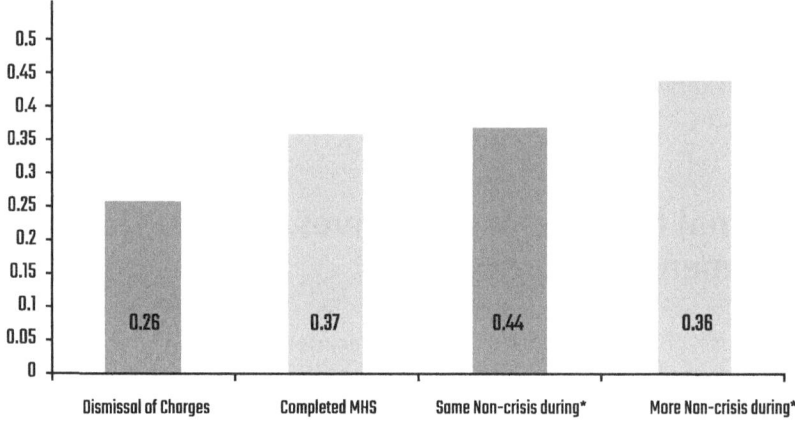

Fig. 5.1 Predicted number of arrests two years after exiting *City* MHC (*Note* *Referent category is less non-crisis treatment during)

completion—occurring at different points in the process help explain reduced recidivism patterns among this population. (see Fig. 5.1).

## Incentives

At the beginning of MHC, during the opt-in phase, the offer to enter MHC has a lasting effect on recidivism.[4] Clients (and MHDT defendants) who were offered a dismissal of charges after successfully fulfilling the conditions of the court decreased their chance of being charged with a crime by 82%, when compared to those who do not receive the dismissal offer.[5] The predicted probability for experiencing at least one arrest for an individual who was offered a dismissal of charges is 26% (or 61% if not offered a dismissal of charges). Thus, an offer to dismiss charges reduces the predicted probability of first arrest by 35%. The unique story from the quantitative data from *City* MHC is the role of incentivized compliance, starting with an offer to dismiss charges during the opt-in stage. The relationship between incentives and opting-into MHC is revealed through court observations and interviews, while the link between incentives and post-court success comes from the empirical analysis. These findings speak to the balance of the "carrot and stick." Without more "carrots" for participation—court program incentives such as dismissal of charges and supportive resources (especially housing) throughout the court program—fewer clients will opt-into MHC and be successful. A probation officer stated, "there's obviously an incentive for the defendants to [opt-into MHC] so that they can get the charges dismissed at the end of two years and successful completion" (emphasis added). This explanation is consistent with client accounts of success. Avoiding a criminal record is imperative for housing access and labor market opportunities. Clients are motivated by such offers and people who are motivated may be more likely to avoid future criminal justice contacts.

While not distinct to MHCs, the offer of dismissing charges and its possible association with recidivism might be more common in treatment courts than traditional courts. In *City* MHC, 32% of defendants were offered this incentive. In interviews, some MHC team members suggested that there is a greater tendency toward offers of dismissal in MHC than in traditional court because of MHC organizational goals and institutional structure (as detailed in Chapter 4). As one MHC team member[6] stated, "overall, I think MHC gets more dispositional continuances [dismissal of charges] than mainstream courts." Similarly, another team member thought the rates of dismissal offers were comparable to other problem-solving courts (e.g., community court) and "while it occurs in [traditional court], and is not unique to MHC, it is probably higher in MHC."

Socio-demographic factors are associated with *City* MHC participation and these patterns are also carried over to the offer of dismissing charges after successful completion of MHC. Of those that were offered a dismissal of charges, clients were more likely to be male (61%), white (66%), and younger (the average age of incentive-recipients was 34 compared to 39 of the general MHC cohort). But given that men were over-represented in MHC, women received a dismissal offer at a greater rate. Women make up 27% of the population but 39% of all dismissals offered (where men represented 73% of the population but 61% of dismissal offers). Similarly whites represent 62% of the total MHC sample but 66% of those clients offered a dismissal of charges. There appears to be a sex- and race-disparity benefitting whites and women in the offer to dismiss charges. This finding is in line with impressions from team members that younger, white women are more likely to be offered a dismissal of charges and that, in general, the court is "tougher" on men. Researchers find similar disparities in court termination (Ray and Brooks Dollar 2013) and the selection process (Luskin 2001), raising questions about parity along racial/ethnic, sex and age dimensions in MHCs.

The offer for a dismissal of charges, and possibly the associated socio-demographic patterns, reflect MHC team members' assessments of risk and amenability to treatment and court conditions. One team member stated, "People who get a dispositional continuance [dismissal of charges] are much more likely to have little or no [criminal] history and already come into the court with a lower likelihood of recidivism." Clients who were offered to have their charges dismissed also had fewer average arrests in the two years prior to entering the court (3 arrests vs. 5 arrests in the whole cohort). The *City* MHC data are in line with research related to the likelihood of being accepted into MHC (Luskin and Ray 2015) and chances of general diversion from the criminal justice system (Luskin 2001). Not unexpectedly, a greater percentage of those clients offered a dispositional continuance successfully completed the court program (70% vs. 40% in the whole cohort).[7]

**Beyond the Offer to Dismiss Charges**

Interview data with MHC team members and clients shed light on possible mechanisms to explain the significance of a client being offered a dismissal of charges for their participation in the court and their reduced criminal behavior. Dismissal offers "sets the tone, they [clients] are much more hopeful… I do see that in people' face and attitudes" suggested a judge. The offer itself represents a strong incentive for behavioral compliance, motivating defendants toward fulfilling treatment and court obligations. Though clients may not understand why they are given an offer, it can motivate their behavior and shape their perception of fairness. For example, in response to questions about why they opted-into MHC, several clients declared that they chose to opt-in because the charges would be dropped upon successful completion of court obligations. Monique indicated that the offer was a clear incentive to stay in court. She went on to discuss how this altered her substance use by saying, "I turned down a drink or a drug and I knew I had to do a UA and did not want to go to jail. I was also a lot better off in court." In the interview she also explained that she tried hard not to do anything to jeopardize her dismissal offer: "I never missed a court date and faced whatever they were going to give." This was even the case when she was using drugs and alcohol and afraid of the sanctions that might be administered for her non-compliance. She was less worried given that her case was in MHC, as opposed to traditional court, and she characterized the court as "better for me because they were more lenient."

Monique's experience was similar to that of other clients, albeit she was more candid about the role the offer played in her compliance and overall court experience. I asked Vicki if she would recommend MHC for someone else and she stated, "If it was a situation where it is worth it, like doing this and not having it go on our record, I would absolutely tell them to do it, yes." Not having a criminal record was clearly an incentive for many clients, but not all. A judge clarified, "A deferred sentence is not all that meaningful. The dismissal can because that means it ends, but the fact of their criminal record doesn't matter to many people, in my opinion." This was not the case for clients that I interviewed, the offer to dismiss their charge(s) was a clear incentive. But the effect of this incentive is reduced for those with lengthy records. For Shima the offer was positive, she stressed how she perceived her MHC experience altered her entire trajectory: "I'm so happy that I got into mental health court this last time, because I would be in prison if I was in regular court."

A second way a dismissal offer may influence a client's experience in MHC is through perceptional changes of the client for <u>both</u> MHC team members and clients themselves. Both of these changes are captured in the remarks of a probation officer (emphasis added):

> But there's another thing that we might be tapping into here with the [dispositional] continuances and that's how the <u>client perceives</u> the fact that the city is offering a dispositional continuance and what that might say about the way the <u>city is viewing</u> the case, the way the court's viewing the case and more specifically how they are viewing the client.

The probation officer explained how the offer to dismiss charges is qualitatively different from other court incentives and how these differences may play a role in its effect on recidivism, even years later (emphasis in original):

> And I think when someone walks in [MHC] and the city says, 'Well, a suspended sentence,' and it's just sort of 'business as usual' but when the city recommends a dispositional continuance, there's an underlying message there that says <u>we believe in this person, we believe in this client, we believe in this client's likelihood to succeed</u> and our reflection of our belief in the client is the offering a dispositional continuance.

On one hand, MHC team members might approach a case or a client differently, on the other hand, clients might be more motivated to alter their behavior because of the team's support and belief in their success. Both influences may be occurring simultaneously. The probation officer concluded by saying that the offer to dismiss charges "may create an additional <u>incentive</u>, besides just trying to keep [the charge] off the record. That is, someone believes in me and I want to do good by them, whether it's the court or the city" (emphasis added). This sentiment was echoed in how MHC client talked about their experiences in court. Several clients stated that the MHC team "believed in them" and that they wanted the court to be "proud of them" and "did not want to disappoint them." These comments reflect that relationships developed between MHC team members and MHC clients. Reflecting the closeness and respect, clients wanted to meet their high expectations. Clients summarized the influence of the MHC team—initially at a distance—"took the time to care about me," that they were "in it together," and that "the court and all the lawyers contributed to [graduation from MHC]. I did not do this by myself."

A few MHC team members did not believe that a dismissal offer changed how attorneys or judges worked with cases or defendants. However, a skeptic team member suggested that during court reviews "clients were reminded of their dispositional continuance" to encourage compliance and motivate the client. From my observations, the initial offer can shape incentives toward behavioral compliance and how defendants are perceived in the court.

Interestingly, in *City* MHC, there was large variation in the speculated rate of dismissals offered by team members, as well what the optimal number of dismissal offers. A probation officer characterized the court's offer to dismiss all charges as "rare" and did not see a downside to offering more dismissals, even proposing MHCs "[offer] them to all clients and see where that might lead." This probation officer followed by clarifying that the MHC could always revoke the offer if the client is non-compliant, but saw great potential in truly shifting the incentive structure of the court as a matter of practice. This opinion was clearly in opposition to a prosecutor who thought that the rate of dismissals was "about right" and that in "many cases you cannot justify it to the community" in terms of the severity of the offense or the threat to public safety. During an interview with a judge I asked about whether he would be more inclined to accept or even encourage offers to dismiss charges upon successful completion of the court given the statistical evidence presented in this chapter. He responded with a resounding "Yes!"

## Expanding Court Program Incentives

Giving a more generous offer at opt-in seems to incentivize behavioral compliance, suggesting a differential court experience that ultimately results in reduced recidivism. While incentives matter, especially in the early stage of court selection and opt-in, it is only one factor in the larger court program. Expanding court program incentives throughout the process is a next step to advance the goals of MHCs. In reference to graduation—the ultimate incentive—a defense attorney reflected, "I know the certificate at the end, that is pretty standard and acceptable, and a great moment for everybody." She also advocated for more rewards throughout the process. While continual participation is incentivized by highly contextualized responses to non-compliance, as illustrated in the previous chapter, there is room for extension and a favorable environment toward expanding incentives within much of the team.

MHCs also commonly incentivize participation by offering defendants exclusive resources, such as housing and treatment access, but multiple team members suggested that additional incentives might be even more important in times of limited court resources. A defense attorney talked about MHC "being a hard sell" for clients not facing a lot of jail time or for those who have to plea to the charge(s). The same attorney insinuated that incentives were a large part of the decision-making process: "We are not getting the things we need to make people's success more possible. I think it all goes back to the carrot or the stick," implying the court needs to offer more carrots.

Judges were also cognizant of the issue and were brainstorming on ways to expand the structure of incentives for clients to enter and succeed in MHC. A judge suggested that perhaps we could explicitly "give credit for individuals opting-in." Another judge offered the following insight about expanding "perks" given the "more rigorous process" of MHC:

> So we are talking about how we could increase some of the perks, lessening the jurisdiction. It is really difficult to determine what is the optimal time for an individual to be in mental health court? That is always an issue. The prosecutor typically wants two years,[8] so they want two years of jurisdiction, but an individual will opt-into mental health court. They are going to try it out for a while on mental health conditions of release and then they opt-in. So instead of the two years… we have suggested they might want to adjust, give credit for individuals opting-in.

The judge also suggested exploring other incentives to offer clients including "increasing dispositional continuances, stipulated order of continuance (SOC's).[9] There is a recognition that dismissal offers are not "true" diversion.[10] The defense wants me to lighten up on the abstain condition." He was not promoting all of these new incentives but was open to an open dialogue around incentives, especially in light of statistical evidence that they improve client outcomes.

Another judge was also more practical and direct about this issue, saying "I don't see any reason why we couldn't use true incentives—cash, gift cards, whatever. I've seen that used in specialty courts in a very low level." He went on to describe what a creative approach to incentive might look like in practice: "Everybody in compliance today gets to draw a ball and then we will pick a number and whoever matches gets a $25 gift card or whatever. That is just a way to say thank you." In addition to a gift card this judge saw few limits to what could be included, naming such possibilities as "medical treatment, dental treatment, medicine, job training, education, food…" He advocated for a client-specific set of incentives whereby the court expands the social services offered. Furthermore, this judge upheld a forward looking time horizon that included "in whole, short term and long term" not only at the beginning and then at the end for those that make it through. He, like other team members, suggested that clients need support and incentives throughout MHC.[11]

While a prosecutor advocated for more incentives throughout the court program, he also expressed caution:

> I think there is a place for vouchers, food vouchers and gas vouchers and transportation vouches. But again, it all has to come back with the integrity of the court. A lot of people think, well, why don't you do a fish bowl, where they go up and if they are in compliance they get to take something out of the fish bowl. But then there is this element of well, look at the types of cases that we are dealing with, and does that have integrity to the audience members and the people who there? What does a victim [feel], who maybe went through a devastating domestic violence case, and doesn't have access to the resources that he is getting in the court?

He called for an awareness of how incentives might be perceived, especially in the felony-drop down cases, by victims and court observers. Similarly, a defense attorney also wanted more incentives, but she was skeptical about how to do this well: "I think some of the rewards are so corny that people bring up. I don't know, I don't want to give someone a candy bar for doing something. I think that is just a little demeaning." She discussed the positive graduation certificate as an incentive but declared that there needs to "be something more" than the graduation ritual.

Offering a dismissal in *City* MHC may have some long-term implication on behavioral change in MHCs. It may also extend to other court contexts[12] and broader society. However, the different incentive structure in *County* MHC complicates the applicability of this incentive structure—dismissals—to the felony court context. While not offering a clean record, the incentives in *County* MHC are to reduce felony cases to misdemeanors. This "hybrid approach" is similar to the offer to dismiss charges in *City* MHC as it is, in effect, dismissing the felony charge and replacing it with a less-serious misdemeanor charge. In an interview, a probation officer explained the *County* incentives:

So the benefit of coming into our court [MHC] is you lose the felony, you don't have the felony conviction, you don't get points, you don't risk going to prison, and the most [prison time] you can get is one year, maybe two if they do two misdemeanors consecutive.

Several probation officers expressed concerns about the trend toward more felony dropdowns citing "dangerousness" and "fit" for MHC given its current mission. A judge declared, "the debate really happens on the felony side" given "public demands" to respond to the seriousness of the charges. Another MHC team member stated, "in many cases you cannot justify [a charge dismissal] to the community" because of the severity of the offense or the threat to public safety. A defense attorney articulated greater risk for felony cases:

> The potential for disaster is higher, because a trespasser, a criminal trespasser, if they reoffend, it is back to the doorway. If an assaultive stabber or whatever, reoffends, it is a high likelihood that it is a serious violent offense so the stakes are a little bit higher and we are looked at a little more closely.

These concerns about higher risk clients limit dismissal offers or charge reductions in felony cases.[13] This poses a challenge as this is where second generation MHCs are increasingly heading (taking felony charges) (Redlich et al. 2005). Recent reserach suggests there is real promise in the level of supervision seen in MHCs for defendants with felony charges, as evidenced by reduced recidivism among completers (Ray et al. 2015b), reduced risk of violence from clients (McNiel et al. 2015), and greatest reductions in criminal justice costs (Steadman et al. 2014). But complexities and tensions remain around the amount of incentives offered. Aside from incentives, the management of mental health issues is central for many clients in MHC.

## Mental Health Treatment

Alongside reductions in criminal recidivism, reductions in clinical symptoms or increases in treatment (access and usage) is a major outcome of MHCs (Griffin and DeMatteo 2009). Throughout the *City* MHC program, the shift toward non-crisis mental health treatment and overall management of mental illness is influential in reducing client re-arrest. Clients who received more non-crisis treatment during court (when compared to their non-crisis treatment before entering the court) have significantly lower odds—64%—of being charged with a new crime than those who received less non-crisis treatment during court.[14] The predicted probability of a client's first arrest after exiting MHC for those who received less non-crisis treatment[15] during MHC is 67% compared with 37% and 47% for the same non-crisis treatment during court and more non-crisis treatment respectively. A client's improved management of their mental health needs and compliance with a mandated treatment regimen during MHC is another marker of success. Improved management is often represented by a shift from one form of mental health contact to another (from crisis to non-crisis), toward preventative mental health treatment. This change signifies improved treatment engagement, which is central a goal of MHCs. However, even despite these improvements, mental health stability still poses a tremendous challenge for clients.

Proponents of a medical model of crime believe that part of the cause of criminal behavior is untreated mental health (Miller and Johnson 2009; Schneider et al. 2007), which is a foundational premise of MHCs (albeit, a controversial perspective; see discussion in Chapter 2). It is assumed that part of the underlying cause of criminal delinquency is addressed by the MHC program, which links clients with appropriate mental health treatment, and therefore successful MHC clients are expected to have lower rate of recidivism. For many team members, success was understood through the prism of treatment, directly related to the stabilization in managing one's mental illness. In speaking about the mission of MHC, one probation officer described it as:

> So, you know, the idea being that if you change something in their mental health treatment, either how much, whether they're taking meds or participating in treatment, and encourage them and sort of hold them accountable to do it, it will decrease their legal problems because the legal problems are tied to the mental illness.

He did acknowledge that it does not work out so simply in practice. While the application of the court's mission involves much more than mental health treatment, analysis reveal that individuals who increased their participation in preventative mental health treatment and reduced their unplanned, crisis treatment experienced reductions in recidivism.

Part of the effect of mental health stability on recidivism is that clients learn to accept and manage their mental illness while participating in MHC. Research suggests that MHCs may have clinical implications for the treatment of defendant's mental illnesses by increasing treatment referral, access to treatment in the community, and engagement (Keator et al. 2013; Boothroyd et al. 2003; Trupin and Richards 2003), as well as improving psychosocial functioning (Cosden et al. 2005). How clients experience the court process—especially perceptions of fairness—is related to reduced recidivism (Wales et al. 2010) and improved attitudes towards recovery (Kopelovich et al. 2013). Others suggest that the quality of services received need to be assessed to better identify if and how MHC's improve clinical status (Boothroyd et al. 2005).

Many team members expressed high hopes for what some of the clients can achieve, linking mental health treatment and taking medications to positive life changes. In his approach as a probation officer, he told clients that success is "only attainable if you are going to be continually following through with the regimen… The correlation between you taking your meds and not using drugs, to getting a job and having your family back." Another probation officer shared a story of success that centered on a client's "understanding her mental illness and medication." She entered *County* MHC on stalking charges. It was through the "tight structure… and balance of the therapeutic-ness of the court with the criminal court part" that led to her ultimate success from probation's perspective. The criminal part refers to the power of the court to sanction non-compliance (i.e., jail). In this case, the contact with probation even included daily medication monitoring in her probation officer's office. The MHC team "just kind of won [her over] and turned things around for her." Now she is regularly taking her medication, is a massage therapist and lives independently. She has "a really changed life," which is recognized by her mother who shared her gratitude: "You [probation officer] gave me my daughter back."

Even though the reduction in criminal behavior is notable for clients connected with scheduled mental health treatment, this often involves a mandatory pharmaceutical component, raising ethical concerns. To receive some of the benefits of improved mental health treatment—for individuals and society through lower rates of criminal offending—there is an expansion and deepening of the net. While coercive treatment and medication monitoring is a contentious issue in the literature and among some mental health advocates (Hughes and Peak 2013), it is routinely a part of opt-in recommendations. Most MHC team members suggested that this requirement was not problematic because the court is voluntary; clients who object to taking prescribed medications would choose not to opt-into MHC. Requiring MHC clients (and MHDT defendants) to take prescribed medications is also buttressed by public support, largely driven by fear and perceptions of dangerousness of mentally ill individuals (Pescosolido et al. 1999). While not minimizing concerns about coercion and mandated medication, mandatory treatment and possible medication may reflect part of the MHC tradeoff and explain dampened enthusiasm by some.

Aspects of the MHC program may be able to offset some coercion concerns such as social support embedded in relationships with team members. Clients who perceive the MHC to be coercive had diminished perceptions of recovery and perception of coercions were predictive of higher levels of criminal justice involvement a year later (Pratt et al. 2013). For example, MHC clients who perceived the MHC as fair (an element of procedural justice) had more favorable perceptions of recovery (Kopelovich et al. 2013) and were more positive about the court program (Munetz et al. 2014). The voluntary nature of MHCs might explain lower levels of perceived coercion. In an informal conversation with a client in *County* MHC, Marcus stated that he was glad he "chose" to do MHC, reflecting his agency. He declared, "I do not know where I would be without MHC!" Marcus mentioned the trouble with accepting his mental illness. As a young man, he assumed that his mental health symptoms were developmental and related to lifestyle issues (e.g., marijuana use), rather than mental illness.

Beyond its impact on recidivism, MHCs aim to connect clients with treatment, specifically mental health treatment. In addition to awareness of mental illness and changing habits about treatment since opting-into MHC, the social support of the team has been critical. Shima pronounced, "I am really grateful," as she listed off several team members by name including a probation officer and defense attorney. Her appreciation referred to assistance with treatment and providing social support. She went on to state, "I have never had anyone help me with my meds. I was out there homeless and on drugs. I appreciate the court offering me this chance to get my life together." Many clients offered genuine thanks and appreciation to the court at various points in the court process, much of which referenced the MHC team's social support system assisting with mental health management.

Predictions of long-term behavioral changes around mental health management are complex. A court liaison described the challenge: "You can't force somebody to take medications. They can be with us for two years, and dubbed a success story. As soon as they are done with probation, they can stop taking their medications. You can't force somebody to do that, they are free and human." The same challenge pervades substance use. In practice, the management of mental health treatment in MHC often includes chemical dependency treatment. From the quantitative analysis it is not clear how mental health management interacts with sobriety because the data set does not include measures of chemical dependency. However court observations and interviews show that MHCs need to actively manage clients with co-occurring issues.

Succeeding in MHC and staying clear of the criminal justice system in the future is not simply about managing mental health treatment or taking prescribed medications and some argue that link is weak (Fisler 2015; Steadman et al. 2011). It may be factors such as housing and social support, primarily or in combination with treatment, that lead to reductions in criminal recidivism as suggested by the qualitative data. In addition to mental health treatment and insight into mental illness, the structure and support that the program and team offer often culminates into completion of the MHC program.

## Graduation[16]

Graduating from MHC is itself an achievement. At the completion of the court, the positive effects of the graduation ritual and all it represents carries over to clients' lives. Completing MHC reduces the likelihood of being charged with a new crime. Those who completed MHC reduce their odds of being charged with a new crime by 66%, when compared to those who did not successfully complete the court. The predicted probability of experiencing a first arrest for those who completed MHC is 36% (or 62% for individuals who did not completed MHC). Completing MHC reduces the likelihood of first arrest by 26%. Growing research specifically highlights the importance of completing and graduating from MHC in reducing reoffending rates (Burns et al. 2013; Hiday and Ray 2010; McNiel and Binder 2007; Moore and Hiday 2006; Ray 2014). Based on *City* MHC data, fewer or no prior arrests is the strongest factor associated with graduating from MHC. In addition, being white, younger and female also increased the odds of graduation.

Court completion and graduating from MHC is an important ritual and marks success in the court program. A successful graduation is a culmination of hard work on the part of the client and a dedicated team. Treatment management and compliance are critical to graduating from MHC. The final court appearance for clients showcase what it means to succeed in MHC. Even a defense social work and unyielding critic of MHC reflected on graduations and the success of many participants as "gratifying."

During a graduation ritual, a client receives a certificate, the judge comes down from bench and shakes the client's hand—a noticeable reduction of physical and social distance—and then the audience applauds. The importance of the physical movement of the judge from an elevated status position from the upper bench to the physical level of the client cannot be overstated. Often clients hug MHC team members, who offer words of praise to the client. Clients are also often joined by family, friends, case managers and others to witness the event. Sometimes clients capture the moment with a photograph. Consider one such graduation in *City* MHC:

*Judge*: It [the case] is coming to a close.
*Probation*: He has been in compliance. He has had some ups and downs… He's been a pleasure to work with. We will *not* see him back in court.
*Prosecution*: Dismiss charges. Congratulations!
*Defense*: Congratulations!
*Judge*: I am happy to hear all of the positive comments.

*Client*: Thank you... It really did get me into shape. I have done everything that I can do to make sure those things do not happen again. This [the court] has kept me going in a good direction. In the beginning I did not want to do this [MHC] but as time went along it was clear that it was helping me. Thank you.
*Probation*: Congratulations! (presents certificate)
*Client*: Thanks to everybody. I thought it was corny [when others got a certificate] but now it feels really good. I will be seeing you... No I won't! (laughter) But if I see you on the street I will say "Hi." Thanks.

Stating that he will say "hi" if anyone from the court sees him on the street is an acknowledgment of all that the client has achieved; he is now a regular member of society, unburdened by stigma. The client is suggesting that MHC team members do not need to look away in embarrassment—nor does the client need to look away in shame—if they see each other in public. He is now a restored citizen, with the rights, responsibilities and, importantly, status which that implies. Graduation also reduces the social distance and status differences between the client and the professional staff symbolized by the handshakes, hugs, and ritual displays of affection.

All clients I interviewed spoke positively about the graduation ritual, expect one (see Chapter 7 for Vicki's story). For some it was very emotional, as in the case of Monique and Shima. The success of Monique's journey through MHC is well described in her graduation ritual (as briefly described in the introduction). The full court dialogue around her graduation showcases the emotions and reintegration underneath this climatic closure.

*Probation*: I am pretty excited today! Monique is in full compliance. I am requesting that the charges be dropped. She has been in court for two years. I took over her case from another probation officer and we established a good working relationship. In her time in the court she had a record of doing very well and then earlier this year she did some experimentation of what it might be like without her meds

|  |  |
|---|---|
|  | and it did not go how she expected. But she got back on track. Since that time she has been newly committed to sobriety and treatment. She has acquired some skills along the way. I am really pleased with her progress and have enjoyed working with her. She should be really proud of her accomplishments. |
| *Prosecutor*: | The City is also very pleased. It's quite an accomplishment. The City is happy to dismiss the two charges. The City wishes her the best of luck. |
| *Defense*: | I am so happy for Monique. I have been working with her for two years. There were some hiccups along the way but she never said, 'I want to throw in the towel.' She always stayed committed. She's ending on a high note. She knows what she needs to do to <u>not</u> see her here again. I could not be more happy for her. (emphasis in original) |
| *Judge*: | I want to congratulate you. I know it has been hard. You persevered through the difficulties and you continued on. The Court is happy! Now I think you know that you are going to get a certificate today. [He reads the certificate]. |

The judge then stepped down from the bench to shake Monique's hand and congratulate her, while Monique held up her certificate exclaiming, "It makes it official!" Everyone laughed and then clapped. As she exited the court I heard the probation officer say, "You are always welcome back but *never* come back!" (emphasis in original). This ritual was so powerful because everyone was focused on the conversation— even those in the audience waiting for their case to be heard. There was no "texting" or milling around which is too often the case in MHC.

Shima also expressed lots of emotion—happiness and appreciation— around her graduation from both *County* and *City* MHCs. She detailed her first graduation from *County* MHC:

> It was very tearful, because at that time I believed that someone actually took the time to care for me... I know they cared about other clients, but they went out, I believe, out of the way to make sure that I was going to be okay. The graduation was very tearful. I really wasn't able to speak that much. Judge [name] made her speech – 'it is wonderful to finally see you

get out of here.' She said something really kind, and the prosecutor even said, 'We really want the best for you and we are so happy to see you finally graduate'... and then they asked me if I wanted to speak, and I could not. The tears would not stop. I still get kind of emotional about that graduation, because it felt – there were clients there, there were other people. It wasn't just me in that courtroom. They were telling them, 'See this is an example, you all sitting there, you can do this.' As soon as I graduated and I knew I was free.

Her account underscores the power behind this positive emotional event. Reflecting on her graduation in *City* MHC, she stated similarly that, "It was good … It went well, they care for you. They want to make sure you are graduating because you have earned it. You have done it and now it is time for you to leave. You are not in my court and don't ever come back ever." In court as she graduated the judge stated "We want the best for you. We are so happy to see you graduate!" The prosecutor echoed the same congratulations and added "I'm so proud of you!"

For others, like Jennifer, graduation gave her a sense of closure and symbolized moving on. Jennifer stated, "When I finished with mental health court, I feel like shedding part of my past and moving forward." For her it represented the start of a new stage in her life. As I was witnessing her graduation she expressed happiness and a sense of relief as her entanglements with the court had come to a successful end. Although no tears were shed, there was emotional energy on her part and in the courtroom.

It was not only the female clients who expressed emotions about their graduation from MHC (although women did more freely express emotions in interviews). A male client shared similar sentiments during an interview as he reflected on his graduation. Robert, a less expressive and talkative client, concisely stated that his graduation was "great" and "made me feel good." With a smile on his face, he reflected on the role of the judge and excitedly shared that everyone, "the whole gang was in on it." He concluded, "It is uplifting. I've never been through nothing like that… I never accomplished nothing like that before."

A similar level of excitement and emotional energy was seen in other cases. Here is an example of a client and her final day in court:

*Judge*: I see a big smile on your face today. This is going to be the last time you are here.
*Client*: I hope so!
*Probation*: [Name of client] has maintained full compliance. She has really done well. She is graduating early to accommodate the start of the school for her son. She's done really well, particularly the last 6 months. There was a medication change. She's jelling with her therapist. She agrees to continue to see her [therapist] even though not under the mandate from the court. It has been a pleasure to work with her. To see her growth and development. She's always been in compliance. There is clarity in her thinking and her judgements. She is setting goals and making great progress. I'm hoping that she will get in contact with us later to tell us show she is doing. She has an inspiring arch.

The judge asked if she wanted to say anything. She addressed the court with a simple statement, "I wanted to say thank you." The judge responded, "It was a pretty easy case for a judge. You made it easy. That was the hard work of yourself. This is one of the reasons I like this court." The judge came off the bench and awarded her the certificate and everyone clapped and she hugged her probation officer. It was an even more emotional scene than normal with the usual clapping intensified by the presence of her six-year old son in the audience.

Member of the MHC team and clients saw the graduation ritual in similar ways. A probation officer, recalling a graduation of a client who worked primarily with another probation officer, described the powerful experience:

I walked up to him, shook his hand and told him 'congratulations and that [name of regular probation officer] was proud of him.' He goes, 'Man, never did I think I would shake the judge's hand. They came up to me, they got off the bench, and they approached me' and they said, 'Good job, I'm proud of you,' and shook my hand. It was a completely different experience that this guy has ever had in a court.

MHC team members view graduations as so important that a court liaison suggested having one day a month set aside where all the graduations occurred to really emphasize the accomplishments and enhance the ritual.

These graduations are not isolated incidents nor spontaneous celebrations but rather planned rituals with specific social functions. Graduation ceremonies showcase emotional energy and a collective experience. They emphasize the social relationships that were created and, in some cases, will be missed.

After graduation, clients are not tethered to MHC anymore, nor accountable at various review hearings and mandatory meetings with probation officers, treatment providers and case managers. Many clients realized the need to stay on the treatment planas laid out by the court but now they will need to choose to do so without the structure and support of the court. For some, housing might stipulate certain aspects such as sobriety, but the majority of clients are now largely on their own. The data show that MHC completers do recidivate less. In *County* MHC a judge described "a tremendous success rate" touting a 75% graduation rate as a marker of success.[17]

## Structure and Social Support

The support and structure of MHCs are the two features that are central to reduced recidivism and are connected to incentives, mental health treatment, and court completion. In addition to assistance with treatment, team members provide social and emotional support, financial resources (i.e., connecting clients with benefits) and access to housing. The court structure provides a framework to offer support and accountability to incentivize compliance.

Almost all team members and clients mentioned structure and support when discussing success in MHC. Some examples of success were particularly dramatic and were more about support and stability than a lack of criminal justice involvement. Take, for example, a "favorite success in our court" imprinted in the memory of a defense attorney. She described the client as being in a "deep depression" with debilitating consequences. At times, he simply could not leave his apartment but then "something about treatment had changed at some point. All of a sudden, I saw him smile for the first time." This has been after meeting with him for more than a year. By the end of court she recounted "He re-engaged in a relationship with his dad… He had rebuilt a relationship with his family. He was willing to leave his apartment. He was going to be able to keep that housing for a long time." While these transformations are possible, they are often only realized in part; they hinge upon the team support and structure of the court.

For a probation officer, it was the contrast for clients from the outside world with its limited structure to the supportive structure of MHC that made a difference, especially those with misdemeanor charges. But he offered caution beyond the probationary period in MHC.

> [Those] who have struggled mightily with whether it is conforming to rules and regulations of society, whether it is not following through with medical regimens and medication regimens, my perspective is that you do this, you see these benefits, and hopefully it is going to change and alter your behavior down the road to where you don't need mental health court telling you that you need to do these things. You are going to start seeing the benefits of changing your behavior and changing your lifestyle to where ultimately you can live independently without the structure that you have become so dependent on.

To improve the chances for long-term behavioral change among clients, the program has to provide structure and social support and ways to translate them into the real world once a client is out of MHC such as seeking help before things spiral downwards). A court liaison suggested that when the team is working well, finding collaboration amidst difference benefits the clients, "On the cases where probation and liaisons and the prosecution and defense all see together, those are the situations where people benefit the most. If we could have a team that truly does act like that all the time that would be best."

In response to my question about what constitutes success, one probation officer realistically shared that "unfortunately the court has a lot of variables attached to it." He stated, "everybody in the court has a role in success." But it is clear from court data and interviews that probation officers represent a "key role," a point expressed by many probation officers and a majority of clients. This may not be surprising given the frequency of contact between clients and probation officers. Self-described as being "really in the trenches," probation officers work reactively and pro-actively: "We can either catch something before it starts" and then alert case managers "keeping the court apprised of what's going on" or react to alarm bells from case managers. MHC team members, especially probation officers, are confident in their expertise and felt that they "know a whole lot about what was going to have them be successful, what kind of needs they had."

A prosecutor argued that the "tools and resources" offered to MHC clients, as opposed to other parts of the criminal justice system, accounts for the reduction in recidivism. In fact, this prosecutor reviews how a client did in the court, whether it was good or bad, and then makes the following speech at every graduation:

> I hope you continue on – something personal about what is going on with them and we don't ever want to see you back here again, unless you are visiting or you are a juror. They all laugh. I say, 'I am serious, that is the goal.' We invest two years of resources, time, court, money, funds, to their lives, and those who really take advantage of it, I think are successful.

When detailing some success stories of clients with bipolar disorder, a court liaison stated that they "consistently do the best." In his account, prior to entering MHC "they had no support, they had no structure, they had no family, they had no reason to stay clean, and just giving them a bit of a push and setting them up with a little bit of things helps." After time in MHC, "They stay on their meds. They have structure. They have somewhere to stay. They are not using drugs anymore and that's what they need."

A probation officer reminds clients, especially those in recovery, that MHC and sobriety is a long-term commitment and patience is tantamount. He offered an example of how he talks to clients:

> 'Look, you know, you're 45 years old, it took you 40 years to get this fucked up, there is no way that you're going to get fixed in 40 days, it might take more than 40 months, you have to be patient with the process. Things do not get fixed overnight.' And that patience is incredibly difficult. Um, you get frustrated, you know, you've been an alcoholic for 20 years and you get sober and you've been sober for three months, yet, your whole life hasn't changed, you're not suddenly working and driving a car and having an apartment and connecting with your family, but you do what you thought you were supposed to do, you got sober, so where's the good stuff? When's it coming? It's like, 'Look, man, you've got to have patience, please be patient, just stick with it, hang in there.'

Supporting clients also means helping them to be patient with themselves and the process.

In MHCs, there was an effort to acknowledge the presence and role of family members in the client's life and court process and in some cases hear from them directly. Sometimes the social support structure provided by MHC team members verged on a pseudo family, especially in cases with minimal family presence. In Braithwaite's (1989) work on reintegrative shaming he refers to the family model, specifically parents, but his insights can be applied to the team model in MHCs. Take, for example, a probation officer's description:

> It's like some people kind of get adopted by the whole team... And I think they know we like to see them, and that's why [name] the front-desk person knows him, yeah. I try and remember those people.

In describing relationships with probation, clients made a family analogy. Robert said that his probation officer was central to his success: "He was like a brother to me. He saw hope in me." This account was mirrored and expanded upon by Shima:

I know all the girls up there at the receptionist's desk. Sometimes I felt that we were more than acquaintances. I went out and bought them earrings, little treats, and I knew they liked chocolate. The ladies [at the front desk at probation] were always kind. I can't remember the names – that is not a big deal, but they went out of their way to care for me and talk to me and make sure that I was okay... I felt like it was kind of a family. That is what I told my therapist – 'I feel like they are family, because they took the time to ask me how I was and [name of probation officer] could call my bullshit... that is when I knew that I needed to be honest when I did relapse, even though I knew I wasn't going to have a UA [urine analysis] done. I had to tell them.'

Shima called the team members a "kind of family." Given her life experiences and lack of social support and stability, this was, not surprisingly, necessary for her success. Clients who referred to team members with family metaphors were those with limited external family support. For Shima, building these relationships was related to compliance. She often talked about "tough love" and went so far as to characterize her most recent probation officer as "like a brother to me." She went on to state, "He could have sent me to jail for the time that I messed up, but he saw some hope in me." Before entering *City* MHC, Shima also spent some time in *County* MHC and reflected on her relationship with probation in that court: "I was able to talk to [probation officer], even though at that time I had my therapist. It was nice because I know she was going to keep me out of trouble, but it was my responsibility to do it." She summarized the team support structure and how it influenced her experience in *City* MHC, "I actually was very grateful for him, as a probation officer... He was awesome. He worked so hard for me."

While others did not use the language of family or kinship, the level of social support they received from the MHC team, especially probation, emulates familial expectations. In the case of Shima she recounted that it was more than just housing that helped her be successful:

They were there. I knew I could pick up the phone and go... 'Hey, I need to see you. I know you have other clients,' and they would open up their

## 5 Reducing Recidivism and Pathways to Success

door and say, 'Listen, just come in. If you feel like drinking, you need to come in and see us, or go see you therapist.'

For some clients these emotional commitments were sometimes counterproductive. Some clients talked about not wanting to let team members down with their non-compliant behavior. For example, Jennifer told me that "I didn't want to disappoint people. When I got that second charge, I felt like I disappointed them, and it made me feel like a bad person, bad girl."

There is a danger in falling into paternalism which can be counterproductive. In a few cases, I observed judges who were overly critical and personally judgmental, which can spoil a positive ritual. For instance, the following exchange was rare but highlights the damaging, heavy-handed approach judges can sometimes take. In this case, the judge used a hostile and stigmatizing and tone in admonishing the client personally:

*Judge*: Why are you hanging around with him? I do not think he is good for you.
*Client*: I don't think that my boyfriend choice is a legal issue.
*Judge*: Well I am just suggesting that you be more careful about who you choose to spend time with for the sake of your recovery and stability.

Following this exchange, the client was clearly offended by the line of questioning and the judge's argumentative and shameful tone reminiscent of reintegrative shaming (Braithwaite 1989). It is often a fine line between providing supportive advice and insulting paternalism. Although the judge tried to reframe the comment in terms of compliance issues and success in the court program, it fell flat and seemed insincere. The paternalistic tone reinforced stigma and shame. Clients in the court and team members were obviously uncomfortable afterward by this affront to therapeutic justice.

For clients with strong ties to the MHC team, once they are no longer in MHC they struggle to re-create or replace the social support and structured accountability outside of the court. As the courts are focused on what happens while clients are in MHC this is a concern but not a priority. Even though MHCs are currently under-resourced, investment in graduates might enhance long-term success.

## Liminal Stage

MHC represents a transitional stage for some clients, making it difficult to move on to the next phase of their lives. Time spent under court supervision, often about two years, dragged on for some clients, making it hard for them to fully prepare for life after court. Shima explained that her two years in *City* MHC "felt like, to be honest with you, four years, and actually it really wasn't." For Robert, this was acute with the threat of jail looming making MHC ever-present in his everyday life:

> Just knowing that to have that time hanging over your head… It is not too good of a feeling, because you can get into jail at any time if you mess up… Yeah, I just wanted time to hurry up and pass, and get off this. I thought it would never go by, though. Man, the first year it was kind of slow, but it wasn't nothing compared to the second year. The second year was slow.

This was also true for Jennifer, who said, "I think of it more as a stage." For her, the time in MHC coincided with a different phase of her life, one that she is trying to leave behind. It held a symbolic power. While she was trying to move on it was hard when entangled with the court and its requirements. Upon graduating Jennifer reflected, "I feel like shedding part of my past and moving forward." Although she worked hard not to let the court and its obligations control her life, "I'm just trying to live my life and give it the attention it deserves but my life doesn't revolve around that, really." Although but she did reflect that it was difficult to be fully independent with court obligations.

Monique offered a clear account of how hard it is to achieve a functional status, such as employee, while in MHC. She stated that it would be hard to manage work with the many court obligations:

> Your life outside is on hold [when in MHC]… It kept me busy for two years… I didn't really try to get a job or do anything much when I was on probation, because I had treatment two times a week, and then probation three times a week, and then court. Then I had medical appointments I needed to make and then I had a lot of stuff to do… I was spending a lot of time at the bus stop, waiting on a bus.

A bus analogy is fitting, as clients often shared that they were trying to get to a new destination (e.g., permanent housing, sobriety, mental health stability) but that the process was slow and not direct, involving lots of waiting time and delays. The circuitous path that clients often take reflects the challenges in mental health management amidst limited resources and general instability.

It is not enough to have MHC be a part of clients' daily thoughts to keep them in compliance. It is probably a necessary, but not a sufficient condition, for court success. This was clear in the case of Monique, who said, "I had my PO [probation officer] and my UA's at the forefront of my mind. I had to keep that in mind all the time." Even though MHC obligations were always on her mind, Monique told me "I did use again and got in trouble and went right back into the court system." There is a balance between managing court commitments and making behavioral changes to avoid criminal entanglements. Many clients are successful despite these challenges, while others experience multiple setbacks.

## Broadening the Idea of Success

Complete criminal desistance is a desirable outcome, but it is not the only way to measure MHC efficacy and maybe unrealistic with this population. If we rely only on one rubric, such as criminal recidivism, we will not capture all the ways that MHC might be successful. Even within criminal recidivism we might need to broaden our notion of success to include when a former client commits fewer crimes, or less serious crimes, of if there's a longer duration between violations. Underneath changes in recidivism patterns are other forms of behavioral change, some of which can be understood as successful outcomes, even if they are not coupled with recidivism. Broadly speaking, social welfare and wellbeing are useful measure of success (Johnston 2012).

Success is relative even in the case of criminal recidivism. A defense attorney clarified that recidivism needs to be framed in comparative terms, "do people commit new crimes when they are in the court—all the time, but less so, I would say than if they had nothing and they were just, OK, you're done, see you later." A probation officer offered a similar account of success: "We can recognize the successes as being, maybe they are not out robbing somebody, but they have a dirty UA. That to me is a move in the right direction. They may not be living with their family, they may be estranged from their kids, but they are not homeless. They are in clean and sober housing." Even a judge espousing a "more nuanced approach" highlighted the relativity of recidivism, "we look at …how long it was before we see someone come back into court."

Success in MHCs is complicated. As opposed to a binary understanding of success and failure, success is best understood on a continuum. The idea is that "you should help people be in a better position than they were when they came in [to MHC]" suggested a prosecutor. Part of the challenge in evaluating success or failure of MHCs, and problem-solving courts more generally, is the complex needs of clients. Multiple probation officers explicitly alluded to the grayness in understanding success: "the court is also learning that successes are not always black and white." Success means different things for different people and is relative to where clients were and where they are now. In many ways MHCs' continuum of success is antithetical the rest of the criminal justice system which has clearer boundaries, guidelines, and outcomes.

Focusing on recidivism, a judge suggested that even small amounts of time away from the criminal justice system reflects some level of success. He summarized with this client account:

> When you think about the person who is on the street, using every day, and mentally ill, and now they are coming in court, and for three months we've maintained sobriety and maintained coming to court. Then maybe they use and maybe they reoffend, but we had three months of sobriety

and no involvement with law enforcement. So for three months the community was better off than it was before... That is a marker of some measure of stability. Then we've gotten some stability in the community. It is not forever, but it is something.

This judge made a distinction between "aspirational" and "intermediary" goals and the need to measure and celebrate the "intermediary steps."

For some team members, altered criminal behavior or reduced contact with the criminal justice system was not central to their definition of success—but in fact even tangential—to other important life changes, such as housing for a formerly homeless client. A judge detailed a similar view:

> We want this person to be better, not only just sort of altruistically – I am a person and I want to see people do better in their lives – but also from a systemic point of view, if they are doing better, they are not committing new crimes. They are not creating victims, causing resource drains... On all side, it is we just want to help them get better, it will help everybody.

These factors may be obvious, but achieving them and reducing reoffending trends is a real challenge—one that some MHC clients do indeed achieve, but many fall short of.

Success can be measured in terms of individualized progress in line with a treatment orientation. All team members talked about measuring success "on an individual basis" or "individualized success." It is important to recognize where clients are starting from to fully capture their success trajectory. A probation officer detailed this "roller coaster" perspective:

> Most of the time we don't get them to the top of the mountain... So a lot of times we don't see them get all the way up there, but, you know sometimes we do. You know, like I've had lots of clients that when we started working with them, it's just... I mean this sounds cliched, they were homeless, they were not on meds, they were psychotic, and, they had nothing. And now they've got housing, and now they

show up for their appointments, and now they um, you know, they are getting their GED. Or they've got a part-time job or a full-time job. Sometimes they get there and they fall back down the mountain a little bit. Because, nothing, very rarely do we grow, and we just keep growing and growing and growing, right? I mean, we have our setbacks, and especially with mental illness... I've seen, it's a lot of a rollercoaster. As long as we're kind of climbing back up to the top again, you know. Of course you gotta go to the bottom to climb back up to the top, and so, sometimes, we get to ride the full ride, we do all the ups and downs.

Success for some clients was different from success for other clients. As another probation officer explained, MHC is centered on the clients themselves and their ability to engage: "I think it definitely gives people the avenue and the opportunity to be a success, to get what they need in structure and treatment... It will work if the client wants it to work." In a similar reference to the court being inherently individualized, a defense attorney stated that is why the court is successful, referencing a specific case: "the court catered his plan to exactly what this guy could accomplish, and it was a success."

While team members were positive and hopeful, they also unmistakably understood the complexity of evaluating success. A harm-reduction orientation influenced notions of success, with team members holding this perspective as less rigid and more optimistic about success in MHC. Take the following account by a judge as an illustration of successful client outcomes:

> Put on your mental health hat, and realize that 100 percent compliance is really not the goal here. Them showing up, them going to their medication appointments, then maybe having a dirty UA for alcohol but three clean UA's throughout the month, that's success. So I think they play a really big role in how they perceive and treat the people that they are seeing.

Taking a similar approach, a defense attorney reiterated that MHC is not about checking boxes: "[A client] didn't attend every case management meeting. That isn't success to me. That is where we are all about checking boxes, but that's not—you can't do that with mental health, you can't. His success was about engaging with treatment and rebuilding social relationships." Similarly, a court liaison focused on stability:

> I do think reduction of recidivism is one of those ways to measure it [success], but also is there increased stability. If they do have more episodes, are they shorter in length? Are they able to start naming and using coping skills? The same ways you would measure is someone progressing in treatment. That is the same way you would measure is somebody progressing in this court. People, like I said, we are dealing with chronic bad choice makers. Are they making <u>fewer</u> bad choices? (emphasis added)

For many clients whether the court was successful was relatively straightforward. In response to a simple question of whether their lives are better because of experiences in MHC, all but one client said yes, some resoundingly. Clients recognized the multifaceted aspects of MHC, noting that it is the whole system that makes it work. In response to a question about whether they could improve the court process or features Robert responded, "No, they got a pretty good system down there." Although many clients were positive about the court structure and support, offering few if any recommendations for improvement, there are some clear limitations to what MHCs can do.

## Success Within Limits

Team members who work within the court system know the imperfect picture of success. Recognizing the structural limits, a prosecutor aptly stated, "We have a lot of huge success stories and some failures, too, but I think that is [true] in any system." Several features of the court— availability of resources and team functionality—influence client success. Some of the limits, as stated by a probation officer, are directly related to the court itself, such as the supportive structure making clients too dependent:

We see it all the time, sabotaging – getting ready to get off mental health care, there are charges, they go on warrant, they get picked up. It is, you did so well for so long, and it is no different from somebody who is institutionalized. They don't know how to live without the structure.

For clients who are higher functioning (higher level of organization) and have more social and fiscal resources, the demands of MHC were not onerous but for others they proved intense and in some case too difficult. In thinking about who the court works best for and which groups are less successful, a probation officer clearly stated that those who are "super personality disordered people" and another probation referred to as "drugs primary" are not the best "fit" for the court.

Alignment between a client's mental illness diagnosis and the mandated treatment is important. A court liaison articulated this point,

> I would say that the most successful ones who have been brought into the court are the ones who do fit the standard criteria, because, again, they have an actual mental illness that is driving this, as opposed to an Axis II. You have to treat that very differently. The treatment programs that we recommend to 99 percent of the time are not built for Axis II.[18]

This position was reflected by others, including a prosecutor who referred to a situation "when someone's behavior is really just criminal and not related to their mental illness." While the court is expanding its criteria—even if informally—to include a broader range of mental illness, the treatment programs need to be adjusted to align with eligibility modifications. To see further reductions in criminal recidivism research suggests that mental health treatment needs to target impulsivity and other common criminogenic needs (Peterson et al. 2010).

Other team members were less forgiving in their understanding of success, placing the responsibility directly on the clients. For long-term behavior change an assertion of agency—abandoning previous "feelings of helplessness or hopelessness" in the words of a probation officer—is crucial and clients have to do their part. Even believers of the court model such as a court liaison stated bluntly, "Some people can't be helped." Another court liaison proclaimed, "Mental health court, for me, is we are going to provide you access to the things you need.If you use them, you will do better, you will actually have a chance. If you decide not to use them, you will be in jail."

Many team members held an optimistic view and saw how successful clients reduced the burden on society leading to reductions in criminal justice costs as well as corollary reductions in other arenas such as hospital and emergency room visits. Research suggests that some problem-solving court models reduce costs, especially those taking felony charges (Steadman et al. 2014). A judge thought that part of MHC success is about reduction in fiscal and social costs. He promoted a "social justice standpoint"—accessing social services—as opposed to a normal "criminal justice standpoint" that relied almost exclusively on criminal recidivism.

Even those in *County* MHC who were more critical of the courts shifting mission, the team dynamics, and questions about costs, were still positive. A probation officer stated, "Yes, it has been successful for some, and they are the people who have actually been able to find the right treatment modality for, the people who got plugged into something that finally clicked for them." Another team member commented:

> Yeah, absolutely, I think it is a really great program. I think we do have some flaws, and probably do get an amount of cases that maybe are not appropriate for mental health court. But it is very difficult, also, to tell from the beginning what is going to be successful and what isn't.

Team members raised serious concerns limiting the courts ability to be more successful, including drifting away from the initial mission, judicial leadership, costs and client attitudes and behaviors associated with the MHC program. Despite these real concerns, they all expressed great hope in the possibilities of MHC when done well. In fact, those who do not believe in the mission of MHC rotate out of the court quickly; team members who remain are those that believe in the court's mission and are hopeful of successful outcomes in line with therapeutic justice.

## "Frequent Flyers"

Despite efforts to halt or least slow down the "revolving door" of criminal justice, MHC are beset by a similar trend as the broader criminal justice system: repeat offenders. Certainly there are "frequent flyers"—an oft-repeated phrase about individuals who repeatedly return to the criminal justice system—in MHC—such as the case of Shima and Norm. A probation officer remarked,

> [Those] who are mentally ill but have such a bad… you know, crack problem, and they just don't… they just don't quite have, they're not at the point where they could participate and be successful. And so, rather than trying again, usually we've tried with them, we stop trying and try to work out the most simple deals we can.

Not all team members saw repeat clients so negatively. For instance, a defense attorney supported multiple chances as therapeutic outcomes take time: "we have clients who have gotten their third and fourth chances, and it has been on that third or fourth chance that it all clicked."

Many who recidivate and end up back in MHC are those with co-occurring disorders. Multiple cases in MHC by some clients raise questions about its effectiveness. As a probation officer jokingly told me, "some clients need MHC for life." The intent was not meant to be punitive but reminiscent of the lack of structure and support once a client graduated or exited MHC. Another probation officer clarified why this is the case: "there are some people we talked about how they need probation for life, just in the sense that the structure really helps them, and they like it." While this argument is untenable and would unlawfully deepen the net, it underscores a crucial limitation of MHCs given the larger deficits in the mental health system and social safety net. Repeat clients continue to come into MHC with each new criminal charge due to the flagging system and their mental illness. "We have had people graduate and be successful and found out a year later that they hadn't been taking their meds for the last three months. Oh, because they were people who were able to make it look like they had it altogether" stated a defense attorney. In a few rare cases, MHC clients (or MHDT defendants) make headlines and the entire court program innovation comes under scrutiny.

## Worst-Case Scenarios

MHCs cannot prevent worst-case scenarios as far as the public understands it: a person with severe mental illness, often off their medication or otherwise disconnected from treatment, who kills someone, often at random, and because of access to deadly weapons. Ironically, while some MHCs around the country emerged in response to a dreadful event, MHCs cannot prevent these crimes from happening. The rarity of such tragic events makes them a less meaningful focus of court programming. All team members, especially probation officers, emphatically stated "No" in response to my question about whether MHCs could in fact prevent such worst-case scenarios. Of course, the counter factual scenario cannot be assessed—there may have been individuals who would have committed serious crimes if not for the accountability and support of the court. As a probation officer put it, "So you're talking about trying to measure the absence of something, you know what I mean? And it's really difficult… But, maybe that week in jail [as a sanction or revocation] prevented something else… prevented [name of client] from killing that guy downtown." What is known is there are individual who, despite having been connected with MHCs, have committed serious acts of violence. While this is far from a normal occurrence, it is a clear limit to MHCs' ability to curb crime. How many tragic events did not occur is unknowable as described a defense attorney: "It is hard to say [if MHC's prevent worst-case scenarios] because maybe some of the people who have come through and been successful, having not done that, would have been on the front page."

There is a real fear by some team members to offer MHC to individuals with serious criminal histories who are deemed dangerous. A defense attorney suggested that if we "let them into the court in the first place. They have only been here for a month, so why are we just going to pull the plug [and revoke]?" suggesting that a longer investment by the team is needed for clients that opt-into MHC. This tension often leads to a short stay in MHC based on early non-compliance and strong negative sanctioning. A defense attorney expressed the weightiness of such cases: "if they do drugs again, they are going to go and kill somebody, so revoke." Contrarily, another defense attorney asserted that the team needs to give the defendant a chance to make it work as "these are the people that need the help the most. This is what the court is designed for, not the people that are minimal risks, that are less likely to commit more crimes." Her position, echoed by others and vehemently opposed by some, was that if the courts want to have a great effect, then accepting clients who pose a greater risk is inescapable.

The uncertainty, described as "hit and miss" by a judge, suggests that it is hard to ascertain which cases will end in disaster. "You give it your best shot" and "consider everything that has been given to me" noted a judge wishing for more assurances. A judge suggested that the "number one item" why judges do not want to preside over MHC was fear—"somebody from the court is going to take a life and I'm [judge] to blame." Recognizing that there are no easy answers and that sometimes there are "spectacular failures… when they [clients] have committed a higher-level crime… every step forward we are making a positive impact" stated a judge. We have to "move the ball forward" he concluded. Another judge echoed the "complicated balancing… of public safety issues,"and political impact as judges are "worried about… having their name on the front page [of the newspaper]."

Prosecutors were aware of public concerns about safety too. They often referenced them in court hearings. A prosecutor stated that the court's ability to avoid worst-case scenarios is "unknowable," but she was optimistic in her assessment:

> We have had horrific offenders be successful. We have had offenders kill people when they have gotten out of mental health court, so we can only control so much. We can't keep them on supervision for the rest of their lives. I wish we could, but I feel like if everybody on our team makes the best effort that they can, we have a chance to make a difference in those dangerous cases.

A probation officer specifically cited the lack of public awareness about MHCs and criminal behavior, as well as frenzied media coverage. In thinking about court effectiveness, he also warned not to "correlate them [clients] being on probation to not committing crimes."

While probation officers and the sanctions ordered by the court may be able intervene in criminal pathways, a client can be "totally compliant right in front of my face, walk out this door, get high, get behind a car and kill somebody... We are not in control of their behaviors."[19] Interestingly MHC team members referenced drug use and relapses as the critical intervening variable to dangerous behavior and did not directly associate mental illness with violence. Despite the potential for such rare events, team members were more optimistic and personally understood their position on the team in altering client trajectories, in the words of a prosecutor "you have the possibility of changing an individual's life."

In addition to reducing criminal reoffending, as illustrated by *City* MHC data and buttressed by other research studies across the country I find that these courts do much more to help clients succeed, but with notable constraints. Many team members stated that society is asking the courts to do something they cannot; there is a great need for earlier points of intervention in the lives of people with severe mental illnesses as well as reform to the civil commitment system. It is remarkable what MHCs are able to achieve, amidst these limitations and fears, as witnessed through the stories of clients themselves. The narratives of the profiled clients in the following chapter clearly convey success—albeit imperfect and nonlinear.

# Notes

1. *County* MHC team members were less optimistic about MHC successes and cited cost concerns. A probation officer reluctantly stated that, "I feel like we're not [successful]. I think it's really irresponsible, with as expensive as this program is to run." However, this team member went on to qualify, that despite all of the problems, there are successes: "Oh, yes. Yes, absolutely." In a similar pessimistic assessment, another probation officer remarked, "I think it's a popular program and it appeals to people, on an emotional level, and it's politically popular, but honestly when I think of how much it costs to run, I couldn't even say whether or not I think it should keep going."

2. A modified version of some of this section was published previously (see Snedker et al. 2017).
3. No comparable data was available for *County* MHC.
4. Either a deferred sentence or suspended sentence.
5. Ironically, even though charges are dismissed for defendants who were offered a dismissal of the charges and successfully completed the MHC, they may not disappear completely. In the words of a prosecuting attorney, "the record still exists." A defendant's record will indicate that a charge has been legally dismissed, however the charge and final adjudication will still remain on their criminal record.
6. I use the term team member in the discussion of dismissal offers as opposed to professional positions given the sample size of the follow-up interviews and issues of confidentiality.
7. While there were likely selection bias in which clients are offered a dismissal of their charge that are not captured in the statistical models, the significance of the dismissal offer variable remains in all models (with controls), suggesting that the effect of the offer represents more than selection bias.
8. There is some variation in jurisdiction length. For example, in *County* MHC prosecutors routinely ask for two years of supervision for felony cases but routinely ask for one year to eighteen months for grows misdemeanors.
9. A SOC is a specialized form of a dispositional continuance.
10. True diversion would mean no jail time.
11. Interestingly, Veteran's Court (presided over by the same *County* MHC) has more incentives built in, such as coins for major achievements.
12. The role of court program incentives suggests a possible application to traditional court. In a study of MHC non-completers, dismissing charges once defendants returned to traditional court was associated with reduced criminal recidivism (Ray et al. 2015a, 2015b); this finding reinforces the notion that dismissing charges even outside the MHC context can have a suppressive effect on new criminal charges. While this study cannot parse out how a defendant is processed once their case is revoked from MHC, taken together these studies suggest there is an effect of the offer to dismiss charges and/or the actual dismissing of charges on criminal desistance in both court systems.
13. Quantitative data are not available from *County* court to analyze if this incentive structure—offering misdemeanor charges for felony charges—has a similar reduction on recidivism.

14. This county agency that collected this data defined "non-crisis" services as routine outpatient services that are part of a person's structured treatment plan and "crisis" is a term used for services given for urgent or emergent mental health issues.
15. In the statistical analysis we were unable to control for mental health diagnosis or condition due to limitations in the data, however we control for whether the issue of competency was raised during a defendant's time in court.
16. Much of this section on graduation rituals comes directly from a Snedker (2016).
17. Detailed data is not yet available to researchers for analysis. *County* MHC is undergoing an evaluation in 2018.
18. Axis II of the American Psychiatric Association's DSM-IV includes personality disorders.
19. A *County* MHC client was charged with an egregious random murder. The assailant was diagnosed as bipolar and in 2017 his cases (DUI) were transferred to MHC (Green, *Seattle Times*, January 17, 2018). He did not have a significant criminal history or violence and was in compliance with the courts conditions prior to the episode. This rare case illustrates the challenges in preventing worst-case events as there are not always clear signs of a severe downward spiral.

# References

Anestis, Joye C., and Joyce L. Carbonell. 2014. "Stopping the Revolving Door: Effectiveness of Mental Health Court in Reducing Recidivism by Mentally Ill Offenders." *Psychiatric Services* 65 (9): 1105–12. https://doi.org/10.1176/appi.ps.201300305.

Boothroyd, Roger A., Norman G. Poythress, Annette McGaha, and John Petrila. 2003. "The Broward Mental Health Court: Process, Outcomes, and Service Utilization." *International Journal of Law and Psychiatry* 26 (1): 55–71. https://doi.org/10.1016/S0160-2527(02)00203-0.

Boothroyd, Roger A., Cynthia Calkins Mercado, Norman G. Poythress, Annette Christy, and John Petrila. 2005. "Clinical Outcomes of Defendants in Mental Health Court." *Psychiatric Services* 56 (7): 829–34. https://doi.org/10.1176/appi.ps.56.7.829.

Braithwaite, John. 1989. *Crime, Shame and Reintegration*. Cambridge, UK: Cambridge University Press.

Burns, Padraic J., Virginia Aldigé Hiday, and Bradley Ray. 2013. "Effectiveness 2 Years Postexit of a Recently Established Mental Health Court." *American Behavioral Scientist* 57 (2): 189–208. https://doi.org/10.1177/0002764212465416.

Christy, Annette, Norman G. Poythress, Roger A. Boothroyd, John Petrila, and Shabnam Mehra. 2005. "Evaluating the Efficiency and Community Safety Goals of the Broward County Mental Health Court." *Behavioral Sciences & the Law* 23 (2): 227–43. https://doi.org/10.1002/bsl.647.

Cosden, Merith, Jeffrey K. Ellens, Jeffrey L. Schnell, Yasmeen Yamini-Diouf, and Maren M. Wolfe. 2003. "Evaluation of a Mental Health Treatment Court with Assertive Community Treatment." *Behavioral Sciences & the Law* 21 (4): 415–27. https://doi.org/10.1002/bsl.542.

Cosden, Merith, Jeffrey Ellens, Jeffrey Schnell, and Yasmeen Yamini-Diouf. 2005. "Efficacy of a Mental Health Treatment Court with Assertive Community Treatment." *Behavioral Sciences & the Law* 23 (2): 199–214. https://doi.org/10.1002/bsl.638.

DuBois, Lios, and Teri Martin. 2013. *Mental Health Court Evaluation*, 1–77. Portland, OR: Law & Policy Associates.

Fisler, Carol. 2015. "When Research Challenges Policy and Practice: Toward a New Understanding of Mental Health Courts." *The Judges' Journal* 54 (2): 8–13. http://www.courtinnovation.org/sites/default/files/documents/JJ_SP15_54_2_Fisler.pdf.

Griffin, Patricia A., and David DeMatteo. 2009. "Mental Health Courts: Cautious Optimism." In *Problem-Solving Courts: Justice for the Twenty-First Century*, edited by P. Higgins and M. B. Mackinem, 91–113. Santa Barbara: Praeger.

Hiday, Virginia A., and Bradley Ray. 2010. "Arrests Two Years After Exiting a Well-Established Mental Health Court." *Psychiatric Services* 61 (5): 463–68. https://doi.org/10.1176/appi.ps.61.5.463.

Hughes, Shannon, and Terry Peak. 2013. "A Critical Perspective on the Role of Psychotropic Medications in Mental Health Courts." *American Behavioral Scientist* 57 (2): 244–65. https://doi.org/10.1177/0002764212458273.

Johnston, E. Lea. 2012. "Theorizing Mental Health Courts." *Washington University Law Review* 89 (3): 519–79.

Keator, Karli J., Lisa Callahan, Henry J. Steadman, and Roumen Vesselinov. 2013. "The Impact of Treatment on the Public Safety Outcomes of Mental

Health Court Participants." *American Behavioral Scientist* 57 (2): 231–43. https://doi.org/10.1177/0002764212465617.

Kopelovich, Sarah, Philip Yanos, Christina Pratt, and Joshua Koerner. 2013. "Procedural Justice in Mental Health Courts: Judicial Practices, Participant Perceptions, and Outcomes Related to Mental Health Recovery." *International Journal of Law and Psychiatry* 36 (2): 113–20. Elsevier Ltd. https://doi.org/10.1016/j.ijlp.2013.01.004.

Luskin, Mary Lee. 2001. "Who Is Diverted? Case Selection for Court-Monitored Mental Health Treatment." *Law & Policy* 23 (2): 217–36.

Luskin, Mary Lee, and Bradley Ray. 2015. "Selection into Mental Health Court: Distinguishing Among Eligible Defendants." *Criminal Justice and Behavior* 42 (11): 1145–58. https://doi.org/10.1177/0093854815601158.

McNiel, Dale E., and Renée L. Binder. 2007. "Effectiveness of a Mental Health Court in Reducing Criminal Recidivism and Violence." *American Journal of Psychiatry* 164 (9): 1395–403. https://doi.org/10.1176/appi.ajp.2007.06101664.

McNiel, Dale E., Naomi Sadeh, Kevin L. Delucchi, and Renée L. Binder. 2015. "Prospective Study of Violence Risk Reduction by a Mental Health Court." *Psychiatric Services* 66 (6): 598–603. https://doi.org/10.1176/appi.ps.201400203.

Miller, JoAnn, and Donald C. Johnson. 2009. *Problem Solving Courts: A Measure of Justice*. Lanham: Rowman & Littlefield.

Miller, Sarah L., and Abigayl M. Perelman. 2009. "Mental Health Courts: An Overview and Redefinition of Tasks and Goals." *Law & Psychological Review* 33: 243–58. https://doi.org/10.3366/ajicl.2011.0005.

Moore, Marlee E., and Virginia Aldigé Hiday. 2006. "Mental Health Court Outcomes: A Comparison of Re-arrest and Re-arrest Severity Between Mental Health Court and Traditional Court Participants." *Law and Human Behavior* 30 (6): 659–74. https://doi.org/10.1007/s10979-006-9061-9.

Munetz, Mark R., Christian Ritter, Jennifer L. S. Teller, and Natalie Bonfine. 2014. "Mental Health Court and Assisted Outpatient Treatment: Perceived Coercion, Procedural Justice, and Program Impact." *Psychiatric Services* 65 (3): 352–58. https://doi.org/10.1176/appi.ps.002642012.

Pescosolido, Bernice A., John Monahan, Bruce G. Link, Ann Stueve, and Saeko Kikuzawa. 1999. "The Public's View of the Competence, Dangerousness, and Need for Legal Coercion of Persons with Mental Health Problems." *American Journal of Public Health* 89 (9): 1339–45. https://doi.org/10.2105/AJPH.89.9.1339.

Peterson, J., J. L. Skeem, E. Hart, S. Vidal, and F. Keith. 2010. "Analyzing Offense Patterns as a Function of Mental Illness to Test the Criminalization Hypothesis." *Psychiatric Services* 61 (12): 1217–22. https://doi.org/10.1176/appi.ps.61.12.1217.
Pratt, Christina, Philip T. Yanos, Sarah L. Kopelovich, Joshua Koerner, and Mary Jane Alexander. 2013. "Predictors of Criminal Justice Outcomes Among Mental Health Courts Participants: The Role of Perceived Coercion and Subjective Mental Health Recovery." *International Journal of Forensic Mental Health* 12 (2): 116–125.
Ray, Bradley. 2014. "Long-Term Recidivism of Mental Health Court Defendants." *International Journal of Law and Psychiatry* 37 (5): 448–54. Elsevier Ltd. https://doi.org/10.1016/j.ijlp.2014.02.017.
Ray, Bradley, and Cindy Brooks Dollar. 2013. "Examining Mental Health Court Completion: A Focal Concerns Perspective." *Sociological Quarterly* 54 (4): 647–69. https://doi.org/10.1111/tsq.12032.
Ray, Bradley, Brittany J. Hood, and Kelli E. Canada. 2015a. "What Happens to Mental Health Court Noncompleters?" *Behavioral Sciences & the Law* 33 (6): 801–14. https://doi.org/10.1002/bsl.2163.
Ray, Bradley, Sheryl Pimlott Kubiak, Erin B. Comartin, and Elizabeth Tillander. 2015b. "Mental Health Court Outcomes by Offense Type at Admission." *Administration and Policy in Mental Health and Mental Health Services Research* 42 (3): 323–31. https://doi.org/10.1007/s10488-014-0572-2.
Redlich, Allison D., Henry J. Steadman, John Monahan, John Petrila, and Patricia A. Griffin. 2005. "The Second Generation of Mental Health Courts." *Psychology, Public Policy, and Law* 11 (4): 527–38. https://doi.org/10.1037/1076-8971.11.4.527.
Sarteschi, Christine M., Michael G. Vaughn, and Kevin Kim. 2011. "Assessing the Effectiveness of Mental Health Courts: A Quantitative Review." *Journal of Criminal Justice* 39 (1): 12–20. Elsevier Ltd. https://doi.org/10.1016/j.jcrimjus.2010.11.003.
Snedker, Karen A. 2016. "Unburdening Stigma: Identity Repair Through Rituals in Mental Health Court."*Society and Mental Health* 6 (1): 36–55. http://journals.sagepub.com/doi/abs/10.1177/2156869315598203.
Snedker, Karen A., Lindsey Beach and Katie Corcoran. 2017. "Beyond the 'Revolving Door'? Incentives and Criminal Recidivism in One Mental Health Court." *Criminal Justice and Behavior* 44 (9): 1141–1162. https://doi.org/10.1177/0093854817708395.

Schneider, Richard D., Hy Bloom, and Mark Heerema. 2007. *Mental Health Courts: Decriminalizing the Mentally Ill.* Toronto: Irwin Law.

Steadman, Henry J., Allison Redlich, Lisa Callahan, Pamela Clark Robbins, and Roumen Vesselinov. 2011. "Effect of Mental Health Courts on Arrests and Jail Days: A Multisite Study." *Archives of General Psychiatry* 68 (2): 167–72. https://doi.org/10.1001/archgenpsychiatry.2010.134.

Steadman, Henry J., Lisa Callahan, Pamela Clark Robbins, Roumen Vesselinov, Thomas G. McGuire, and Joseph P. Morrissey. 2014. "Criminal Justice and Behavioral Health Care Costs of Mental Health Court Participants: A Six-Year Study." *Psychiatric Services* 65 (9): 1100–4. https://doi.org/10.1176/appi.ps.201300375.

Trupin, Eric, and Henry Richards. 2003. "Seattle's Mental Health Courts: Early Indicators of Effectiveness." *International Journal of Law and Psychiatry* 26 (1): 33–53. https://doi.org/10.1016/S0160-2527(02)00202-9.

Wales, Heathcote W., Virginia Aldigé Hiday, and Bradley Ray. 2010. "Procedural Justice and the Mental Health Court Judge's Role in Reducing Recidivism." *International Journal of Law and Psychiatry* 33 (4): 265–71. Elsevier Ltd. https://doi.org/10.1016/j.ijlp.2010.06.009.

# 6

## Stories from Clients: How Mental Health Courts Can Change Lives

Beyond criminal recidivism, the core of MHC success lies in its capacity to benefit the lives of its clients. Much can be learned about what works and what does not work in MHC through the reflections of clients themselves and voices. Case histories of seven *City* MHC clients provide insights into the lived experience of the more successful clients in MHC. One probation officer generated a list of possible clients from which I recruited. From my court observations and experiences with probation officers, clients who were more successful were more inclined to speak with me resulting in a biased sample of the more successful clients (See Appendix A for full details on sampling method and client characteristics). Those clients who experienced revocation from the program might understandably have a different perspective from the clients portrayed in this chapter.

Personal stories have been a largely untapped source of data in previous studies of MHCs.[1] They help researchers uncover the factors clients feel have altered their life trajectories, exemplifying the ways in which experience in MHC influences their quality of life, including the management of mental illness and substance use, housing stability, employment status and family relations. These histories also address specific connections between clients and MHC staff to explore how the court process fosters—or impedes—better outcomes for clients. Although these stories do not reflect every client's experience, they do reveal the potential of MHCs, as well as the struggles that beset many clients. All seven of these clients graduated from MHC, but their lives after exiting the court show varying degrees of success.

A probation officer highlighted the importance of qualitative examinations of client experience: there is a "lot of value to these courts that you don't get with the numbers." Speaking with clients, listening to their stories and investigating their cases through court documents reinforce the findings from previous research. Client narratives show what lies behind the statistical relationships discussed in the previous chapter, including managing mental illness and sobriety. They also show that the offer to dismiss charges after successful completion of the probationary period is another determinant of MHC success. Procedural justice—perceptions of fairness and respect in the court—and social support also mediate success in MHC. The stories that follow go beyond quantitative data to unearth a deeper human story.

## "It Has Ruined My Taste for Alcohol": Sobriety, Incentives and Social Support

Monique's case highlights the role that alcohol abuse plays in the management of mental illness and ultimate success or failure in court. Monique's graduation from MHC—albeit without complete compliance or perfect abstinence—reveals the importance of sobriety, incentives that foster compliance, and the power of social support from MHC team members. Monique explained, "This whole ordeal, from beginning to end, it has ruined my taste for alcohol. I don't even like alcohol at all anymore. I can't even stand to taste beer, a wine, whiskey, vodka. I don't want it!" When I probed her further she admitted the emotional gravity of the MHC experience saying, "If I did drink I would feel so bad about it. The guilt. Everything I had to go through ruined my taste for it."

Monique is a sociable and optimistic white woman and in her early fifties. Her entry into MHC began in 2012 with several assault charges and a harassment charge. She does not know how she was referred to MHC: "They found out I was mentally ill and they siphoned me to that courtroom." After two full years on probation, she graduated MHC in 2014. During our interview Monique was friendly and easy to converse with, she laughed during our conversation and clearly enjoyed the time that we spent together at a local coffee shop.

Monique's upbringing in Oregon held many challenges, including the death of her mother when she was two and subsequent abandonment by her father. Despite her early childhood trauma, she and her brother were adopted and well cared for. She recounted an active and busy childhood revolving around "sports, horses, and dogs." However, things started to go awry in her teenage years when she ran away from home and went to her grandmother's house in Canada. She quickly returned to Oregon to her adoptive parents and finished high school, but things soon went downhill. At seventeen she was married, and by nineteen she was divorced with two small children. Remarkably, Monique persevered and graduated from college. Ultimately, however, the combination of untreated mental illness and alcohol abuse proved disastrous. The next several decades of her life were characterized by a "series of treatment centers for drugs, alcohol, and mental health." During this time, Monique was unable to care for her children, who went to live in Canada with extended family members. Monique ultimately became involved in the criminal justice system—a place she never expected to find herself—but she conceded that this might have unexpectedly improved her life.

In our conversations, Monique talked casually about her mental illness: "You know this is mental health court, so I have a mental disorder." Her first recognition of her mental health issues was after college when she "went hitchhiking on a spree and was kind of out there on a limb, not making any sense in what I was doing." This episode led to a three-month stay in a mental institution. But symptoms associated with her mental illness manifested much earlier, coinciding with early alcohol use. She confessed, "I have been an alcohol abuser since I was a teenager." Like so many clients in MHC, her substance abuse and mental illness are interconnected. Monique stated it succinctly:

> There were a lot of times when I think I drank in order to deal with my mental health. A lot of times. Right now, if I wasn't taking medication, I probably would be out on a limb again and drinking. It has just been my pattern, throughout my life. It is hard to break. I do good for a while, so I get in trouble, or I am out there using and drinking, and I get in trouble.

She talked about being hospitalized several times prior to entering MHC, but she "never took care of the underlying problem."

Initially, Monique hesitated to opt-into MHC, but chose to because the charges would be dropped if she successfully completed the court obligations. In line with the findings presented in the preceding chapter, the importance of incentives is clear: "I did not want those assault charges on my record. I wanted those charges dropped... I do not know how I got [the dismissal of charges] but I am sure glad I did." The offer to dismiss her charges shaped her behaviors by providing an incentive to comply with court obligations; Monique did not want to risk losing her favorable sentencing recommendation or receive other negative sanctions.

The case of Monique highlights the role of negative sanctions to incentivize compliance. Monique talked about the times she drank and used drugs and was able to evade court sanctions. Monique felt guilty that she was neither sober nor drug-free throughout the court and that sometimes she lied about it, getting caught and spending time in jail. Reflecting on that experience, she stated, "Jail was terrible. I do not ever want to go back there again." She also knew that she could not fail to appear for her court appearances either: "I never missed a court date and faced whatever they were going to give. It was a lot nicer to go in there when nothing was wrong with the review." Monique's anxiety going into court was reduced if she had a good report, which was largely driven by her sobriety. Accountabilitywas critical for Monique: "During the time I was on probation, the monitoring of my life and what I was doing was good for me 'cause it kept me on the straight and narrow.... The court reinforced that idea [sobriety]."

In the early stages of the court process, resources and support proved important in connecting her with temporary housing. At the time of the interview, Monique was in housing that she secured on her own but she lamented the continual challenges in housing due to stigma of mental illnessconsistent with research on discrimination (Corrigan et al. 2003). It was not clear that she was in any danger of losing her housing due to her mental illness, but she perceived that having mental health challenges increased her vulnerability to eviction (both informal and formal, see Desmond 2016). Monique emphasized the importance of the MHC team in her success. Members of the MHC team provided Monique with social support over the two years of probation, without which it is not clear that Monique would have graduated from MHC. She spoke of them as a "good team" and specifically talked about the hard work of her two probation officers (one retired during her time in court). The second probation officer would not "play games with her" about sobriety issues. She also expressed gratitude for the court liaison saying, "she is a great lady and she really cares." While she did not have any "real relationship with the lawyers," Monique felt that they kept her informed about the court process and procedures. In speaking about the MHC team, she complemented them for "putting a lot into me." The mental health treatment facility also played a key role in her story. Now that she has graduated from MHC and is without the structure of the court, her treatment provider will be even more critical in the management of her mental illness.

Monique's graduation ritual (described in detail in the Introduction and in Chapter 5) encapsulated her successful journey through MHC. In reflecting on it, Monique stated, "I really appreciated the fact that they cared so much about whether or not I graduated or not. Instead of just saying, 'okay, you are done, dismiss charges.'" The ritual proved powerful due to the relationships she made with team members and the long journey she had undertaken toward the better management of mental illness and sobriety.

Monique has had little social support since her graduation from MHC.She relied on the team while in MHC. Monique told me that her daughter provides some support but does not have time to check in on her. I was surprised at the end of the interview when Monique mentioned that she is currently married and had been for over a year. The home is not alcohol free. Monique claimed that her husband "drinks like a fish," but that "he doesn't push it on me – he wouldn't drink around me at all if I asked him not to, but I don't care if he drinks."

When I asked if he ever attended her court reviews to support her she laughed and saying "No! Because he's packing [carries a gun]. He does not want to go to the hassle of security." Alcohol at home raise serious concerns about Monique's ability to stay "clear and sober," which she acknowledged is necessary to her staying out of trouble and staying on medication. Monique's time is unstructured and she is not currently working, relying on a fixed-income that largely goes to pay the rent. At the time of the interview she did not express any plans to seek employment.

Monique felt positively about her experience in MHC and recommended it other others: "I think that the court has its place. I think it is a good thing. We need a justice system in place for people that are mentally ill… I know there are other people like me. I am not the only one… It needs to stay in place." Monique identified cultural differences between the practices of MHC and the traditional court system. For her, as well as other clients, MHC was a qualitatively distinct experience from the rest of the criminal justice system and other problem-solving courts (she had contact with drug courts). Despite Monique's graduation from MHC, at the time of the interview a few months after court completion, it was uncertain how she will fare and how well she will do without the support, oversight and accountability of the MHC team. Her case highlights the often-critical role of substance abuse in MHC cases, as well as the potential for intimates to undermine health and progress. For almost two years, Monique did not have any new criminal law violations. However, in summer of 2016 Monique was brought back to court on two counts of property destruction, which were later dropped and dismissed without prejudice.[2]

## "It's a Way to Build Healthy Habits": Sobriety, Treatment and Identity

Jennifer's case, like Monique's, underscores the importance of controlling alcohol and other substances for the successful management of mental illness. Jennifer graduated from MHC after several tries. Her story underlines the importance of sobriety, treatment, and support for change in personal and social identity. Looking at her investment in MHC, Jennifer commented that she is "trying to think about it as a way to build healthy habits, rather than you have to do this and this and this." She also talked about gaining perspective and seeing how far she has come since her entry in MHC: "I still have my struggles, but when I don't feel like I'm doing very good, I look at where I was not so long ago, and that makes me feel a lot better."

Jennifer is a serious and nervous white woman and in her mid-thirties. Her entry into MHC began in 2010 with a theft charge. In the subsequent five years before she graduated from MHC in early 2015, she accumulated several more theft charges and a criminal trespassing charge. Her case was unusual as she spent longer than average time in MHC. Like many of the more successful clients, the court offered to dismiss Jennifer's charges after she graduated from MHC. Given that she had a clean criminal record before entering MHC this was a clear incentive to opt-in. At the time of her interview, she had approximately six months before finishing the court's conditions and graduating. During the interview at a hipster coffee shop, Jennifer readily answered my questions, although at times she struggled with her answers. She agreed to the interview to support the research project despite not desiring the social interaction. Jennifer is clearly smart and determined, but exhibited visible anxiety. She constantly tapped on the table throughout our hour-long conversation.

Having grown-up in the Pacific Northwest, Jennifer talked about her normal childhood with a supportive family and her love for sports and animals. After college Jennifer moved to a new city on the West coast to be with her older sister, with whom she is close; they had attended college together. After completing college, Jennifer was by most accounts on track for a successful career in nursing. However, five years into working in her chosen field, her "addiction got in the way" resulting in the suspension of her nursing license. That moment marked the beginning of a drastic decline in her life, triggering several jail stays and a lifelong struggle with chemical dependency and mental illness.

As with Jennifer and Monique, symptoms of mental illness often precede substance abuse. The tendency to rely on alcohol and other substances—"I am not just an alcoholic. I will use anything"—to self-medicate and curb the effects of anxiety, depression and other mental health issues was woven into Jennifer's story. She also described suicidal thoughts that began at a "pretty young age," with suicide attempts beginning later. In a forthright manner, Jennifer shared a dark description from her past self: "I never pictured myself living older than 25. Growing up, I never saw my life – I thought either I would get in an accident or I'd kill myself." During her college years, Jennifer actively sought help for her mental illness, with limited success, claiming that medications helped her "to get addicted to [illicit] substances."

For Jennifer, there came a point when alcohol could not dampen the severity of her mental health symptoms: "Eventually it was not working because I was depressed and alcohol is a depressant. I got super-disabled, where I just drank and used drugs and didn't have any support." Her mental health issues coupled with substance abuse had debilitating effects. Jennifer recounted the spiral of self-destruction that ensued, "I hated myself. I always wanted to die. I didn't want to stay sober, and I was whittling myself, getting in real bad relationships." The pattern of self-destruction culminated in a year-long stay in a mental hospital and eventually jail. For her, substance use, mental illness and criminal behavior were interconnected: "I think all of my suicide attempts have been under the influence, generally alcohol. And pretty much the crimes I have committed."

Jennifer saw her addiction as a disease and was critical of the court's "punitive [response] for relapsing." However, she also readily acknowledged that the accountability and the threat of jail pressured her to stay away from alcohol and other illegal substances:

> I guess, honestly, it [MHC] has helped support my sobriety. I have been trying to get sober for 10 years, and the consequences of using and drinking while I am there is jail time. So I did end up getting that a few times, and instead I have to stay out of there. It was such a hard thing for me to go through that… the jail time for me is horrible.

Oversight and support from the court is helpful, but at the same time clients often worry about how well they will do without the review hearings, UA testing and judicial accountability after they leave the court. Jennifer mentioned that the court hindered her feeling fully responsible: "In some ways I don't feel like I really own my sobriety because there is always outside forces that are watching me. I have to get slips signed." Recognizing this as important to her future success in managing substance abuse, Jennifer was not waiting to graduate from the court to make positive changes: "I am trying to own it now, because I just want my life to be better."

For Jennifer, MHC was limited in its positive social support. The majority of the effect it had on her level of compliance was through negative sanctions—jail. Despite her frustration with her probation officer, who was the one who recommended jail, Jennifer talked about him fondly and about having a "connection to him on a personal level." Even Jennifer admitted that jail is a productive sanction for her as she does community service in her work anyway. Although the sting of jail as a sanction still pained her, Jennifer willingly took ownership—"it is my fault"—of the relapses that landed her in jail. The connection with her probation officer and her sense of personal responsibility may prove critical to her success in the court.

Other clients spoke extensively about the MHC team in providing social support and credited them for at least some of their success. This was not Jennifer's experience. She talked candidly about addiction and credits herself, her treatment counselor and the court for her new path. In her case, even though she had another counselor for chemical dependency, a mental health counselor had the biggest impact on her sobriety and management of her mental illness. Her counselor believed in her and helped her believe in herself. This affirming client-patient relationship came about through mental health treatment mandated by the court. I asked her about her social support network beyond her counselor and she was actively "building one," including a stronger relationship with her sponsor. She characterized herself as "socially challenged" and acknowledged that building relationships with some MHC team members was hard especially in group settings. Her sister was "supportive" and "always there" and her parents were generally supportive "in kind of a non-hands-on way." The geographic distance from her family added to the emotional distance. Jennifer battled with perceived disappointment that her alcohol abuse causes them, "I was raised religiously and the fact that I even drank was shocking. I was a good girl in high school." She went on to tell me that she wanted to comply with the court conditions because she does not want to "get another charge" or spend more time in jail. But it was more than that; stealing does not "fit with who I am as a sober person." It was clear that her self-identity had changed in MHC.

Jennifer was not putting her life on hold while in MHC. Professionally, she was trying to get her licenses reinstated and was currently working part-time at a local homeless shelter. Jennifer's struggle with mental illness and addiction provided her insight and connection with other MHC clients and influences her vocational path. She plans to work with the same population: "My experience put me in the direction that I am going in…I want to do nursing there [homelessness center]. I want to stay where I'm at, because I love the company. I love what I do." Jennifer's identities as nurse and counselor give her meaning, purpose and social status.

Jennifer proclaimed that her "life has gotten better, a lot less chaotic" since entering MHC. She admitted that she committed many thefts before being charged, but that shoplifting was in her past. However, Jennifer's life did not "revolve around" MHC the way it did for other clients. She stated that she was "just trying to live my life and give it the attention it deserves. I'm not in this structure, the court thing, then the mental health stuff is less of my destiny, a less of a focus." In some ways, Jennifer is atypical of MHC clients. She is high functioning with education and practical skills that make her employable. She regarded herself as "mentally organized and competent" in comparison with others, distancing herself from other MHC clients helped to form her renewed positive identity. While in MHC, she worked part-time as a counselor, while taking on-line courses to work toward reinstating her health professional credentials, and selling handmade accessories. She was exemplary in her determination and industriousness.

Like many clients, the biggest challenge ahead for Jennifer seems to rest on sobriety. Despite her success with MHC and subsequent graduation, Jennifer gave a mixed assessment of her experience, "I think more positive than negative." After some silence and contemplation she added, "I don't know at this point what my life would look like if I didn't have that [MHC], but I think maybe, at least maybe it is helping me get that solid bit of sobriety with people looking over my shoulder." She was optimistic about her future. As of fall 2017, after graduating two years prior, Jennifer has had no further contact with the criminal justice system.

## "It Helped Humble Me Down": Faith, Support, and Tools for Living

Isaiah's case highlights the role of personal faith, humility, social support and a structured environment in providing necessary life skills. Isaiah credited the court for helping him to "get the tools he needs," to learn new skills and apply them to his life: "Before I didn't have the tools that they gave me, and I didn't know how to use the tools. Or I did know how to use it, but I was still young on using them." Then Isaiah specified the newly acquired abilities and their potential:

> Just how to get along, how to be a great person, how to handle certain situations… It teaches me how to get along, how to follow directions, abide by the laws, to be honest and with integrity… it [MHC and support groups] helped humble me down.

Isaiah is a quiet and amiable black man in his mid-thirties. He characterized himself as "open-minded" and "responsible." He emphasized that he is a "Christian man" who tries to center his life on his faith. A native to the Pacific Northwest, Isaiah described his childhood as fine but challenging at times, being the middle child of five children. Being raised by both of his parents in a "Christian home" provided a solid foundation of faith. As a child, he liked sports and loved computers, especially building and rebuilding them. While he did not graduate from high school, Isaiah worked at an early age in low-level service work and then at a local mechanics shop. He still enjoys working with his hands and doing mechanical work. He married and divorced early and has four children with two mothers (none of whom he married). While he wasn't particularly forthcoming in details about his personal life, he was pleasant to converse with and earnestly answered all of my questions to the best of his ability, asking for clarification, with me often repeating or rephrasing questions to make sure he understood what I was asking. During the course of our interview, Isaiah was soft-spoken and respectful. He smiled a lot during our conversation and seemed to enjoy the time that we spent together at a local coffee shop.

Isaiah's entry into MHC began in early 2015 with an assault charge. He offered a brief account of the incident: "I got into it with my father, I guess. They [prosecutor] said I hit him, but I didn't. I pled guilty, though, took a plea bargain. So that's how I got into court." It is clear why he pled guilty—he received a deferred sentence—but less clear why he was not offered a dismissal of the charge. He clarified why he opted-into MHC: "So I can get everything, like... mentally get everything stable." In talking about his mental health diagnosis, which occurred in his late twenties, Isaiah shared how his family "tried to help" and that they gave him "a lot of family support." His relationship with his family made the altercation with his father and subsequent no contact order painful for him. After one and a half years on probation, the court was considering his case for early graduation. In the court review preceding our interview, his probation officer asked the team both on and off the record (in the pre-court meeting and during the court review hearing) to consider an early graduation for Isaiah, given his record of compliance saying, he has "gotten a lot out of the court." The prosecutor and judge stated that the team would consider this request at the next hearing, approximately three months later, in mid-December 2016, which did happen. Isaiah was very excited about this prospect, which clearly increased his acclamation for the court when he described it as "a great choice," saying he would recommend MHC to others in similar circumstances.

It is clear from our conversation that his devout faith "grounded" him, helping him to "do right." Examples of his humility occurred at many points during our conversation; he told me he's "just looking for the tools that I need in life... just learning how to get through life." He readily acknowledged that he cannot handle his mental health challenges alone and the he needs guidance. Isaiah talked about religion and various practices, including meditation that aided him in his daily life. When I asked him what he needed to stay successful (especially after he exits the court) his response centered on his faith: "The Lord first, but with the tools and everything that the court gave me, I'm using that and that is going to keep me on track, on the right track."

Isaiah told me that the court was critical to the management of his mental illness and that the support he received motivated him: "I am working with a lot of places, a lot of people that work in the system, programs. I stay in touch with them, and they are keeping me... [being] supportive." He credited the MHC; it provided the groundwork and skills that he is planning to take with him beyond the court:

> Structure, so they give me structure. It helps me build a great foundation. So my foundation is pretty strong, based on the court, the information that they give me and what they set for me. I use that, and I will continue using it even after the court, after I finish with probation.

Many of the life skills that he learned or were reinforced by the court revolve around how to handle everyday challenges.

During his time in court Isaiah has always been in compliance with the court's treatment plan and conditions of sentence. In fact, in his most recent court review, all parties referenced his excellent record, which is atypical of MHC clients. It was clear in court and in our interview that he was proud that he was in full compliance. The court's structure and support system helped him immensely. Mostly he credited his probation officer for this smooth path through MHC. The "tools" that he so readily talked about are related to what he learned from probation. Isaiah described his probation officer as a person who "gives great advice" and was a "great inspiration." He told me that he takes the guidance and instruction that probation and the court offer him and he "uses it" in his life. Although his probation officer played a primary role in this socialization process, he also specifically mentioned the importance of judges:

> I listen to them. I look up to them, so whatever information they give me, I take and I use. I use everything that they have given me.

Everything, tools they have given me to learn. I apply it to my life. The judges have been great.

The supportive team clearly affected Isaiah and he took pride in the social relationships formed and his skill development. When I probed further for specifics on how the team had aided him, he talked about "staying on a pattern that I am given" and abiding by the "structure" of the court.

Housing assistance is critical for many clients in MHC. When Isaiah entered the court he was homeless. The court helped connect him with temporary housing, which then helped him to secure transitional housing. At the time of the interview, he lived in temporary subsidized housing and the housing agency was assisting him to find more permanent housing. Isaiah was grateful to the team members for helping him to acquire housing and was hopeful about having stable permanent housing before exiting the court: "I am waiting for a one bedroom apartment or a studio. As soon as I get that, then I can reap the benefits of everything that I learned." Isaiah is an example of someone who gained a lot from the resources the court provides, most notably the structure, social support and social services (e.g., housing). The support from the court was especially consequential given that Isaiah received limited family support; he informed me that he does have his "mother and some friends" for support, but did not elaborate.

In the past, substance abuse was an issue for Isaiah but it had nothing to do with the incident that landed him in the criminal justice system. At the time of the interview, he had been sober for over a year and a half. He continued to go to "groups" and stayed connected with his sobriety support system, even though these activities were not mandated by the court. He realized that he needs the supportive structure to stay on the right path. Isaiah informed me that "the court had me seeing a lot more things and gave me a lot more tools to use," all of which were helpful in the management of his continued sobriety.

In our interview, he was optimistic about the future. He hoped that in the coming years he will secure stable housing, have a job and pursue his education. Importantly, he desired to develop a "great relationships" with his children. Although he currently sees them, he wanted to be more involved in their lives. However, he realized the challenges he still faces, such as his search for permanent housing, employment, management of his mental illness and his court obligations, take precedence over his long term goal of improving his relationship with his children. As a result, he was waiting to focus on other important relationships once he was more settled: "I am working on myself right now." Expecting a lot of himself, he talked about trying to be a "good citizen" and felt that he can be successful. In response to the question of whether or not his life is better now than when he entered the MHC one and a half years ago, he responded unequivocally, "Yes, definitely, definitely!" Even when I pushed him to identify some gaps in the court program, he told me that "It has done a lot." At the end of our conversation Isaiah concluded that choosing to participate in MHC was a good choice—asserting his agency in the process—and that "the system works!" A few months after we spoke, in late 2016, he graduated from MHC compliant with all his conditions. While exemplary as a client, the lack of structure post-graduation may become an issue. But as of the fall of 2017 Isaiah has had no further contact with the criminal justice system.

## "Just Keeping My Nose Clean": Staying Sober, Compliance and Supportive Housing

Robert too struggled with sobriety. After graduating from MHC, the continuation of supportive housing—an alcohol-free environment with support services on site—has been instrumental for Robert's long-term behavioral change. He explained his plan for staying out of jail: "Just keeping my nose clean, and just keep up the good work. Don't get too serious about this. Just keep up the good work."

Robert is a sweet and shy white man in his early sixties, but his appearance and self-presentation suggested that he was much older. The deleterious effects of homelessness, alcoholism and severe mental illness were readily apparent. I spoke with Robert several months after he graduated from MHC in 2014. Unlike the other clients I met with, Robert and I talked in the common room of his supportive housing apartment building which he preferred to a local coffee shop. We sat down at a table away from the other residents who were playing cards, reading and conversing. Robert seemed slightly nervous when speaking with me. He spoke politely, softly and sparingly. Despite my gentle probing, it was difficult to get Robert to give detailed responses. His demeanor did not match his self-description in the beginning of the interview as an "easy going guy."

Robert first entered MHC in 2012 on an assault and criminal trespassing charge. He opted-into MHC with a reduced sentence of two months with no jail time—referred to as a suspended sentence, which requires a guilty plea. It was his first offense and unclear to me why he was not offered a dismissal of charges. He explained it "was just stupid stuff around alcohol, basically, not stealing or anything like that... I never was a thief, just not a good thing." His alcohol addiction began after he became homeless about fifteen years ago: "It is just rough, not having a place to call home. I took the only way I could deal with it was to be drinking on the streets." Robert was not homeless when he entered MHC and did not rely on the court for housing assistance, but his impression was that the court helped people with housing. Even though he was dealing with criminal charges and recovery, he stated that his life was much better now because he was not homeless.

When talking about how the court influenced his life, Robert came back to his sobriety. Almost with amazement, Robert reported that he saw his time in court positively; "I'm glad I did this [MHC], because I never seen this side of me ever in my life." Although he relapsed while in the court, he was surprised that "they didn't throw me in jail" and "gave me a second chance." He credited this generous reaction to the timing of his relapse—a full year into the two years of probation—and the support from his probation officer. Fear of going to jail has been a strong motivator: "I'd never jeopardize going to jail."

Mental health issues were clearly present in Robert's case but he kept the personal details private. He stated that "I have problems there [mental illness], too, but not out of the ordinary or anything, not blacking out or anything." He credited the onset of his mental illness to "pretty much about the same time" as homelessness and alcoholism. Robert sought to normalize his situation and distance himself from others in MHC and in his supportive housing facility. When talking about his residence he noted, "I've got it all right here… There is all kinds of support here" including the Alcoholics Anonymous meetings which he attends. In an attempt to destigmatize his housing, he made clear that while "you are always around sober people" other tenants can live here too: "anybody, it is not just for drug addicts, it is for anybody." The social support in Robert's life outside his housing and treatment was minimal. Robert talked about "having friends" but offered no details. He seemed disconnected from his family and his only son was not a source of support for him, but they do "talk to each other."

When discussing his plan for life after MHC he talked about needing to "go to meetings and keep up the good work." He referenced his case manager at his mental health treatment facility several times and his intention to continue to meet with him even if not mandated by the court. Like many other clients, Robert also credited his probation officer for support; he was the person, often the only person, who "saw some hope in me." His positive view of the entire MHC team was apparent: "I have nothing but good things to say about it. They have good people there. They were really supportive, the courts."

Robert was hopeful and optimistic at the end of our interview. He recently experienced a powerful graduation ritual. In our discussion about his life after the court, he revealed, "It is kind of hard… I have never been without the courts helping me along. Yeah, it is kind of scary, but I can do it." Robert was able to stay out of the criminal justice system for one full year after MHC graduation and has maintained his supportive housing. Unfortunately, Robert ended up back in court a year later with a new criminal law violation for assault. This time he decided not to opt-into MHC but his case and all subsequent hearings were held in MHC with his prior MHC probation officer. His case is under the MHDT path, which includes mandated mental health treatment without the additional support and oversight offered in MHC. Given his prior history in MHC and relationships with team members, he will probably receive more support than is typical of MHC opt-outs. He pled guilty and received a suspended sentence. While he opted-into

MHC the first time because "I thought it would be easier for me," I asked him if that turned out to be true and he responded frankly "No, not in the long run. Now that I think about it, it was, oh, man, I never want to go through that again, believe me." His prior experience clearly influenced his unwillingness to opt-in a second time.

On August of 2016, I met up with Robert in the hallway outside the courtroom. He was pleased to see me and sweetly referred to me as "The Professor." Despite being back in MHC—on the MHDT track—he was doing well. He was now in permanent housing (before he had been in temporary housing) which he believed would assist him with stability and sobriety. During the court review, Robert was found to be in full compliance, his probation officer offered a long preamble to the probation review:

> Robert was last in court at the end of June where he was in full compliance. He is just doing great right now. I supervised him in MHC a few years ago and he genuinely participated in the court. Even during that time he struggled a bit with sobriety. When Robert completed MHC and was no longer under the authority of the court that contributed to this case. He spent some time in jail. He comes to see me once a week for a UA. He is positive and upbeat. He is meeting with his case manager and attending groups. He's doing tremendously well. Terrific job. I could not be more proud. He just celebrated a birthday – 65 years old – and one year of sobriety.

The defense attorney briefly re-emphasized the same sentiment. Robert responded to the judge, "I just want to thank the court especially [name of probation officer]. He's more like my case manager than my probation officer." The judge congratulated him on his sobriety and was very encouraging. Robert hugged his probation officer as he left the courtroom. In early 2017, after being in full compliance with the court conditions, he completed the court conditions early—six months before the end of the two-year probationary period. Because of the way he was supervised ("MHC lite")—with frequent reports and regular reviews—the team (especially his p[robation officer) wanted to acknowledge his hard work so he was presented with a certificate similar to MHC graduates.[3]

Although not an overwhelming success, Robert's case is also not an abject failure. His case does, however, raise questions about introducing some kind of support post-MHC and the therapeutic and resource differences between the MHDT track and full MHC. Many clients may need multiple stays in MHC, a point referenced by many team members on some clients needing MHC for life. While he might have benefited from a longer probationary period in MHC, net widening arguments urge inquiry into alternative therapeutic interventions. As of fall of 2017, Robert has kept his record clean and has not returned to MHC.

## "I Don't Have to Keep Going Back to Bad Situations": Trauma, Trust and Responsibility

Shima's case illustrates the potential of MHC to help highly vulnerable and disadvantaged clients. The MHC team in both courts were vital to her success in and out of the courtroom. Shima is still trying to overcome childhood and adult trauma. The holistic MHC approach recognized the complex issues that Shima brought with her and provided much needed social support. The trust formed with team members helped her to take responsibility for her actions and choices: "I believe it [MHC] has embedded in me that I don't have to keep going back to bad situations. I don't need to hurt myself to believe that I'm still breathing. It made me believe that I don't need to get in trouble no more. I am fresh now."

Shima is a slight, pleasant Asian woman in her mid-forties. She grew up on the West coast after immigrating as a young child for adoption. She was re-adopted at age ten by a more loving "spiritual" family. Despite this more stable family environment, Shima characterized her youth as lonely: "I was very quiet. I kept to myself. I played by myself a lot." Shima struggled in school, leading to a placement in special education; the associated negative label affected her self-esteem and self-confidence. During our interview, Shima was friendly, willing to share her story, and clearly enjoyed the time that we spent together at a downtown coffee shop. In a follow-up email, Shima expressed gratitude writing, "Thank you so much for letting me share some of my experiences."

Shima's first contact with the criminal justice system dates back to 1990. What followed were years of minor traffic infractions (e.g., speeding, driving without a license), many domestic violence violations and several assault charges. Domestic violence charges against an ex-boyfriend landed Shima in *City* MHC in 2012. She received a suspended sentence for one charge and the court dismissed the others (violations of a domestic violence order). Like Monique, Shima was unsure why she opted-into the court but deduced that it must have been because of the "reduction" offered by the court: "I thought I was going to prison when they opted me in, obviously I am going to take that deal." She spent time in both *City* and *County* MHCs.

Shima described her growing up years as sheltered and controlled. She felt that she had few opportunities to exert any agency and lacked fundamental socialization, leaving her ill-equipped to make informed choices: "I grew up very naïve. I didn't know about drugs, didn't know what swearing meant... I didn't know nothing about sex... I didn't ask questions." As a teenager, Shima's family blamed her for being sexual assaulted by a family member. This led to a stay in a mental hospital, the first of many visits to the mental health ward which she described as "living in hell." Discharged from the institution at age sixteen, she "ran away from home. It was the only choice I had." Years later things turned around for Shima when she fell in love with and married an African American man. Sadly, both families disapproved of their interracial marriage. Tragedy struck again when her husband unexpectedly died of a heart attack. Shima teared up when she remembered him, telling me how much she loved him and needed him: "He loved me for who I was... I lost him. He was my best friend. He did everything for us—making sure we were happy, making sure we had money, making sure we were fed, all the things that a husband would do. I was lost."

With two small boys, Shima was unprepared to take on the role of the sole family caretaker. She lacked even the most basic life skills: "I didn't even know how to do bills." Despite the family tensions, she spent time with her in-laws, which proved disastrous. They were "alcoholics" and encouraged her to drink and take Valium to cope with her bereavement. Coupled with the tremendous loss and the lack of constructive social support, Shima began to drink: "So I start just drinking it and I couldn't stop… I never drank with my husband." This began the cycle of alcohol abuse that plagued her for years to come. The shock of being widowed, coupled with alcohol abuse, led to self-mutilation. Numbed by the loss of her husband, Shima cut and even stabbed herself to "feel like I was alive." During the interview, she pulled up her sleeves to show me the dozens of marks and stitch wounds on her arms.

Unable to function independently, let alone raise her children, extended family members took custody of her boys. Painfully, she confessed, "they were my babies but I didn't know how to take care of them because drinking was involved and I had to make a choice. That choice was to give them up." Some years later, she entered a romantic relationship and had a daughter but her partner was unable to handle her alcoholism. Now, her daughter lives with her father but she has frequent contact. In fact, her daughter's father served as the payee for her disability benefits and he and his new wife allowed Shima to stay with them on occasion to spend time with her daughter. Overwhelmed by feelings of guilt and failure, she was only now getting reconnected with her adult sons, but she saw their grief and feelings of abandonment as barriers.

Shima's journey through *County* MHC included several jail sanctions but she ultimately graduated. When I met her, she was in *City* MHC and while she still had some violations—missing meetings, relapse—she was largely in compliance. She admitted, "when I was in probation I had a really hard time keeping my appointments, even for my health." The court sanctioned her with day reporting for violating court conditions.During her time in *City* MHC, Shima was indicted on a new theft charge; the case was automatically diverted to MHC. Both the defense and the prosecuting attorneys argued that the theft charge should be dismissed with prejudice (a ruling where charges cannot be refiled later) given Shima's compliance in MHC. The judge granted the request and dismissed the case in the "interest of justice."

Shima's graduation from *City* MHC represented a turning point in her life. Her renewed sense of self was profound: "I have been sober for almost two years, and I need to realize that things are well." For Shima, the accountability to probation was critical: "I know [probation officer] was going to keep me out of trouble" but so was judicial oversight. In reflecting on of one of the judges, Shima said the judge "put faith in me."

Shima knew it is her "responsibility to do it" now that she has graduated from the court. While in MHC Shima received a lot of social support from various team members across both courts saying,"I felt that they always work for me." It was the support and the consequences for problem behavior that influenced Shima. The relationship with MHC team members lead to greater honesty and encouraged her to take on more responsibility. Other clients shared stories of social relationships built with MHC team members but none were as acute as Shima's account. She felt that while she was in court she was "going to be taken care of." She also received housing assistance early in the court process; her MHC probation officer arranged for her placement in temporary sober housing, which proved to be important for her stability. At the time of the interview, Shima informed me that she currently lives with a friend.

In her final reflection of her time in both courts, she summarized that overall, "It did help me." She has even recommend MHC to others: "If you are still in the regular court and they [court] aren't doing nothing for you, you need to ask your attorney about mental health court… they will help you. That is what mental health court is all about."

She admitted that she did "mess up" while in court but the message from the team influenced her life: "You hear other people telling you that you have so much to live [for]… They [MHC team] remind me that they believe in me, and I need to start believing in myself." Toward the end of our interview she confessed, "I still mess up." She worried about her ability to stay sober despite two years of sobriety: "I can stop drinking for today, I'm going to say today. Tomorrow, you never know." It was clear that Shima draws from the support and encouragement she received from team members, which enhanced her self-esteem and sense of agency. How well she will do without the court's support and oversight is unknown. Once again, Shima's case suggests that some post-MHC support, in her case related to housing stability and sobriety, would be beneficial. Shima had no new criminal law violations for almost three years, but as of summer 2017 she was back in MHC on an assault charge. Shima is currently on MHC conditions of release at the opt-in phase. While disappointing, three years of law-abiding behavior without the support and structure of MHC is partial success.

## "Meth Has Been My Downfall. It Destroyed My Life": Drugs, Jail and Structure

Norm's case reinforces the destructive power of substance abuse and how it causes entanglements with the criminal justice system. When I interviewed Norm he was about one year into his two years of probation. Norm's ultimate success or failure hinges on his ability to stay away from controlled substances. He knows that they are destructive and he wanted a better life: "Well, my mental health and the drugs of my choice don't work well together, the stimulants, methamphetamines—they make me delusional… Meth has been my downfall. It destroyed my life… I want to stay off meth."

A large white man in his late forties, Norm was soft-spoken despite his size. His striking blue eyes and amiable affect were inviting. We spent time conversing at a downtown coffee shop.He characterized his upbringing as middle class, stating that he "started out really good." His early onset of drug use in junior high school was his "downfall" leading to drug charges in his late teens. Yet by the age of thirty, he had stopped using drugs and has been clean for over ten years. It was unclear what triggered a reoccurrence of using but that was when he "got in trouble with the court." This was the first of many charges revolving around drug use. Norm's long journey in MHC started in 2001 on an assault charge, which he asserted "was a misunderstanding" and he was "flagged into MHC." The first case went well and was "pretty easy." He successfully graduated from MHC and it was not until 2014 that things went badly again due to drugs. On a visit to a treatment provider, under the influence of methamphetamines,

Norm "got mad" at his case manager and threw a bottle through "the administrative window." The court classified the incident as property destruction and assault. Norm contested the assessment of his behavior as assault: "I didn't even assault her, it just <u>appeared</u> like I assaulted her" (emphasis in original). Although he admitted that he did break the window he emphasized his lack of a motive, "I didn't mean to break the window, to be honest." Each time Norm entered MHC—with several years and in one case almost a decade between crimes—the charges remained on his record but are set to be dismissed at the end of the assigned probationary period (referred to as a suspended sentence).

Surprisingly, he later divulged that he was grateful it happened, "Thank God for getting arrested this time, because now I'm pretty adamant about never using methamphetamines again. Because of the negative effect. I might use other drugs again." During our interview Norm readily disclosed painful details about his life struggles. Talking about his mental illness, he noted it "makes everyday living hard. If it wasn't for that, I could probably get by okay." Norm seemed well equipped to handle his mental illness when he is not on drugs; staying on his medication has "never been a problem for him." Unfortunately, Norm thought he was capable of knowing which drugs he can handle without adverse effects, as he told me, "I know what my bad drugs are" and detailed the types of drugs he can "handle." I asked Norm how important the abstinence requirement of the court is and he affirmed that it is "very important." Even though he often failed to comply with this condition he recognized the need to be "clean and sober." He confessed, "no one supports me in my sobriety." His support network was limited to "one solid friend" who never used drugs and one case manager. It was unclear if he plans to continue to see his case manager after it is not mandated through the court; Norm informed me "I usually can't figure out what to say when I'm with her [case manager]." In response to questions about his family, he mentioned his mother and father who live in the area and support him; his father sometimes came to court with him. Norm was not married and does not have any children. In many ways, he was alone without much positive support, and he claimed that "everyone else is out for themselves."

The main impediment to his drug use was negative sanctions—jail time—imposed by the court.When talking about why he opted-into MHC the second time, Norm mentioned housing, but the third time he opted-in he revealed it was to avoid jail. Jail was a clear form of deterrence: "I didn't want to do any jail time at all… Because jail is so bad. That is what it is for me. I hate jail." Despite his abhorrence of jail, the pull of drugs was often greater. When talking about two meetings he missed—which he disliked terribly—I asked him if the court told him that if "you missed two meetings by the time of your next review you are going to spend two days in jail, would you go to those meetings?" And he stated, "Yeah."

When reflecting on what worked for his first time in MHC, Norm suggested, "I had more structure in my life… I was living in a clean and sober home. My depression was being treated properly. I had a girlfriend. I was socializing, and I was able to stay clean and sober." The court did provide Norm with temporary housing, which was the "the main reason" he opted-into MHC. During his second time in MHC, he spent a lot of time in jail for abstinence violations, even when claimed he was "90 percent medication compliance." He estimated the total time as "about 60 days in jail, over three to four different visits," at which point he plead guilty and the court counted his time served. He wanted to get out of the court and jail so he could "start using drugs." Norm blamed the judge for being "a stickler"; he felt the judge's overly punitive approach ignored the progress he was making. From a net-widening perspective, if Norm was going to continue violating the abstinence requirement and receiving jail sanctions, it would be less punitive to revoke him from MHC. The limitation is that he was under no supervision or structure and recidivated back into MHC.

The structure of the court was good for Norm although it frustrated him. For example, he reluctantly conceded that both daily reporting and drug tests (UA's) worked for him: "I was taking pee tests three times a week, and then two times a week… I couldn't use at all. Now I am only taking pee tests once a week, and I can use." Like some other clients, he worked the system so that he used in-between drug tests. Norm suggested that a different kind of incentive would help him work. He explained:

> I think if I got a job that would help. I was painting, and if I got a good painting job that would take care of everything… I like to paint. I could buy me a car and an apartment, and get me back in shape, and then I could get a girlfriend, and things would work out.

While it is unlikely that a job would eradicate all his problems, work denotes meaning and status and helps to organizes one's time. From Norm's perspective, getting a job was hard without a car, but that being a painter was a "doable goal" but not within the realm of the court: "The court can't get jobs." I probed further about utilizing social service agencies and he adamantly stated,

> I don't think that social services help with squat. Their advice is eat better and exercise… The jobs they have to offer are washing dishes or reporting to a recycling plant. Those are job that is hard on you [physically]. More than on the average person, I get tired easy and I get frustrated easy.

His current living environment made his situation worse: "It is low income and nobody works. Everybody is dirty, everybody takes drugs." He wanted to be around "normal, healthy people" which helps with his depression, but given his living situation and the time he spent in court, normal exchanges were infrequent. There was a powerful moment during our conversation when he drifted off and stared blankly out of the coffee shop window. We were in a downtown coffee shop located on a high floor overlooking the streetscape below. At about the half-way point of the interview Norm disclosed his need to find the right environment in order to feel "normal." I asked him a follow-up question about being normal and he went quiet. At first I was alarmed, given his history of mental illness and drug abuse, but I patiently waited for several minutes. He calmly responded to my question, "I feel normal right now." He elaborated why this moment was so normal, "we look like two regular people talking in the coffee shop."[4] The gravity of his statement struck me immediately. While this is a routine social exchange for many, for Norm it was noteworthy because it was exceptional.

Despite being in compliance for over one year of a two-year probationary period, in 2016 Norm was back in court on a new assault charge. The court granted Norm an "easy sentence" noted his probation officer and revoked the prior MHC case with credit given for time served. The new case has limited obligations outside the structure of MHC. It is unlikely to go well for Norm given his need for drug testing and court-sanctioned accountability. In fact, in June of 2017 he was booked on another assault charge. Again, Norm pled guilty to one charge of assault, taking credit for time served. Unfortunately, it seems likely that this pattern will continue.

## "It is Not That Big of a Deal": Mindfulness, Compliance and Education

Vicki's case highlights some of the limits of MHC. The contrast between Vicki's story and the others is striking. However, when considered in light of her social class it is clear that Vicki had a greater stock of resources to draw upon. Lacking client "buy-in" to the process, the emotional and behavioral benefits of court rituals failed Vicki and all that remained was tedious compulsory procedures and "going through the motions." Vicki characterized her time in court as "Pretty fine. It is just going in and jumping through hoops. It is not that big of a deal, just go in there, and, oh, you are in compliance, okay, great and then you go. It is just going downtown every month."

Vicki is an articulate and strong-willed white woman in her early thirties. Vicki entered MHC in 2013 with two assault charges and one obstruction charge. Her offer into MHC included dismissing one of the assault charges and an obstruction charge. A second assault charge was pending dismissal based on court completion. Throughout her time in MHC she was in full compliance, barring one violation based on a misunderstanding that was not sanctioned. Her compliance resulted in an early graduation (eight months before expected termination date) from MHC. I spoke with Vicki a few months prior to her graduation in 2015. We meet in a local coffee shop, just hours before she was to meet her estranged husband in an attempt to reconcile. The anxiety around the forthcoming encounter loomed in the background.

Growing up in a West coast city with a seemingly normal childhood, Vicki's life looked promising. Vicki spent several years on the East coast graduating from a well-known undergraduate institution and then attended an elite university for graduate training in teaching, specializing in mathematics. During this time Vicki met her husband and was married in her mid-twenties. Her marriage brought her back to the West coast and for the next three years things went well in her teaching job and marriage. Up to this point, her life followed the expected normative trajectory of an upper-middle class upbringing.

Vicki candidly talked about her mental illness and the associated pain and damage that it caused. Things quickly fell apart as Vicki painfully described:

> Then in 2012, everything came crashing down because I, for the first time in my life, became manic. I didn't know what was going on [with my mental health]. My husband didn't know what was going on. It started over several months. It was springtime and things were getting crazier. Everything was very busy. I wasn't sleeping enough. We were arguing a lot… that was terrible.

Not knowing how to react, Vicki disclosed that he "started getting scared of me" and "at one point he decided to call 911, and they came and took me away." She recounted the "unpleasantness" of the episode and shared that similar episodes occurred five times over the course of two years. After she got out of the hospital the first time she felt like her "life was over, everything was blah, and I went into a depression." Never having experienced mental illness before, this came as a shock and led to despondency, which further strained her relationship and her own self-esteem.

An incident with her husband, who was returning to their apartment with two of his friends to pick up his things, brought Vicki to MHC. She described the incident in great detail and found the charges illegitimate. She detailed a yelling match that ensued between her husband's friends and Vicki as she tried to close the door so she could get dressed (as she had been in the shower). She recounted what occurred when the police arrived:

They see me trying to shove them out of the door. So that is assault. I wasn't hitting anybody, I wasn't hurting anybody, I was just trying to get them out. Then, of course, they arrest me, and I'm the problem, even though they are coming to my apartment and trying to force their way in… they just listened to him, 'Oh, she's crazy, take her away.'

Her husband's inability to cope with her mental illness weighed heavily on Vicki. It put a tremendous strain on their marriage to the point of separation. Vicki was visibility upset sharing her sense of betrayal and abandonment.

In the early stage of MHC, Vicki was also in a confidential civil proceeding. During the hearing, attorneys raised competency issues in her absence. The court retracted the competency evaluation order one month later. She gave no credit to MHC in managing her mental health: "The court doesn't do anything for that… all the services they offered me. They all sound like things for people in crisis." Although Vicki did not acknowledge it, the court process and associated mandated treatment did seem to increase her awareness of her condition and facilitated subsequent management. As in the cases of Monique and Jennifer, the court created incentives for Vicki to enter MHC by dropping the assault charge; "if I finished the term then it would be off my record… I absolutely couldn't have anything like this in my record, because then I could never get a job as a teacher." Vicki planned to continue to see her therapist and psychiatrist beyond MHC. She knew that she was "not the same person anymore." Mental illness had become a wedge between her and husband. Despite her love for him, she doesn't think he is "strong" enough to handle mental illness at center stage in their lives.

One of the conditions the court imposed on Vicki were limits to her mobility. She was considering leaving and moving back to the city where she grew-up. Although Vicki blamed the court for restricting her movements, she later admitted that it was her marital discord that impeded making any major life decisions: "Until I can figure out what is going on with me and my husband, everything is pretty much crap." Even when she referred to the family support she came back to her marriage and that she was the only one who can "figure things out."

Unlike many of the other clients I got to know, substance abuse was not a driving force in Vicki's life and did not represent an impediment to success in MHC or in the management of her mental illness. She informed me that she drank "frequently" and smoked marijuana "occasionally" while in the court program. She described the abstinence requirement of MHC and the drug testing as a "bit of a charade." She declared, "I am not an alcoholic and I'm not addicted" and she clarified that one has to be careful about drinking and taking medicine but she was "not on the medications anymore."

During the time Vicki spent in court—watching the proceedings and outcomes of other cases—she felt out of place, "some people in here are really messed up… it makes me feel like I don't really belong there." MHC did not occupy much of Vicki's life, she stated, "I don't really think about it [MHC] that much," but also admitted she was looking forward to not worrying about the court conditions, especially restrictions on drinking and smoking marijuana. For her, leaving the court represented "one more thing I don't have to think about or worry about."

Vicki made it clear to me she does not "<u>need</u> the court" (emphasis in original). She was always in compliance with court conditions and graduated substantially early (16 months after arrest date). Despite her success in the court and early graduation, she declared that MHC "gave me nothing." In court—even at her graduation—she exhibited no observable emotions.In reconstructing her case, the court's program appeared to have fallen flat with Vicki for several reasons. She came into the court based on a contested charge; she did not believe the case was legitimate and thus her experience was tainted by feelings of injustice. She was "angry and mad" about it and defiantly asserted, "I don't think that I should be having to go through this [MHC] and have sanctions. I didn't do anything." It appeared that her sense of moral superiority limited what she gained from MHC.

Given Vicki's assessment of MHC, I asked her if she would have preferred going through the traditional court system. Despite her objections, it was clear to her MHC was a better option: "It is important that I did this [opt-into MHC], because I didn't have to go in front of an actual court and be judged. If they had found me guilty, then I would have had it on my record forever, and that would be terrible. I couldn't even deal with that."

For some clients, MHC works by rebuilding a damaged social identity. For others, it worked because it offers a clean slate. Vicki is squarely in the second camp. Most clients do not dispute their charge(s). Many are in need of stable housing. Most have limited social support. Although suffering from a serious mental illness, Vicki was otherwise well-equipped to function in society independently; she had social support from family and friends, housing, an advanced education and realistic job prospects (especially having avoided a criminal record).Despite her lack of buy-into MHC, she capitulated in many ways to the demands of the court. However, her defiance kept her emotionally distant from the team and the process. And though Vicki did not abstain from all substances during her time in MHC, she was in full compliance and graduated the court with her charges dismissed substantially earlier than the average case. What Vicki's case underlines is that the court has less to offer people like her and MHC is most beneficial to those with profound needs and those experiencing greater social marginalization. Vicki continued to stay clear of the criminal justice system as of the fall of 2017. A pattern that will likely continue.

## Client Success Trajectories

Case histories provide valuable insights into how and why MHCs shape client's lives. Client narratives reveal the process by which the court reduces (and fails to reduce) criminal behavior. The use of incentives and sanctions throughout the court process influence clients' perceptions, treatment support and social relationships. These factors effect client court experiences and post-court trajectories beyond reductions in criminal behavior. Quantitative analysis in the previous chapter shows that incentives at opt-in (dismissal of all charges) are particularly important for behavioral outcomes during and after exiting the court. This is clear in three of the profiled cases (all women), and not coincidentally, the most successful ones. Court observations and interviews also illustrate the importance of a collaborative MHC team, positive and negative sanctions, judicial approach, and management of chemical dependency (the theme of sobriety is evident in five of the seven case histories). The connection between mental health symptoms, substance use and crime for many MHC clients is evident. In general, clients benefit from the structure and social support that the MHC process and team offers. The majority of clients I spoke with lacked family social support and resources impeding their ability, in many cases, to be fully successful (Vicki's case is a clear exception). Many clients found it difficult to navigate the court system, which was exacerbated by vulnerabilities and disadvantages. Poverty was a common denominator for clients that I spoke with, adding to the challenge of navigating the justice system (Lens 2016). Many of these themes—sobriety, social support from the team, and importance of a job—were evident in success stories from other problem-solving courts (Berman and Feinblatt 2005). Previous research on problem-solving courts focuses almost entirely on judges, but case histories reveal the critical role that probation officers play in the success or failure of clients in MHC.

These stories are powerful. The lives of these clients before entering MHC are difficult, creating impediments to court success. Unambiguously successful cases do occur, but partial success is more common. Success, understood more broadly, can mean a longer interval between criminal offenses, stable housing, or reduced substance abuse, and better management of mental illness. It is important to keep in mind that we do not know how much worse off these clients would have been without the intervention of the court.

Beyond the seven cases profiled, I had numerous informal conversations with clients illustrating positive effects. One such conversation in *County* MHC occurred during court after a client had been in court the previous day for court watch.[5] Sherman, a young man his mid-twenties explained to me, "I do not know where I would be without mental health court!" He talked about how his experience in MHC changed his life trajectory and the relationships made in court encouraged him not to give up. He mentioned the trouble he had with accepting his mental illness. As a young man, Sherman assumed that his mental health symptoms were developmental and related to lifestyle issues (substance use). The court helped him accept that it was mental illness and to make constructive changes to his life. Due to the frequency of his court appearances in MHC, I observed Sherman several times. It was clear in his hearings—through his responses to the positive affirmations from team members (especially the judge) with smiles and optimism and connections with other clients—that at least some part of the court review process, including the sanction of court watch, refreshed him. He revealed that these exchanges gave him the strength to continue the struggle to stay clean and comply with his treatment regimen. Sherman described the connection to the MHC team and the social support they provided as central to his success.

The court does not work for all clients. In fact, several team members mentioned clients that committed suicide while in MHC leading them to reflect on the court's response and if something could have been done differently to alter the client's fate.It is unrealistic to expect that the court can fully address mental illness, substance use and the paucity of social support in many clients' lives. There is no simple solution to managing mental illness. Part of the response must occur outside the criminal justice system. While efforts within the criminal justice system like MHCs can alleviate some of the problems individuals with mental illness face, it cannot remedy the broader social ills at play—limited mental health care, skill deficits and limited employment opportunities, insufficient disability and welfare benefits, among them. The courts have an important role to play as they mediate client contact with the criminal justice apparatus. If we are clear about what MHCs are able to do (and not do), success may become more widespread. The next chapter suggests reforms and a set of "best practices" to improve MHCs, and other strategies of therapeutic justice.

# Notes

1. Berman and Feinblatt (2005) detail three success stories one from community court, drug court and domestic-violence court.
2. The case was dismissed due to "proof problems" but can be brought again.

3. In his case, the certificate stated successful completion from *City Municipal Court Mental Health Probation*, <u>not</u> MHC. This was a unique case and a clear exception.
4. He further detailed that no one in this coffee shop would guess that he suffered from mental illness and was in the court system and I was a professor interviewing him as a part of a research project. We were just two people conversing over a coffee and tea. This exchange and interpretation of its social significance reinforced the importance of reducing stigma and negative labels for clients in MHC.
5. Snedker (2016: 43).

# References

Berman, Greg, and John Feinblatt. 2005. *Good Courts: The Case for Problem-Solving Justice*. New York: The New Press.

Corrigan, Patrick, Vetta Thompson, David Lambert, Yvette Sangster, Jeffrey G. Noel, and Jean Campbell. 2003. "Perceptions of Discrimination Among Persons with Serious Mental Illness." *Psychiatric Services* 54 (8): 1105–10. https://DOI.org/10.1176/appi.ps.54.8.1105.

Desmond, Matthew. 2016. *Evicted: Poverty and Profit in the American City*. New York: Crown Publishing Group.

Lens, Vicki. 2016. *Poor Justice: How the Poor Fare in the Courts*. Oxford: Oxford University Press.

Snedker, Karen A. 2016. "Unburdening Stigma: Identity Repair through Rituals in Mental Health Court." *Society and Mental Health* 6 (1): 36–55. http://journals.sagepub.com/doi/abs/10.1177/2156869315598203.

# 7

# Conclusion: From Therapeutic Justice to Social Work Criminal Justice

MHCs, when oriented toward therapeutic justice, provide hope in the lives of individuals with mental illness involved in the criminal justice system. However, the future of MHCs depends on reforming certain key practices, including modifying aspects of court organization and cultural practices. Some MHCs are already embracing such changes; others will need to do so to remain relevant and effective. With improvements, MHCs hold tremendous potential as a model of criminal justice that can be both effective and more humane.

MHCs represent an alternative to jail (as a condition of sentence)[1] for individuals with mental illness. However, intervening to improve the lives of a socially vulnerable population represents the welfare-enhancing promise of MHCs. Taken together, the evidence presented in this book illustrates how MHCs work and can positively influence clients' lives. The implications are enormous for those clients who benefit from the support and structure of MHCs. However, there are many who are not eligible or who do not opt-into MHC, and thus cannot experience any of the benefits or resources the court has to offer. Moreover, not all MHC clients are successful (or even partially successful). Many do not reap benefits from the court experience.

MHCs are not a panacea to the issue of overrepresentation of people with mental illness in the criminal justice system. MHCs are not preventative. Courts in general are reactive entities; they cannot start a relationship with an individual before he/she is accused of offending. Individuals come to the court system through an arrest, and it is at that point that MHCs become an option. Although becoming a client in MHC benefits many individuals, it does so under the surveillance of legal agents and the looming threat of jail. But MHCs do have proactive elements (e.g., frequent probation and review hearings) as a part of their structure and culture. Many raise concerns about the appropriateness of the criminal justice system as the site for this intervention (Boldt 2009). Expanding prevention-focused practices will increase the therapeutic tendencies of the court.

Researchers who assess MHCs label them as a "promising practice" (Liu and Redlich 2015)—which is a step below "best practice." Researchers place an "emphasis on empirical evidence and its application toward best practice" (Heilbrun et al. 2015, 1) to improve how governmental entities interact with people who have mental illness. In line with "evidence-based practice" and "best practices," the reforms proposed in this chapter come from the case studies, interviews and court observations of *City* and *County* MHCs, as well as the research literature on MHCs. Achieving therapeutic justice fully requires a series of shifts and changes as outlined in the following pages.

Prior to the implementation of key reforms, MHCs must clarify the court's mission, aligning it with their practices and resources. Multiple models are possible, but alignment is critical. Specific MHCs need to either re-center around their original mission of MHCs, with a singular focus on severe mental illness and low-level offenders. Or MHCs need to alter practices and resources to better align with a revised mission around a broader understating of mental illness with a less direct relationship to criminal behavior and/or expand to include more serious offenses (more in line with the social scientific evidence). A change in mission might be appropriate in many courts, as long as the necessary resources develop alongside. It is to the proposed reforms, based on developing "best practices," that I now turn.

## Implementing Reforms for MHCs: Toward Social Work Criminal Justice[2]

MHCs and other problem-solving courts are already innovations within the criminal justice system, but they can innovate further. Therapeutic justice—a philosophical orientation for MHCs detailed throughout the book—can best be achieved through practices reflecting what I call a kind of *social work criminal justice*. This idea is similar to a "social justice standpoint," as advocated by a MHC judge and similar to a public-health model approach for courts proposed by legal scholar Adam Benforado (2015). A *social work criminal justice* approach to MHC necessitates a further shift in the balance between a social control model and a model of care, stressing the latter. A social work-oriented court is a hybrid—not a complete social service agency nor a traditional criminal justice one. Whatever the therapeutic orientation of the court, punitive elements are ever present as judges still dole out real punishments, sometimes at odds with a therapeutic focus. As the name suggests, criminal justice elements—such as accountability and punishment—cannot be abandoned entirely but can be de-emphasized more.

Elements of *social work criminal justice* already exist in current MHC practices. Having both a defense social worker and a court liaison with social work training as part of the MHC team, which is already in place, sets the foundation for this model. MHCs can incorporate more practices from the social service world and perhaps be explicit about the merger of two systems under a social work criminal justice paradigm. MHCs are already understood as "blended institutions" (Miller and Johnson 2009) where legal and social work worlds become entangled.

Pushing the balance further toward social work and away from criminal justice may seem impossible to some, including some with training in social work. But MHCs are already—to some extent—operating counter to traditional court practices. The traditional adversarial way of doing criminal justice, by almost any measure, is not working. Jails and prisons are full, despite unprecedented reductions in crime rates nationally and people with mental illness are incarcerated at high rates.[3] A social work tendency is already present in MHCs, but there is no consensus on taking it to another level. In line with my recommendation of *social work criminal justice*, I propose several reforms for the future of MHCs. The reforms modify and extend reforms of problem-solving courts suggested by others but focused more specifically to MHC.[4] These reforms return to the original paradigm shifts associated with MHCs (as detailed in Chapter 2), which differentiate MHCs from the traditional court model. The reforms outlined in Table 7.1 push MHCs further toward therapeutic and collaborative orientations and addresses some of the hazards of problem-solving courts around accountability, measuring effectiveness and realistic expectations (Berman and Feinblatt 2005).

Table 7.1 MHC reforms: From therapeutic justice to social work criminal justice

| Orientation | Guidelines | Practices |
|---|---|---|
| Therapeutic | Incentives | ~ Lessen abstinence requirement<br>~ Therapeutic approach to non-compliance<br>~ Variable jurisdictions<br>~ Offer more dismissal of charges<br>~ Gift cards for compliance<br>~ More housing |
| | De-stigmatize | ~ Change the court name<br>~ Expand stigma-reducing court practices |
| | Diversity | ~ Opt-in more clients<br>~ Felony tracks or felony courts<br>~ Relax eligibility and amenability assessments<br>~ Minority recruitment |
| Collaborative | Court management | ~ Court program coordinator<br>~ Run the court calendar effectively<br>~ Judicial consistency<br>~ Reform team rotation practices<br>~ Strengthen relationships with services providers |
| | Team member training/recruitment | ~ Initial training<br>~ Continuing education<br>~ Hire diverse MHC team<br>~ Quarterly retreats |
| | Collecting, analyzing and using data | ~ Court statistician for problem-solving courts<br>~ Regular external evaluation |
| | Publicity | ~ Public awareness campaign |

## Therapeutic Orientation: Adopting Harm Reduction

MHCs can more formally embrace harm-reduction philosophies and practices. In the words of a judge, who presided over clients with "minor charges," the court is "a door to help." A harm-reduction orientation focuses on therapeutic issues, acknowledging the harm that criminal justice experiences impose on clients. Many team members suggested that they have been practicing "harm reduction" for a long time without labeling it as such. A modified harm reduction approach prevails in the two MHCs in this study, leading to a nuanced—and often less punitive—understanding of the review process (as detailed in Chapter 4). However, it is far from uniform and remains unformalized. A defense social worker suggested that the "court is behind" in its approach as "harm reduction is being embraced elsewhere… [including] harm reduction housing" with evidence of effectiveness (Ritter and Cameron 2006).

### Incentives

MHCs have the capacity to draw in more clients at varying stages of the court process. As detailed in Chapter 5, there are many ways to increase incentives. A defense attorney surmised, "I think the problem is we are not offering benefits to enough people," so expanding benefits would increase the inducement to consider MHC.

Four incentives are worth serious consideration. First, directly in-line with a harm-reduction approach, MHCs can incentivize participation and client "buy-in" by moving away from zero-tolerance with regard to abstinence,[5] without abandoning it entirely. In many ways, addiction is the biggest stumbling block for MHC clients. I observed countless examples of how substance abuse—both alcohol and drugs—derailed many clients from being successful in MHC. For many clients, struggling with substance abuse, total abstinence does not seem to work. Under the requirement of abstinence, MHCs' focus shifts to sanctions and the management of sobriety, overshadowing other mental health concerns of their clients.

Sanctions can be counterproductive to therapeutic justice and management of substance use issues. While abstinence is still the goal, in practice, a more nuanced understanding should prevail so that substance use violations alone do not lead to revocation from the court. More fluid, less zero tolerance responses to addiction often occur in the practices of the court. This reform might address concerns that many of the MHC team members I interviewed had about MHCs turning into *de facto* drug courts. If the sobriety provision cannot be reformed, another solution it to have a distinct track within MHC or a separate Co-Occurring Court that explicitly deals with clients with mental illness and chemical dependency issues.

A second reform would formally reduce the length of the court's jurisdiction, which is typically "too long"—cited many team members—for misdemeanors cases; this often happens informally through early graduations and on a case-by—case basis as a condition of sentence. It is not clear that a standard two-year probationary period is necessary for the stabilization of individual's mental health or for the therapeutic benefits of the court to be realized. The two-year probationary period may be a reflection of administrative ease—that's what other non-specialty courts do—or legal allowance rather than based on a scientific analysis of effectiveness. While there is some disagreement about jurisdiction length, especially from prosecutors who prefer the *status quo* (longer probationary period) and some judges (even suggesting a five year jurisdiction as a possibility in line with current practices for DUI and domestic violence cases). The bigger challenge is determining the "optimal time for an individual to be in mental health court," as summarized a judge. Research data on varying jurisdictions for clients can inform a sliding jurisdiction scale for practical purposes.

Third, MHCs can increase the number of dismissal offers, especially in misdemeanors cases, given the suppressive effect such offers have on criminal recidivism (as detailed in Chapter 5). In the case of misdemeanor crimes, if the court dismissed more cases this could be an effort towards decriminalizing mental illness. On the other hand, if it goes to the other extreme and offers everyone a dismissal of charges some might argue it has become more of a service provider than a court, raising questions about governmental oversight over social services if in fact it becomes a key way to access resources. This has implications for equity and justice issues. Others, like a defense attorney, suggested that having all cases under one Superior Court would be smoother and linked it to the incentive structure: "Then if it is a misdemeanor, it is a straight up dismissal if you comply. If it is a felony, you get a misdemeanor. Then it gives everyone incentive to comply."

Lastly, MHCs can facilitate more housing services and other resources—a "critical mass" as described by others (Schneider et al. 2007). Stable housing is essential for MHC success. The lack of housing options was often a source of frustration expressed by many team members. For instance, a court liaison recalled cases where "we have people where everything is ready to go. They are amenable to treatment. Their entire treatment plan is ready, and there is no housing." This poses additional challenges for people who are homelessness or require in-patient treatment programs or other forms of supportive housing. In addition, efforts to centralize and offer "wraparound" services for clients in one location would reduce complex scheduling which often leads to missed appointments and non-compliance.

Part of the discussion around expanding incentives is the need for increasing resources. A defense attorney summarized the problem that was reiterated by many: "there hasn't been the creation of a lot of services to match our current needs. We are just doing more with less and serving a more difficult population." A judge noted, "The perks have seem to have lessened over time, because housing used to be a priority for individuals who would opt-in." The lack of resources left one defense social worker to characterize the work process as "robotic," being at the "mercy of court resources." Working under tremendous constraints, professionals in the MHC referred to the available resources as "not good enough." A court liaison described it this way: "There is always a resource problem… we know there are not enough psychiatric beds. They are trying to reduce the funds they pay mental health providers so then you get bigger caseloads." Necessary reforms include expanding the allocation for housing, in- and out-patient treatment programs especially for clients with co-occurring conditions, psychiatric beds, psychiatric evaluations as well as in-house services, such as anger management and domestic violence prevention. Unfortunately addressing this concern is not directly under the court's control. Funding comes from governmental sources and services are provided by city agencies and various non-profits organizations. Bringing in court leaders on city/county/state funding priorities might be required to match the funding allocation with the need.

My suggestions are consistent with recommendations that the government should incentivize behavioral compliance or induce desired behaviors by entering into contracts with individuals (Winick 1991). Part of offering more incentives to clients is about warding off the "therapeutic state" that Wexler (1973, 338) counsels against. He suggested making the treatment alternative "more attractive—or at least no less attractive—than the traditional criminal alternative." In many ways things haven't changes much since Wexler's early writings: it is the lack of resources that limits what the courts are capable of achieving and expanding incentives requires matched financial investments.

## De-Stigmatize

Part of a social work-oriented criminal justice agenda is about reducing stigma around mental illness. Exaggerated connections between mental illness and criminal behavior frames media coverage and feeds stigma. In reality, criminal behavior for many MHC clients is often better understood as a consequence of multiple factors, rather than being directly caused by mental illness. Court rituals can serve to reduce some of the stigma people with mental illness experience. Graduations represent an effective reward ritual, but MHCs could expand stigma-reducing practices prior to gradation, such as a more therapeutically-oriented sanctioning process and other rewards (e.g., tokens, gift cards) throughout the program.

The negativity around mental illness is impossible to avoid completely, but the name of the court may add to, not reduce, social stigma. The name of the court—with mental health in its title—was identified by MHC team members and clients as problematic. It may discourage some individuals, who might really benefit from the structure and support of MHC, from participating. There are some alternatives which do not use "mental health" in the title. Courts should consider alternatives such as Behavioral

Health Court, Alterative Court Program, Therapeutic Court, or simply Treatment Court. *County* MHC created a separate diversionary program, shifting the language to "Therapeutic Alternative Unit." *City* MHC is considering a name change, according to a judge. This represents more than a symbolic reform, and one that a number of MHCs are taking nationally.[6] Less specific court titles could also include clients with co-occurring mental health and substance abuse issues without naming them publicly.

## Diversity

To broaden their therapeutic effect, MHCs can serve a more diverse client base. This includes taking in higher risk clients as well as more clients from racial and ethnic groups currently underrepresented in MHCs (when compared to the greater jail population in the surrounding area). Diversity of risk in the client pool is somewhat controversial. Many team members argued that MHC works well for the "high functioning participants" rather than the more severely impaired people the court was initially created to help. The result is that many of the "neediest individuals" are left behind and seen in the MHDT track or traditional court with fewer resources to address complex defendant's needs.

To address this critique, MHCs can expand who they help in three specific ways. First, they could allow defendants to opt-into MHC at later stages of their case, by creating an easy pathway in *City* MHC for MHDT defendants to become MHCs clients. Second, the court could consider broadening the eligibility requirements, as the population that the court was intended to address may be close to capacity or already served. Many team members referenced clients with a diagnosis of post-traumatic stress disorder (PTSD) as a possible group that could be added to the court docket. A defense attorney critically stated, "I know it [eligibility criteria] is based on the access to care criteria and how you get benefits" but "there are people, I think, with severe PTSD who could benefit from our court, but we don't have the resources to help them." More access to some components of MHCs might prove beneficial to a broader range of defendants. Third, MHCs could create distinct tracks, including a "MHC lite" for clients with less complicated needs and less risky clients, as well as a path for clients with co-occurring disorders. In general, adopting a more harm-reduction orientation, argued a defense attorney, would "capture some of those people who are in the margins."

In practice, MHCs courts already create individualized plans and vary supervision and intervention, based loosely on risk and needs assessments of client, but perhaps more formal tools could aid (not replace) this process such as the risk-needs-responsivity (RNR) concept (see Andrews and Bonta 2003). Under this model some argue that mental illness is a response factor as opposed to a risk factor for criminality (Fisler 2015). Such tools allow for the risk and needs of clients to drive the appropriate level of intervention, possibly improving assessments and monitoring, giving more resources and attention to higher-risk, higher-need defendants. A judge described how a "high needs, high risk" approach could lead to court reorganization:

> We ought to differentiate across the board in the way we deal with them [clients], and perhaps the low need, low risk people should be dealt with in the general trial courts for personal deterrence and general deterrence, and the high needs, high risks should be dealt with as we do with specialty courts.

Differing slightly, another judge suggested that the courts focus heavily on needs, to best align client needs with what the court can offer. Prior judges have worked on restructuring the intake criteria and creating "roadmaps" to assist in the selection process but from the perspective of this judge "improvement is still needed."

Taking clients with higher needs and risks is potentially dangerous and politically perilous, but if MHCs want to have more successes for more people, it is one path forward. There is some support among judges for this refocusing, while simultaneously advocating for more diversion in the case of lower-level offenses,

> Therapeutic courts work best when they are really serving high risk, high needs people, which means do we need to be serving the shoplifters? Maybe those are the cases that should be diverted and not filled on

criminally at all. But the high risk high need folks are the ones that are not safety able to get well and manage their recovery without the oversight of a court and probation, and tend to do well, and both they and the community really benefits from that.

Accepting riskier clients will ultimately mean more failures, but a greater potential for success and a wider circle of beneficiaries. Expanding to a true felony MHC is one way forward.

The lack of minority representation in MHC clientele was met with a degree of frustration from some members, especially women and minorities and those with social work expertise. Questions arose around who was missing from MHC and for which groups was it most useful. Of the seven profiled "success" stories discussed in Chapter 6, three were offered the best incentive to opt-in (dismissal of charges), all of whom were women and two were white women. The quantitative analysis reported in Chapter 5 also illustrates the effects of court program incentives and suggests that a greater awareness of sex and racial/ethnic disparities is needed in MHCs, especially during the opt-in decision-making process, to address differential participation and success rates. Criminal history and a lack of amenability represent key obstacles for many minority clients, but a richer understanding of the role of cultural factors in help-seeking behaviors and stigma management and structural factors in criminality might alleviate some underrepresentation in the court.

In a contemplative response, a judge talked about how the court needs to have conversations about "implicit bias" and "intersectionality issues" implying especially that race/ethnicity and social class overlap to effect outcomes. In detailing some of the best success stories she commented that both clients were white who "I suspect had other resources in their lives." She went on to confess that she thinks about race daily and "loses sleep over it" but even with her awareness of a "cultural and communication divide" she did not always have "the tools to break it." Expanding notions of whom MHC can work for will ultimately expand the pool of participants to include more minority clients. This is a key reform to respond to the clear underrepresentation of minorities, especially blacks and Hispanics, in MHCs.

## Collaboration: Management and Education

MHCs deviate from the traditional court model with an emphasis on collaboration. "Buy-in" to the mission of MHCs is first and foremost to court performance. A well-functioning team that talks to one another, respects and trusts one another, even when members differ, leads to less adversarialism, benefiting clients. Encouraging respect and listening, are prerequisites for a functioning team. Several MHC team members expressed concerns about certain team members being able to communicate effectively, especially in *County* MHC. Others expressed time-pressure as a culprit. A court liaison recounted, "I'm not sure about the collaboration. I'm not sure what that means, and we don't have time to talk as a team about things like privileged communication."

### Court Management

The first step to better manage the court calendar and team is to hire an effective court program coordinator to oversee the organization and management of the court and to help the team "get what they need [such as training]" suggested a defense attorney. When MHCs lack a competent, well-trained court program coordinator it causes much frustration among team members. The goal, according to a defense attorney, should be to "run the calendar... so that it is less traumatic to the clients." Managing the court calendar and being efficient and effective in working with clients are important goals, and is somewhat lacking in both courts.

There are inherent challenges that come with working in a highly bureaucratic system. A court liaison suggested, "I think if we could just cut through the bureaucracy and cut through the red tape and do what has to be done," the court will be more successful. Judges are crucial to the flow of the court calendar. Too often contemporary criminal justice relies heavily on efficiency, sometimes at the expense of effectiveness; a tradeoff noted by Warren (1998) in a tabular comparison between traditional court process and "transformed" court process in problem-solving courts (cited in Rottman and Casey 1999). The process in MHCs is slower, as it takes time to build relationships and trust, for the sake of addressing complex social problems. If punishment was the primary motivator for MHCs, then efficiency would reign supreme, but the shift in emphasis away from efficiency concerns is necessary for outcomes reflecting therapeutic justice. The trade-off between efficiency and effectiveness must be recognized. The goal of efficiency—at times—has to be subservient to other goals. The priority cannot be to get through as many cases in the fewest number of minutes. It is not that MHCs should ignore efficiency, but rather highlight effective practices, which at times must be expedient (such as during express review hearing) and at other times be time-consuming (during opt-ins and graduations). A graduation ritual is a *prima facie* example of court inefficiency, but while sometimes time-consuming, it can be very effective for the MHC graduate and other observers (as detailed in Chapter 5).

A judge spoke about "judicial efficiency and economy" as goals but warned against "equating efficiency to being fast." He understood efficiency as "using the right words, being respectful of people's time" and he does remind himself to "try to slowdown" and take "one case at a time." His concerns were more about "what's going on [with a client]… and what can I do to make this person not come back [to court before scheduled review]." In linking the pacing of the court to levels of compliance, a judge noted that "I tried really hard to move people along when they are in compliance, and then take the time when there was a problem."

The main determinant of how efficient and effective the court process is the tone set by the judge. The irony is that sometimes judges try to move things along to be more efficient, but it actually distracts from the flow of the court. The running of the court is more appropriately set collaboratively, by the prosecuting and defense attorneys, who are most familiar with the cases and the client issues.

Beyond effective court and calendar managment, stability, communication, and a balance of power were seen as important and in need of reform to strengthen teamwork.[7] MHC teams have to balance stability with longevity among team members; considering re-rotation of key players might be a model. There is an "extensive learning curve" in the words of a prosecutor that encourages a longer rotation period but another prosecutor suggested that if there is too little rotation the "team gets too comfortable."

A probation officer stated, "You want to have that consistency across the board." It is not just judicial stability that is important but also stability among prosecution. The stability is achieved through personnel and in approach, as a court liaison described, "Like the judge, we have different prosecutors on different days." I observed that different prosecutors working on different days led to variation in prosecutorial consistency and court practices, frustrating members of the defense. A court liaison echoed this account and blamed it on a lack of resources—too few prosecutors.

Of course, too little movement can thwart new members and new ideas. A defense social worker claimed that the "status quo" around leadership "prevented the court from growing and generating new ideas… such as harm reduction." Too much stability can lead to a power imbalance, as is the case in *County* MHC. This was the source of much tension as there was no "counterweight to the strong leadership in prosecutors' office" and the defense was left the "powerless… [the] step-child of the court," whereby "everything we do is put under the microscope," complained the same defense social worker. Similarly, a defense attorney described their position under a strong prosecutor's office as reduced to a "persistent chirping bird." Even judges were cognizant of the power disparioty as "the prosecutor can maintain too much control… They can serve as the gatekeepers to the court." A big impediment to the team's collaboration was lack of transparency and inclusion of all team member's voices in the decision-making process, especially by "people on the ground" not just supervisors suggested a defense attorney. That does not mean that all positions are equal, but they should all be voiced and heard. This was particularly apparent in *County* MHC. The legal liability for probation was a grave concern given they perceived a lack of "voice" in the opt-in decision-making process. In fact, one of the probation officers was being deposed in a civil lawsuit the same week I interviewed him. It was not just probation officers who voiced this concern and its negative influence on the team's effectiveness. For example, a court liaison stated, "Everyone is safe except for the probation officers. So that creates a lot of tension and anger when they feel they don't have a voice."

In the two MHCs I studied, one court (*City* MHC) was more collaborative than the other. However, recent structural changes —with the defense agency contract—is currently threatening its ability to continue to collaborate to the extent that it has in the past. The overarching organization representing public defense attorneys recently changed, prompted by a legal suit to expand the number of defense attorneys working in MHC. Now the three public defense agencies are under the same umbrella. In theory, this change would improve exposure of MHCs to the legal community and, possibly, the general public. However, in practice, this exposes the court to more attorneys practicing in treatment courts who do not have training or the necessary professional interest to work with clients with mental illness. The new defense agency represents a serious challenge to the collaborative model. A court liaison talked about the new defense law firm noting, "[they] don't talk to me unless they want to." Although the new defense attorneys have been invited to the pre-court meetings, they mostly do not attend. From a judge's perspective the new agency and the associated lawyers were "less willing, or unwilling, to engage in the collaborative aspect, so they want to… waive any of their clients' right for the long-term benefit." This may ultimately hamper the court's ability to encourage defendants to opt-in. This could be disastrous for the future of *City* MHC as familiarity with the court, "buy-in" and trust amongst the members are pivotal for a workable team.

Beyond the internal team and associated legal agencies, there is room for better communication and collaboration with community service providers to enhance smoother transitions for clients. Even in MHC hearings "deference" can be given to case managers or other treatment agency representatives present on behalf of clients (e.g., such as moving the case forward in the court calendar) suggested a defense attorney. More collaboration also offers greater assistance with earlier intervention in ways that benefit clients. Agencies can also follow-up with the team if a client "starts to spiral out of control," as a probation officer suggested. There is a danger that better communication between providers, housing and social service agencies could be as a tool for net-widening social control (see Chapter 2 and Castellano 2011); a probation officer noted that a tighter relationship would "enhance accountability and reduce client manipulation." MHCs can reach out to the other agencies with a therapeutic orientation. For example, police officers sometimes attend court reviews, but relationships between police and MHCs can be strengthened. When arrests happen, police officers might learn to "flag" cases for MHC on the initial citation.

## Team Member Training and Recruitment

The MHCs in this study had most of the components for a good specialty court, except both lacked comprehensive and mandatory training for their team (Skeem et al. 2006).[8] All team members expressed interest in and had some background in mental illness, some quite extensive in terms of educational credential and work history in the area of mental health, but received little or no training once hired in MHC. A probation officer described the process as "trial by fire." Many probation officers had been with the court since its inception, before any training was developed. Another probation officer summarized the structural problem:

> There's nothing built into the system so that when a new staff person comes in, particularly attorneys, who have no training—why should they—in mental illness. Judges, who are really just attorneys, who have no training in being judges or, mental illness or chemical dependency besides what they got, you have these… people have no consistent training.

A prosecutor reflected about the early days, without training, when the court "limped along." Training across the team is needed.

All team members stated something to the effect of "the agency does not provide training," while they did get some "on the job training" from co-workers. In the case of judges, they talked about being "paired" with or "shadow[ing]" the previous judge. In fact a judge told me that she "demanded it" and how she "begged them to orient me [to MHC]." However, there was very little, if any, mandated training and many members suggested that education of staff was a "priority" for reform. Given the dual role that probation officers hold in working with clients who are mentally ill, probation officer training and support may be critical in improving outcomes for clients (Skeem et al. 2007). Beyond effective training in one's own position a judge suggested "cross-training"—learning about the science around mental illness as well as other team members positions. He highlighted that just because you know the law and have judicial experiences, it does not mean you will be an effective judge as MHC is "vastly different, which requires new [non-legal] skill development."

Once basic mental health training for team members is implemented, continuing educational opportunities can supplement earlier training. Workshops and educational seminars could include the connection between criminal behavior and mental illness and how "those two worlds collapse," as a court liaison put it. Conducting trainings with city departments across all of the municipalities in collaboration with a defense team, as suggested by a prosecutor, would educate those connected to the criminal justice system, even tangentially, so they know it is an alternative to incarceration.

In addition, cultural training might partially address racial and ethnic client disparities. Beyond training and continuing education, MHC team can expand their racial and ethnic diversity through reformed hiring practices and "promote diversity on the bench" as a judge advocated. Several were critical of the underrepresentation of racial and ethnic minorities among court professionals, calling for a more diverse MHC team as a first step in addressing issues of racial/ethnic equity within the courts. Having a more diverse MHC team might increase the cultural competency of court. Since, decisions about eligibility and sanctions are discretionary and subjective, cultural competency is paramount. A defense social worker directly linked the lack of racial/ethnic representation in the MHC team to the disproportionate number of minorities found eligible during the opt-in process and the higher failure rate for minority clients.

Training and hiring practices shape the level of collaboration within the MHC. Ways to further enhance collaboration and team building—beyond initial training and hiring—are also needed. Beyond position specific training, collaboration within the MHC team requires a functional team with clear definitions and recognition of each team members' role and level of expertise. Team members offered such ideas as retreats and outside mediators to ensure that communication is multi-directional. Straying from a teamwork model in both orientation and practice threatens the efficacy of MHCs.

## Collecting, Analyzing and Using Data

To improve, MHCs can collect useful data on clients and the court process and make the data available for statistical analysis.[9] Findings can inform court reforms to achieve the best outcomes for clients. Therapeutic jurisprudence, as an interdisciplinary project, calls for linking social scientific inquiry and law (Winick 1996). Up to now, social science contributions to the study of MHCs have largely been in the field of psychology. Sociology and other fields have much to offer to in the assessment of therapeutic jurisprudence; this book contributes to this effort through a case study design showing some of the therapeutic and antitherapeutic outcomes of MHCs.

Using social scientific inquiry to promote an understanding of MHCs beyond the specific case studies, MHCs can gather and make data more easily available to researchers to perform analyses. A court liaison suggested using data to inform "evidence-based practices" and having meetings to talk about the data and then "make changes." Many, including a court liaison, spoke about data as critical to "frame" court assessments, evaluate effectiveness and to "give a picture to not only us, but the county, to the nations of these that work." For many team members, not collecting and using data was "irresponsible" and "horrifying," as several probation officers described it. A probation officer suggested placing revoked or unsuccessful cases under the microscope, referring to them as "forensic autopsies" to be examined by the team.[10]

Many team members took the court on "faith," they believe that it works but they "have no proof" in the words of a prosecutor. In the past, there was some precedence in *County* MHC to collect and use statistics, but that was abandoned with a specific staff departure. Ideally, the court manager would have basic statistical skills or be able to work with a court social scientist/statistical analyst. MHCs could share an analysist position with other problem-solving courts. MHCs should also have comprehensive evaluations performed by a third party regularly (at least every 5–7 years) but must also be cognizant of the challenges—dynamism and variation—with evaluating effectiveness of MHCs and follow informed recommendations (Wolff and Pogorzelski 2005).

**Publicity**

Beyond education within the MHC team, educational outreach should expand more broadly in the criminal justice system and legal communities.[11] Some research argues that what MHCs and problem-solving courts are doing is a prototype for practices that traditional courts ought to adopt (Berman and Feinblatt 2005). A judge, who advocated this position, suggested that this would involve "flipping the paradigm on its face" and retooling mainstream courts to the model of MHCs. He argued that specialty courts are the "proper way" as they "address the underlying problem." He further intimated that if,

> general courts adopted the methods that we are using in the really intense specialty courts, then the general courts would have the same sort of outcome… which again are multifaceted and better for everybody, including the defendant.

He believed that a lack of resources is behind the failure to reshape the way courts operate in the mainstream criminal justice system.[12] While keeping MHC intact many offered hope in applying methods and practices in MHC "outside of specialty courts into a more generalized approach" stated a judge.

Importantly, the public at large needs to be educated about MHCs and mental illness. The public is unfamiliar with the criminal justice process, especially problem-solving courts. Education around mental health awareness and the MHC process in the community is also a viable way of addressing the racial and ethnic make-up of the court. All team members suggested that the public was "oblivious" or knows little or nothing about MHCs and other treatment courts. There is an opportunity to invest in the public knowledge and awareness about MHCs. A court liaison stated, "I think it is a real shame, the fact that we have a great model here, and it is better than most other courts like it, and we are not selling it."

A public awareness campaign could extend MHCs reach and support. It also might open collaborations with other organizations and help to divert individuals from jails and the courts entirely.[13] Most team members thought there would be greater community "buy-in" if the public was more informed. This is especially important given the link between mental illness and violence portrayed in the mass media. A court liaison characterized our society as being "so fearful but then never wants to provide services or money to actually combat that."

However, if the public were more aware of these courts and their effectiveness, the public might be more willing to pay for services to reduce the social and economic costs.

## Tradeoffs of "Net-Widening"

MHCs aimed toward therapeutic justice do indeed widen the net. A consequence of therapeutic justice is a tradeoff to new and sometimes stronger nets (see Chapter 2 for an extensive discussion). At its best, MHCs are responsive to the public concerns about safety and act as a stabilizing force in society, while bringing a social work lens to criminal justice. But at its worst, MHCs criminalize mental illness and furthers the reach of the criminal justice system. Some of the limits of treatment courts to bring about therapeutic justice are related to their placement in the criminal justice system itself. MHC reformers must be cognizant of the overarching criminal justice system, which limits the potential of MHCs. MHCs do add additional layers of monitoring and surveillance—hence newer and denser criminal justice nets. Some, but not all, concerns about nets can be countered—or could be—by additional treatment assistance, social support, and housing assistance.

The exploration of MHCs contributes to our general understanding of how the criminal justice system and mental health are linked. An examination of these two MHCs allows for a better understanding of the broader issues surrounding MHCs with local, national and international implications. The problem-solving court movement has gained momentum in other common law countries such as England, Wales, Australia, Canada, Ireland and elsewhere (for a comparative study of the problem-solving court movement see Nolan 1999; for a focused study of Canada see Schneider et al. 2007; for a general discussion see Schneider 2010). Investigating the impact of problem solving courts, and mental health courts specifically, is important for both domestic criminal justice policies and for courts in other countries. The U.S. is an important case to study MHCs given its weak social welfare state. Other industrialized countries may not need to rely as much on problem-solving courts with stronger (mental) health apparatuses and more generous welfare benefits and available social services.

While MHCs are unlike other courts in the criminal justice system, reflecting a significant shift in social policy, the therapeutic model offers insights to MHCs and criminal justice more broadly. But more research is needed to guide additional reforms. Future research is needed to examine the implications of expanding, strengthening, and introducing new nets. More work can be done in both a scholarly and policy direction to better understand the association between MHCs and other diversionary frameworks. In addition, researchers need to carefully consider the role that incentivized sentences play in curbing criminal behavior. Furthermore, future work should explore other institutional incentives, and the sanctioning process, with an eye toward possible socio-demographic determinants. Future research needs to more fully examine responses to non-compliance and explore if patterns of MHC sanctioning influence after-court criminal recidivism. More data on the cost effectiveness of MHCs is needed to evaluate the social and fiscal costs and benefits of these courts.

It is important to make changes to MHCs with a clear awareness of what MHCs can and cannot do. Despite the benefits that MHCs provide clients, and team members working within the court, there are structural and cultural limitations to what MHCs can accomplish. MHCs must work within societal constraints; they cannot fundamentally alter the structural inequalities that shape clients' lives. MHCs cannot be expected to ameliorate fundamental social conditions that influence criminal trajectories including unsupportive family, economic hardship, policing that criminalizes mental illness, and inadequate housing policy. MHCs cannot be expected to address the inadequacies of other social systems and a weakening social safety net, nor can MHCs be expected to fill the void in the mental health apparatus. Furthermore, MHCs are embedded within a society that constructs mental illness as a criminal justice problem (Erickson and Erickson 2008) and uses the criminal justice system as a service delivery model to address serious mental illness in our society.

MHCs, while a softer hand of the criminal justice system, is still part of a punitive system. Yet, MHCs can, and do, operate in a therapeutic way. Even within the limited parameters, MHCs can address issues of homelessness (or lack of affordable housing), health care needs (mental health primarily), and limited social support networks and resource accessibility (through the MHC team) on an individual level. The court program can help clients better navigate the governmental and service agencies that provide much needed resources, such as housing and treatment.

## Prevention Prior to MHC

A prevention perspective demands intervention prior to court entry and, in many cases, prior to police contact. There are multiple points of intervention prior to MHCs whereby defendants with severe mental illness can be completely diverted from the criminal justice system (for example the Sequential Intercept Model, see Griffin et al. 2015; see also Bernstein and Seltzer 2003; Schneider et al. 2007; Seltzer 2005; Thompson et al. 2003). Ideally, MHCs would work more directly with prior points of intervention (e.g., police) as well as post-MHC intervention points (e.g., court re-entry). For example, prevention prior to MHC could be done through police Crisis Intervention Teams (as detailed in Chapter 2). In the city at the center of this study, a working CIT program should create less contact with MHC, as a CIT officer explained, ideally "we do not make a lot of arrests" but rather divert people to the hospital, shelters, or other social service agencies. A Mental Health Professional suggested that the CIT police team can make it so that some incidents involving people with serious mental illness do not become front page news, by intervening and de-escalating the situation.

Given that individuals have been charged with a crime, MHCs are mostly post-booking diversions. Other diversions which redirect individuals from being processed in the criminal justice system are largely pre-booking. Interventions prior to ever stepping into a jail or a courtroom have been successful in the lives of people with mental illness.[14] Moving away from the criminal justice end of the spectrum by offering more pre-trial diversions translates into treatment, in lieu of punishment, not in addition to punishment. More diversionary (treatment as a true alternative) practices will reduce fears about the dangers of the therapeutic state (e.g., Wexler 1972–1973). All the clients I interviewed mentioned that earlier intervention might have helped them, especially those who were homeless such as Jennifer, Shima, Norm and Robert.

## Final Thoughts

While the book was going to press, I followed up with the seven clients discussed in Chapter 6 by accessing their court records.[15] I began the book with Monique's case, as it seemed to symbolize success and optimism. However, in 2017 Monique returned to MHC on assault and harassment charges, three years after graduation from MHC. Her mental stability had deteriorated. The judge ordered a competency evaluation, ultimately finding that Monique was unable to proceed with her case due to a lack of competency. While previously in MHC, she was able to manage her mental health and limit her drinking, but once Monique graduated from MHC the lack of stability and structure had deleterious effects. Her case highlights two critical weaknesses of the current MHC model. First, after clients graduate from MHC they are untethered from the criminal justice system with no support or oversight. Some clients might benefit from a model for continual sponsorship after leaving MHC, such as the "peer model" where MHC graduates assist other clients as they go through the court process. As the peer serves in a leadership and supportive role it may reinforce client success and confidence. A court liaison described it in the following way:

> They help get the other person to appointments, provide some encouragement. They can be available to talk to. They have a limited but still very good role. They are that person who has been there and say, 'Hey, I know what you are going through, I support you.' That's nice.

Team members suggested expanding the program to keep formerly MHC clients connected with the court in a leadership capacity. The peer model is "somewhat limited," according to one court liaison, but could be expanded. Monique might have benefited from serving as a peer model to other clients.

Second, a client's mental health can worsen after MHC oversight is removed, sometimes leading to destabilization and fluctuating competency. When judges rule, after receiving competency evaluations, that a defendant[16] is not able to proceed he/she is referred to the state's mental hospital for further evaluation. In many cases, given the strict standards of civil commitment, individuals are held for a short period of time and then released back into society with little or no support. As in the case of Monique, she needs assistance and structure but, as far as I am aware, is not currently under the supervision or care of any institutional body.

Work needs to be done to bridge the gap between criminal and civil systems (as well as speed up the competency process with more psychiatric evaluators). From a net-widening perspective, severing the ties with the court for graduates and/or those who are not eligible due to competency concerns is in many ways desirable, but there is a need to expand organizational responses and services to link the civil and criminal domains. Resources must be provided to connect those who are found not competent to stand trial or enter MHC, but do not reach the standard for involuntary civil commitment, to services. The court is a critical point of intervention that often goes unexploited, mostly due to the lack of available resources. While there are "bridge" programs to fill this gap, they are limited in funding and number of outreach workers. Even with sufficient resources, the court would still be limited in filling this gap—those individuals with mental illness that are unable to proceed in MHC but do not reach the level for civil commitment—as they cannot compel individual to take advantage of services, whereas courts can mandate treatment for MHC clients.

As for the other clients, as of the fall of 2017, Jennifer, Isaiah, Robert and Vicki have had no further contact with the criminal justice system. After three years of no contact with the criminal justice system, Shima is currently on MHC conditions of release at the opt-in phase. It is not clear if she will try MHC again and if she does whether or not it will work to curb her criminal involvement for a longer period of time. Norm was also back in court in the summer of 2017 on an assault charge and he chose to serve his time and not opt-into MHC. Shima and Norm's cases are similar to Monique's in that the lack of support and structure after graduation likely contributed to their recidivism.

To achieve therapeutic justice, courts oriented toward individuals with mental illness must proceed differently and with greater awareness of the anti-therapeutic tendencies of the criminal justice system. On their own, MHCs are not enough to curb contact with the criminal justice system for the majority of clients, no matter how dedicated the team, or how wanting a client is to avoid the criminal justice system. At its best, courts oriented towards therapeutic justice can be responsive to social problems (mental illness and criminality, safety, homelessness, low-income housing) and potentially provide a stabilizing force in society, leading to improvements in the quality of life for a vulnerable section of the population. At its worst, these courts can punish multiple statuses—the "triple stigma" of criminal, mentally ill and addict (Hartwell 2004),—and lead to additional stigma and extensive time entangled with the criminal justice system.

The courts in this study—when lead by a knowledgeable and empathetic judge and a strong team—can be supportive and therapeutic, reduce social stigma for clients, and provide a model for a more humane, treatment-oriented criminal justice that lowers recidivism rates. Although MHC effectiveness for some portion of the population is indeed a hopeful development, my optimism is tempered by clear recognition of the limitations of MHCs as they proceed into the next decade. Improvements that build on the strengths of the MHC model and address some of its weakness, as well as address gaps in the public health and social service delivery model for people with mental illness, are important steps forward.

## Notes

1. MHC clients may receive jail as a sanction so opting-into MHC does not remove jail completely.
2. Some of these recommendations can also be implemented in traditional courts and the broader criminal justice system.

3. 2016 data released from the FBI's Uniform Crime Reports show that homicide rates increased for the second year in a row, possibly reflecting an uptick in violent crime. Despite these increases, the national homicide rate is lower (by about a half) than decades ago.
4. According to the Center for Court Innovation, there are six principles required for problem-solving courts to be effective: (1) Better information to team (such as training); (2) community engagement; (3) Collaboration; (4) Individualized Justice; (5) Accountability; and (6) Outcomes (cost-benefit analysis) (see Wolf 2007).
5. This is increasingly a challenge as more states have recreational marijuana laws, making access easier and the activity less stigmatizing.
6. See http://www.samhsa.gov/gains-center/mental-health-treatment-court-locator/adults, for a list of MHC names across the country.
7. In addition, all team member should be on the same pay/benefit structure (e.g., city or county employees depending on the court). This was a large source of tension for *County* MHC and the outside agency funding the court liaisons. This has largely been remedied with recent contract negotiation expanding the state benefits and pay structure for more categories of team members.
8. The prototype for a specialty agency around mandated mental health treatment includes five components: exclusive mental health caseloads, reduced caseloads, sustained officer training, active integration of (internal and external) resources to meet client needs and problem-solving strategies.
9. Despite support from many of the team members in both MHC's, the process was exceedingly bureaucratic and time-consuming and in some cases data was just unavailable. This was much more the case in *City* MHC than in *County* MHC. In *City* MHC, it was difficult and time-consuming the get access to the pre-court meetings as well as get permission to interview the professional staff. This was directly related to the presiding judge at the time of collecting interview data. In *County* MHC I was invited to attend the meeting and had many informal conversations with the sitting judge; a real contrast to the suspicion that surrounded and limited access to *City* MHC. This is problematic for future researchers who want and should be able to study our nation's courts. Collaboration between the court system and academic research should be encourage and not thwarted. More efforts should be

made to create meaningful relationships between public entities (such as the MHC's) and the academy and the public.
10. The process of selecting on the dependent variable (case revocations) will not yield representative data or population-based estimates, but it represents a great tool for understanding what does not work.
11. For several years there was a legal clinic for law students taught by a MHC defense lawyer affiliated with a local university law school. During the clinic, law students read about mental illness and the law and had hands-on training, spending time with MHC clients and addressing the court (under supervision of professor/counsel). Due to funding priorities, this program—aimed at educating and re-socializing law students—was terminated. "Integrating behavioral sciences into the legal system" (Wexler 1996, 170) extends to law schools so that when lawyers practice law, and in some cases rise to the bench, they should be more aware. Legal clinics represent a viable reform to educate the broader legal community and future lawyers. In 2018 a new class at the same law school offered a course on "Lawyering in a Problem-Solving Court" examining the drug court model, and then moving on to mental health court, veterans court, and other types of treatment courts. Linking coursework back to practical experience is preferable.
12. The same judge used the case of Veteran's court as a way forward due to federal funding: "The policy, the way Veteran's Court is, is the way that we should have all of our courts operate, but we don't have the resources to do it. One of the great things about Veteran's Court specifically is that the federal government pays for a lot of it."
13. The city in this study has a law enforcement assisted diversion program diverting individuals to community-based services rather than jail and the court system.
14. For example in Broward County, Florida the MHC is a voluntary pre-adjudication program, that is, it diverts people into treatment before they face trial if they agree to follow the court's direction.
15. I followed up with clients based on *City* MHC records. It is possible that clients might have become involved with other courts in the region or other states. I am unable to verify if they are in another jurisdiction.
16. I use the term defendant as client is reserved for those that can demonstrate the ability to give consent and who opt-into MHC.

# References

Andrews, D. A., and J. Bonta. 2003. *The Psychology of Criminal Conduct*. 3rd ed. Cincinnati: Anderson.

Benforado, Adam. 2015. *Unfair: The New Science of Criminal Injustice*. New York: Crown Publishers.

Berman, Greg, and John Feinblatt. 2005. *Good Courts: The Case for Problem-Solving Justice*. New York: The New Press.

Bernstein, Robert, and Tammy Seltzer. 2003. "Criminalization of People with Mental Illnesses: The Role of Mental Health Courts in System Reform." *The University of the District of Columbia Law Review* 7: 143–62. https://doi.org/10.3366/ajicl.2011.0005.

Boldt, Richard C. 2009. "A Circumspect Look at Problem-Solving Courts." In *Problem-Solving Courts: Justice for the Twenty-First Century*, edited by Paul Higgins and Mitchell B. Mackinem, 13–32. Santa Barbara: Praeger.

Castellano, Ursula. 2011. *Outsourcing Justice: The Role of Nonprofit Caseworkers in Pretrial Release Programs*. Boulder: Lynne Rienner Publishers.

Erickson, Patricia, and Steven Erickson. 2008. *Crime, Punishment, and Mental Illness: Law and the Behavioral Sciences in Conflict*. New Brunswick: Rutgers University Press.

Fisler, Carol. 2015. "When Research Challenges Policy and Practice: Toward a New Understanding of Mental Health Courts." *The Judges' Journal* 54 (2): 8–13. http://www.courtinnovation.org/sites/default/files/documents/JJ_SP15_54_2_Fisler.pdf.

Griffin, Patricia A., Mark Munetz, Natalie Bonfire, and Kathleen Kemp. 2015. "Development of the Sequential Intercept Model: The Search for a Conceptual Model." In *The Sequential Intercept Model and Criminal Justice: Promoting Community Alternatives for Individuals with Serious Mental Illness*, edited by Patricia A. Griffin, Kirk Heilbrun, Edward P. Mulvey, David DeMatteo, and Carol A. Schubert, 21–39. Oxford: Oxford University Press.

Hartwell, Stephanie. 2004. "Triple Stigma: Persons with Mental Illness and Substance Abuse Problems in the Criminal Justice System." *Criminal Justice Policy Review* 15 (1): 84–99. https://doi.org/10.1177/0887403403255064.

Heilbrun, Kirk, David DeMatteo, Heidi Strohmaier, and Meghann Galloway. 2015. "The Movement Toward Community-Based Alternatives to Criminal Justice Involvement and Incarceration for People with Severe Mental Illness." In *The Sequential Intercept Model and Criminal Justice: Promoting*

*Community Alternatives for Individuals with Serious Mental Illness*, edited by Patricia A. Griffin, Kirk Heilbrun, Edward P. Mulvey, David DeMatteo, and Carol A. Schubert, 1–20. Oxford: Oxford University Press.

Liu, Siyi, and Allison D. Redlich. 2015. "Intercept 3: Jails and Courts." In *The Sequential Intercept Model and Criminal Justice: Promoting Community Alternatives for Individuals with Serious Mental Illness*, edited by Patricia A. Griffin, Kirk Heilbrun, Edward P. Mulvey, David DeMatteo, and Carol A. Schubert, 78–94. Oxford: Oxford University Press.

Miller, JoAnn, and Donald C. Johnson. 2009. *Problem Solving Courts: A Measure of Justice*. Lanham: Rowman & Littlefield.

Nolan, James L. 1999. *Legal Accents, Legal Borrowing: The International Problem-Solving Court Movement*. Princeton: Princeton University Press.

Ritter, Alison, and Jacqui Cameron. 2006. "A Review of the Efficacy and Effectiveness of Harm Reduction Strategies for Alcohol, Tobacco and Illicit Drugs." *Drug and Alcohol Review* 25 (6): 611–24. https://doi.org/10.1080/09595230600944529.

Rottman, David, and Pamela Casey. 1999. "Therapeutic Jurisprudence and the Emergence of Problem-Solving Courts." *National Institute of Justice Journal* 240 (July): 12–19.

Schneider, Richard D. 2010. "Mental Health Courts and Diversion Programs: A Global Survey." *International Journal of Law and Psychiatry* 33 (4): 201–6. Elsevier Ltd. https://doi.org/10.1016/j.ijlp.2010.07.001.

Schneider, Richard D., Hy Bloom, and Mark Heerema. 2007. *Mental Health Courts: Decriminalizing the Mentally Ill*. Toronto: Irwin Law.

Seltzer, Tammy. 2005. "Mental Health Courts a Misguided Attempt to Address the Criminal Justice System's Unfair Treatment of People with Mental Illnesses." *Psychology, Public Policy, and Law* 11 (4): 570–86. https://doi.org/10.1037/1076-8971.11.4.570.

Skeem, Jennifer L., Paula Emke-Francis, and Jennifer Eno Louden. 2006. "Probation, Mental Health, and Mandated Treatment: A National Survey." *Criminal Justice and Behavior* 33 (2): 158–84. https://doi.org/10.1177/0093854805284420.

Skeem, Jennifer L., Jennifer Eno Louden, Devon Polaschek, and Jacqueline Camp. 2007. "Assessing Relationship Quality in Mandated Community Treatment: Blending Care With Control." *Psychological Assessment* 19 (4): 397–410. https://doi.org/10.1037/1040-3590.19.4.397.

Thompson, Michael D., Melissa Reuland, and Daniel Souweine. 2003. "Criminal Justice/Mental Health Consensus: Improving Responses to

People with Mental Illness." *Crime and Delinquency* 49 (1): 30–51. https://doi.org/10.1177/0011128702239234.

Warren, Roger K. 1998. "Reengineering the Court Process," Madison, WI, Presentation to Great Lakes Court Summit, September 24–25.

Wexler, David B. 1973. "Therapeutic Justice." *Minnesota Law Review* 57: 289–338. https://doi.org/10.3366/ajicl.2011.0005.

———. 1996. "Therapeutic Jurisprudence and the Criminal Courts." In *Law in a Therapeutic Key: Developments in Therapeutic Jurisprudence*, edited by David B. Wexler and Bruce J. Winick, 157–70. Durham: Carolina Academic Press.

Winick, Bruce J. 1991. "Harnessing the Power of the Bet: Wagering with the Government as a Mechanism for Social and Individual Change." *University of Miami Law Review* 45 (4): 737–816. https://doi.org/10.3366/ajicl.2011.0005.

———. 1996. "The Jurisprudence of Therapeutic Jurisprudence." In *Law in a Therapeutic Key: Developments in Therapeutic Jurisprudence*, edited by David B. Wexler and Bruce J. Winick, 645–68. Durham: Carolina Academic Press.

Wolf, Robert V. 2007. *Principles of Problem Solving Justice*. Center for Court Innovation. Retrieved from https://www.courtinnovation.org/sites/default/files/Principles.pdf.

Wolff, Nancy, and Wendy Pogorzelski. 2005. "Measuring the Effectiveness of Mental Health Courts Challenges and Recommendations." *Psychology, Public Policy, and Law* 11 (4): 539–69. https://doi.org/10.1037/1076-8971.11.4.539.

# Appendices

## Appendix A: Methodological Appendix

This book draws from two highly contextualized studies of MHCs—*City* and *County*—using a mixed-methodological approach. The qualitative portion of the study is primary which includes two components. First, I conducted fieldwork by observing court proceedings and gathering detailed observations of reviews and hearings. Both courts are open to the public. *City* MHC is held on Monday–Thursday from 1:30 to 5:00 p.m. (or earlier if all cases are processed) and when necessary on Fridays (10:30 a.m.). *County* MHC hears cases in the city center on Tuesday and Wednesday from 1:30 to 5:00 p.m. and on Thursdays from 2:30 to 5:00 p.m. (or earlier if all cases are processed).

In *City* MHC I observed court periodically (usually one time per week) from 2010 to 2013 and daily for a three month period in 2013 and the periodically in 2016. In 2013 I attended the pre-court meeting for a two week period. I observed *County* MHC periodically (usually one time per week) in 2013 and daily for a three month period in 2013 with unprecedented access to the pre-court meeting for three weeks. For both courts I took extensive field notes on the social, organization and physical features of the court process and its actors; this includes taking notes on objects, actors, acts, activity, events, timing, goals and feelings—all of which are essential elements of ethnographic research and field note philosophy (Spradley 1980; Bailey 2007).

The book draws heavily from qualitative interviews with MHC team members from both courts and clients from *City* MHC. The majority of interviews with team members took place in 2013 while judges were interviewed in 2016. Team member interviews shaped the judicial interview protocol. I conducted 48 in-depth interviews in total. All interview respondents completed an informed consent. The majority, 41 in total, were with MHC team members equally split with 19 from each court and the remaining from other service agencies/providers. The breakdown by position is as follows and detailed below (See Table A.1): judges ($n = 8$), prosecuting attorney ($n = 6$), defense attorneys ($n = 6$), social workers ($n = 4$), probation officers/counselors ($n = 7$), court liaisons/court monitors ($n = 4$), court program coordinator ($n = 2$), victim's advocate ($n = 1$), social services/housing personnel ($n = 1$), and crisis prevention police personnel ($n = 2$).

Recruitment for interviews with MHC team members was done in three ways. First, I introduced (or re-introduced as I had already met many of them when I observed court prior) myself to the team at their pre-court meeting with a written summary describing the project and handing out my business card with contact information. After the meeting I sent a follow-up email to the team members including a brief summary of the project. Lastly, I met and spoke with team members informally before, during and aftercourt. I sent formal written letters of introduction to fourteen (past and present) judges.

I interviewed all the defense attorneys, prosecuting attorneys, and social workers affiliated with MHC in the summer of 2013. There was one court liaison, due to medical issues, was unable to agree to an interview before retirement. Eight judges agreed to an interview, five of whom were currently or recently the presiding MHC judge (3 from *County* and 2 from *City*), and the other three judges were intermittently in *City* MHC. The response rate was astounding as all members of the team, except a few judges, agreed to an interview, making a population of the MHC team during 2013 as opposed to a sample.

Table A.1  MHC Team Interview List

|  | Position | Sex (male/female) | Race/ethnicity (minority) | Follow-up interview |
|---|---|---|---|---|
| *County* MHC | Judge | Male | | |
| | Judge | Male | Yes | |
| | Judge | Female | | |
| | Prosecutor | Female | Yes | X |
| | Prosecutor | Female | | |
| | Prosecutor | Male | | X |
| | Defense Attorney | Female | | |
| | Defense Attorney | Female | | |
| | Defense Attorney | Female | | X |
| | Social Worker | Male | | |
| | Social Worker | Female | Yes | X |
| | Social Worker | Male | Yes | |
| | Probation Officer | Female | | |
| | Probation Officer | Male | | X |
| | Probation Officer | Male | | |
| | Court liaison | Male | Yes | |
| | Court liaison | Female | Yes | |
| | Court Program Coordinator | Female | | |
| | Court Program Coordinator | Female | | |
| | Victims Advocate | Female | | |
| *City* MHC | Judge | Male | Yes | |
| | Judge | Female | | |
| | Judge | Male | | |
| | Judge | Male | | |
| | Judge | Male | | |
| | Prosecutor | Female | Yes | X |
| | Prosecutor | Female | | |
| | Prosecutor | Male | Yes | |
| | Defense Attorney | Female | | X |
| | Defense Attorney | Female | | X |
| | Defense Attorney | Female | | |
| | Social Worker | Female | Yes | |
| | Probation Officer | Male | | |
| | Probation Officer | Male | Yes | |
| | Probation Officer | Male | | X |
| | Court Liaison | Female | | |
| | Court Liaison | Female | Yes | |
| Miscellaneous | Social Service Provider | Male | | |
| | Police Sergeant | Male | | |
| | Mental Health Professional | Female | | |

Nine MHC team members (from defense, prosecution and probation) were also contacted for follow-up questions based on quantitative results.

The interviews probed questions on many aspects of the court process. The interview protocol included questions across six main domains: (1) professional role; (2) mission and comparison to other courts; (3) collaboration and court process; (4) mental health court effectiveness; (5) future of mental health courts; and (6) public perceptions. There were slight modifications for judicial interviews and for police and mental health professionals. (See Appendix B for interview protocols for team members, judges, police and clients).

In addition I interviewed seven clients from *City* MHC in 2014–2015. A probation officer (who had worked for the court since shortly after it began) compiled a list of high functioning clients (and IRB requirement) with a variety of experiences (both positive and negative) with MHC. I recruited clients after one of their court hearings in the hallway outside of the court room. I introduced myself and the project and handed each client a brief written summary of the project and my business card with my contact information. I asked them if I could interview them about their experiences in MHC. I made it clear that I had no position or relationship with the court system and cannot assist with their case in any way and that agreeing or not agreeing to the interview will not impact their court process (positively or negatively). All of these points were reiterated in the informed consent.

Of the eleven clients on my list, seven agreed to be interviewed, one refused, one failed to show-up for our scheduled interviews, and one was in the process of fighting new felony charge in another court. MHC client interviews included questions across six main domains: (1) background and prior life experiences; (2) experiences in MHC; (3) review process and court appearances; (4) relationships to the MHC team; (5) impact of the court on daily life; and (6) court improvement. I also reconstructing their cases from court records and court observations of hearings and reviews.

Interviews lasted approximately 60 minutes (with follow-up interviews lasting about 30 minutes), were audio-recorded and took place in a court office or conference room for team members and in local coffee shops with clients. For client interviews, I purchased a beverage for each client as well as offered them a $25 gift card for agreeing to an interview.

All interviews were transcribed by one of two transcribers and all conducted and coded by the author. All statements are confidential and team members are referred by their professional role (e.g., defense attorney) and not linked to the court in which they work and pseudonyms are used for all client references. For those professionals with whom there were less than three in that position he/she is referred to simply as MHC professional staff.

The interview data were coded thematically to explore the practice of therapeutic justice, examine the relationship between court outcomes and court process features and explore the relationship between team members and clients. While as a researcher I am critical of the perspective that clients and team members offer I also must take their words truthfully. I recognize that team members good intentions may not always translate that way in practice and try to highlight such discord.

The quantitative data comes from administrative information on 136 MHC clients and MHDT defendants who exited the court in 2008. I gained permission to access and use this data from the municipal MHC and the county's treatment agency. These data combine information from several sources and governmental agencies. The first portion of the data come from local government records and the court's public information website. The second portion comes from the county's public agency that provides mental health and chemical dependency services to defendants involved in the MHC. These data provide information on the frequency of a defendant's participation in non-crisis mental health treatment, defined as routine outpatient services that are part of a defendant's structured treatment plan. The final portion of data were obtained from criminal justice organizations, such as the local police department, local county jail, and the state court system. This segment of the data includes information on defendants' arrests in the state, which is used to measure criminal recidivism in this analysis. The complete data set combines information from various sources together through individual defendant identification numbers. The final dataset combine all of these data sources into one dataset set, stripped of personal identifiers.

The quantitative data analysis referred to in Chapter 5 was published with Lindsey Beach and Katie Corcoran in *Criminal Justice and Behavior*. Using a cohort of exiters from the court in 2008 and reoffending up to 2 years post-court exit, analyses compare MHC clients to MHDT defendants. We analyzed three aspects of criminal recidivism through quantitative model exploring how MHC influences criminal recidivism. We employed three separate analytical procedures. First, a logistic regression model estimated the odds of being charged with a criminal offense within two years post-exit. The second was an event history model (Cox proportional hazard model), which estimates the time to first criminal charge (within two years of court exit The third model was a negative binomial regression, used to explore the number of charges defendants accumulate during two years post-exit. The statistical analysis operationalized the possible effect of incentivized participation (dismissal offer) on criminal recidivism. We utilized measures of preventative mental health treatment to determine if increased treatment participation during court is associated with lower criminal recidivism post-exit. Additionally, we assess if full MHC participation (MHC clients)—which includes the full support of court actors, access to resources, and high levels of behavioral monitoring—influences criminal recidivism. Analytical models controlled for key demographics and prior criminal history to minimize selection bias issues. The predicted probabilites presented in Chapter 5 were generated from the logistic regression analysis.

All portions of the project have been approved through the University of Washington's Human Subjects Division (#452199) and Seattle Pacific University. Seattle Pacific University accepted the University of Washington's approval of this research.

# Appendix B: Interview Protocols

## Interview Protocol for MHC Team Members

1. Please state your position/role (e.g., judge, defense attorney, social worker, liaison, etc.). (Also mention any prior position in [MHC])

    a. How long have you been in the court in your current role? Describe your specific role within the MHC? Did you undergo any special training for this position in MHC?
    b. Why did you become involved in the MHC?

2. How would you describe what Mental Health Courts do? What is the goal of MHC?

   a. What makes them different from traditional or mainstream courts? Other problem-solving courts? How is *City's/County's* MHC approach distinct?
   b. What is the importance of the court's dual role—as both a competency court and therapeutic court?
   c. How has the MHC changed since its inception almost 15 years ago (in 1999)?

3. MHCs are often described as "collaborative" based on "teamwork." How accurate is that characterization in your experience in MHC? What is your role on the team?

   a. How does the pre-court meeting impact the workings of MHC?
   b. What is the role of the judge in MHC? Describe the power of the judge in MHC? Do Judges have too much power? Too little? How much judicial variation is there? Does their role differ from mainstream court? Other problem-solving courts?

4. Do you think the MHC court works? Describe.

   a. How do you evaluate success? Which outcomes?
   b. For which clients does it work well and which ones does it not work well? What are some of the problems or limitations? Can you describe a case (with no identifiers) that captures the strengths and/or weakness of the MHC?
   c. How much does MHC "tailor" the court for individual client's needs?
   d. What is the role of stigma or shame in MHC? What role do sanctions play?
   e. Why do so few opt-in? Will this impede the court's success?
   f. Is it true that many MHC clients spend more time under the supervision of the criminal justice system if they opt-in to MHC? Is this a problem?

5. What do you think is the future of MHCs?

   a. What are some of the challenges facing the future success of this MHC?

6. How do you think the public perceives the MHC?

   a. How do you address public concerns about public safety and mentally ill offenders?
   b. Can MHCs play a positive role in reducing infrequent "worst-case scenarios'" where an individual with mental illness randomly targeted an innocent civilians in public?

7. Is there anything else I should know about the MHC?

## Interview Protocol for MHC Judges

1. What is your role/or has been your role in mental health court? How did you become a judge in MHC?

   a. *If sitting judge*: Are you glad you are a MHC judge?
   *If past judge*: Would you seek this appointment again?
   *If pro tem*: Would you seek a term as a judge in MHC?
   b. Did you undergo any special training for this position in MHC? Do you think judges need additional resources or education to be a successful MHC judge?

2. Can you describe what it is like to be a judge in MHC? How does this differ from mainstream/traditional court?

   a. What makes an effective MHC judge?
   b. What are your thoughts about the sanctioning process in MHC? When a client is out of compliance, do you take a harm reduction approach, a graduated sanctions or another perspective?

      i. How important is the abstinence requirement?

c. What is the role of discretion as MHC judge (more or less than traditional court)?
   d. How important is the language that is used in court (e.g., client, response, team)?
3. MHCs are often described as "collaborative" based on "teamwork." How accurate is that characterization in your experience?
   a. What is your role as judge on the team?
   b. What is the importance of your absence in the pre-court meeting?
   c. In what ways do you see adversarialness in the court process?
4. What is the importance of the court's dual role—as both a competency court and therapeutic court?
5. Do you think the MHC court work? For which clients does it work well and which ones does it not work well? Can you think of any examples?
   a. Do enough defendants opt-in? Do the "right" defendants opt-in? (In District ask about felony drop-downs). Would you like to see more people in MHC?
   b. What is your perspective on offering more dismissal offers as an incentive to opt-in to MHC? (Quantitative analysis from *City* MHC show that those defendants offered a dismissal of their charges—even if it was not granted—had lower incidences of reoffending.
   c. MHC's originated in response to tragedies. Can MHCs play a positive role in reducing infrequent "worst-case scenarios'" where an individual with mental illness randomly targeted an innocent civilians in public?
6. Scholars raise *legal* and *ethical* concerns with MHC.
   a. Lack legitimacy (e.g., neutrality, due process, and open justice).
   b. Punitive. Clients may be treated more harshly (spend more time under the supervision of the criminal justice system) if they opt-in to MHC than if they had opted out?
   c. Racial disparities in who is offered MHC. (privileges whites, women, younger individuals)

d. Coercive treatment (forced to use pharmaceutical drugs that some consider to be controversial)
7. What are some of the challenges facing the future success of MHCs? What are some reforms that might benefit MHCs? (Research data; training; etc.)
8. Is there anything else I should know about the MHC? Can you recommend other judges I should speak to?

## Interview Protocol for MHC Clients

1. Tell me a little about yourself? What was it like when you were growing up? Can you recall any memories from your childhood?
2. What stage are you in the process of MHC? How long have you been in the MHC? Can you describe your experiences in MHC?
   a. Why did you opt-in to this court? Did you have any reservations? If yes, how do you feel about those reservations now?
   b. What are some of the benefits and/or challenges to being in this court (as opposed to mainstream court)?
3. Has your overall experience been positive? Negative? Describe.
   a. What were your reviews like?
   b. Were you always in compliance? If not, what happened when you were not in compliance? How fair was the process?
4. What has your relationship been like with MHC staff?
   a. Judges? Did you feel the judges were respectful? Where you respectful of the judges? Did you feel that that judges wanted to work with together with you? Were your experiences different with different judges?
   b. Defense attorney?
   c. District attorney/City?
   d. Social workers?
   e. Liaison?

f. Who aided you the most in the MHC process? Who offer little or no assistance?
5. How is your everyday life different now after being in the MHC? Do you have a better quality of life since entering MHC? In terms of:
   a. Management of mental health conditions
   b. Management of substance abuse (if applicable)
   c. Finding stable housing (if applicable)
   d. Finding work (if applicable)
   e. Any other way that MHC has impacted your life?
6. How do you think the MHCs could have worked better for you? What do you think the MHC could do to help increase your quality of life and others like you?

   a. Would you refer others to opt-in to MHC? Why or why not.
   b. Are there specific improvements to the court that you can recommend based on your experience?

# Interview Protocol for Police Officers and Mental Health Professional (MHP)

1. Please state your position/role (e.g., police officer, mental health professional, etc.)?

   a. How long have you been in your current role? Why did you take on this role? Did you undergo any special training for this position?
2. How would you describe what CIT does?
   a. How do you address public concerns about public safety and offenders who are mentally ill?
   b. How does it fit within policing?
   c. Does it connect with the LEAD (Law Enforcement Assisted Diversion) or other similar programs?
3. What is your relationship to MHC?
   a. How is this partnership different from traditional criminal justice?

4. Do you think CIT works? Describe. How do you evaluate success? Which outcomes?

   a. What are some challenges or problems with the CIT program? Reforms?

5. How do you think CIT influences public perceptions of police and criminal justice system?

   a. Can CIT play a positive role in reducing infrequent "worst-case scenarios'" where an individual with mental illness randomly targeted an innocent civilians in public? What about MHCs?

6. Is there anything else I should know about CIT and the relationship to MHC? Are there any officers that you can recommend that I speak to?

# Appendix C: Quantitative Analysis on Recidivism for MHC Clients and MHDT Defendants

Table C.1 Descriptive statistics for MHC clients and MHDT defendants

| Variable | MHC participants | MHDT participants | All participants |
|---|---|---|---|
| Sex n (%) | | | |
| Male | 44 (72%) | 50 (74%) | 94 (73%) |
| Female | 17 (28%) | 18 (26%) | 35 (27%) |
| Race n (%) | | | |
| White | 40 (66%) | 40 (59%) | 80 (62%) |
| Non-white | 21 (34%) | 28 (41%) | 49 (38%) |
| Noncrisis MH treatment n (%) | | | |
| Increased during court | 33 (54%) | 23 (34%) | 56 (43%) |
| Decreased during court | 18 (30%) | 20 (29%) | 38 (30%) |
| Stable during court | 10 (16%) | 25 (37%) | 35 (27%) |
| Dismissal of charges n (%) | | | |
| Offered | 26 (43%) | 15 (22%) | 41 (32%) |
| Not offered | 35 (75%) | 53 (78%) | 88 (68%) |
| Court completion n (%) | | | |
| Successful | 33 (54%) | 32 (47%) | 65 (50%) |
| Unsuccessful | 28 (46%) | 56 (53%) | 64 (50%) |
| Age | | | |
| M (SD) | 38 (11.23) | 38 (11.77) | 37.96 (11.48) |
| Range | 18–60 | 19–76 | 18.5–75.5 |
| Prior criminal charges | | | |
| M (SD) | 3.72 (3.09) | 5.41 (6.04) | 4.61 (4.93) |
| Range | 0–18 | 0–26 | 0–26 |
| Dependent variables | | | |
| Any criminal charge (2 years) n (%) | 26 (43%) | 37 (54%) | 63 (49%) |
| Days until first criminal charge | | | |
| M (SD) | 513 (275) | 439 (288) | 474 (283) |
| Range | 1–731 | 18–731 | 1–731 |
| Total criminal charges (2 years) | | | |
| M (SD) | 1.82 (3.24) | 2.56 (3.76) | 2.21 (3.53) |
| Range | 0–15 | 0–14 | 0–15 |
| Sample size | 61 | 68 | 129 |

*Note* MHC = mental health court; MHDT = mental health diagnosis and possible treatment

*Source* (Snedker et al. 2017)

**Table C.2** Logistic Regression, Cox Proportional Hazard, and Negative binomial Regression (NB) Models predicting first arrest, time until first arrest, and number of arrests, respectively, unstandardized coefficients displayed ($N = 129$)[a]

| Variable | Model 1 | | | Model 2 | | | Model 3 | | |
|---|---|---|---|---|---|---|---|---|---|
| | Logit | Cox | NB | Logit | Cox | NB | Logit | Cox | NB |
| Female | 0.68 (0.44) | 0.62* (0.28) | −0.02 (0.35) | 0.82 (0.50) | 0.57* (0.29) | 0.25 (0.35) | 0.99 (0.55) | 0.58* (0.29) | 0.26 (0.36) |
| White | −0.32 (0.41) | −0.08 (0.27) | −0.46 (0.31) | −0.01 (0.43) | 0.20 (0.28) | −0.20 (0.30) | −0.04 (0.45) | 0.14 (0.28) | −0.19 (0.30) |
| Age | −0.04 (0.10) | −0.02 (0.06) | 0.03 (0.08) | −0.09 (0.11) | −0.07 (0.07) | −0.02 (0.08) | −0.17 (0.11) | −0.10 (0.06) | −0.05 (0.08) |
| Age[b] | 0.00 (0.00) | 0.00 (0.00) | 0.00 (0.00) | 0.00 (0.00) | 0.00 (0.00) | 0.00 (0.00) | 0.00 (0.00) | 0.00 (0.00) | 0.00 (0.00) |
| Prior charges | 0.16** (0.05) | 0.01*** (0.02) | 0.12** (0.03) | 0.10 (0.05) | 0.08** (0.03) | 0.06 (0.03) | 0.07 (0.05) | 0.07* (0.03) | 0.04 (0.03) |
| Noncrisis[b] | | | | | | | | | |
| More during | — | — | — | −0.83 (0.52) | −0.59 (0.32) | −0.57 (0.33) | −0.96 (0.55) | −0.62 (0.32) | −0.70* (0.33) |
| Same | — | — | — | −1.19* (0.59) | −0.86* (0.39) | −1.01* (0.41) | −1.25* (0.61) | −0.90* (0.38) | −1.07** (0.41) |
| Eligible/opt-in | — | — | — | −0.50 (0.42) | −0.23 (0.27) | −0.37 (0.32) | −0.31 (0.44) | −0.15 (0.27) | −0.19 (0.32) |
| Completed MHC | — | — | — | −1.18* (0.46) | −0.74* (0.31) | −1.15** (0.35) | −1.07* (0.48) | −0.64* (0.31) | −1.19** (0.35) |
| Dismissal of charges | — | — | — | — | — | — | −1.48** (0.54) | −0.74* (0.35) | −0.95* (0.38) |
| Constant | 0.48 (1.90) | — | −0.27 (1.55) | 3.12 (2.20) | — | 1.79 (1.54) | 5.37* (2.40) | — | 3.04 (1.61) |
| Pseudo $R^2$ | 0.12 | — | 0.04 | 0.19 | — | 0.08 | 0.24 | — | 0.09 |
| Alpha | — | — | 2.24 (.46) | — | — | 1.65 (.37) | — | — | 1.56 (.35) |

Note MHC = mental health court
[a]All dependent variables are based on arrests within 2 years of exit from the court
[b]Less during is the referent category
*$p < 0.05$; **$p < 0.01$; ***$p < 0.001$

# References

Abramson, Marc F. 1972. "The Criminalization of Mentally Disordered Behavior Possible Side-Effect of a New Mental Health Law." *Hospital and Community Psychiatry* 23: 101–5.

Alexander, Michelle. 2012. *The New Jim Crow: Mass Incarceration in the Age of Colorblindness*. New York: The New Press.

Almquist, Lauren, and Elizabeth Dodd. 2009. *Mental Health Courts: A Guide to Research-Informed Policy and Practice*. New York: Council of State Governments Justice Center.

Andrews, D. A., and J. Bonta. 2003. *The Psychology of Criminal Conduct*. 3rd ed. Cincinnati: Anderson.

Anestis, Joye C., and Joyce L. Carbonell. 2014. "Stopping the Revolving Door: Effectiveness of Mental Health Court in Reducing Recidivism by Mentally Ill Offenders." *Psychiatric Services* 65 (9): 1105–12. https://doi.org/10.1176/appi.ps.201300305.

Angermeyer, M. C., and H. Matschinger. 2003. "The Stigma of Mental Illness: Effects of Labelling on Public Attitudes Towards People with Mental Disorder." *Acta Psychiatrica Scandinavica* 108 (4): 304–9. https://doi.org/10.1034/j.1600-0447.2003.00150.x.

Austin, James, and Barry Krisberg. 1981. "Wider, Stronger, and Different Nets: The Dialectics of Criminal Justice Reform." *Journal of Research in Crime and Delinquency* 18: 165–96.

Bailey, Carol A. 2007. *A Guide to Qualitative Field Research*. 2nd ed. Thousand Oaks, CA: Pine Forge Press.

Beach, Lindsey R. 2016. "Unlocking the Black Box of Mental Health Court Case Processing : An Event History Analysis of Extralegal Characteristics & Behavior on Case Revocation." MA thesis, University of Washington.

Beckett, Katherine. 1999. *Making Crime Pay: Law and Order in Contemporary American Politics*. Oxford: Oxford University Press.

Beckett, Katherine, and Steve Herbert. 2009. *Banished: The New Social Control in Urban America*. Oxford: Oxford University Press.

Benforado, Adam. 2015. *Unfair: The New Science of Criminal Injustice*. New York: Crown Publishers.

Bentham, Jeremy. 1969. "An Introduction to the Principles of Morals and Legislation." In *A Bentham Reader*, edited by Mary Peter Mack, 86–87. New York: Pegasus.

Berman, Greg, and John Feinblatt. 2001. "Problem-Solving Courts: A Brief Primer." *Law & Policy* 23: 125–40.

———. 2005. *Good Courts: The Case for Problem-Solving Justice*. New York: The New Press.

Bernstein, Robert, and Tammy Seltzer. 2003. "Criminalization of People with Mental Illnesses: The Role of Mental Health Courts in System Reform." *The University of the District of Columbia Law Review* 7: 143–62. https://doi.org/10.3366/ajicl.2011.0005.

Birgden, Astrid, and Tony Ward. 2003. "Pragmatic Psychology Through a Therapeutic Jurisprudence Lens: Psycholegal Soft Spots in the Criminal Justice System." *Psychology, Public Policy, and Law* 9 (3–4): 334–60. https://doi.org/10.1037/1076-8971.9.3-4.334.

Boldt, Richard C. 2009. "A Circumspect Look at Problem-Solving Courts." In *Problem-Solving Courts: Justice for the Twenty-First Century*, edited by Paul Higgins and Mitchell B. Mackinem, 13–32. Santa Barbara: Praeger.

Boothroyd, Roger A., Norman G. Poythress, Annette McGaha, and John Petrila. 2003. "The Broward Mental Health Court: Process, Outcomes, and Service Utilization." *International Journal of Law and Psychiatry* 26 (1): 55–71. https://doi.org/10.1016/S0160-2527(02)00203-0.

Boothroyd, Roger A., Cynthia Calkins Mercado, Norman G. Poythress, Annette Christy, and John Petrila. 2005. "Clinical Outcomes of Defendants in Mental Health Court." *Psychiatric Services* 56 (7): 829–34. https://doi.org/10.1176/appi.ps.56.7.829.

Braithwaite, John. 1989. *Crime, Shame and Reintegration*. Cambridge, UK:Cambridge University Press.

Bronson, Jennifer, and Marcus Berzofsky. 2017. *Indicators of Mental Health Problems Reported by Prisoners and Jail Inmates, 2011–2012*, 1–17. Washington, DC: U.S. Department of Justice. https://www.bjs.gov/index.cfm?ty=pbdetail&iid=5946.

Burns, Padraic J., Virginia Aldigé Hiday, and Bradley Ray. 2013. "Effectiveness 2 Years Postexit of a Recently Established Mental Health Court." *American Behavioral Scientist* 57 (2): 189–208. https://doi.org/10.1177/0002764212465416.

Canada, Kelli E., and Amy C. Watson. 2013. "'Cause Everybody Likes to Be Treated Good': Perceptions of Procedural Justice Among Mental Health Court Participants." *American Behavioral Scientist* 57 (2): 209–30. https://doi.org/10.1177/0002764212465415.

Casey, Timothy. 2004. "When Good Intentions Are Not Enough: Problem-Solving Courts and the Impending Crisis of Legitimacy." *SMU Law Review* 57: 1459–520. https://doi.org/10.3366/ajicl.2011.0005.

Casey, Pamela, and David B. Rottman. 2000. "Therapeutic Jurisprudence in the Courts." *Behavioral Sciences & the Law* 18: 445–57.

Castellano, Ursula. 2011. *Outsourcing Justice: The Role of Nonprofit Caseworkers in Pretrial Release Programs*. Boulder: Lynne Rienner Publishers.

Castellano, Ursula, and Leon Anderson. 2013. "Mental Health Courts in America: Promise and Challenges." *American Behavioral Scientist* 57 (2): 163–73. https://doi.org/10.1177/0002764212465616.

Chase, Deborah J., and Peggy Fulton Hora. 2000. "The Implications of Therapeutic Jurisprudence for Judicial Satisfaction." *Court Review* 37: 12–21.

Christy, Annette, Norman G. Poythress, Roger A. Boothroyd, John Petrila, and Shabnam Mehra. 2005. "Evaluating the Efficiency and Community Safety Goals of the Broward County Mental Health Court." *Behavioral Sciences & the Law* 23 (2): 227–43. https://doi.org/10.1002/bsl.647.

Clear, Todd R., and Natasha A. Frost. 2014. *The Punishment Imperative: The Rise and Failure of Mass Incarceration in America*. New York: New York University Press.

Corrigan, Patrick, Vetta Thompson, David Lambert, Yvette Sangster, Jeffrey G. Noel, and Jean Campbell. 2003. "Perceptions of Discrimination Among Persons with Serious Mental Illness." *Psychiatric Services* 54 (8): 1105–10. https://doi.org/10.1176/appi.ps.54.8.1105.

Cosden, Merith, Jeffrey K. Ellens, Jeffrey L. Schnell, Yasmeen Yamini-Diouf, and Maren M. Wolfe. 2003. "Evaluation of a Mental Health Treatment Court with Assertive Community Treatment." *Behavioral Sciences & the Law* 21 (4): 415–27. https://doi.org/10.1002/bsl.542.

Cosden, Merith, Jeffrey Ellens, Jeffrey Schnell, and Yasmeen Yamini-Diouf. 2005. "Efficacy of a Mental Health Treatment Court with Assertive Community Treatment." *Behavioral Sciences & the Law* 23 (2): 199–214. https://doi.org/10.1002/bsl.638.

Daicoff, Susan. 2000. "The Role of Therapeutic Jurisprudence Within the Comprehensive Law Movement." In *Practicing Therapeutic Jurisprudence: Law as a Helping Profession*, 465–92. Durham: Carolina Academic Press.

Desmond, Matthew. 2016. *Evicted: Poverty and Profit in the American City*. New York: Crown Publishing Group.

Dollar, Cindy Brooks, and Bradley Ray. 2015. "The Practice of Reintegrative Shaming in Mental Health Court." *Criminal Justice Policy Review* 26 (1): 29–44. https://doi.org/10.1177/0887403413507275.

DuBois, Lios, and Teri Martin. 2013. *Mental Health Court Evaluation*, 1–77. Portland, OR: Law & Policy Associates.

Erickson, Patricia, and Steven Erickson. 2008. *Crime, Punishment, and Mental Illness: Law and the Behavioral Sciences in Conflict*. New Brunswick: Rutgers University Press.

Ewick, Particia;, and Susan S. Silbey. 1998. *The Common Place of Law: Stories from Everyday Life*. Chicago: University of Chicago Press.

Feeley, Malcolm M., and Jonathan Simon. 1992. "The New Penology: Notes on the Emerging Strategy of Corrections and Its Implications." *Criminology* 30: 449. http://scholarship.law.berkeley.edu/facpubs.

Finkle, Michael J., Russell Kurth, Christopher Cadle, and Jessica Mullan. 2009. "Competency Courts: A Creative Solution for Restoring Competency to the Competency Process." *Behavioral Sciences & the Law* 27: 767–86. https://doi.org/10.1002/bsl.

Fisher, William H., Eric Silver, and Nancy Wolff. 2006. "Beyond Criminalization: Toward a Criminologically Informed Framework for Mental Health Policy and Services Research." *Administration and Policy in Mental Health and Mental Health Services Research* 33 (5): 544–57. https://doi.org/10.1007/s10488-006-0072-0.

Fisler, Carol. 2015. "When Research Challenges Policy and Practice: Toward a New Understanding of Mental Health Courts." *The Judges' Journal* 54 (2): 8–13.http://www.courtinnovation.org/sites/default/files/documents/JJ_SP15_54_2_Fisler.pdf.

Ford, Matt. 2015. "America's Largest Mental Hospital Is a Jail." *The Atlantic*, August 10, 2015. https://www.theatlantic.com/politics/archive/2015/06/americas-largest-mental-hospital-is-a-jail/395012/.

Foucault, Michel. 1995. *Discipline and Punish: The Birth of the Prison*. 2nd ed. New York: Vintage. https://doi.org/10.2307/2065008.

Freiberg, Arie. 2001. "Problem-Oriented Courts: Innovative Solutions to Intractable Problems." *Journal of Judicial Administration* 11 (January 2001): 8–27.

Fritzler, Randal B. 2003. "10 Key Components of a Criminal Metnal Health Court." In *Judging in a Therapeutic Key: Therapeutic Jurisprudence and the Coirts*, 118–23. Durham: Carolina Academic Press.

Galanter, Marc. 1974. "Why the 'Haves' Come out Ahead: Speculations on the Limits of Legal Change." *Law & Society Review* 9 (1): 95–160.

Garland, David. 2002. *The Culture of Control: Crime and Social Order in Contemporary Society*. Chicago: University of Chicago Press.

Gerring, John. 2007. *Case Study Research: Principles and Practices*. Cambridge: Cambridge University Press.

Goffman, Erving. 1959. *The Presentation of Self in Everyday Life*. Anchor Books. New York.

———. 1961. *Asylums: Essays on the Social Situation of Mental Patients and Other Inmates*. New York: Anchor Books.

———. 1986. *Stigma: Notes on the Management of Spoiled Identity*. New York: Simon & Schuster.

Goldkamp, J. S., and C. Irons-Guynn. 2000. "Emerging Judicial Strategies for the Mentally Ill in the Criminal Caseload: Mental Health Courts in Fort Lauderdale, Seattle, San Bernardino, and Anchorage," 1–83. http://www.ncjrs.gov/pdffiles1/bja/182504.pdf.

Goodale, Gregg, Lisa Callahan, and Henry J. Steadman. 2013. "Law & Psychiatry: What Can We Say About Mental Health Courts Today?" *Psychiatric Services* 64 (4): 298–300. https://doi.org/10.1176/appi.ps.201300049.

Griffin, Patricia A., and David DeMatteo. 2009. "Mental Health Courts: Cautious Optimism." In *Problem-Solving Courts: Justice for the Twenty-First Century*, edited by P. Higgins and M. B. Mackinem, 91–113. Santa Barbara: Praeger.

Griffin, Patricia A., Henry J. Steadman, and John Petrila. 2002. "The Use of Criminal Charges and Sanctions in Mental Health Courts." *Psychiatric Services* 53 (10): 1285–89.

Griffin, Patricia A., Mark Munetz, Natalie Bonfire, and Kathleen Kemp. 2015. "Development of the Sequential Intercept Model: The Search for a Conceptual Model." In *The Sequential Intercept Model and Criminal Justice: Promoting Community Alternatives for Individuals with Serious Mental Illness*, 21–39. Oxford: Oxford University Press.

Harcourt, Bernard E. 2006. "From the Asylum to the Prison: Rethinking the Incarceration Revolution." *Texas Law Review* 84: 1751–86.

Harris, Alexis. 2016. *A Pound of Flesh: Monetary Sanctions as Punishment for the Poor.* New York: Russell Sage Foundation.

Hartwell, Stephanie. 2004. "Triple Stigma: Persons with Mental Illness and Substance Abuse Problems in the Criminal Justice System." *Criminal Justice Policy Review* 15 (1): 84–99. https://doi.org/10.1177/0887403403255064.

Heilbrun, Kirk, David DeMatteo, Heidi Strohmaier, and Meghann Galloway. 2015. "The Movement Toward Community-Based Alternatives to Criminal Justice Involvement and Incarceration for People with Severe Mental Illness." In *The Sequential Intercept Model and Criminal Justice: Promoting Community Alternatives for Individuals with Serious Mental Illness*, edited by Patricia A. Griffin, Kirk Heilbrun, Edward P. Mulvey, David DeMatteo, and Carol A. Schubert, 1–20. Oxford: Oxford University Press.

Hiday, Virginia A., and Bradley Ray. 2010. "Arrests Two Years After Exiting a Well-Established Mental Health Court." *Psychiatric Services* 61 (5): 463–68. https://doi.org/10.1176/appi.ps.61.5.463.

Hora, Peggy Fulton, William G. Schma, and John T. A. Rosenthal. 1999. "Therapeutic Jurisprudence and the Drug Treatment Court Movement: Revolutionizing the Criminal Justice System's Response to Drug Abuse and Crime in America." *Notre Dame Law Review* 74: 439–538.

Hughes, Shannon, and Terry Peak. 2013. "A Critical Perspective on the Role of Psychotropic Medications in Mental Health Courts." *American Behavioral Scientist* 57 (2): 244–65. https://doi.org/10.1177/0002764212458273.

James, Doris J., and Lauren E. Glaze. 2006. *Mental Health Problems of Prison and Jail Inmates*, 1–12. Washington, DC: U.S. Department of Justice. http://bjs.gov/content/pub/pdf/mhppji.pdf.

Johnston, E. Lea. 2012. "Theorizing Mental Health Courts." *Washington University Law Review* 89 (3): 519–79.

Kaiser, Kimberly A., and Kristy Holtfreter. 2016. "An Integrated Theory of Specialized Court Programs: Using Procedural Justice and Therapeutic Jurisprudence to Promote Offender Compliance and Rehabilitation." *Criminal Justice and Behavior* 43 (1): 45–62. https://doi.org/10.1177/0093854815609642.

Keator, Karli J., Lisa Callahan, Henry J. Steadman, and Roumen Vesselinov. 2013. "The Impact of Treatment on the Public Safety Outcomes of Mental Health Court Participants." *American Behavioral Scientist* 57 (2): 231–43. https://doi.org/10.1177/0002764212465617.

Kopelovich, Sarah, Philip Yanos, Christina Pratt, and Joshua Koerner. 2013. "Procedural Justice in Mental Health Courts: Judicial Practices, Participant Perceptions, and Outcomes Related to Mental Health Recovery." *International Journal of Law and Psychiatry* 36 (2): 113–20. Elsevier Ltd. https://doi.org/10.1016/j.ijlp.2013.01.004.

Kushel, Margot B., Judith A. Hahn, Jennifer L. Evans, David R. Bangsberg, and Andrew R. Moss. 2005. "Revolving Doors: Imprisonment Among the Homeless and Marginally Housed Population." *American Journal of Public Health* 95 (10): 1747–52. https://doi.org/10.2105/AJPH.2005.065094.

Lens, Vicki. 2016. *Poor Justice: How the Poor Fare in the Courts*. Oxford: Oxford University Press.

Liu, Siyi, and Allison D. Redlich. 2015. "Intercept 3: Jails and Courts." In *The Sequential Intercept Model and Criminal Justice: Promoting Community Alternatives for Individuals with Serious Mental Illness*, edited by Patricia A. Griffin, Kirk Heilbrun, Edward P. Mulvey, David DeMatteo, and Carol A. Schubert, 78–94. Oxford: Oxford University Press.

Lurigio, Arthur J., and Jessica Snowden. 2009. "Putting Therapeutic Jurisprudence into Practice: The Growth, Operations, and Effectiveness of Mental Health Court." *Justice System Journal* 30 (2): 196–218. https://doi.org/10.1080/0098261X.2009.10767926.

Luskin, Mary Lee. 2001. "Who Is Diverted? Case Selection for Court-Monitored Mental Health Treatment." *Law & Policy* 23 (2): 217–36.

Luskin, Mary Lee, and Bradley Ray. 2015. "Selection Into Mental Health Court: Distinguishing Among Eligible Defendants." *Criminal Justice and Behavior* 42 (11): 1145–58. https://doi.org/10.1177/0093854815601158.

Mack, Kathy, and Sharyn Roach Anleu. 2010. "Performing Impartiality: Judicial Demeanor and Legitimacy." *Law & Social Inquiry* 35 (1): 137–73. https://doi.org/10.1111/j.1747-4469.2009.01180.x.

McNiel, Dale E., and Renée L. Binder. 2007. "Effectiveness of a Mental Health Court in Reducing Criminal Recidivism and Violence." *American Journal of Psychiatry* 164 (9): 1395–403. https://doi.org/10.1176/appi.ajp.2007.06101664.

McNiel, Dale E., Naomi Sadeh, Kevin L. Delucchi, and Renée L. Binder. 2015. "Prospective Study of Violence Risk Reduction by a Mental Health Court." *Psychiatric Services* 66 (6): 598–603. https://doi.org/10.1176/appi.ps.201400203.

Menkel-Meadow, Carrie. 1992. "Is Altruism Possible in Lawyering." *Georgia State University Law Review* 8 (2): 385–419. https://doi.org/10.3366/ajicl.2011.0005.

Metzl, Jonathan M., and Kenneth T. MacLeish. 2015. "Mental Illness, Mass Shootings, and the Politics of American Firearms." *American Journal of Public Health* 105 (2): 240–49. https://doi.org/10.2105/AJPH.2014.302242.

Meyer, John W, and Brian Rowan. 1977. "Institutionalized Organizations: Formal Structure as Myth." *American Journal of Sociology* 83 (2): 340–63. https://doi.org/10.1086/226550.

Miller, JoAnn, and Donald C. Johnson. 2009. *Problem Solving Courts: A Measure of Justice*. Lanham: Rowman & Littlefield.

Miller, Sarah L., and Abigayl M. Perelman. 2009. "Mental Health Courts: An Overview and Redefinition of Tasks and Goals." *Law & Psychological Review* 33: 243–58. https://doi.org/10.3366/ajicl.2011.0005.

Moore, Marlee E., and Virginia Aldigé Hiday. 2006. "Mental Health Court Outcomes: A Comparison of Re-arrest and Re-arrest Severity Between Mental Health Court and Traditional Court Participants." *Law and Human Behavior* 30 (6): 659–74. https://doi.org/10.1007/s10979-006-9061-9.

Morse, Stephen J. 1999. "Craziness and Criminal Responsibility." *Behavioral Sciences & the Law* 17 (2): 147–64. https://doi.org/10.1002/(SICI)1099-0798(199904/06)17:2<147::AID-BSL336>3.0.CO;2-X.

Munetz, Mark R., and Patricia A. Griffin. 2006. "Use of the Sequential Intercept Model as an Approach to Decriminalization of People with Serious Mental Illness." *Psychiatric Services* 57 (4): 544–49. https://doi.org/10.1176/ps.2006.57.4.544.

Munetz, Mark R., Christian Ritter, Jennifer L. S. Teller, and Natalie Bonfine. 2014. "Mental Health Court and Assisted Outpatient Treatment: Perceived Coercion, Procedural Justice, and Program Impact." *Psychiatric Services* 65 (3): 352–58. https://doi.org/10.1176/appi.ps.002642012.

Nolan, James L. 1999. *Legal Accents, Legal Borrowing: The International Problem-Solving Court Movement*. Princeton: Princeton University Press.

Nolan, James L., Jr. 1998. *The Therapeutic State: Justifying Government at Century's End*. New York: New York University Press.

———. 2001. *Reinventing Justice: The American Drug Court Movement*. Princeton: Princeton University Press.

———. 2003. "Redefining Criminal Courts: Problem-Solving and the Meaning of Justice." *American Criminal Law Review* 40: 1541–65. https://doi.org/10.3366/ajicl.2011.0005.

Paik, Leslie. 2011. *Discretionary Justice: Looking inside a Juvenile Drug Court*. New Brunswick: Rutgers University Press.

Perlin, Michael. 2013. "'The Judge, He Cast His Robe Aside': Mental Health Courts, Dignity and Due Process." *Mental Health Law & Policy Journal* 3 (1): 1–29.

Pescosolido, Bernice A., John Monahan, Bruce G. Link, Ann Stueve, and Saeko Kikuzawa. 1999. "The Public's View of the Competence, Dangerousness, and Need for Legal Coercion of Persons with Mental Health Problems." *American Journal of Public Health* 89 (9): 1339–45. https://doi.org/10.2105/AJPH.89.9.1339.

Peterson, J., J. L. Skeem, E. Hart, S. Vidal, and F. Keith. 2010. "Analyzing Offense Patterns as a Function of Mental Illness to Test the Criminalization Hypothesis." *Psychiatric Services* 61 (12): 1217–22. https://doi.org/10.1176/appi.ps.61.12.1217.

Petrila, John. 1996. "Paternalism and the Unrealized Promise of Essays in Therapeutic Jurisprudence." In *Law in a Therapeutic Key: Developments in Therapeutic Jurisprudence*, 685–705. Durham: Carolina Academic Press.

Petrila, J. 2003. "An Introduction to Special Jurisdiction Courts." *International Journal of Law and Psychiatry* 26 (1): 3–12.

Pfeiffer, Mary Beth. 2007. *Crazy in America: The Hidden Tragedy of Our Criminalized Mentally Ill.* New York: Carroll & Graf.

Poythress, Norman G., John Petrila, Annette McGaha, and Roger Boothroyd. 2002. "Perceived Coercion and Procedural Justice in the Broward Mental Health Court." *International Journal of Law and Psychiatry* 25 (5): 517–33. https://doi.org/10.1016/S0160-2527(01)00110-8.

Pratt, Christina, Philip T. Yanos, Sarah L. Kopelovich, Joshua Koerner, and Mary Jane Alexander. 2013. "Predictors of Criminal Justice Outcomes Among Mental Health Courts Participants: The Role of Perceived Coercion and Subjective Mental Health Recovery." *International Journal of Forensic Mental Health* 12 (2): 116–25.

Ragin, Charles C. 1992. Introduction: Cases of "What is a Case?" In *What Is a Case? Exploring the Foundations of Social Inquiry*, edited by Charles C. Ragin and Howard S. Becker, 11th ed., 1–52. New York: Cambridge University Press.

Ray, Bradley. 2014. "Long-Term Recidivism of Mental Health Court Defendants." *International Journal of Law and Psychiatry* 37 (5): 448–54. Elsevier Ltd. https://doi.org/10.1016/j.ijlp.2014.02.017.

Ray, Bradley, and Cindy Brooks Dollar. 2013. "Examining Mental Health Court Completion: A Focal Concerns Perspective." *Sociological Quarterly* 54 (4): 647–69. https://doi.org/10.1111/tsq.12032.

Ray, Bradley, and Cindy Brooks Dollar. 2014. "Exploring Stigmatization and Stigma Management in Mental Health Court: Assessing Modified Labeling Theory in a New Context." *Sociological Forum* 29 (3): 720–35. https://doi.org/10.1111/socf.12111.

Ray, Bradley, Cindy Brooks Dollar, and Kelly M. Thames. 2011. "Observations of Reintegrative Shaming in a Mental Health Court." *International Journal of Law and Psychiatry* 34 (1): 49–55. Elsevier Ltd. https://doi.org/10.1016/j.ijlp.2010.11.008.

Ray, Bradley, Brittany J. Hood, and Kelli E. Canada. 2015a. "What Happens to Mental Health Court Noncompleters?" *Behavioral Sciences & the Law* 33 (6): 801–14. https://doi.org/10.1002/bsl.2163.

Ray, Bradley, Sheryl Pimlott Kubiak, Erin B. Comartin, and Elizabeth Tillander. 2015b. "Mental Health Court Outcomes by Offense Type at Admission." *Administration and Policy in Mental Health and Mental Health Services Research* 42 (3): 323–31. https://doi.org/10.1007/s10488-014-0572-2.

Redlich, Allison D. 2005. "Voluntary, But Knowing and Intelligent? Comprehension in Mental Health Courts." *Psychology, Public Policy, and Law* 11 (4): 605–19. https://doi.org/10.1037/1076-8971.11.4.605.

Redlich, Allison D., Henry J. Steadman, John Monahan, John Petrila, and Patricia A. Griffin. 2005. "The Second Generation of Mental Health Courts." *Psychology, Public Policy, and Law* 11 (4): 527–38. https://doi.org/10.1037/1076-8971.11.4.527.

Ritter, Alison, and Jacqui Cameron. 2006. "A Review of the Efficacy and Effectiveness of Harm Reduction Strategies for Alcohol, Tobacco and Illicit Drugs." *Drug and Alcohol Review* 25 (6): 611–24. https://doi.org/10.1080/09595230600944529.

Rottman, David, and Pamela Casey. 1999. "Therapeutic Jurisprudence and the Emergence of Problem-Solving Courts." *National Institute of Justice Journal* 240 (July): 12–19.

Sarteschi, Christine M., Michael G. Vaughn, and Kevin Kim. 2011. "Assessing the Effectiveness of Mental Health Courts: A Quantitative Review." *Journal of Criminal Justice* 39 (1): 12–20. Elsevier Ltd. https://doi.org/10.1016/j.jcrimjus.2010.11.003.

Scheff, T. J. 1974. "The Labelling Theory of Mental Illness." *American Sociological Review* 39 (3): 444–52.

Schneider, Richard D. 2010. "Mental Health Courts and Diversion Programs: A Global Survey." *International Journal of Law and Psychiatry* 33 (4): 201–6. Elsevier Ltd. https://doi.org/10.1016/j.ijlp.2010.07.001.

Schneider, Richard D., Hy Bloom, and Mark Heerema. 2007. *Mental Health Courts: Decriminalizing the Mentally Ill.* Toronto: Irwin Law.

Selman, Donna, and Paul Leighton. 2010. *Punishment for Sale: Private Prisons, Big Business, and the Incarceration Binge.* Lanham: Rowman & Littlefield.

Seltzer, Tammy. 2005. "Mental Health Courts a Misguided Attempt to Address the Criminal Justice System's Unfair Treatment of People with Mental Illnesses." *Psychology, Public Policy, and Law* 11 (4): 570–86. https://doi.org/10.1037/1076-8971.11.4.570.

Silver, Eric. 2006. "Understanding the Relationship between Mental Disorder and Violence: The Need for a Criminological Perspective." *Law and Human Behavior* 30 (6): 685–706. https://doi.org/10.1007/s10979-006-9018-z.

Skeem, Jennifer L., Paula Emke-Francis, and Jennifer Eno Louden. 2006. "Probation, Mental Health, and Mandated Treatment: A National Survey." *Criminal Justice and Behavior* 33 (2): 158–84. https://doi.org/10.1177/0093854805284420.

Skeem, Jennifer L., Jennifer Eno Louden, Devon Polaschek, and Jacqueline Camp. 2007. "Assessing Relationship Quality in Mandated Community Treatment: Blending Care with Control." *Psychological Assessment* 19 (4): 397–410. https://doi.org/10.1037/1040-3590.19.4.397.

Skeem, Jennifer L., Sarah Manchak, and Jillian K. Peterson. 2011. "Correctional Policy for Offenders with Mental Illness: Creating a New Paradigm for Recidivism Reduction." *Law and Human Behavior* 35 (2): 110–26. https://doi.org/10.1007/s10979-010-9223-7.

Slobogin, Christopher. 1996. "Therapeutic Jurisprudence: Five Dilemmas to Ponder." In *Law in a Therapeutic Key: Developments in Therapeutic Jurisprudence*, 763–93. Durham: Carolina Academic Press.

Slovenko, Ralph. 2002. "The Transinstitutionalization of the Mentally Ill." *Ohio Northern University Law Review* 29: 641–60. https://doi.org/10.3366/ajicl.2011.0005.

Snedker, Karen A. 2016. "Unburdening Stigma: Identity Repair through Rituals in Mental Health Court."*Society and Mental Health* 6 (1): 36–55. http://journals.sagepub.com/doi/abs/10.1177/2156869315598203.

Snedker, Karen A., Lindsey Beach and Katie Corcoran. 2017. "Beyond the 'Revolving Door'? Incentives and Criminal Recidivism in One Mental Health Court." *Criminal Justice and Behavior* 44 (9): 1141–1162. https://doi.org/10.1177/0093854817708395.

Spradley, James P. 1980. *Participant Observation.* New York: Holt, Rinehart & Winston.

Steadman, H. J., M. W. Deane, J. P. Morrissey, M. L. Westcott, S. Salasin, and S. Shapiro. 1999. "A SAMHSA Research Initiative Assessing the Effectiveness of Jail Diversion Programs for Mentally Ill Persons." *Psychiatric Services* 50 (12): 1620–23. https://doi.org/http://dx.doi.org/10.1176/ps.50.12.1620.

Steadman, Henry J., Lisa Callahan, Pamela Clark Robbins, Roumen Vesselinov, Thomas G. McGuire, and Joseph P. Morrissey. 2014. "Criminal Justice and Behavioral Health Care Costs of Mental Health Court Participants: A Six-Year Study." *Psychiatric Services* 65 (9): 1100–104. https://doi.org/10.1176/appi.ps.201300375.

Steadman, Henry J., Susan Davidson, and Collie Brown. 2001. "Mental Health Courts: Their Promise and Unanswered Questions." *Psychiatric Services* 52 (4): 457–58. https://doi.org/10.1176/appi.ps.52.4.457.

Steadman, Henry J., Allison Redlich, Lisa Callahan, Pamela Clark Robbins, and Roumen Vesselinov. 2011. "Effect of Mental Health Courts on Arrests and Jail Days: A Multisite Study." *Archives of General Psychiatry* 68 (2): 167–72. https://doi.org/10.1001/archgenpsychiatry.2010.134.

Steadman, Henry J., Allison D. Redlich, Patricia Griffin, John Petrila, and John Monahan. 2005. "From Referral to Disposition: Case Processing in Seven Mental Health Courts." *Behavioral Sciences & the Law* 23 (2): 215–26. https://doi.org/10.1002/bsl.641.

Stolle, Dennis P., David B. Wexler, Bruce J. Winick, and Edward A. Dauer. 2000. "Integrating Preventative Law and Therapeutic Jurisprudence: A Law and Psychology Based Approach to Lawyering." In *Practicing Therapeutic Jurisprudence: Law as a Helping Profession*, edited by Dennis P. Stolle, David B. Wexler, and Bruce J. Winick, 5–44. Durham: Carolina Academic Press.

Sutton, John R. 2001. *Law/Society: Origins, Interactions, and Change*. Thousand Oaks: Pine Forge Press.

Thompson, Michael D., Melissa Reuland, and Daniel Souweine. 2003. "Criminal Justice/mental Health Consensus: Improving Responses to People with Mental Illness." *Crime and Delinquency* 49 (1): 30–51. https://doi.org/10.1177/0011128702239234.

Torrey, Fuller E. 1997. *Out of the Shadows: Confronting America's Mental Illness Crisis*. New York: John Wiley & Sons.

———. 2014. *American Psychosis: How the Federal Government Destroyed the Mental Illness Treatment System*. Oxford: Oxford University Press.

Torrey, Fuller E., Aaron D. Kennard, Don Eslinger, Richard Lamb, and James Pavle. 2010. "More Mentally Ill Persons Are in Jails and Prisons Than Hospitals: A Survey of the States." May: 1–22. http://www.

treatmentadvocacycenter.org/storage/documents/final_jails_v_hospitals_study.pdf.

Trupin, Eric, and Henry Richards. 2003. "Seattle's Mental Health Courts: Early Indicators of Effectiveness." *International Journal of Law and Psychiatry* 26 (1): 33–53. https://doi.org/10.1016/S0160-2527(02)00202-9.

Tyler, Tom R. 1996. "The Psychological Consequences of Judicial Procedures: Implications for Civil Commitment Hearings." In *Law in a Therapeutic Key: Developments in Therapeutic Jurisprudence*, 3–15. Durham: Carolina Academic Press.

Vogel, Wendy M., Chan D. Noether, and Henry J. Steadman. 2007. "Preparing Communities for Re-Entry of Offenders with Mental Illness Wendy." *Journal of Offender Rehabilitation* 45 (1–2): 167–88. https://doi.org/10.1300/J076v45n01.

Wales, Heathcote W., Virginia Aldigé Hiday, and Bradley Ray. 2010. "Procedural Justice and the Mental Health Court Judge's Role in Reducing Recidivism." *International Journal of Law and Psychiatry* 33 (4): 265–71. Elsevier Ltd. https://doi.org/10.1016/j.ijlp.2010.06.009.

Warren, Roger K. 1998. "Reengineering the Court Process," Madison, WI, Presentation to Great Lakes Court Summit, September 24–25.

Watson, Amy, Patricia Hanrahan, Daniel Luchins, and Arthur Lurigio. 2001. "Mental Health Courts and the Complex Issue of Mentally Ill Offenders." *Psychiatric Services* 52 (4): 477–81. https://doi.org/10.1176/appi.ps.52.4.477.

Wexler, David B. 1973. "Therapeutic Justice." *Minnesota Law Review* 57: 289–338. https://doi.org/10.3366/ajicl.2011.0005.

———. 1996. "Therapeutic Jurisprudence and the Criminal Courts." In *Law in a Therapeutic Key: Developments in Therapeutic Jurisprudence*, 157–70. Durham: Carolina Academic Press.

———. 2000a. "Practicing Therapeutic Jurisprudence: Psycholegal Soft Spots and Strategies." In *Practicing Therapeutic Jurisprudence: Law as a Helping Profession*, edited by Dennis P. Stolle, David B. Wexler, and Bruce J. Winick, 45–68. Durham: Carolina Academic Press.

———. 2000b. "Therapeutic Jurisprudence and the Culture of Critique." In *Practicing Therapeutic Jurisprudence: Law as a Helping Profession*, 449–64. Durham: Carolina Academic Press.

Wexler, David B., and Bruce J. Winick. 1991. "Therapeutic Jurisprudence as a New Approach to Mental Health Law Policy Analysis and Research." *University of Miami Law Review* 45 (5): 979–1004.

Whitaker, Robert. 2010. *Mad in America: Bad Science, Bad Medicine, and the Enduring Mistreatment of the Mentally Ill*. Philadelphia: Basic Books.

Wilson, James Q., and George L. Kelling. 1982. "Broken Windows: The Police and Neighborhood Safety." *The Atlantic* (March): 29–38.

Winick, Bruce J. 1991. "Harnessing the Power of the Bet: Wagering with the Government as a Mechanism for Social and Individual Change." *University of Miami Law Review* 45 (4): 737–816. https://doi.org/10.3366/ajicl.2011.0005.

———. 1994. "The Right to Refuse Mental Health Treatment: A Therapeutic Jurisprudence Analysis." *International Journal of Law and Psychiatry* 17 (1): 99–117. https://doi.org/10.1016/0160-2527(94)90039-6.

———. 1996a. "The Jurisprudence of Therapeutic Jurisprudence." In *Law in a Therapeutic Key: Developments in Therapeutic Jurisprudence*, edited by David B. Wexler and Bruce J. Winick, 645–68. Durham: Carolina Academic Press.

———. 1996b. "The Side Effects of Incompetency Labeling and the Implications for Mental Health Law." In *Law in a Therapeutic Key: Developments in Therapeutic Jurisprudence*, 17–58. Durham: Carolina Academic Press.

Winick, Bruce J., David B. Wexler, and Edward A. Dauer. 1999. "Preface: A New Model for the Practice of Law." *Psychology, Public Policy, and Law* 5 (4): 795–99. https://doi.org/10.1037//1076-8971.5.4.795.

Wolf, Robert V. 2007. *Principles of Problem Solving Justice*. Center for Court Innovation. Retrieved from https://www.courtinnovation.org/sites/default/files/Principles.pdf.

Wolff, Nancy. 2002. "Courts as Therapeutic Agents: Thinking Past the Novelty of Mental Health Courts." *Journal of the American Academy of Psychiatry and the Law* 30 (3): 431–37. http://jaapl.org/content/30/3/431.full.pdf.

Wolff, Nancy, Nicole Fabrikant, and Steven Belenko. 2011. "Mental Health Courts and Their Selection Processes: Modeling Variation for Consistency." *Law and Human Behavior* 35 (5): 402–12.

Wolff, Nancy, and Wendy Pogorzelski. 2005. "Measuring the Effectiveness of Mental Health Courts Challenges and Recommendations." *Psychology, Public Policy, and Law* 11 (4): 539–69. https://doi.org/10.1037/1076-8971.11.4.539.

Yngvesson, Barbara. 1994. "Making Law at the Doorway: The Clerk, the Court, and the Construction of Community in a New England Town." In *Law and Community in Three American Towns*, edited by Carol J. Greenhouse, Barbara Yngvesson, and David M. Engel, 54–90. Ithaca: Cornell University Press.

# Index

## A

Accountability 44, 92, 144, 153, 156, 166, 232, 237, 250
Alcohol 234
  abuse 62, 167, 207, 230, 231, 236, 238, 243, 244, 249, 267
  sobriety 168, 176, 198, 232, 233, 237, 238, 242–246, 250, 260, 268
  use 37, 164, 234, 236, 258
Amenability. See Court liaison; Eligibility; Opt-in

## B

Buy-in 281
  client 2, 87, 102, 133, 201, 214, 216, 235, 255, 258, 259, 267
  court team 32, 109, 274, 277
  judges 32, 108, 110

## C

Case study 16, 17
  design 15
  sampling strategy 16
City mental health court 16–19, 34, 46, 48, 49, 59, 60, 65, 70, 73, 74, 85, 89, 93, 95, 98–100, 104, 115, 122, 176, 183–185, 187, 191, 277
Civil commitment 9, 50, 52, 175, 286
Client anxiety 116, 121, 136–140, 143, 165, 232, 235, 236
Client background 231, 235, 239, 243, 247, 251, 256
  criminal history 88, 96, 99, 188, 189, 199, 235, 248, 273
Client case histories 17, 21, 229
  Isaiah 116, 134, 138, 239, 241, 243, 287
  Jennifer 56, 66, 98, 116, 134, 139, 159, 166, 171, 174, 202, 210, 234, 238, 287

Marcus 197
Monique 1, 59, 65, 83, 116, 123, 134, 138, 143, 164, 168, 170, 188, 200, 230, 234, 285
Norm 98, 135, 153, 159, 160, 167, 168, 251–255
Robert 119, 134, 138, 167, 202, 207, 210, 243, 245–247, 287
Sherman 260
Shima 69, 98, 119, 135, 159, 170, 174, 176, 189, 197, 200, 201, 207, 210, 247, 250, 287
Vicki 49, 123, 133, 168, 189, 255, 257–259, 287
Client self-identity 99, 235, 238, 247, 249, 250, 254, 258
Competency 48, 73
  court 16, 18, 48, 49, 73
  dynamic nature of 49, 61, 172, 286
  evaluation 10, 35, 50, 54, 61, 257, 285, 286
  hearing 49–51, 73
  lack of 52, 54, 175, 285
  legal definition of 49
  restoration 61
Compliance 21, 62, 103, 138, 141, 156, 158, 160, 199, 208, 241, 255
  medication 35, 67, 196
  subjective nature of 153, 178
  treatment 66
Conditions of release 55, 62, 65, 84, 88–91, 97, 101, 103, 105, 141, 175, 188, 287. *See also* Treatment, plan
  abstinence (drugs and alcohol) 91, 101, 145, 155, 167, 192, 232, 252, 258, 267

mental health treatment 67
Co-occurring conditions 9, 13, 44, 60, 67, 86, 88, 149, 155, 176, 198, 218, 231, 232, 235, 251, 260, 271
County mental health court 16–19, 34, 35, 40, 48, 49, 57, 65, 66, 70, 71, 74, 85, 89, 90, 99, 118, 122, 160, 161, 165, 183, 204, 217, 260, 274, 276
  felony drop down 19, 57, 65, 87, 99, 175, 184, 193, 194
Court liaison 40, 46, 85, 86, 89, 94, 97, 100, 121, 265
  and amenability 87, 121, 176
  eligibility determination 87, 88, 176
Court physical environment 29
Court program coordinator 274
Court reviews 1, 20, 50, 68, 71, 90, 137, 140, 141, 144, 167, 264
  express 159, 160, 171, 275
Crime control 5
  broken windows theory 5, 18
  public safety 15, 17
  smart on crime 6
Crime type 3, 7, 57
  drug 7
  felony 16, 19, 57, 65, 72, 74, 194
  misdemeanor 5, 12, 16, 19, 57, 59, 62, 99, 184, 268
  property 9
  violent 9, 35, 155, 194, 219
Criminal record 14, 99, 175, 187, 259
Critiques of mental health courts 57, 60, 61, 63, 66, 68, 69, 93, 107, 236, 287. *See also* Selection, bias

ethical issues 61, 67, 69, 97, 102, 196
legitimacy 35, 45, 55, 133
paternalism 31, 54, 75, 108, 113, 193, 209
therapeutic jurisprudence 38, 71
therapeutic state 31, 61, 102, 170, 270, 285

### D

Dangerousness 10, 35, 100, 155, 194, 197, 219, 220, 272
Defense attorneys 40, 51, 85, 89, 115, 116, 277
  client representation 117
  preventative lawyering 117
  relationship to clients 42, 48, 53, 62, 67, 139, 176, 197
  relationship to team 42, 47
Defense social workers 40, 120, 265
Diversion 13, 14, 58, 192, 249, 271, 273, 283–285
  pre-charge 6, 284
Diversity
  in court clients 93, 187, 271, 279
  in court team 95, 273, 279, 281
Drug 287. *See also* Conditions of release; Treatment, chemical dependency
  addiction 7–9, 13, 62, 86, 155, 167, 216, 235
  test 87, 102, 104, 146, 166
  use 37, 96, 153, 189, 221, 234, 242, 251, 253, 258, 267
Dual roles 49, 108, 124, 154, 278

### E

Education 96, 149, 238, 242, 247, 259, 278, 279, 281
Eligibility
  and amenability 90, 100, 103, 188, 273
  assessment 72, 85, 279
  criteria 18, 59, 73, 85, 86, 216, 271
  diagnosis 84, 86
  expanding 72, 73, 216, 271
  and opt-in 60
Emotional response 102, 132, 200, 202–204, 230, 258
Employment 234, 238, 242, 253, 259

### F

Formal law 30, 31

### G

Gender 9, 121, 187, 199, 202, 273
Goffman, Erving 11, 47, 132
Graduation 1, 162, 166, 171, 185, 187, 188, 190, 191, 193, 198–200, 203, 206, 230, 233, 234, 239, 243, 245, 249, 270, 275
  early 91, 240, 255, 258, 268

### H

Harm reduction 20, 63, 70, 120, 154, 156, 214, 267, 287. *See also* Sanctioning approaches, harm reduction

Housing
  court help with 33, 37, 60, 70, 97, 98, 213, 232, 242, 250, 253, 269
  homelessness 13, 18, 36, 37, 58, 59, 88, 106, 212, 242, 244, 269

Imperative
  punitive 4–6, 44, 131
  rehabilitative 4–6, 12, 37, 109, 131
Incentives 57, 65, 98, 99, 106, 160, 185–193, 232, 253, 257, 268–270, 283, 287. *See also* Sentencing outcomes, dismissal
  and compliance 21, 190
  opt-in 21, 60, 84, 93, 98, 192, 267, 273
  perverse 60, 100
Individualization 31, 37, 44, 45, 53, 90, 155, 157, 178, 191, 213, 214, 268, 272
Informality 46, 47, 52, 56, 65, 162

Jail 12, 84, 107, 235
  client fear of 2, 59, 87, 100, 102, 174, 192, 232, 236, 244, 253
  increased time in 61–65, 68, 70, 71
  revolving door 1, 13
  threat of 157, 166, 174, 210, 236, 264
  treatment access in 11, 61, 172
Johnston, E. Lea 35, 61

Judges 6, 41, 46, 50, 51, 70, 108, 114, 122
  decision making 65, 66, 68, 113, 114, 165, 176
  demeanor 111, 112, 114, 134, 153, 199, 209, 275
  discretion 42, 68, 86, 134, 174, 177
  effectiveness 108, 111–114, 134, 165, 253, 278
  efficiency 112, 136, 137, 275
  encouragement 2, 68, 91, 108, 115, 142, 143, 153, 159, 161, 165, 167, 203, 204, 246
  relationship to clients 43, 94, 108, 110–112, 123, 133, 135, 136, 142, 199, 241
  relationship to team 41, 46, 112–115, 136, 143
  therapeutic orientation 43, 109, 110, 122, 123, 161
Juvenile court 4, 6

Language choice 17, 53, 54, 163, 166, 271
Look-see 90

Mass incarceration 6, 15, 33
Media coverage
  crime 5, 6, 9, 35, 220, 270, 281
  mental illness 9, 10, 35, 218, 220, 270, 281
Mental health court
  effectiveness 136, 143, 158, 183, 218, 274

efficiency 47, 49, 50, 52, 53, 66, 90, 136, 165, 274, 275
equality in 157, 162, 178, 187, 269, 283
evaluations of 15, 185, 279, 280
first generation 13, 16, 19, 45
limits of 33, 52, 122, 140, 156, 217, 218, 220, 255, 261, 283, 286, 287
national landscape 13
organization 136, 160, 165, 187, 191, 192, 204, 263, 272, 274
second generation 13, 16, 19, 72, 194, 217
structure 205, 215, 218, 241, 242, 253, 257
Mental health system 4, 10, 52, 58, 231, 236, 248
access to 98
community care 9, 10, 14
deinstitutionalization 9–11, 15, 58
problems in 9, 35, 61, 62, 93, 218, 221, 269
transcarceration 11
transinstitutionalization 11
Mental illness
bipolar disorder 67, 86, 206
connection with criminal behavior 7, 12, 32, 34–36, 88, 195, 216, 236, 270
criminalization of 8, 10, 11, 14, 33, 35, 58, 176, 282
decriminalization of 33, 55, 62, 69, 268
depression 96, 236
diagnosis 9, 18, 34, 54, 57, 73, 95
insight 54, 57, 124, 140
in jails and prisons 4, 8–11, 15, 59, 264, 265

medical model 11, 195
personality disorders 216
self-medicating 232, 236
stigma of 9, 53–56, 93, 112, 132, 163, 168, 200, 209, 233, 238, 270, 271, 287
training in 12, 40, 49, 59, 109, 111, 114, 277, 278
and victimization 12
MHDT 84, 103–105, 124, 245, 246, 271, 287. *See also* Opt-out
mental health court lite 105, 246, 272
Mission 17, 19, 31, 33, 35, 36, 41, 52, 73, 109, 195, 217
alignment 264
drift 71–73, 75
model drift 73, 75

N

Net widening 20, 31, 57, 69, 75, 91, 98, 100, 107, 167, 172, 176, 247, 253, 277, 286
deeper nets 61, 62, 102, 197, 218
new nets 57, 66, 282, 283
stronger nets 57, 60–62, 68, 70, 105, 176
Non-adversarialism 14, 37, 42, 47
Non-compliance 63, 68, 141, 146, 151, 175, 177
contextualization 159, 168
medication 67, 68, 172, 201
new charge 90, 146, 212, 235, 249, 255
relapse 66, 167, 168, 221, 237, 244, 268
subjective nature of 163, 178
treatment 68, 118, 177

## O

Opt-in 18, 20, 62, 85, 89, 96, 97, 105, 106, 186, 197, 219, 271, 273. *See also* Court liaison; Eligibility
  and amenability 18, 85
  client decision 118, 188, 192, 232, 243, 248, 253
  constrained choice 102, 105
  guilty plea 91, 99, 192, 240, 244
  hearing 91, 92
  voluntary 64, 67, 69, 88, 89, 95, 102, 105, 197
Opt-out 57, 70, 84, 89, 103–105, 124, 176, 263, 287. *See also* MHDT
Outcomes. *See* Graduation; Recidivism; Reintegration; Sanctioning types, revocation

## P

Police 5, 9, 15, 58, 59, 277
  Crisis Intervention Team 58, 59, 284
Power dynamics in court 29, 41, 42, 52, 74, 111, 113, 136, 199, 204, 276
Pre-court meetings 18, 45–48, 89, 113, 139, 162, 164, 277
Probation
  duration of 62, 63, 91, 103, 192, 210, 235, 247, 268
  review frequency 67, 71, 104, 140, 141, 144, 166, 167, 264
  reviews 140, 141, 143, 159, 167
Probation officers 41, 70, 72, 74, 75, 105, 115, 118, 123, 157, 176, 177, 260, 278
  dual roles 118
  legal liability 276
  relationship to clients 106, 118, 119, 122, 135, 143, 150, 176, 197, 206, 209, 237, 241, 245
  relationship to team 118, 119, 122
Problem-solving court 4, 6, 8, 14, 31, 56
  drug courts 7, 14, 37, 68, 144, 147, 157, 164, 234, 268
  movement 6, 39, 264, 282
  specialized populations 3, 7, 8, 14, 56, 72
Procedural justice 20, 132, 137, 158, 159, 162, 230
  client perception 120, 132, 133, 135, 188, 196, 197
  give voice 134, 140, 153, 170
  judicial usage 133, 165
  showing concern 135
Progressive ideals 4
Prosecutors 40, 58, 100, 118, 148, 220
  adversarialism 41
  collaboration 39, 71
  discretion 42
  relationship to clients 40
  relationship to team 165, 276
Psycholegal soft spots 117
Public opinion
  crime 5, 13, 17
  mental illness 10, 17, 36, 197, 281
Public safety 31, 32, 40, 50, 70, 145, 146, 172, 174, 194, 220
Punishment 63, 65
  changing forms of 4, 6, 8
  culture and 5
  decreasing 37, 173, 267
  increasing 68, 70

new penology 5
theories of 61

## Q

Qualitative data 15, 16, 20, 21, 30, 59, 229
Quantitative data 17, 20, 185, 279

## R

Race 9, 93, 187, 199, 271, 273, 287. *See also* Diversity
  bias 94–96, 273
  cultural sensitivity 94, 95
Recidivism 12, 20, 31, 32, 65, 70, 132, 183, 185, 188, 190, 191, 194, 195, 198, 204, 234, 245, 251, 253, 255
  number of new charges 186, 198, 211
  revolving door 37, 72, 218, 252, 282, 287
  time between charges 212
Reforms 6, 86, 97, 149, 191, 192, 204, 210, 215, 219, 247, 263, 264, 267–269, 272, 278, 285
Reintegration 32, 33, 64, 68, 149, 184, 196, 200, 202, 243, 247
Reintegrative shaming 207, 209
Religion 238–240, 247
Resources 101, 187, 273
  access through mental health court 33, 45, 59, 60, 69, 70, 84, 100, 104, 107, 191, 193, 217, 242, 269
  lack of 36, 269, 276, 286
Rights 38, 45, 46, 51, 61, 68
  speedy trial 89, 99
  to treatment 10
  trial by jury 99
Risk 96, 146, 188, 194, 220, 271–273
Risk-need-responsivity 272
Rituals 2, 21, 91, 132, 139, 158, 178, 198, 199, 201, 204, 233, 246, 270, 275, 287. *See also* Graduation

## S

Sanctioning approaches 41, 144, 162, 177
  graduated sanctions 144, 145, 147, 151, 157, 165
  harm reduction 104, 120, 141, 144–146, 148, 150, 165, 270
  hybrid model 145, 147, 154
  increasing compliance 164, 167, 170, 232
  second chances 156, 164, 244
  zero tolerance 120, 145, 267
Sanctioning types
  jail 145, 146, 165, 168, 172, 173, 175, 217, 253
  other 146, 166, 168, 169, 172, 249
  positive 158, 160, 161, 255, 258, 270
  revocation 96, 99, 166, 175–177, 184, 188, 191, 220
Selection
  and amenability 18, 86
  bias 93, 96, 188
  preferred 96, 188, 220, 271
Selection process 20, 83, 85, 124, 188
  referral stage 59, 65, 85, 93, 231

Sentencing outcomes
  deferred 99, 189, 240
  dismissal 62, 186–188, 190–193, 199, 200, 230, 232, 235, 248, 252, 255, 268, 273
  reduced 62
  suspended 99, 244, 248
Sequential Intercept Model 13
Social control 6, 11, 12, 31, 57, 58, 68, 265
  mental illness 4, 9, 11
  as opposed to a system of care 11
Social safety net 98, 218, 282, 283
Social science 35, 38, 88, 185, 280
  socio-legal studies 3
Social support 176, 190, 198, 204, 205, 207, 208, 218, 230, 233, 237, 240–242, 245, 247, 250, 252, 260, 261
  lack of 36, 208, 285
Social work criminal justice 21, 31, 265
Stability 90, 195, 215, 233, 238, 246, 250, 268
Success
  causes of 133, 143, 186, 188, 194–196, 198, 206, 230, 253, 260, 261
  client perceptions 215, 243
  understandings of 21, 183, 184, 195, 211, 212, 216, 217, 247, 260

T
Team 107
  adversarialism 39, 47, 74, 120, 164, 175
  collaboration 34, 39–43, 47, 74, 113, 114, 118, 137, 145, 164, 184, 206, 274, 276, 279
  model 37, 39, 40, 43–46, 53, 56, 74, 115, 121, 122, 141
  relationship to clients 190, 199, 202, 208, 233, 237, 242, 245, 250, 259
  turnover 108, 115, 122, 217, 275
Therapeutic
  agents 20, 107, 108, 116, 118, 120
  anti-therapeutic 38, 52, 55, 117, 119, 121, 136, 140, 144, 172, 287
  jurisprudence 20, 30, 37–39, 44, 45, 52, 90, 107
  justice 20, 21, 30, 31, 55, 75, 107, 118, 123, 124, 135, 137, 265, 275, 287
Traditional court 29, 32, 41, 62, 101, 103, 287. *See also* Opt-out
  adversarialism in 7, 39, 41, 42, 74
  compared to mental health court 32, 37, 38, 44, 45, 56, 109, 122, 123, 131, 133, 134, 148, 187, 234, 281
Transitioning out of mental health court 205, 209, 218, 233, 237, 242, 245, 247, 250, 258, 285, 286
Treatment
  chemical dependency 66, 90, 176, 198
  coercive 35, 66, 67, 197
  crisis mental health 195
  intensity 63, 66, 70
  mental health 32, 36, 66, 90, 104, 176, 198, 216, 233, 237, 257

non-crisis mental health 185, 194, 195, 297
plan 20, 34, 44, 66, 89, 90, 204
providers 66, 69, 90, 233, 277
Trust 41, 94, 106, 119, 121, 122, 124, 143, 247, 275

### V
Victim advocate 40

### W
Wexler, David 30, 31, 38, 39, 61, 102, 170, 270
Winick, Bruce 38, 49

The manufacturer's authorised representative in the EU is Springer Nature Customer Service Centre GmbH, Europaplatz 3, 69115 Heidelberg, Germany. If you have any concerns regarding our products, please contact ProductSafety@springernature.com

Printed and bound by CPI Group (UK) Ltd, Croydon, CR0 4YY
23/03/2026
02076739-0008